The publisher and the University of California Press Foundation gratefully acknowledge the generous support of the George Gund Foundation Imprint in African American Studies.

Workers on Arrival

Workers on Arrival

BLACK LABOR IN THE MAKING OF AMERICA

Joe William Trotter, Jr.

UNIVERSITY OF CALIFORNIA PRESS

University of California Press, one of the most distinguished university presses in the United States, enriches lives around the world by advancing scholarship in the humanities, social sciences, and natural sciences. Its activities are supported by the UC Press Foundation and by philanthropic contributions from individuals and institutions. For more information, visit www.ucpress.edu.

University of California Press
Oakland, California

Library of Congress Cataloging-in-Publication Data

Names: Trotter, Joe William, 1945- author.
Title: Workers on arrival : black labor in the making of America /
    Joe William Trotter, Jr.
Description: Oakland, California : University of California Press, [2019] |
    Includes bibliographical references and index. |
Identifiers: LCCN 2018028905 (print) | LCCN 2018031716 (ebook) |
    ISBN 9780520971172 (Epub) | ISBN 9780520299450 (cloth : alk. paper)
Subjects: LCSH: Working class African Americans—History. | African
    Americans—Employment—History.
Classification: LCC HD8081.A65 (ebook) | LCC HD8081.A65 T77 2019 (print) |
    DDC 331.6/396073—dc23
LC record available at https://lccn.loc.gov/2018028905

Manufactured in the United States of America

28   27   26   25   24   23   22   21   20   19
10   9   8   7   6   5   4   3   2   1

I dedicate this book with love to my three brothers among the "Trotter-14"—Rahmaan Rasheed (James Edward), Otis, and David Wayne

CONTENTS

ILLUSTRATIONS

ACKNOWLEDGMENTS

A long time in the making, this book has benefitted from the research, feedback, and encouragement of many institutions, colleagues, students, friends, and family members. As a work of synthesis, *Workers on Arrival* builds upon the pioneering contributions of numerous scholars. Thus, I am happy to extend my sincere gratitude to all who helped to make this book possible. Along the way, however, I have incurred special debts and wish to extend special gratitude to my longtime friend Earl Lewis, University of Michigan and past president of the A. W. Mellon Foundation; Leslie Harris, Northwestern University; Dennis Dickerson, Vanderbilt; Ron Lewis, University of West Virginia; Clarence Lang, Kansas University; Rhonda Williams, Case Western Reserve University, now at Vanderbilt; Donna Murch, State University of New Jersey, Rutgers; and Lisa Matterson, University of California–Davis.

In 2015, Carnegie Mellon University's Center for Africanamerican Urban Studies and the Economy (CAUSE) celebrated its twentieth anniversary with a state-of-the-field conference on black urban history since the transatlantic slave trade. Papers and comments presented at this conference reinforced work on all phases of this synthesis. Participants included, to name a few, Davarian Baldwin, Trinity College; Marcus Hunter, UCLA; Carol Anderson, Emory University; Leslie Alexander, Ohio State University, now at the University of Oregon; Michael Gomez, New York University; Richard Blackett, Vanderbilt; Samuel Black, the Heinz History Center, Pittsburgh; Laura Grantmyre, Point Park University; and Larry Glasco and Rob Ruck, both at the University of Pittsburgh.

Each year, a CAUSE postdoctoral fellow visits Carnegie Mellon to conduct uninterrupted research and writing on his or her own book. As I worked on this project, I enjoyed helpful interactions and conversations with postdoctoral fellows Kwame Holmes, University of Colorado; Millington Bergeson-Lockwood, U.S. Embassy, Malawi; Scot Brown, UCLA; Stephanie Boddie, Baylor University; and Waverly Duck, University of Pittsburgh. At the same time, indispensable to progress on this book were opportunities to share my ideas with others in a variety of public and academic settings at home and abroad: the Urban History Association; the Association for the Study of African American Life and History; the American Historical Association; the National Museum of African American History and Culture in Washington, DC; and programs in African American and U.S. history at Newcastle University and Queens College in the United Kingdom. Special thanks to historians Marcus Rediker, University of Pittsburgh and director of the Annual E. P. Thompson Lecture; Benjamin Houston, Newcastle University, UK; Brian Kelly, Queens College, Belfast, UK; and Emma Hart, University of St. Andrews, UK.

For their ongoing support, I am indebted to CAUSE advisory board members Eric Anderson, School of Design; Edda Fields-Black, Department of History; James P. McDonald, BNY-Mellon Global Philanthropy (retired); Kenya Boswell, BNY-Mellon Foundation of Southwestern Pennsylvania (president); Afeworki Paulos, Social and Decision Sciences and Librarian (retired); Nico Slate, Department of History; Gabrielle Michalek, librarian; and H. LaRue Trotter, teacher. In the larger Pittsburgh metropolitan community, I acknowledge, in addition to BNY-Mellon, the Giant Eagle Corporation, Nancy and the late Milton Washington, and the Falk family fund (before it disbanded) for supporting the research mission of CAUSE and scholarship under the Giant Eagle Professorship in History and Social Justice. Making this work possible at Carnegie Mellon, however, is the consistent support of current and recent department heads Donna Harsch and Caroline Acker; deans Richard Scheines, John Lehoczky, Ramayya Krishnan, and Ilker Baybars (CMU-Q); provosts Mark Kamlet and Farnam Jahanian; and presidents Jared Cohen, Subra Suresh, and now Farnam Jahanian.

In the Department of History, this book benefitted from ongoing conversations with colleagues Wendy Goldman, my coeditor on a recent collection of essays, *The Ghetto in Global History;* Nico Slate, a specialist on transnational black history; and Lansiné Kaba, Distinguished Visiting Professor of History at the CMU-Qatar campus in the Middle East. I am especially grateful to Lansiné and Dean Baybars for arranging lectures on the book in-progress at the Qatar campus. Graduate and undergraduate students also encouraged work on this book through their energetic and critical reactions to ideas presented in classes and seminars on the subject: most notably Clayton Vaughn-Roberson, David Busch, Levi Pettler, Bennett Koerber, Andrew Masich, Avigail Oren, Cassie Miller, Michael (Takashi) Matsumaru, Fidel Campet, Kevin Brown, Russell Pryor, Jessica Klanderud, Germaine Williams, Brad Sommer, and Derek Handley, to name a few. Special thanks to Clayton for bibliographical work for this book.

It has been a joy working with the University of California Press and its entire production team. Editor Neils Hooper's interest proved key as I sought to transform an earlier history of blacks in urban America into a more focused history of black workers from the transatlantic slave trade to recent times. For her thorough read and editing of an earlier draft of the book manuscript, I am grateful to Susan Whitlock, the development editor for the UCP. Thanks also to copyeditor Barbara Armentrout for her diligent work on the final version of the manuscript. Before this book took its current shape as a labor and working-class history, it also benefitted immensely from anonymous readers at Penguin Press and the Oxford University Press.

Staff members provided indispensable assistance for this book. I acknowledge with great appreciation Gail Tooks and Natalie Taylor, business managers; Jesse Wilson, webmaster and photographer; and especially Hikari Aday, program coordinator and assistant to the director of CAUSE. Hikari not only helped to carve out space in my schedule for bringing this book to completion but also tracked down permissions for the book's artwork.

Finally, as in all of my endeavors, I owe my greatest debt of gratitude to the love of my life, H. LaRue Trotter, my fourteen siblings (one deceased), and a host of nieces and nephews.

They continue to inspire, energize, and give purpose to my life and labor. Words cannot express how grateful I am for their deep wellsprings of love and support over the years. On a very personal note, however, as the eldest of four men among the "Trotter-14," I dedicate this book with love to my three brothers: Rahmaan Rasheed (James Edward), Otis, and David Wayne.

PROLOGUE: FOREGROUNDING
THE BLACK WORKER

African Americans have a unique history of labor exploitation and wealth creation on American soil. Along with the labor of men and women of diverse ethnic groups, black workers are critical to any discussion of the nation's productivity, politics, and the future of work in today's global economy. Yet, too often, popular, journalistic, public policy, and academic analyses treat the black poor and working class as consumers rather than producers, as takers rather than givers, and as liabilities rather than assets. Recent media discussions about the sources of political conservatism and the future of American democracy place the white working class at center stage, largely ignoring the role of African Americans, women, and other nonwhite workers. Some of this commentary went so far as to suggest that white workers are "oppressed, not so much by capital but by cultural elites and coddled minorities." Indeed, increasing numbers of white workers consider themselves members of a "new minority" or "strangers in their own land" in the face of persistent demands for equal treatment by previously neglected women and racial minorities. Many of these workers need government aid to help make ends meet because their jobs provide insufficient pay and benefits to cover medical and living expenses, yet this need wars with their entrenched perception of social welfare programs as doles for African Americans and minority workers—some undocumented immigrants—with an insufficient work ethic to warrant such support.[1]

Workers on Arrival hopes to intervene in discussions and debates about the future of the city, the nation, and American democracy by restoring the broader historical context of African American workers as producers, givers, and assets. Drawing upon the conceptual and substantive insights of nearly a century of research, *Workers on Arrival* focuses on black urban labor and working-class history, documenting the movement of urban black workers from the periphery of the African American working class during the first three hundred years to its center during the twentieth century. It calls attention not only to the ongoing coercive dimensions of this process but also to the equally important ways that people of African descent gradually forged transnational liberation movements to free themselves from both local and global forms of inequality. As such, this study examines the lives and labor of black workers within the larger context of urban capitalist development, community formation, and politics from the transatlantic slave trade to recent times.

During the first three centuries of European residence in North America, enslaved agricultural laborers fueled the growth of early capitalism as a transnational phenomenon. Brought here through the African slave trade specifically for their labor—hence, the title *Workers on Arrival*—African Americans produced wealth not only through their labor power and toil without pay but also as "commodities" bought and sold for profit in the capitalist marketplace. They were the most exploited and unequal component of the emerging modern capitalist labor force. Nonetheless, enslaved seventeenth-, eighteenth-, and nineteenth-century black workers facilitated the growth of the early city alongside poor and working-class whites, many of whom were disfranchised and unfree indentured servants. Some African Americans worked as skilled craftsmen and women (using knowledge they brought from the old country as well as training they acquired in the New World), but most labored as "common," "manual," "general," "unskilled," or "household" workers.

From the beginning, African Americans used the unique conditions of the urban environment to open up pathways to their own emancipation. A free wage-earning black proletariat gradually emerged within the bowels of urban slavery. As historian Seth Rockman shows, both free black and white laborers lived "a hand-to-mouth existence characterized by minimal control" over the fruits of their own labor.[2] But early white wage earners enjoyed gradually increasing access to the vote, state power, and their own political, social, and labor organizations, while the vast majority of their African American counterparts remained linked to their enslaved brothers and sisters through systems of legal and extralegal disfranchisement, economic exploitation, and racial inequality.

The Civil War and the emancipation of some four million enslaved people fundamentally changed the conditions and experiences of the black working class. Freedom transformed African Americans from a predominantly enslaved agricultural proletariat into a rural, sharecropping, and wage-earning working class. Unlike the pre–Civil War black working class, the postbellum black working class claimed full citizenship rights under the law. Whereas only small numbers of enslaved blacks gained access to wage labor and clawed their way into the free, wage-earning working class, emancipation opened up the free labor force to all African Americans, urban and rural alike. The postbellum black working class took a huge step forward, but emancipation and proletarianization was an exceedingly complicated and mixed process. Between the end of the Civil War and the beginning of World War I, white workers, elites, and the state joined forces and forged a new white supremacist system—a series of formal and informal policies and social practices—that stymied the development of a fully free black working class.

The Jim Crow system subverted the promise of some avenues to freedom and independence, forcing African Americans to make new decisions. Emancipated rural blacks initially sought land ownership and even share-cropping over wage labor as the surest routes to economic emancipation and full citizenship, but, frustrated by the roadblocks white supremacy put in their way, rising numbers of sharecroppers and wage-earning farmhands abandoned the land for wage work in rural industrial coal mines, lumber mills, and railroad construction projects as well as the rapidly industrializing cities. While urban blacks remained a minority component of the working class well into the twentieth century, the emergence of a predominantly free rural and rural industrial workforce reinforced the growth of the urban working class. During the late nineteenth and early twentieth centuries, growing numbers of southern rural migrants swelled the ranks of urban black communities. As the alliance between the white elite and white workers weakened and broke down in the face of rising white workers' demands and labor strikes, black workers gained access to previously all-white jobs, including steel and meatpacking plants, as strikebreakers. These postbellum and early Jim Crow–era developments paved the way for the beginning of the Great Migration and the development of the black industrial working class during the inter–world war years of the early twentieth century.

But the making of the black working class involved far more than the story of what jobs were available when. Throughout their history, working African Americans built on their economic contributions to forge vigorous movements for freedom, independence, and access to civil and human rights. From the inception of the transatlantic slave trade through the Civil War, they challenged capitalist control of their labor through frequent movement from place to place, initially as enslaved fugitives and later as free wage earners of color; revolts and plots to revolt; entrepreneurial pursuits; and, most of all, the creation of a plethora of community-based institutions. Working-class black community organizations helped to set the stage for the anticolonization and antislavery movements that culminated in the outbreak of the Civil War and the fall of slavery. But the black freedom struggle was by no means limited to the quest for emancipation and full citizenship on U.S. soil. Until the onset of the Civil War, black workers had embraced the idea of resettlement elsewhere (including the Caribbean, Canada, and West Africa) alongside their struggle for freedom in the new republic.

While the latter idea persisted into the postemancipation era, a variety of postbellum developments undercut the appeal of emigration projects. In addition to opportunities to enter previously all-white workplaces as free workers and as strikebreakers, African Americans also formed their own labor organizations to fight racial discrimination in the workplace and open up new jobs for themselves and their families. They also gradually moved into all-white labor unions and challenged the color line within the organized white labor movement as well as corporate structures. African Americans and their working-class white allies advanced broad multiracial demands for better working conditions, higher wages, and access to viable mechanisms for addressing their grievances against unfair labor policies and practices. The interracial labor movement dramatically expanded under the impact of the Great Depression and the emergence of the New Deal political coalition during the 1930s.

Nonetheless, as their numbers rose in the urban industrial economy, black workers soon encountered mob violence, racial job ceilings, and color lines in the economic, housing, and community life of the metropolis. Thus, alongside their escalating engagement in the development of a broader multiracial labor movement, urban black workers and their communities created a new and more diverse Black Metropolis, their own urban public sphere, or city within the city. They envisioned the Black Metropolis not only as a bulwark against mob violence and exclusion from essential social and commercial services but also as a launching pad for assaults against Jim Crow in the organized labor movement, key sectors of the industrializing economy, and the housing market. They also regularly protested the official and unofficial use of state power to reinforce the economic advantages of white over black workers.

As the abolitionist movement of the antebellum years ultimately secured the fall of slavery, so the Modern Black Freedom Movement toppled the twentieth-century segregationist order. This achievement reduced the incidence of poverty, lifted significant numbers of poor and working-class blacks into the middle class, and narrowed the racial gap in access to citizenship rights and equal employment opportunities. Even so, as suggested by the rise of the Universal Negro Improvement Association during the 1920s, the explosive growth of the Nation of Islam during the 1950s and early 1960s, and the Black Power phase of the Modern Black Freedom struggle during the late 1960s and early 1970s, the increasing integration of blacks into the industrial working class and their slow ascent into the ranks of the middle class were by no means a linear process that moved inexorably from historic patterns of exclusion to inclusion. The color line remained strong, and black nationalism persisted among the repertoire of African American strategies for economic democracy, political citizenship, and human rights.

More recently, despite significant progress during the height of the Modern Black Freedom struggle, the deindustrialization of the urban economy soon undercut gains for poor and working-class black families. Unemployment, poverty, environmental health hazards, and incarceration of young blacks dramatically increased during the final years of the twentieth century. These changes not only signaled the resurgence of interracial conflict along the color line on the one hand and intraracial class conflict on the other, they also ushered in greater internal friction within the deindustrializing black urban working class itself. Intraclass conflicts intensified with the eruption of drug wars, black on black street violence, and family disputes as the number of households headed by women with children sharply increased. Whereas black women had forged strong cross-class institutional and political alliances during the industrial era, poor and working-class black women exerted increasing independence over their own organizations and movements for social change during the closing decades of the twentieth century.

The ability of *Workers on Arrival* to assert the centrality of the African American working class to an understanding of U.S. history rests on certain crucial contributions to historical study. During the late twentieth century, historical scholarship moved labor and working-class history from the periphery to the center of our understanding of the United States as a multiracial and multiethnic nation. The lives of immigrant and American-born workers, black and white, men and women, "skilled" and "less skilled," gained increasing attention in popular and academic discussions of the nation's history.[3] Though African people did not share in white privilege with Italian American and other Euro-American groups, their lives overlapped with the conditions and social struggles of workers from a variety of ethnic and nationality backgrounds. These experiences included not only unequal and inadequate wages and working and living conditions, and struggles to eradicate inequality within and beyond the workplace, but also intellectual movements to create and sustain more inclusive portraits of U.S. history as a whole. Despite criticism of these "bottom-up" perspectives, social historians advanced the notion that "class, ethnicity, gender, sexuality, and so on were often more meaningful historical" experiences than the nation for large numbers of Americans.[4]

Meanwhile, radical global perspectives on U.S. history "from above the nation" have enabled new insights into enslaved African and African American workers as producers in the world economy.[5] Building upon the pioneering insights of twentieth-century African American scholars from W.E.B. Du Bois and Eric Williams to Ira Berlin, Nell Painter, and many others, early twenty-first-century scholars of American capitalism and democracy place enslaved African Americans at the center of these global processes. In his groundbreaking study, *River of Dark Dreams: Slavery and Empire in the Cotton Kingdom,* historian Walter Johnson accents the global impact of enslaved African labor on both sides of the Atlantic: "The fortunes of cotton planters in Louisiana and cotton brokers in Liverpool, of the plantations of the Mississippi Valley and the textile mills of Manchester, were tied together through the cotton trade—the largest single sector of the global economy in the first half of the nineteenth century."[6]

Sven Beckert's *Empire of Cotton: A Global History* treats cotton and enslaved African labor not only as an experience shared with other cotton workers around the globe but also as the critical linchpin of the worldwide "Industrial Revolution." Employing the concept of "war capitalism" to underscore the coercive dimensions of enslavement and the early development of modern capitalism, Beckert shows how the "cumulative result of this highly aggressive, outwardly oriented capitalism" enabled Europeans "to dominate the centuries-old worlds of cotton, merge into a single empire centered in Manchester, and invent the global economy we take for granted today."[7] In his innovative study, *The Half Has Never Been Told: Slavery and the Making of American Capitalism,* historian Edward Baptist documents the immense suffering endured as well as the subsequent memories of enslavement that African people and their descendants carried forward into the future. *The Half Has Never Been Told* illuminates how African people developed a profound and enduring understanding of the myriad ways that their forced labor leavened the rise of the modern worldwide capitalist economy and facilitated the gradual spread of democracy among people of European descent:

> The idea that the commodification and suffering and forced labor of African Americans is what made the United States powerful and rich is not an idea that people necessarily are happy to hear. Yet it is the truth. And that truth was the half of the story that survived mostly in the custodianship of those who survived slavery expansion. . . . The half not told ran like a layer of iridium left by a dinosaur-killing asteroid through every piece of testimony ex-slaves, such as Lorenzo Ivy, left on the historical record: thousands of stanzas of an epic of forced separations, violence, and new kinds of labor.[8]

As recent studies of capitalism and slavery make clear, the history of the black working class is linked to the rural political economy of staple-crop production—tobacco, rice, sugar, and especially cotton. African Americans remained a predominantly rural southern people well into the twentieth century. In the postbellum years, they also continued to fuel the expansion of the modern capitalist economy through their labor as disfranchised sharecroppers, farmhands, household workers, and general laborers. Consequently, until recently, the preponderance of scholarship on black workers explored the conditions and experiences of agricultural workers and to some extent rural industrial coal miners, lumber workers, and railroad laborers. However, under the impact of the Great Migration and the transformation of African Americans into a predominantly urban people during the twentieth century, research on black urban, labor, and working-class history gradually emerged as a new specialty within American and African American Studies. By the opening years of the new millennium, this scholarship had illuminated a broad range of topics, themes, regions, localities, and issues in the development of black labor history from its commercial-era beginnings through the initial phase of deindustrialization during the mid-twentieth century.[9]

Comprehensive analyses of the intersections of race, work, and gender relations strengthened the growing body of urban labor studies and reinforced the utility of historical perspectives for understanding a series of daunting issues in contemporary African American and U.S. life. In her study of rural and urban labor, *American Work: Four Centuries of Black and White Labor,* for example, historian Jacqueline Jones analyzes the variety of occupations pursued by African Americans. She also accents "the 'racial' conflicts" that emerged around issues of work and economic inequality and "remain the moral burden of this country's history."[10] Nearly a decade later, Nancy Maclean focused her attention on the impact of the Modern Black Freedom and feminist movements on questions of exclusion and inclusion from work and political democracy. "How did a society that for centuries took for granted the exclusion from full participation and citizenship of the majority of its members (namely, Americans of color and all women) become one that values diversity and sees as an achievement the representation of once excluded groups in prominent positions? Not only workplaces have changed but also the nation's political map."[11] More recently, historian Ira Berlin linked successive African and African American migrations since the transatlantic slave trade to shifting capitalist demands for labor. In his view, "The great crossings [national and transnational, industrial and preindustrial, and beyond] cannot be understood apart from the ever-changing demands of global capitalism and its voracious appetite for labor, [black and white,] men and women—whether slave or free."[12]

These approaches, and others, not only inform the key overlapping arguments of this book but also help to shape its structure. *Workers on Arrival: Black Labor in the Making of America* is divided into two closely interconnected parts. Part 1, "Preindustrial Beginnings" (chapters 1, 2, and 3), locates the roots of the black urban working class in the rise of the transatlantic slave trade and the forced migration of some fifteen million African people to North America during the colonial era. These chapters show how a small but growing fraction of urban black workers helped to construct the colonial city and usher in the American Revolution and the emergence of the new republic. Chapter 1 illustrates how large-scale European immigration into the nation's cities coupled with the intense labor demands of southern cotton agriculture during the early nineteenth century not only curtailed African American access to freedom under the law but also limited the employment of free people of color as artisans, factory hands producing goods for national and international markets, and household and general laborers in the most lucrative segments of the urban domestic and personal service workforce. Although most preindustrial black workers, enslaved and free, lived and worked in multiethnic neighborhoods (though increasingly segregated along color lines by the beginning of the Civil War), these chapters document how early black urbanites nonetheless encountered day-to-day intimidation, mob violence, and movements to recolonize free people of color on African soil.

Chapter 2 sketches African Americans' early attempts to build community as a way of bettering life conditions. It examines how black urban workers and their families forged tenuous interracial alliances with selected white residents and used the unique economy, culture, and politics of both the city and the nation, which they helped to create, to broaden channels for wage-earning employment, self-emancipation, independent institutions, and movements to abolish slavery; stymie the African colonization movement; and end restrictions on the citizenship rights of free people of color. This chapter also shows how class conflicts, aggravated by internal color and gender distinctions, gradually emerged within the African American community by the beginning of the Civil War. In addition to documenting the role of the Civil War in the emancipation of enslaved people, chapter 3 also illustrates how postbellum federal, state, and local governments allied with white supremacists and constructed a new racially stratified Jim Crow system, which in turn established the socioeconomic and political backdrop for the transformation of the black class structure during the early twentieth century.

Part 2, "The Twentieth Century" (chapters 4, 5, 6, and 7), examines the rise of the urban industrial working class under the impact of the Great Migration and its collapse in the face of deindustrialization and increasing globalization during the final years of the twentieth century. Chapter 4 shows how a racial "job ceiling" and "color line" in the residential and community life of the city accompanied the increasing movement of black workers into jobs and housing with higher pay and better living conditions, while chapter 5 documents diverse struggles against the Jim Crow order. Black workers and their communities both unified and clashed over the deployment of diverse liberal, interracial, proletarian, and nationalist strategies for liberation and full citizenship rights for black men, women, and children.

Chapter 6 documents how the complicated interplay of industrial employment, new neighborhoods, and the emergence of the militant Modern Black Freedom struggle dismantled the segregationist system and inaugurated a new equal-opportunity regime, including "affirmative action," to eradicate color as well as gender lines in employment, education, housing, and social programs receiving support from the public treasury. In addition to illustrating how the black industrial working class rapidly declined as the Jim Crow edifice collapsed, the Great Migration came to a close, the manufacturing sector dissipated, and the interracial labor movement dwindled during the late twentieth century, chapter 7 discusses the rise of a new African American urban politics to address the demands of African American life in the emerging postindustrial age. This chapter also considers the meaning of new waves of immigrants from Latin America, the Caribbean, Asia, and Africa. Finally, the concluding epilogue reflects on the implications of U.S. labor and working-class history for today's African American community, work, and democracy. It concludes that current global class and race relations are not entirely new, but deeply rooted in the nation's past with profound implications for the future.

PART ONE

———

Preindustrial Beginnings

ONE

Genesis of the Black Working Class

BY THE LATE EIGHTEENTH CENTURY, the enslaved African population had increased to well over a thousand in each of five cities: New York, Boston, Philadelphia, Charleston, and New Orleans. In the wake of the American Revolution, the free wage-earning black population had also expanded alongside the enslaved black working class. These black workers, both enslaved and free, fueled the rise of the early American city as they also enhanced the wealth and power of urban slaveowners and employers. Working as general laborers, domestic servants, building and construction laborers, deckhands, sailors, ship pilots, artisans, and factory workers, African people were indispensable to the growth and development of the new nation. Despite their crucial contributions to the rise of preindustrial America, however, free workers of color were not rewarded with increased opportunities and rights. In the first half of the nineteenth century, they encountered sharp competition from rising numbers of European immigrants, mostly from Germany and Ireland. At the same time, they lived and worked under the burden of racially restrictive labor legislation; a vigorous, white-led African recolonization movement; and mob violence. As a result, free blacks lost access to increasing numbers of jobs in the skilled crafts as well as the most coveted general labor and household-service occupations. Still, they were active participants in the making of their own lives as well as the New World social order.[1]

THE COLONIAL GENERATION

The first urban black workers and their children cleared and leveled land, cut firewood, and prepared ground for the erection of buildings, for crop cultivation, and for burying the dead.[2] In 1723, among 88 survivors of one slave voyage to New Orleans, 50 enslaved men dug drainage ditches along the Mississippi River and constructed levees; 35 raised buildings on the company's plantation; and another 3 returned to work in the seafaring transatlantic trade system.[3] France may have founded New Orleans and Louisiana, "but it was slaves from Senegal to Congo who laid the foundation," historian Lawrence Powell concludes in his study of the city's history.[4] Similarly, within months of Charlestown's founding in 1670, the demand for enslaved blacks became so intense that buyers sometimes came "very nearly to Blows" wrangling over "who should get the good Slaves." Enslaved people toiled "in the streets of Charles Town, in the Anglican church and in the market, and in gentry dining rooms, kitchens, and stableyards."[5] For their part, early Afro–New Yorkers worked on the establishment and maintenance of the Dutch bouwerys (farms), Fort Amsterdam, and public roads. They also burned limestone and oyster shells for use in outhouses and for interring the dead. Only "a great deal of money," promises, and "bribe[s]," the Dutch West India Company declared, would induce white workers to perform such labor on behalf of the colony's survival and development.[6]

In Philadelphia, the *Pennsylvania Gazette* regularly advertised for slaves suited for both rural and urban labor, including household service. As indentured white servants increasingly "reneged on their contracts" and searched for "less restrictive employment" opportunities, one of Philadelphia's most active slave traders vigorously urged the "more general use of Slaves" over free white workers.[7] Bostonians, too, hoped to recruit "slaves sufficient to doe" all their general labor and household work. In 1740, an English visitor observed the use of black men as servants: When the Boston "ladies ride out to take the air in a chaise or chair . . . they have a negro servant drive them. The gentlemen [also] ride out here as in England . . . with their negroes to attend."[8]

African people helped to build and service the colonial city not only as general laborers and household and domestic workers but also as skilled craftsmen and craftswomen. Wealthy European merchants, artisans, and diverse business owners purchased, trained, and employed Africans as brick masons, carpenters, cabinetmakers, sailmakers, bakers, coopers, and tailors, among other trades. By the eve of the American Revolution, slaveholders encouraged black Philadelphians to learn trades and placed a large "share of the ordinary trades of the city in their hands." The *New York Gazette* as well as the *Boston News Letter, Boston Chronicle,* and *Boston Gazette* regularly carried ads for the purchase of slave coopers, carpenters, joiners, tailors, bakers, blacksmiths, and sometimes printers. In 1719, when a New York colonial court sentenced an African American blacksmith to death for theft, his owner, also a blacksmith, asked the court to spare the slave's life, arguing that he himself was a "very poor Lame and Antient man" and that he had "nothing whereby to sustain himself but what is procured by the Labour of the said Negro man."[9]

Blacks worked in an even broader range of skilled crafts in the urban South than in the North. New Bern, Petersburg, Richmond, and other smaller southern towns and cities employed significant numbers of enslaved craftsmen, but skilled blacks found their greatest opportunities for artisan labor in New Orleans, Charleston, and later to some extent Baltimore. Between 1750 and 1779, Charleston probate records revealed that no less than 73 percent of the city's artisans owned slaves upon their death. White artisans worked and cooperated "with slaves on a daily basis as blacks and whites learned their trades together." On one occasion, a carpenter, Thomas Bennett, sought "immediately a handy white lad and two negro boys as apprentices to carpenter's trade." Between 1770 and 1799, Charleston's white artisans placed twice as many newspaper advertisements for black as for white workers. In 1728, the governor of Louisiana reported "placing negroes as apprentices with all the workmen who we think are good and honest men, and if the same practice had been followed when they were first sent to the colony, we could at present do without several white men." By 1732, numerous New Orleans tradesmen and merchants owned blacks "whom they housed and trained in their shops." An estimated 15 percent of the city's enslaved people resided in artisan households, and some 25 percent of all the city's tradesmen "lived with slaves."[10] Enslaved African people not only cultivated the land and built the levees, but also "framed the houses, plastered the walls, and shingled the roofs. As well they forged the tools that made the barrels that stored the tobacco and indigo, which were then carried to market in wagons and carts that their hands built and kept in repair."[11]

In 1790, Baltimore's craftsmen and craftswomen accounted for one quarter of the city's slaveholders as well as a quarter of all enslaved blacks. Two decades later, Baltimore's artisans and manufacturers had increased to 35 percent of slaveowners, with 30 percent of the city's enslaved population. Significant numbers of Baltimore's enslaved blacks had gained skills as carpenters, blacksmiths, and lumber-mill hands in surrounding rural areas before moving to the city. At the turn of the nineteenth century, historian Charles Steffen notes, two-thirds of Baltimore's wealthiest fifty-two craftsmen owned one or more slaves. Enslaved skilled workers stood at the "top of the slave occupa-tional hierarchy," and shipbuilders claimed the lion's share of enslaved blacks, "with a mean average" of about six slaves per firm among them.[12]

Artisans deployed a wide range of skills and know-how within the context of specific crafts. They took pride in their specialized tools, higher earnings, greater autonomy in the workforce, and "mastery of the expertise required to produce material objects their communities needed and valued." Before the advent of woodworking machinery of various types, especially planing machines, African American carpenters performed this work by hand much like their West African kinsmen. In precolonial West Africa, canoe builders had carved out "massive tree trunks, larger even than the giant cypress that boat slaves would hollow in South Carolina." According to historian and urban sociologist W. E. B. Du Bois and his co-author Augustus Dill, in the American colonies these artisans could thus take a "single-tree" from the forest and carve out "a hundred other things too numerous to mention." The African American carpenter "in those days was also the 'cabinet maker,' the woodturner, coffin maker, generally the pattern maker, and the maker of most things made of wood." Similarly, the African American blacksmith "in the days of slavery was expected to make any and everything wrought of iron. He was to all intents and purposes the 'machine blacksmith,' 'horseshoer,' 'carriage and wagon ironer and trimmer,' 'gunsmith,' [and] 'wheelwright.'"

Before their forced migration to South Carolina, some enslaved Africans had worked on the construction of the Barbadian city of Bridgetown. African artisans not only constructed the city's buildings but also "crafted their orna-mental embellishments." More than those of any other North American city, Charleston's eighteenth-century buildings showed the distinct imprint of West African–influenced Barbadian culture, including intricate "wrought ironworks" on the galleries of buildings, gates, and "garden walls flanking the street."[13] While some contemporary observers described black artisans as "tolerable good," other observers used such terms as "first rate" and "excel-lent," especially in advertisements for the return of runaway craftsmen.[14]

While most black artisans were men, women also worked in the skilled trades. As early as July 1763, the *Providence Gazette* advertised for the return of a 38-year-old runaway named Dinas, described as a "skilled seamstress." The owner of another runaway female slave described her as a skilled "needle-woman." In New York, according to historian Leslie Harris, enslaved African American women, "like the white women of artisan families, assisted the men in their skilled tasks as necessary." Free black women were also prominent among the hardworking "artisans and tradespersons who lived above their own shops" in Charleston by the late eighteenth century. Moreover, similar to male migrants from surrounding farms and plantations across the early American North and South, large numbers of black women (some fugitives) migrated to cities from the countryside, where they had learned to spin thread, weave cloth, and sew. In Georgia, the state not only mandated that landowners plant five hundred acres of mulberry trees for every five hundred acres of land for the development of the silk culture but required that black slave women be sent to Savannah "at the proper season every year" to gain training in the craft of "reeling and winding silk." According to one scholar, revolutionary and early America represented a kind of "golden age" of the black artisan, including to some extent women as well as men.[15]

Able-bodied adult men and women carried out the bulk of slave labor, but colonial cities quickly incorporated enslaved children into established work routines. In 1721, one New York slaveholder, Cadwallader Colden, instructed his agent to buy two "well made" black males "about eighteen years of age" and "a negro Girl of about thirteen years old." Colden wanted the young men for general labor and the female to assist his wife, "chiefly to keep the children & to sow." In 1730, the *New York Gazette* advertised "a Likely Negro Girl about 18 Years of Age, and a likely Negro Boy about 16 Years, both born in this City, they can speak good English and Dutch and are bred up to all sorts of House-work." When Phillis Wheatley arrived in New England during the early 1760s, she also embarked upon a well-worn path of domestic slavery for young children in the household of a Boston family. And in 1766, the *South Carolina Gazette* described one 12-year-old as a "handy" girl with experience "waiting in a house and attending children." By hiring young people out, their owners could also earn more than enough to cover their keep. General and household labor of enslaved people, young and old, men and women, freed white men and, to some extent, white women for engagement in alternative professional, skilled, and entrepreneurial activities.[16]

Although poor and working-class whites also labored in such general and household service jobs and buoyed the wealth of colonial elites, enslaved people enriched cities through both their labor and their sale as commodities on the open market. Slaveowners used this distinction to help discipline the enslaved labor force and sharpen the divide between free and slave labor. As historian Daniel Walker notes, the threat of sale was one of the most effective "social-control mechanisms available to slave regimes throughout the Americas, both rural and urban." Enslaved blacks themselves would later recall how some owners "used to say that if we didn't suit him he would put us in his pocket quick—meaning he would sell us."[17]

While their numbers would remain small, the free black population nonetheless slowly increased by the beginning of the American Revolution, rising to 600 in Charleston and to just over 1,000 in Philadelphia and New York. Compared to their plantation counterparts, urban black workers gained substantial access to long-distance travel, informal commercial networks, wage labor, and opportunities for emancipation. At the core of this cluster of forces was the "hiring-out" system, including the Dutch system of "half freedom" in New Amsterdam. This arrangement enabled some enslaved people to find their own jobs, negotiate wages, and, through overwork, earn their own money to purchase their freedom and the freedom of loved ones. This system of labor was by no means limited to the city. Historian Dylan Penningroth estimated that 6 percent of enslaved rural blacks and 31 percent of urban slaves worked under hiring-out agreements by the late antebellum years, and "over a lifetime, their chances of being hired out increased."[18]

Sailors and river pilots figured prominently among the gradually expanding free black population. By the mid-eighteenth century, black men, slave and free, constituted as much as 25 percent of the muster for vessels departing Atlantic port cities for the high seas. Black and white sailors endured an exceedingly hierarchical, violent, and repressive shipboard environment. They weathered the same storms, shipwrecks, and "the same infernally leaking ships." But black sailors worked disproportionately as cooks and stewards and encountered frequent day-to-day assaults on their persons. One sailor, John Jea, later recalled how his white shipmates "used to flog, beat, and kick me about, the same as I had been a dog." Another free black sailor, John Dean, related to Thomas Clarkson, a young British scholar and social activist, how the captain of one ship punished him for a "trifling" infraction "for which he was in no-wise to blame." The captain "fastened him with his belly to the deck, and that in this situation, he had poured hot pitch upon his back, and made incisions in it with hot tongs." Yet despite this context of violent inequality, the open sea nonetheless offered enslaved blacks opportunities to breach the racial divide emerging in the urban Atlantic world, including engagement in interracial working-class mutinies and piracy.[19]

The sailor Olaudah Equiano spent the bulk of his life "either in ports or on ships sailing between ports." Equiano not only learned to read, write, and cipher while still enslaved but obtained permission to hire himself out as an

African people not only entered colonial North America in the holds of slave ships. They also worked as deckhands on numerous vessels that plied the Atlantic during the era of the slave trade. Here, the eighteenth-century Anglo-American artist included an African among white shipmates during a rescue at sea in Havana, based on a real-life event. *Watson and the Shark*, 1778 by John Singleton Copley. Courtesy, National Gallery of Art, Washington, DC.

experienced sailor on the high seas. He soon took advantage of the "working" and hiring-out system to accumulate sufficient funds to purchase his freedom. Somewhat similar to Equiano, the enslaved Charlestonian Thomas Jeremiah learned the pilot's trade and obtained his freedom by the eve of the Revolution. All oceangoing vessels appearing in Charleston Harbor depended on skilled pilots like Jeremiah, "who guided vessels over the bar through the harbor's narrow ship channel." Jeremiah became an experienced pilot, thoroughly acquainted with "the time and direction of the tide, knowledge of the reigning winds; of the different depths of the water." He became a stellar example of how one enslaved African not only became a free wage earner but also transformed himself into an influential member of the free black elite. On one occasion, he was convicted and sentenced to the stocks to receive ten lashes, but he appealed his sentence and received a pardon from the lieutenant governor and commander in chief.[20]

The piloting skills of early American blacks were closely intertwined with knowledge acquired in the Old World. Along with canoe-building, carpentry, and blacksmithing skills, African people brought river navigational skills to the Americas. On the inland and coastal waters of West Africa and the New World, Europeans depended on the skills of African boatmen, and ship pilots connected enslaved people and Europeans to emerging capitalist markets on both sides of the Atlantic. Thus, according to historian Kevin Dawson, "privileged exploitation" marked the lives and labor of enslaved pilots. They exchanged their specialized knowledge for opportunities to cultivate "semi-independent lives within the boundaries of bondage." Although European captains of ships proved competent to steer vessels across the Atlantic, they recognized the expertise of the African boatmen and "willingly entrusted" their lives to these skilled black rivermen. In August 1778, an enslaved pilot steered a fifty-gun British warship through the dangerous passage called Hell Gate, near Harlem, New York. When the white commander countered his orders during a particularly perilous moment in the journey, the black pilot firmly retorted, "You no speak here!" The captain complied and the African successfully guided the ship to safety.[21]

Rivermen and sailors occupied a pivotal place in the development of African American trade networks. As he moved from port to port around the globe, Equiano supplemented his wages through the sale of quantities of rum and sugar. In 1765, when his ship docked in Philadelphia, he quickly engaged the local trade network of enslaved and free blacks and sold a few of his own products "chiefly to the Quakers." On another occasion, Equiano sailed into Charleston Harbor. He hired a crew of enslaved black rivermen to ferry him across the harbor to conduct business. Charleston's black river pilots helped Equiano dispose of his wares. Unlike white Philadelphians, however, Charleston's white men purchased Equiano's sugar and rum, as he later reported, "with smooth promises and fair words" but paid him in debased copper dollars. According to Equiano, one white Charlestonian "took advantage of my being a negro man, and obliged me to put up with those [copper coins] or none, although I objected."[22]

Trade networks, wage labor, and employment on the high seas and inland waterways all contributed to the growing number of free people of color, which in turn broadened opportunities for other enslaved blacks to escape bondage and become free wage earners. Charleston slaveowners complained that runaways hired themselves out to free people of color. After successfully hiding out for eight months, Harry, a carpenter, was finally sighted on King Street in

Charleston. He had apparently secured employment with free black carpenters, "as he is intimate with numbers of them." One low-country resident reported that his Angolan washerwoman "sometimes hires herself to free negroes." Another Angolan slave, a skilled needlewoman, also received employment from "free Negroes and others" during her time away "without permission."[23]

While some free blacks provided significant opportunities for their enslaved counterparts to obtain freedom, others insisted that their own freedom included the right to purchase, own, and employ slave labor on equal terms with their white counterparts. Both New Orleans and Charleston exhibited elements of this process, described by some scholars as a "three-tier" or "three-caste" society, where mixed-race free people of color stood between the large majority of enslaved blacks and their white owners. In this system, the most well-to-do free blacks not only became slaveowners themselves but also allied with white slaveowners to discourage and even help to squash slave rebellions. "Libres," as historian Kimberly Hanger notes, justified the enslavement of most black people in exchange for an opportunity to manumit their own kinsmen and women.

While late eighteenth- and early nineteenth-century Savannah is often treated as a three-tier city, recent scholarship uncovers a greater measure of racial solidarity among free and enslaved blacks in Savannah than in Charleston and New Orleans. Nonetheless, slaveholding was an important indicator of increasing social stratification among blacks in all three of these cities.[24]

REVOLUTION, THE NEW REPUBLIC, AND THE FREE BLACK PROLETARIAT

Under the impact of the American Revolution, the end of the international slave trade in 1808, and passage of the Northwest Ordinance in 1787 prohibiting slavery north of the Ohio River, the free black population dramatically increased during the early nineteenth century. Free people of color rose from no more than about 1,000 at the outset of the period in each city to nearly 2,000 in Boston by the 1830s and 1840s, 10,000 in Philadelphia, 14,000 in New York, 2,000 in Charleston, 3,000 in Washington, DC, 11,600 in New Orleans, and 14,800 in Baltimore (the largest concentration of free blacks in the nation at that time). The majority of urban blacks, free and enslaved, men and women, migrated to southern cities from surrounding rural areas within the South, while northern black communities expanded through the arrival of increasing numbers of southern-born black migrants, particularly from the Upper South and border states of Virginia and Maryland.[25]

By the early nineteenth century, black women outdistanced men in most cities across the urban North and South. In 1850, only Richmond among major antebellum cities reported an excess of black men over women. Antebellum slaveowners increasingly sold able-bodied and skilled black men to the booming cotton-growing regions of the Deep South, leaving cities with disproportionately large black female populations. This phenomenon was not limited to adolescent boys or adult males, but also included young boys under ten years of age. Although New Orleans enacted a law against the sale of children under ten, the greater numbers of female than male children in this group suggest that the law against selling young children was not systematically enforced.[26]

Enslaved and free black women shouldered the twin burdens of reproductive and productive labor. As recent scholars note, the colonial and early national eras witnessed the gradual emergence of the "Atlantic service economy," characterized by the increasing "commodification of reproductive labor." Middle class and elite families turned to poor and working-class women to perform labor that "ladies" of the household increasingly viewed as beneath their station in life. In their detailed analysis of black women's lives in colonial Boston and other New England towns, historians Catherine Adams and Elizabeth H. Pleck underscore the pursuit and use of enslaved women to perform what they describe as "household drudge" work. Among the wealthiest households, enslaved black women and girls polished furniture and the family silver and assisted the "lady" of the house with her clothes and hair, drew her bath, and mended her clothes. Some elite men also preferred "the servant girl to shave them rather than going to a barber." The vast majority of mistresses nonetheless used enslaved women "not as their personal attendant" but rather as heavy-laden domestic laborers—black women were "put to work sweeping, emptying chamber pots, carrying water, washing the dishes, brewing, looking after children, cooking and baking, spinning, knitting, carding, and sewing."[27]

Household labor not only entailed long hours and tedious work—cleaning, cooking, washing, ironing, sewing, or whatever employers demanded—but it also made black women vulnerable to widespread physical and sexual abuse. In Charleston, some slaveowners realized a "superordinate level of accumulation" by forcing enslaved women household workers to perform "sexual acts for money" in addition to their washing, cleaning, and other domestic tasks. In some cases, slaveowners ordered enslaved women to have sex with enslaved men to increase the slave workforce. Among free people of color, live-in single women servants faced the brunt of such sexual and labor exploitation on the job, while married women made up the bulk of washerwomen—a low-paying and exceedingly labor-intensive but preferred job. In 1817, black women made up nearly 80 percent of all washerwomen listed in the Baltimore city directory. Among black female heads of households, laundrywomen accounted for 194 of 231 female heads of households in 1822 and 440 of 526 in 1840. The advantage of this job was that washerwomen worked within their own homes while supervising and caring for young children. Nonetheless, washing entailed carrying heavy buckets of water from hydrants or streams to backyards and kitchens, where the women boiled the water and carried out the heavy labor of scrubbing and lifting water-soaked garments. This work resulted in "aching backs, . . . burning hands from lye soaps and rough washboards." Next, washerwomen hung the clothes out in backyards to dry and then "heated irons on the fire to press the clothes and delivered bundles of clean and pressed laundry to the owners."[28]

Although women increasingly outnumbered men in the urban North and South, employers continued to value men over women in the wage-earning labor market. While enslaved and free black women labored almost exclusively as household workers, enslaved and free black men worked as artisans, general laborers, and factory hands as well as household and personal servants. Some southern industrial promoters hoped to end the region's dependence on northern industrial firms for consumer goods. They looked to African American men as a source of industrial labor "in cotton and woolen factories, . . . in iron furnaces, . . . factories and work shops, . . . in the manufacture of such articles as are now made almost exclusively in the Northern states."

While slave labor gradually disappeared from the northern workforce by mid-century, free and enslaved blacks continued to labor side by side in the industrializing urban South. In most instances, the preference was for enslaved labor. In 1845, the governor of South Carolina wrote to the British abolitionist Thomas Clarkson that "we are beginning to manufacture with slaves."[29] A few years later, in Charleston, April 10–15, 1854, the Southern and Western States Convention passed a resolution affirming that "experiments have fully proven that slave labor can be profitably employed in manufacturing establishments." By 1850, enslaved blacks made up a majority of the laborers at the city's Gibbes and Williams Steam Saw Mill, the Bennett Mill, and the Chisholm Mill. Other industrial firms that hired enslaved workers included West Point Rice

Mills, Horlbeck's Brickyard, and the Charleston Bridge Company. Located on the Ashley River, the West Point Rice Mills employed African American engineers, blacksmiths, carpenters, and coopers among its 160-member slave workforce. Further, the Savannah, Ogeechee, and Altamaha Canal Company, chartered in 1824, leased hundreds of enslaved men from Georgia slaveowners to clear land, dig the channel, and construct the canal locks that connected the Savannah River with the Ogeechee. Savannah's enslaved black men also worked for the Georgia Central Railroad Company, the Upper Steam Rice Mill, the Steam Boat Company of Georgia, and the Savannah Brick Company, to name a few. Historian Whittington Johnson notes, "Nearly all the crew of the Georgia Central Railroad, except the conductors, was composed of slaves; the engineers, firemen, other workers, and construction crews were slaves." In New Orleans, during the 1790s, an estimated 20 percent of "libres," or free people of color, worked in the "manufacturing" sector, mainly as shoemakers and carpenters.[30]

The enthusiasm for slave labor in the manufacturing and other sectors of the urban economy meant that free black men and women almost uniformly worked in jobs defined as less skilled and at lower pay than their enslaved and free white counterparts. At the same time, however, the South's black workers as a whole often occupied a broader range of skilled and manufacturing jobs than their counterparts farther north. This phenomenon was not limited to the Deep South as suggested by the above examples. Baltimore's Maryland Chemical Works employed predominantly adult male black workers to manufacture some thirty different "medicines, pigments, dyes, and industrial chemicals." But the firm was "best known for its alum, used by cloth manufactures as a mordant to set dyes in cloth," characterized by an exceedingly tedious labor process. "Throughout the six-to-eight-month process, laborers stoked furnaces, agitated alum broth, raked up drying alum heaps, and shoveled alum from furnace to cistern and back again, day and night, seven days a week." In Louisville, even though most enslaved and free blacks occupied jobs as janitors, handymen, and household servants, by 1850 over 13 percent of black men occupied jobs as craftsmen compared to 8.2 percent in Cincinnati and about 4 percent in Pittsburgh. More so than their northern counterparts, southern employers often blurred the line between African American male and female laborers and adult and child laborers. One Louisville firm advertised for "100 women and boys for brickyards, draymen, etc., 40 men and boys for ropewalk, 40 men and boys for hotel waiters, and 50 boys and girls for tobacco stemmeries."[31]

Richmond emerged as the premier employer of blacks in the manufacturing sector of the urban economy. It claimed a reputation as "the manufacturing heart of Dixie" and the principal employer of black industrial workers. At the outbreak of the Civil War, the city's enslaved population had increased from fewer than 5,000 in 1820 to over 11,600 in 1860; only 2,500 free people of color lived in Richmond. Moreover, as noted above, Richmond was the only city to consistently count more black men than women. Black men took the lion's share of jobs in the city's expanding manufacturing economy. The city employed black workers in its flour mills, stone quarries, and nearby coal fields as well as in the construction of buildings, canals, and railroads. Most important, as the South's premier tobacco- and iron-producing center, Richmond employed large numbers of enslaved black workers in its leading industrial sector. At Joseph Anderson's renowned Tredegar Iron Company, African Americans performed all available skilled jobs—as puddlers, heaters, and rollers—as well as general labor. In a letter to the editor of a leading Charleston, South Carolina, newspaper, Anderson proudly advertised his firm's reliance on slave labor. He rented and hired enslaved blacks but "preferred to own them." At the core of his workforce were a "lot of 35 men and boys he had specially trained to handle key operations." Black workers also fueled the labor force at the James H. Grant, T. S. Hardgrove, and Talbott Brothers tobacco-manufacturing plants.[32]

Tobacco manufacturing involved enslaved men, women, and children in an intricate and arduous system of production. The tobacco industry revolved around the production of smoking and especially chewing tobacco. Each process entailed lots of heavy lifting, packaging, and repackaging of hogsheads; labor-intensive preliminary work in the tobacco stemmeries, where women worked on the roof of buildings as "pickers" sorting and resorting dried tobacco leaves; and the actual manufacturing of the final product itself. Tobacco manufacturers focused mainly on supplying the huge market for chewing tobacco. By the beginning of the Civil War, Richmond reported some fifty tobacco factories employing no fewer than 3,400 African American workers. Antebellum tourists to the city viewed a visit to a tobacco factory as a high point of their journey, "drawn by the unusual sight [and sound] of black industrial workers coordinating their repetitive motions through song." In the making of chewing tobacco, once women had stemmed and dried the leaves, "skilled black men would mix huge vats of a black, syrupy compound of licorice and sugar into which they would dip the stemmed leaves. . . . In the lump-making room, two-men teams—the lumper (or twister) and his helper, usually a child—jointly labored."[33]

Across the urban industrial South, in Richmond and elsewhere, employers of slave labor reported large annual profit margins, reaching between 7 and 10 percent in most cases and as high as 42–65 percent in other instances.[34]

IMMIGRATION AND THE LIMITS OF FREE LABOR

In addition to the use of enslaved workers in southern industry, free wage earners of color encountered new and more daunting challenges in the urban North and South during the antebellum years. For one thing, Deep South cotton planters required increasing numbers of skilled blacks "to construct quarters for master and slaves and to build and repair barns, presses, and a variety of agricultural machinery." In their seminal essay on the subject, labor historians Ira Berlin and Herbert Gutman concluded, "Slave artisans may have been the first to go west, pulled out of the cities in large numbers by the rapid spread of plantation agriculture across the South. In a time of great economic growth, artisan standing provided scant protection from sale . . . to distant rural workplaces, a process that reduced the number of slave artisans in cities."[35] At the same time, the estimated 3.7 million European immigrants who entered the United States between the American Revolution and 1860 took an expanding range of jobs in the artisan field, the newly developing manufacturing sector, and the most lucrative segments of household, general labor, and personal service employment.[36]

Massive European immigration had its most profound impact on the development of the northern black working class. By 1850, black men holding skilled jobs stood at only 8.3, 5.4, and 5.7 percent, respectively, in Philadelphia, New York, and Boston. In Pittsburgh and Cincinnati, respectively, only 4 and 8 percent of blacks gained jobs as carpenters, shoemakers, masons, and other skilled artisans. Although the South attracted relatively fewer immigrants, significant numbers moved to Richmond, Baltimore, New Orleans, Charleston, Savannah, and other southern cities. By the onset of the Civil War, immigrants had increased to over 20 percent of the total population in Charleston and over 25 percent in Savannah. Predominantly adult men, immigrants made up over 30 percent of the working class in Richmond and 42 percent in Charleston. In 1829, when the Chesapeake and Ohio Canal Company built a waterway just above Georgetown in the District of

Columbia, it initially employed African Americans but quickly replaced them with Irishmen.

Nonetheless, despite heightened competition with immigrant workers, southern free wage earners of color held on to a uniformly higher ratio of skilled jobs than their northern counterparts. In 1850, between 12 and 18 percent of free black men reported employment as artisans in Washington, Baltimore, and Louisville. These figures reached over 60 percent in New Orleans and Charleston, where the size of the free black population remained exceedingly small compared to the number of enslaved African American workers.[37]

In the urban North, black carpenters, plasterers, masons, and other skilled workers found few opportunities for employment even among their white abolitionist supporters. As skilled black artisans moved into the urban North in rising numbers, they repeatedly complained that they "found every door closed against the colored man in a free state, excepting the jails and penitentiaries," and they described themselves as little better off than their brothers and sisters in Virginia. And as their parents encountered these barriers, black youth gained few opportunities to enter the skilled crafts. In 1836, a convention of the New England Anti-Slavery Society reported, "The colored people are almost altogether deprived of bringing up their children to mechanical employments, to commercial business, or other more lucrative occupations, whereby so many of our white laborers are enabled to rise above the drudgery in which they commence their . . . life."[38]

Across the early nineteenth-century economy, free black workers faced increasing confinement to a narrow range of jobs described as general labor and household and personal service. "Competition of the foreigners," Du Bois concluded, pushed Philadelphia's black artisans "more and more to the wall."[39] At the same time, as master craftsmen increasingly expelled blacks from the artisan trades, new northern manufacturing firms hired white over black labor. These included cotton textile mills, machine foundries, and boot and shoe manufacturing firms in New York, Philadelphia, Providence, and Boston, as well as booming iron, shipbuilding, and milling industries in the urban Midwest, most notably Cincinnati and Pittsburgh. By 1850, an estimated 70 percent of Pittsburgh's African American men worked as general laborers, coachmen, and waiters, and in other household service jobs, while 66 percent of Cincinnati's black men occupied only five job categories: boatmen, barbers, laborers, cooks, and waiters.[40]

Increasing numbers of black artisans put the tools of their trade aside and turned to any general labor job that they could find. Frederick Douglass recalled, "Finding my trade of no immediate benefit, I threw off my calking habiliments, and prepared myself to do any kind of work I could get to do." Douglass took jobs sawing wood, carrying hods for bricklayers, sweeping chimneys, and transporting heavy oil casks, among others.[41] In seaports across the country, enslaved and free black dockworkers put in long hours lifting and transporting 500-pound bales of cotton and heavy barrels of rice, sugar, and other bulk products at low pay. In some cases, black dockworkers "would turn three hogsheads . . . upon their ends at once, each . . . weighing one thousand pounds net weight." While black and white seamen earned about the same rate for the same job in northern ports, blacks received lower wages than whites for identical work in southern ports.

As black labor became further devalued, sailing jobs on the high seas as well as the prestigious piloting jobs on the inland rivers became less available to black workers. On the Mississippi, Missouri, and Ohio Rivers, the new steamboat owners and captains excluded blacks from jobs as officers, pilots, captains, engineers, clerks, and mates during the antebellum heyday of steamship travel. The preponderance of both enslaved and free black rivermen worked as laborers, dockhands, roustabouts, cooks, and cabin-cleaning crews. They also labored under harsh conditions. Riverside slaveowners themselves sometimes complained about the "overzealous driving" of enslaved blacks leased to the steamboat companies.[42]

Contemporary elite travelers and observers regularly commented on the growing concentration of blacks in what they called "menial service." A New Orleans doctor summed up this perspective when he observed black people "ever at the elbow . . . behind a table, in hotels and steamboats, ever ready, brush in hand, to brush the coat or black the shoes, or to perform any *menial service* which may be required" (my italics). As early as 1815, a Cincinnati physician described blacks as "disciplined to laborious occupations . . . and menial drudgery."[43] In the minds of white workers, according to a Cincinnati editor, it was largely the evils associated with human bondage that confined free blacks to a limited range of jobs "despised as being the work of slaves."[44] And this perspective proved largely immune to change. In 1793, when the Philadelphia yellow fever epidemic took the lives of some 4,000 whites and 250 blacks, African Americans worked for their distressed white neighbors as "nurses, gravediggers, and drivers of death carts." By carrying out the most dangerous and arduous work associated with the epidemic, black Philadelphians hoped not only to counter white racial hatred against the rising numbers of free people of color but also to secure much needed employment during their early transition from enslaved to free workers. But their sacrifices did little to stem resistance to African American movement up the job hierarchy into skilled artisan positions and the nascent urban manufacturing sector as the nineteenth century got under way.[45]

Martin R. Delany, a migrant from Virginia, observed growing limits on African American employment in Pittsburgh and other expanding antebellum cities. In his famous black nationalist manifesto, issued in 1852, Delany complained, "Our fathers are their coachmen, our brothers their cookmen, and ourselves their waiting men. Our mothers their nurse-women, our sisters their scrub-women, our daughters their maid-women, and our wives their washer-women." Similarly, the early nineteenth-century woman activist Maria Stewart pointedly asked, "How long shall the fair daughters of Africa be compelled to bury their minds and talents beneath a load of iron pots and kettles?"[46] Douglass also chimed in. He described the barber trade as a viable livelihood for significant numbers of blacks, while nonetheless treating it as a lowly craft that exceedingly able blacks sometimes pursued for lack of other, more remunerative and professional alternatives. Describing the barber J. M. Whitfield as "the Colored Poet of America," Douglass lamented that Whitfield's talents were confined to his barbershop. It "is painfully disheartening," Douglass said, "that talents so commanding, gifts so rare, poetic powers so distinguished, should be tied to the handle of a razor and buried in the precincts of a barbershop." Douglass, Delany, Stewart, and other free people of color did not decry domestic service labor per se, but they believed that it should not be the primary station of an entire people. Delany explained that the occupation of servant was not necessarily degrading "to one or a few people of a kind; but a whole race of servants are a degradation to that people."[47]

Even as blacks protested limits on their access to skilled jobs, they denounced the displacement of blacks from their previous strongholds in low-wage and low-prestige jobs. The barbering trade had emerged as one of the most lucrative among early nineteenth-century black men. Following the Revolution, increasing numbers of white men had abandoned it as a "servile" trade, inimical to the values of the new republican nation. African Americans soon took the lion's share of barbering jobs in the urban North and South, securing the niche by developing an elaborate system of apprenticeships for young men and opening innovative "first class" barbershops. Catering to an exclusively elite white clientele, these establishments emerged in the heart of expanding business districts in Baltimore, Charleston, Philadelphia, New York, and other cities. Black barbershops not only provided "expert"

THE ILLUSTRATED LONDON NEWS

No. 1078.—VOL. XXXVIII.]   SATURDAY, MARCH 9, 1861.   [WITH A SUPPLEMENT, FIVEPENCE

DEBATING IN FRANCE.

THE emancipation of political speech in France is not only an accomplished fact, but its accomplishment has been as nearly as possible brought about by the act of the Emperor himself. It is a well-known legal maxim that a man may for certain purposes perform certain acts as completely by his agent as by himself. In the recent debate in the French Senate Prince Napoleon must be taken to have directly represented his Imperial cousin. If while this new-born orator was speaking there had been any doubt whether he was delivering his own sentiments merely, the overt congratulations of the immediate Ministers of the Crown, as well as the tone adopted in the subsequent discussion by those unattached members of the Government whose duty it is to defend the Administration in the Chambers, would set the question at rest, while, if reports be true, the Emperor in person has given his fiat to the course taken and the line of argument adopted by his relative. Indeed, it must be presumed that it was fully understood that the privilege of debate was a reality, or even M. de la Rochejaquelein, possessing as he does all the temerity, not to say recklessness, of an impassioned partisan, would hardly have ventured to afford such a test of his quality in reference to free discussion as is to be found in his speech. If the address of this senator was anything, it was an almost fierce declaration of the Legitimist creed, and England at least has to thank him for the decided manner in which the feelings and the wishes toward her have been elicited. On the two main subjects which were

under consideration on the occasion in question we know what the views of the party of reaction in France are. As regards Italy and England, there can be no mistake what would be the policy of those whose dreams for France are a restoration under Henry V. As certainly and as clearly has there been demonstrated to the world the policy of France de facto in both these respects.

Apart from its striking character as a great oratorical display, amounting almost to a phenomenon, the speech of Prince Napoleon was a masterly exposition of the policy of France. It is not to be expected that the declarations of the Prince are binding on the Government; but even if his words were no more than quasi prophecies founded on political calculations they would be of great significance and of no little importance. But it is evident that the process of ratiocination in his mind originated in a conception of the ideas of the Emperor; and as he traced the course pursued by that potentate in reference to the Roman question it was palpable that he had fathomed the Imperial policy. If in some respects that policy has been apparently inconsistent, that inconsistency was almost inseparable from the peculiar position held by the "Eldest Son of the Church;" but, if the creation of Prince Napoleon proves anything, it shows that the object from first to last has really been the deposition of the temporal power of the Pope. The phraseology of the Prince—when he founded an argument for the retirement of the Pontiff to the cul-

tivation of a spiritual supremacy on the geographical situation of the city of Rome—was almost identical with the phrase, now become nearly proverbial, of "the Pope in a Palace with a garden." On the question of Italian unity the opinions of the nearest cousin of the French Crown were equally if not more explicit; while no more decided tribute could be paid to the policy which has been pursued by England in reference to this subject than the angry ravings of the Legitimist speakers, or the close reasoning and cogent arguments of the liberal Imperial party. The part taken in this debate by M. Billault, one of the "speaking Ministers," ought not to be overlooked. Necessarily guarded by an official reticence, all that he said confirmed the impression which Prince Napoleon had produced. He pointed out that the speeches of the Legitimist senators had placed the Italian question and the English alliance on an intelligible footing, and it had caused the Assembly which had listened to those addresses to comprehend those subjects as they were assuredly understood by thinking and impartial men of the world. The definition of the English alliance as it came from both the Princely orator and the Ministerial functionary is identical. Prince Napoleon declared it to be an alliance not with this or that Minister, but with the great liberal English people, an alliance by which, though France might have to make some concessions on secondary points, she would defend the

Urban blacks worked in a broad range of household services, general labor, and skilled crafts. The barber trade emerged as one of the most lucrative jobs open to free people of color before the onset of the Civil War. Here, a black barber is shaving a white customer in his shop in Richmond, Virginia. Courtesy, Albert and Shirley Small, Special Collections Library, University of Virginia, Charlottesville.

shaves and haircuts but also sold wigs and diverse personal care items, while also providing a social and political gathering place for white men of substantial influence in the urban political economy. Historian Douglas Bristol notes in his pioneering study of the black barber that these black workers envisioned themselves as skilled "knights of the razor" and transformed a job that whites perceived as "servile" into a badge of accomplishment and even "superiority" rather than "inferiority."[48]

Soon, however, large numbers of Irish and to some extent German immigrants took jobs as house servants, cooks, stewards, barbers, and laborers. In 1853, in a famous editorial, "Learn Trades or Starve," penned following a national black convention in Rochester, New York, Douglass observed, "The old avocations, by which colored men obtained a livelihood, are rapidly, unceasingly and inevitably passing into other hands. Every hour sees the black man elbowed out of employment by some newly arrived emigrant whose hunger and whose color are thought to give him a better title to the place.... White men are becoming house servants, cooks and stewards of vessels, at hotels, they are becoming porters, stevedores, woodsawyers, hodcarriers, brickmakers, whitewashers and barbers." "A few years ago," Douglass concluded, "a white barber would have been a curiosity—now their poles stand on every corner." In New York, municipal officials routinely rejected black applications for licenses to engage in the carrying trade. When black workers ignored such regulations and continued to work despite white resistance, white carters used physical force to drive black men out of this job. As early as the 1830s, New York's *Colored American* magazine protested discrimination against black carters and urged the mayor to use his influence to end the practice. In letters on the condition of the African race, one antebellum "southern lady" reported that legions of "foreigners" of New York had not only pushed blacks out of "all mechanical trades but even out of the most menial labors."[49]

In addition to the challenge of immigration, the place of blacks in the urban economy was further undermined by a plethora of statutes enacted by states and municipalities in the antebellum period. In 1818, the Kentucky legislature prohibited the immigration of free blacks into the state from elsewhere. In 1834, another state law required free black residents to post a bond in order to avoid expulsion from the state. Charleston passed a statute prohibiting the training of slaves for "any mechanic or handicraft trade." The Charleston city council reported that low-grade or what it called "menial" occupations were "necessarily confined to coloured persons." In 1822, the South Carolina legislature had outlawed the practice of "self-hiring" and imposed a penalty on violators, including the possible "forfeiture of the slave" involved. Savannah not only enacted laws that discriminated against free blacks but also levied special burdens on free women of color. The city required any free person of color who settled in the city to pay a fee of $100. Conviction under the law required men to work 100 days to meet the requirements of the law, but women had to labor 125 days before they were released from forced labor on public projects. In New Orleans, the city council enacted a statute in 1822 restricting municipal jobs to white laborers only, although by the 1850s nearly 50 percent of free black men would still be working in skilled jobs.[50]

Federal law prohibited slavery north of the Ohio River, but midwestern state constitutions and legislation nevertheless discriminated against free blacks and limited their access to free territory. Ohio, Indiana, Illinois, and Michigan required free blacks to post bonds (as much as $500) before they could become legal residents in these states. White migrants and immigrants were not required to post such bonds. In New York, whereas white men had unrestricted access to the state's franchise, black New Yorkers had to demonstrate ownership of $250 worth of property to qualify to vote. In order to repeal this restriction, New York blacks formed suffrage committees throughout the state. But by 1860, only Maine, New Hampshire, Vermont, and Massachusetts allowed free blacks full access to the franchise. Both northern and southern states limited the rights of free blacks to testify in court against whites, serve in the militia, marry across racial lines, attend public schools, gain access to public accommodations on an equal footing with white patrons, and even petition their government. In 1839, the Ohio legislature proclaimed that blacks and mulattoes "have no constitutional right to present their petitions to the General Assembly for any purpose whatsoever, and that any reception of such petitions on the part of the General Assembly is a mere act of privilege or policy and not imposed by any expressed or implied power of the constitution."[51]

THE ASSAULT ON FREE BLACKS: COLONIZATION AND THE FUGITIVE SLAVE ACT

Efforts to curtail the presence of free black workers gained increasing elite and working-class white support with the formation of the American Colonization Society (ACS) in 1816. Under the leadership of northern and southern white elites, the ACS established headquarters in the nation's capital and spearheaded a vigorous campaign to recolonize free people of color (presumably with their consent) on African land "or such other places as Congress shall deem most expedient." The organization's constitution expressed the belief that colonization would not only rid the country of free blacks but also prepare "the way for getting rid of slaves and of slavery" within the borders of the continental United States. But the ACS's motives were far from support for the dignity of African Americans. In its publication, the *African Repository,* the ACS repeatedly articulated colonization in racist terms, describing free people of color as "notoriously ignorant, degraded and miserable, mentally diseased, broken-spirited, acted upon by no motive to honourable exertions, scarcely reached in their debasement by the heavenly light." Poor and working-class whites enthusiastically endorsed colonization as a way to remove a major competitor from the labor force, bid up the price of their own labor, and secure a place in the economy and politics of the city and nation alongside white elites. But African Americans viewed colonization, alongside the institution of slavery itself, as the greatest threat to the development of a viable free wage-earning black working class and citizenry.[52]

The African colonization movement had begun well before the incorporation of the ACS. As early as 1787, colonizationist William Thornton arrived in Philadelphia to promote a scheme for returning emancipated slaves to West Africa. He offered African Americans glowing promises of "free land" as well as self-government, schools, and "free trade" with the United States, Britain, and France. Nearly a decade later, Thomas Branagan, an Irish Catholic immigrant and former overseer on a West Indian sugar plantation, also moved to Philadelphia and pushed for the removal of free people of color to an all-black state. Rather than Africa as a destination, Branagan advocated the emigration of blacks to the western edges of the Louisiana Territory. Despite their lofty rhetoric about the possibilities of a free black state, both Branagan and Thornton described free black workers on American soil as "hopelessly degraded," "inferior," and incapable of succeeding in a free society by virtue of white prejudice against free people of color as well as their own deficiencies brought on by generations of enslavement and "degradation."[53]

In his bid to gain cross-class white support for the "repatriation" of black people, Branagan also played on white fears of interracial sex and marriage. In his 1805 anti–slave trade pamphlet, *Serious Remonstrances,* Branagan identified free black men of Philadelphia as a threat to white "racial purity." Upon gaining their freedom, he said, free men of color avidly pursued sex with white women, including by rape and the entrapment of some "white women into the bonds of matrimony." He urged white working-class and poor men to "imagine" their daughters "who have been deluded, and are now married to negroes, living in little smoaking huts, despised and scorned by both blacks, and whites." Similarly, early nineteenth-century white men denigrated enslaved and free black women and treated them as a danger to the sexual morality of white men and boys, although they nonetheless believed that black women "could be mastered and controlled [that is sexually exploited] by white American men."[54]

These ideas gradually helped to create the foundation for the formation of the ACS as a national organization. In 1817, Robert Goodloe Harper, a Baltimorean, originally from South Carolina, published a public letter urging support for the ACS. He declared free blacks permanently scarred by their "habits of thoughtless improvidence," which they presumably "contracted" while slaves, and he exhorted white Baltimoreans to halt this "idle, worthless race." While postrevolutionary northern white allies and some southern whites had supported the gradual emancipation of African people on U.S. soil, following the War of 1812 they elevated recolonization to the center of their programs for the "uplift" of African people. New York City's Manumission Society stimulated the formation of state and local chapters of the ACS, adopted its agenda, and finally disbanded as a separate entity in 1849. ACS chapters had spread to Pittsburgh, Boston, and other northern cities by the 1820s. Influential political, religious, and economic elites formed the Pittsburgh chapter of the ACS in 1826. Founding members included local Presbyterian ministers, lawyers, and cotton-mill owner Rev. Charles Avery. As late as 1852, Pittsburgh colonizationists urged the federal government to use surplus revenue to help recolonize free people of color on African soil. When ACS headquarters opened an office in Boston during the early 1830s, the popular minister Lyman Beecher quickly gathered "a host of New England clergymen in proclaiming the merits of African colonization and asking God to prosper the cause." In 1835, when the ACS encountered increasing difficulties funding its repatriation projects, the Pennsylvania and New York City chapters broke from the parent body and jointly sponsored their own African resettlement projects.[55]

Finally, passage of the Fugitive Slave Law of 1850, kidnappings, and the reenslavement of fugitives and free people of color alike further weakened the position of black workers in late antebellum cities. Black Bostonians lamented the sight of soldiers and policemen marching black fugitives over the grounds of the Boston Massacre, where Crispus Attucks and his white comrades had lost their lives in the fight for independence, and down to Boston Harbor for transport to a life of slavery in the southern states. F. H. Pettis, a Virginian with a law practice in New York, boldly advertised his fugitive-catching services as "IMPORTANT TO THE SOUTH." According to Pettis's ad, New York City contained an estimated "5,000 Runaway Slaves." Furthermore, the ad stated that the new federal law "renders it easy for the recovery of such property." Slave catchers regularly passed through the Ohio Valley cities of Cincinnati and Pittsburgh and other northern cities in search of prey.

In the wake of the Fugitive Slave Law, free blacks and their white supporters repeatedly complained that "unscrupulous whites" jailed free people of color on false pretenses; others claimed these free blacks as their own slaves and then sold them "into perpetual slavery." In the meantime, southern legislators increased their campaign to obliterate the free black population. In 1859, Maryland's Eastern Shore planter and legislator Curtis Jacobs introduced a bill calling for the complete removal of the state's free black population, declaring before the state's House of Delegates, "Nothing short of an ultimate extinguishment of the free negro element . . . will cure the evils we labor under." A similar bill had been introduced into the South Carolina legislature the previous year, expressing the desire of white South Carolinians to "purge our community" of free people of color.[56]

Remarkably, the number of free wage earners of color in the United States continued to increase through the early nineteenth century in the face of kidnappings, reenslavement, and intensifying competition and conflict with white workers. But their proportion of the cities' total populations dramatically declined over time. African Americans dropped from just over 10 percent of New York's total population in 1800 to only 1.5 percent in 1860. Boston's black population also slipped, from its comparatively small 4 percent of the total in 1800 to less than 2 percent by 1860. In 1830, the African American percentage of Philadelphia's total population peaked at 12 percent, Baltimore's at 23 percent, and Charleston's at 57 percent. New Orleans had reached its highest proportion of blacks (63 percent) two decades earlier. At the outbreak of the Civil War, Charleston and New Orleans were no longer majority-black cities.[57] These declines reflected the increasingly oppressive racial conditions that confronted free and enslaved blacks during the turbulent 1850s.

CONCLUSION

Free and enslaved black workers helped to build, develop, and maintain the preindustrial city. Without them, no doubt, economic productivity, infrastructure development, and wealth creation would have slowed considerably in the major cities of the North and South. And, in turn, their efforts also created the beginnings of the African American working class. By the onset of the Civil War, slavery had gradually disappeared in the northern states and much of the urban Upper South, reinforcing the rise of the free wage-earning black working class. Like their enslaved counterparts, increasing numbers of free people of color took jobs as general laborers and domestic and personal servants in a variety of households, the military, and business establishments. Significant numbers of enslaved and free people of color also worked in the skilled crafts as brick masons, carpenters, blacksmiths, dressmakers, and other tradesmen and tradeswomen. Their work experiences represented a complicated blend of Old World knowledge and New World training in the artisan trades.

Yet massive European immigration, mob violence, and the African "repatriation" movement undercut these significant steps toward economic emancipation and citizenship for black people. Hostility toward wage-earning free men and women intensified with the passage of the Fugitive Slave Law of 1850, further dimming prospects for full citizenship. As we will see in chapter 2, early African American workers and their families would not take these limits on their freedom without a fight. Some would draw on an African vision of liberation and move to Canada, Haiti, or Africa to create their own independent homeland outside the United States. But most free people of color would stay and fight for emancipation, economic equality, and full citizenship rights as workers on American soil.

TWO

Building the Early Community

DURING THE EARLY REPUBLIC, African Americans began a dynamic community-building process in the face of extraordinary oppression. Despite the constant threat of violence and harsh restrictions on where they could live and work, early nineteenth-century black workers established their own organizations and forged grassroots social movements to secure their freedom in the new nation. Indeed, the spread of residential segregation only reinforced a vigorous movement for independent black institutions. A cluster of fraternal, religious, and labor organizations emerged at the institutional core of African American community formation. Meanwhile, a handful of early black elites sought stability and advancement through entrepreneurial business ownership and the acquisition of property, which sometimes contributed to intraracial conflict.

The fight for freedom, equality, and citizenship also included African American–led emigration projects focused on Africa, Haiti, and Canada. The quest for an independent homeland was not only a response to declining socioeconomic and political conditions in the United States but also part of an ongoing, deeply rooted commitment to an African vision of liberation. Whether focused on securing freedom within or beyond the boundaries of North America, then, early nineteenth-century African American social struggles were firmly anchored in the rise of independent black institutions crafted against the backdrop of mob violence and increasing racial discrimination in the urban housing market.

In 1829, a mob of some three hundred whites attacked the homes of free people of color in Cincinnati, Ohio. The city's white workers anticipated "high wages, which the sudden removal of some fifteen hundred laborers from the city might occasion." Philadelphia's black community endured three successive nights of violence in August 1834. Hundreds of black workers were forced to abandon their homes. In 1824 and again in 1831, mobs destroyed the homes and property of working-class blacks in Providence, Rhode Island. One of these hardworking blacks was widower Christopher Hill, who supported himself and his family by working odd jobs, frequently as a woodcutter. The mobs not only destroyed his home but also sold his belongings in the nearby town of Pawtucket.[1]

Despite escalating levels of mob violence and threats of violence against early nineteenth-century black communities, in some ways the greater violence they encountered was the daily living conditions in residential areas increasingly segregated by race. A few instances will paint the picture. Beginning with Philadelphia in 1798, most major cities instituted public waterworks to improve health and living conditions, but such works invariably bypassed the poorest neighborhoods with the largest numbers of free people of color. In New York, the Fresh Water Pond neighborhood symbolized the emergence of independent living space among black workers, but the pond itself was polluted. It emitted a foul smell that undermined the quality of life and health in the area. Elsewhere in New York City, a physician reported the condition of a three-story building "inhabited wholly by Negroes": surrounded on three sides by "a number of pig styes and stables," his report stated, "the quantity of filth, liquid and otherwise" made the grounds "almost impassable." In 1833, the Boston city directory listed one-third of black residents inhabiting areas described as "alleys, courts, places, and rear buildings." Similarly, in the late 1840s, a contemporary observer, George G. Foster, described how black Philadelphians occupied the "lofts, garrets and cellars" as well as the "blind alleys and narrow courts" of the city's housing market. As Philadelphia's black workers and their families moved into the "Cedar Street corridor," they often occupied housing described as mere "cabins," "sheds," and "mean low box[es] of wood."[2]

The conditions were no better in southern cities. Contemporary observers and later scholars described Charleston's Neck as an area of "rude little shacks, back alley rooms, and windowless garrets." The Neck contained "flimsy wooden buildings prone to fire, [and was] lined with muddy, unpaved streets, and plagued by poor sanitary conditions." In Baltimore, the dwellings inhabited by free people of color were invariably "small, frame tenements or row houses, generally one-or-two-story. . . . Fire proved to be a constant threat."[3]

Between 1820 and 1860, the index of residential segregation increased from 46 to 59 percent in Boston, from 35 to 49 percent in Philadelphia, and from 16 to 37 percent in New York. By 1852, 75 percent of New York City "streets, avenues, lanes, courts, and places were utterly devoid of black residents." Although Philadelphia neighborhoods remained racially and occupationally mixed, the trend toward a color- and class-segregated city "had received a strong impetus" from new racially biased building and construction policies and from black families themselves as they sought security from mob violence and daily insults through "residential clustering." And in Boston, rising numbers of Irish immigrants nudged blacks out of some of their previous neighborhoods in Ward Two, transforming the city into the nation's most racially segregated city by 1860.[4]

African American workers fought back against the conditions in their daily lives by creating a variety of institutions to improve their collective security, both physical and economic. Some of the earliest recorded community institutions were founded in the northern cities. As early as 1787, a group of Boston hairdressers, cooks, bootblacks, and other workers dominated the charter roster of the Prince Hall Masonic order. Prince Hall, the founding leader of the African American Masonic movement, had himself worked as a skilled leatherworker and soapmaker. The Masons soon formed female auxiliaries and established mutual benefit funds, staged public parades, and served as bulwarks against economic insecurity for their members.[5] Similarly, in 1805, some twenty wage-earning free black Bostonians founded the African Meeting House, later known as the First African Baptist Church. In addition to spiritual and material support, early African American churches and fraternal orders aimed to combat racism against black men and women on the streets of Boston and elsewhere. "Much more on public days of recreation," Hall said, "how are you shamefully abus'd. . . . The arrows of death are flying about your heads; helpless old women have their clothes torn off their backs, even to the exposing of their nakedness."[6]

At the same time that Bostonians founded their first independent institutions, black Philadelphians met in a blacksmith shop and formed the Free

The Bethel African Methodist Episcopal Church, Philadelphia, founded under the leadership of Richard Allen, ex-slave, general laborer, and shoemaker. Courtesy, Library Company of Philadelphia.

African Society (FAS). A mutual benefit and religious organization, the FAS laid the foundation for the African Methodist Episcopal (AME) Church ("Mother Bethel") in 1794. Richard Allen, ex-slave and founding minister of Mother Bethel, had worked in a broad range of jobs—as butcher, woodcutter, day laborer, brickyard hand, salt wagon driver, and shoemaker—before spearheading the founding of the AME Church. Allen would also soon take a hand in collecting and transporting dead bodies during the outbreak of the city's yellow fever epidemic in 1793.[7] Carpenters, shoemakers, church sextons, and a variety of general laborers and household service workers, including William Miller, James Varick, and Peter Williams, Sr., established New York City's African Methodist Episcopal Zion Church (AMEZ) in 1796, Pittsburgh's Bethel African Methodist Church in 1800, and a plethora of other fraternal orders and churches in the northeast and the Ohio Valley in the early years of the nineteenth century.[8]

In the South, too, black workers were leaders in African American community building. Calling themselves the African Methodist Bethel Society, the founding faction of black Methodism in Baltimore included a mix of

A special service at Baltimore's African Methodist Episcopal Church, December 1845. This lithograph features the presentation of a gift to the pastor. Courtesy, Maryland Historical Society, Baltimore.

skilled and general laborers such as blacksmiths and draymen.[9] Morris Brown, a free black shoemaker, and nearly 4,400 enslaved and free blacks broke away from Charleston's white Methodist Church in 1818. They formed a new African Methodist Episcopal Church under the jurisdiction of the independent Philadelphia-based AME denomination. Four years later, however, in the aftermath of Denmark Vesey's slave revolt, authorities destroyed the Charleston church, dispersed its members, and drove the minister from the city in a wave of violent repression. The black church movement had also faced an uphill battle in Savannah, where Andrew Bryan, a slave on the plantation of William Bryan, and other enslaved blacks suffered severe whippings for daring to hold services for their enslaved brothers and sisters in the early aftermath of the American Revolution. The Savannah group persevered, and by early 1788, Bryan received official ordination as a Baptist minister, and the city's First African Baptist Church commenced service. Nearly a year later, Bryan purchased his freedom and served the church as minister until his death in 1812. Under the leadership of Bryan and his successors, the independent African Baptist Church spread across the small-town and urban South.[10]

As suggested by the frequency of the term *African* in the names of early working-class black institutions, their founders were energized by their African heritage. They enthusiastically articulated their institution-building activities in black nationalist terms. Invocations of African culture and identity were not merely rhetorical strategies. They represented a complicated mix of spiritual, intellectual, political, and material commitments and considerations. In his innovative study of nineteenth-century black religion, politics, and ideology, historian Eddie Claude convincingly argues that the founders of early black institutions appropriated the biblical Exodus story to forge a black nationalist consciousness. This narrative of deliverance, retribution, and finally "promised land" provided African Americans with "nation language" that allowed them to critique and challenge enslavement and constraints on their civil and human rights.[11]

Although the precise impact of West African cultural organizations on early African American institutional life is hotly debated in recent scholarship, it seems clear that West African "secret societies" informed the organization, ideas, and practices of early African American churches and lodges. A growing body of historical work makes a strong and convincing case for the impact of African culture on the early urban North as well as the South. Historian Craig Wilder forcefully argues that the "institutional society— from which black churches and denominations arose—was an outgrowth of the surreptitious attempts of the enslaved to preserve African traditions by venerating and caring for the souls of the deceased." Likewise, Leslie Alexander concludes, "In early national New York City, as in South Carolina, the tradition of African secret societies fostered a deep commitment to community building as a race uplift strategy." And historian Leslie Harris outlines how the "Negroes Burial Ground" in New York City, which opened during the late seventeenth century and closed in 1790, "demonstrated the ways enslaved Africans attempted both to hold on to African cultural traditions and to incorporate European traditions into their lives."

However much the traditions of these institutions derived from Africa, their missions were to the people who had been stolen from that land. The African Methodist Episcopal Zion Church provides a clear example: when the state of New York approved the church's incorporation in February 1801, its articles of incorporation specified that only "Africans or their descendants" qualified for membership and election to the board of trustees. The congregation also decreed that church property belonged to "our African brethren and the descendants of the African race."[12]

While early nineteenth-century churches and fraternal orders addressed the spiritual, material, and political needs of their members, urban black workers also countered economic inequality directly through the formation of their own independent labor organizations and entrepreneurial activities, especially in the decade immediately preceding the Civil War. Organized in New York City in 1850, the American League of Colored Laborers aimed to improve the position of self-employed black artisans, while the Baltimore Association of Black Caulkers, founded in 1858, resisted the "concerted effort" of Irish and German immigrants to drive them out of the ship-caulking trade. African American workers not only promoted "union among the people of color in the trades" but also advanced the education of black youth in "agriculture, the mechanic arts and commerce." In a series of national conventions (organized by a network of black activists and attended by delegates from different cities)—in Columbus (1852), Rochester (1853), and Philadelphia (1854 and 1856)—African Americans also passed resolutions endorsing a movement for formal education, including training in the manual trades.[13]

Labor organizations like the American League of Colored Laborers encouraged "every mechanic" to establish his own business and proposed the creation of a fund "to assist colored mechanics to go into business for themselves." The goal, of course, was an independence that would allow free black workers to flourish and create a solid ground from which to continue the fight against inequality. Growing numbers of washerwomen, cooks, coachmen, waiters, barbers, hairdressers, and workers in the seafaring industry arranged their own contracts, lived independently of their clients, and sometimes employed other workers. As Du Bois observed regarding early nineteenth-century Philadelphia, "the whole catering business, arising from an evolution shrewdly, persistently and tastefully directed, transformed the Negro cook and waiter into a public caterer and restauranteur, and raised a crowd of underpaid" workers to "a set of self-reliant, original business men, who amassed fortunes for themselves and won general respect for their people."[14]

ENTREPRENEURSHIP AND PROPERTY OWNERSHIP

The flourishing black businesses Du Bois praised had grown in the wake of initial efforts by Philadelphian Robert Bogle and his successor, Peter

Augustine, an immigrant from the West Indies; together they paved the way for the emergence of a significant coterie of well-known caterers serving Philadelphia's white elite. In other cities, too, the growth of the early black working class opened the door for the rise of a small, well-educated, entrepreneurial, and propertied free black elite. Some of these men and women had an exclusively white clientele, while others served the predominantly working-class African American market. In New York, Thomas Downing's Oyster Bar on Broad Street and Cato's Tavern in a nearby suburb became well-known for serving mostly whites, while the African Grove, an outdoor café or bar where patrons could order food and drinks, operated by William Brown, a retired black ship steward, served an all-black clientele.[15]

Aside from the food and drink industries, barbering represented one of the best routes to business ownership for African Americans. In 1820, the barber John B. Vashon, considered Pittsburgh's leading black citizen, opened and operated the first public bathhouse west of the Allegheny Mountain chain. Another Pittsburgh barber, Lewis Woodson, owned five barbershops in downtown hotels and another two in nearby neighborhoods.[16]

The most prominent northern black entrepreneurs, Boston's Paul Cuffee and Philadelphia's James Forten, built upon their experiences as laborers in the seafaring industry to establish successful fishing and maritime businesses.[17] Cuffee purchased a fleet of ships, sailed to the Caribbean, Sweden, France, and Russia, and launched an ambitious effort to trade with the continent of Africa. Similarly, Forten eventually employed a workforce of some forty men, black and white, and amassed a fortune of $100,000 from the manufacture of sails for leading shipbuilding companies in the northeastern United States.[18]

Southern blacks also used their general labor and artisan skills to develop hotel, catering, dressmaking, carpentry, and other businesses. Unlike their northern counterparts, however, successful southern black business enterprises not only employed free blacks and sometimes white workers but also owned and employed enslaved blacks.[19] As early as 1791, a successful free black caterer owned an enslaved black and on one occasion hired out his service to the city of Baltimore for nearly two weeks. In Charleston, the free black Jehu Jones parlayed earnings from a successful tailoring business into the purchase of a hotel on Broad Street near the white St. Michael's Church. One observer described Jones's hotel as "unquestionably the best in the city." In addition to free blacks, Jones employed a staff of six enslaved men and women to serve his elite clientele of governors, military officials, and

European and U.S. visitors to the city. Charleston also saw the rise of small wood-supply businesses, which accounted for an estimated 50 percent of the city's free black enterprises. Some of the most lucrative of these wood suppliers owned and employed enslaved along with free blacks. Between 1841 and 1865, the free men of color Robert Howard and the brothers Richard Dereef and Joseph Dereef hired large numbers of enslaved blacks, and according to Martin Delany, they effectively supplied "the citizens, steamers, vessels and factories of Charleston with fuel."[20] Slaveowners thus emerged as the wealthiest members of the southern black elite.

North and South, some black women turned their seamstress skills into dressmaking businesses. In the early 1850s, for example, Cincinnati reported "twenty dress-makers and shirt-makers" among the city's small black population. By 1860, Philadelphia reported the largest number of free black dressmakers. But southern cities produced the most profitable dressmaking enterprises among free black women. Savannah, a city without a substantial garment industry, offered significant opportunities in the dressmaking field. Like their male counterparts, the most successful southern black dressmakers also owned and employed slave labor.[21] Dressmaker Leah Simpson, one of Savannah's leading black businesswomen, owned four slaves in 1819 and purchased another in 1820. Catherine Deveaux, another wealthy black seamstress during the 1820s and 1830s, owned property in three different wards of the city. On one of these properties, she built a "Negro house" to accommodate her own enslaved workers as well as perhaps other enslaved blacks hiring and living out on their own. In 1860, Richmond's free women of color reported significant property-holding acquired through dressmaking businesses: "Virginia Cunningham, property valued at $3,452; Elizabeth Beatty, at $2,315; [and] Mary J. Sullivan, at $1,644."[22] Virginia-born ex-slave Elizabeth Keckley became the most renowned and successful of these black women dressmakers. After purchasing her freedom and the freedom of her son through a loan from a white benefactor, Keckley eventually moved to Washington, DC, where she developed a lucrative business making garments for elite white clients, including the wives of Abraham Lincoln, Jefferson Davis, and Stephen A. Douglas.[23]

Southern working-class black women, slave and free, dominated the informal street trade in farm produce, pastries, and other items that they "made themselves" or "purchased wholesale" from other producers. By the late eighteenth and early nineteenth centuries, a mix of enslaved and free black women had transformed garden produce and home-cooked goods into thriving commercial activities in New Orleans, Savannah, Charleston, and other southern cities. According to historian Amrita Myers, "No matter what [southern] state one lived in or visited or whether these women were called hucksters, peddlers, or hawkers, travelers and locals in southern cities found themselves awash in a sea of black women selling everything from fruits and vegetables to oysters, candies, cakes, spruce beer, hot coffee, popcorn, peanuts, rice coquettes, clothes, and handmade crafts." Some of these women, such as Carlotta Derneville of New Orleans, also operated taverns and boardinghouses on streets lining the levee. They served a large but transient population of sailors, soldiers, tourists, and business travelers. In Charleston, Mary Purvis became widely known as the city's "oyster woman." By 1860, Purvis had built viable business connections to the fishermen along the city's busy docks, thus securing a reliable and steady supply of oysters for her street business. Her success and that of other women food vendors underlaid passage of recurring legislation to curb their "control over the city's food supply."[24]

In many cities, African American labor and business pursuits intertwined with a thriving underground economy. In the Five Points district of New York City, Peter Williams (no relation to the AMEZ minister), owner of Almack's Place, and several black female owners of brothels in the area collaborated with white businessmen and women. Together, they helped to create the district's network of underground businesses, including "dance halls, bars, gambling houses, and prostitution." However, whereas white privilege allowed whites engaged in such "shady" business activities to conceal their hand from the public view, black entrepreneurs like Williams and others "were on site nightly in their places of business, associating with customers, and identifying with employees." In other cases the white person was the public face of a business. Savannah's white small-shopkeepers forged "an alliance of convenience" with enslaved and free blacks who provided vendors with produce secured from their own gardens as well as theft from other white households and businesses.

Although a Savannah city statute prohibited blacks, enslaved or free, from selling whiskey, urban blacks nonetheless maintained a lively underground network of "spirituous liquors." Charleston statutes also forbade the sale of liquor to slaves, but illegal local "grog shops" proliferated through the collusion of "local authorities, merchants, and shopkeepers" with enslaved and free blacks. Likewise, in Baltimore, "grogshops and tippling" houses dotted the city's "backstreets and alleys." During the 1830s and 1840s, the city's leading newspapers regularly protested the "little groggeries," where both poor and working-class blacks and whites gathered "to drink and gamble."[25]

African American women dominated the colonial and early American street-vending trades across the urban South. Thomas Waterman Wood painted this portrait of a free black woman in Baltimore, *Market Woman,* in 1858. Courtesy, Mildred Anna Williams Collection, Fine Arts Museums of San Francisco, 1944.8.

As preindustrial black workers intensified their labor organizing and entrepreneurial activities, both legal and extralegal, they also gradually turned to property ownership as another strategy to gain an independence that would counter economic discrimination, enslavement, and disfranchisement. We have already seen that some southern black women dressmakers amassed property in their own names. Elsewhere, in 1825, a white cartman named John Whitehead sold three plots of farmland in New York City to Andrew Williams, a 25-year-old free African American bootblack. Shortly thereafter, another black worker, Epiphany Davis, a general laborer, purchased multiple lots in the area called Seneca Village. Within less than a decade, blacks had purchased no fewer than twenty-four of the fifty lots available for sale. Black workers (primarily household service workers and general laborers) made up the majority of these homeowners.

But the quest for independence through home ownership became a losing battle for the majority of working-class blacks in the urban North and South. Rates of black property ownership remained low and insufficient to change the quality of housing and living conditions in black neighborhoods. Across urban America, black home ownership peaked by the early 1820s and steadily declined until the Civil War. In 1853, the city of New York destroyed Seneca Village to pave the way for development of Central Park. For its part, Philadelphia's black property ownership declined from 11.6 to about 0.72 percent between 1820 and 1850. In the urban South and the nation, Baltimore had the lowest black property ownership rate (5.3 percent) in 1815, and this percentage dropped to only 0.4 percent by 1850.[26] Nonetheless, at least some antebellum blacks found ways to use their limited property holdings to reinforce their community-building activities.

CONTESTING INEQUALITY AND INHUMANITY: ANTICOLONIZATION, ANTISLAVERY, AND EMIGRATION EFFORTS

As the black community and its institutions grew, they provided an effective base from which African Americans launched vigorous movements to fight for their freedom, equal rights, and citizenship in the early republic. Antebellum black workers defined the colonization movement as the greatest immediate threat to the full emancipation of enslaved and free people of color. In mass meetings, newspaper columns, and pamphlets, free wage earners of color repeatedly declared their determination to stay put: "Here we were born, and here we will die," declared a defiant New York City gathering. In January 1817, however, the fight against colonization gained its most dramatic and forceful expression at Philadelphia's Mother Bethel AME church. Some three thousand blacks packed the main floor and balcony of the church on Sixth Street. When James Forten, chair of the gathering, called for a vote on the question of "repatriation" to Africa, the throng delivered in unison a resounding "No!" In resolutions adopted at the meeting, African Americans pledged not only to fight for full citizenship rights for free blacks but also to escalate their opposition to slavery across the land.[27] Although some black leaders such as Allen and Forten had initially endorsed the colonization idea, the massive grassroots opposition at the Bethel meeting squashed such sentiments and forged a strong cross-class consensus.

Over two decades later, black New Yorkers organized a "great anti-colonization meeting" and denounced repatriation as "antirepublican, un-Christian, and 'contrary to reason.'" Moreover, as reports of high mortality among returnees to Africa reached the community, New Yorkers suggested that colonization represented a scheme not only to perpetuate the enslavement of African people but also to "exterminate" them.[28] In 1832, an exasperated Maryland colonizationist remarked that "the prejudices of the coloured people of Baltimore and other large Towns, against African Colonization, are so strong that distributing literature among them would be to throw it away." In New Orleans, despite an aggressive American Colonization Society (ACS) chapter and support from leading newspapers and legislators, free people of color vehemently opposed repatriation on the basis of not only their labor investment in the development of the city and nation but also on the basis of family and community connections in the United States.[29] When white Americans in the African colonization movement escalated their appeals to anti-slavery British activists for support, free blacks sent their own representatives—Nathaniel Paul, Lenox Remond, and later Frederick Douglass—abroad to counter ACS propaganda. According to historian R. J. M. Blackett, the rise of the ACS and African American resistance to it provided the initial catalyst for the emergence of the "transatlantic abolitionist movement." "The *voice* of the free colored people," one contemporary observer declared, "has done more to kill the influence of colonization in Great Britain, than any thing else."[30]

Alongside their fight against the ACS, urban blacks intensified their participation in the broader antislavery movement. They issued radical new calls for the immediate emancipation of enslaved people and equal access to jobs, public institutions, and equality before the law for free people of color. David Walker, a free black man born in Wilmington, North Carolina, just after the American Revolution, moved to Boston during the 1820s and helped to found the anti-slavery General Coloured Association of Massachusetts. At the organization's annual convention in 1829, he urged enslaved black people to throw off the yoke of slavery by physical violence if necessary. Walker's "Appeal," later published and distributed as a pamphlet, became one of the most widely read and influential antebellum political statements on the African American quest for freedom, citizenship, and human rights.[31] Inspired by Walker's ideas, Bostonian Maria Stewart, a well-educated domestic worker, published her own militant pamphlet two years later. In *Religion and the Pure Principles of Morality, the Sure Foundation on Which We Must Build,* Stewart declared that neither "gender nor color" should prevent black women from speaking out on behalf of the race. Likewise, in one of Stewart's speeches, she urged black men to boldly "let their voices be heard" and their hands "raised in behalf of their color."[32]

Stewart, Walker, and other radical black abolitionists gradually attracted a new generation of white allies, including the brothers Arthur and Lewis Tappan of New York and William Lloyd Garrison of Boston. As a militant interracial movement gained ground, anti-abolitionist mobs took to destroying the property of both black and white abolitionists, including the home of Arthur Tappan, the church of the African American Episcopalian minister Peter Williams, Jr., and Garrison's newspaper office. This mob violence exposed sharp cleavages within the interracial movement.[33] In the face of rising attacks, Garrison and the American Anti-Slavery Society articulated a policy of noninvolvement with emerging political parties, disaffiliation with organized religion, and strict adherence to nonviolent tactics, even as proslavery mobs destroyed African American homes, churches, and places of business. While Frederick Douglass and leading Bostonians and Philadelphians (including Charles Remond, William Whipper, and Robert Purvis) supported Garrison, rejecting a focus on "the spirit of violence, both in sentiment and practice," James McCune Smith, Samuel Cornish, and other black New Yorkers embraced the use of violence as a mode of self-defense in the vigorous push for full, unrestricted suffrage for free people of color.[34]

Thus, under the impact of mob violence and ideological and political disputes, the anti-slavery movement frayed. Meanwhile, however, fugitive slaves and free people of color heightened their grassroots activities on behalf of enslaved blacks. Fugitive aid societies, vigilance committees, and Underground Railroad networks proliferated. These activities expanded during the 1830s, then mushroomed during the 1840s and especially the 1850s in the wake of the Fugitive Slave Law of 1850. While white agents and collaborators provided indispensable support to the Underground Railroad, African American fugitives and established working-class black urban communities constituted the backbone of the organization.[35] Ordinary black men and women laborers, dockhands, household servants, artisans, and small-businesspeople accounted for some of the most daring efforts to aid the escape of enslaved people. In early 1836, a group of black New Yorkers boarded a recently arrived ship from Brazil, the *Brilliante,* and helped two of five Portuguese-speaking slaves on board to escape. The New York press described the rescue as the work of "a gang of negroes, some of whom were armed." In 1842, New England African Americans formed the Vigilance Freedom Association and enabled fugitive George Latimer and his family to move from Norfolk, Virginia, to Boston. When authorities arrested Latimer on charges of larceny filed by his owner, the committee not only raised sufficient funds to purchase Latimer's freedom but also sent a massive petition bearing nearly 65,000 signatures to the Massachusetts legislature, urging lawmakers to protect African Americans from fugitive slave catchers.[36]

Harriet Tubman, a fugitive from Maryland's Eastern Shore, became one of the most effective agents on the Underground Railroad. After escaping from slavery herself and making her way to Philadelphia, where she obtained work as a domestic, Tubman saved her earnings and made some twenty trips into slave territory to liberate relatives and friends.[37] But many others, less well-known, assisted enslaved people on their route to freedom. In particular, all along the Ohio, Mississippi, and Missouri Rivers, officials regularly reported slave escapes aided and abetted by black riverboatmen. Historian Thomas Buchanan notes that in both the upper and lower South, "African American boat workers provided a safe passage for fugitives escaping from southern cities and rural plantations." After escaping from slavery, Henry Bibb recalled that he used to observe "the lofty banks of the Ohio River, gazing upon the splendid steamboats," and reflect that he himself "might soar away to where there is no slavery." Another fugitive, John Parker, remembered how the Mississippi River attracted him "like a magnet, for as soon as I was free to move in my own selected direction I made straight for the river."[38]

Not surprisingly, the African American liberation movement looked different in the urban South during the antebellum period. While the incidence of slave revolts disappeared from the northern urban landscape in the wake of the American Revolution and the emancipation of enslaved blacks, slave rebellions and plots to rebel had emerged in the colonial North and South. Early New York City became the site of armed struggles to liberate enslaved blacks in 1712 and again in 1741. During the same period, the Stono Rebellion of 1739 broke out near Charleston, South Carolina. Both northern and southern authorities moved quickly to put down these revolts. But such violent efforts to secure freedom remained a vital part of the repertoire of freedom strategies employed by enslaved workers in the urban South. Under the leadership of Gabriel Prosser, a blacksmith, and aided by free people of color as allies, enslaved blacks planned a revolt to secure their freedom through a massive assault on the city of Richmond in 1800. Beginning in April, several bondsmen, especially artisans—coopers, carpenters, weavers, shoemakers, and blacksmiths—helped to lay the foundation for the revolt through their ease of travel between the city and outlying plantations. Before a storm washed out roads leading into the city and someone alerted authorities to the plot, Prosser and his comrades planned to kill all whites except Quakers, Methodists, and others associated with the abolitionist movement.[39]

Following a trial that took less than a month, authorities hanged Prosser and twenty-seven of his compatriots. Similarly, the free black carpenter Denmark Vesey and his enslaved countrymen devised a plan in 1822 to capture and demolish the city of Charleston and leave the region for Haiti. Authorities soon captured, tried, and executed Vesey and some thirty-five other blacks for conspiring to destroy the city and liberate slaves, but the Vesey plot nonetheless revealed how enslaved and free African Americans challenged Charleston's system of slave patrols, a city guard of one hundred men, and another sixty state guardsmen at the Citadel. On the eve of the Vesey plot, Charleston officials had closed the independent African Methodist Episcopal church. When an official investigating committee found that members of the African church had participated in the Vesey plot, the independent black church movement came under even greater surveillance and suppression in the South, particularly the Deep South.[40]

The brutal suppression of revolts and plots to revolt, mob violence against interracial abolitionists, and persistent colonization efforts to remove free people of color from the country all heightened debates over the efficacy of emigration as a strategy for African American liberation. Over the first half of the nineteenth century, under increasing pressure from hostile municipal, state, and federal authorities as well as working-class and elite whites, some urban blacks reevaluated the notion of emigration and resettlement outside the United States on their own terms. They increasingly made a distinction between African American–led and internally generated emigration programs and the white-led colonization movement that black urban communities had so vigorously opposed.

From the outset of the revolutionary era, some African Americans had supported independent programs of resettlement in Africa. The free African Company of Boston expressed strong disapproval of whites "going [to] settle a place for us. . . . We think it would be better if we could charter a vessel and send some [of] our own blacks." As early as 1810, New York's William Miller delivered a speech before the African Methodist Episcopal Church, declaring that Africa was "destined to reclaim its former greatness and become a center of political power." Miller later urged blacks to explore the possibility of actually moving to Africa or Haiti as sites of independence and self-determination for people of African descent.[41]

Just before the War of 1812, leading African Americans supported a plan for the resettlement of black people in Sierra Leone, an area of West Africa sponsored by the British empire. Under the leadership of Paul Cuffee, the black sailor and owner of a commercial fleet of ships, this program gained the initial support of Richard Allen, James Forten, and Absalom Jones of Philadelphia and Thomas Paul, Prince Saunders, and Robert Roberts of Boston. This plan foundered with the advent of the War of 1812. Later, in 1824, Prince Saunders led a group of some 6,000–7,000 free blacks departing for Haiti. After this project failed, nearly a third of the settlers returned to the United States. Another group of free blacks met in Philadelphia in 1830 and endorsed the exploration of Canada as a site for the relocation of blacks from the United States. By the beginning of the Civil War, some 40,000 African Americans had resettled in Wilberforce, Windsor, Chatham, and a few other Canadian locations.[42]

During the 1840s and 1850s, the independent African American resettlement idea gained even greater support in the work of Mary Ann Shadd Cary, editor of a Canada-based newspaper; Martin Delany, resident of Pittsburgh and coeditor of the *North Star* with Frederick Douglass; and Rev. Henry Highland Garnet, a resident of Troy, New York. Canada, the Caribbean, and West Africa remained favorite targets of these late antebellum proponents of emigration. Shadd Cary advanced her idea on emigration through her widely circulated pamphlet *A Plea for Emigration or Notes of Canada West,* a forty-four-page essay published in June 1852, while Delany advocated a location in

West Africa's Niger Valley in his book *The Condition, Elevation, Emigration, and Destiny of the Colored People of the United States Politically Considered* (1852). For his part, in 1858, Garnet spearheaded the formation of the African Civilization Society and pushed for the development of "a grand centre of negro nationality, from which shall flow the streams of commercial, intellectual, and political power which shall make colored people respected everywhere." Garnet and the African Civilization Society hoped to destroy slavery and the slave trade within the United States and worldwide by opening up the competitive production of cotton on the continent of Africa. Notably, a free black working class was the center of his vision: under the supervision of New World–born black immigrants, Garnett believed, free African labor could potentially produce cotton more cheaply than New World slave-produced cotton and undercut the capacity of slavery to sustain itself on U.S. soil.[43]

INTERNAL SOCIAL CONFLICTS

The early African American community was not immune to a variety of conflicts that undercut solidarity along gender, class, and color lines. For instance, working-class and elite black churchmen alike invoked the biblical injunctions of the apostle Paul that women should remain silent in the church and follow the guidance of men in both spiritual and secular matters. AME and Baptist churches denied women permission to preach the gospel and take public stands on abolitionism, colonization, the Underground Railroad, and other social justice and political movement questions. After Maria Stewart strongly articulated her ideas about liberation, Boston's black community pressured her to leave the public arena. When she departed for New York thereafter, Stewart staunchly defended the right of black and white women to shape the political agenda of the larger community. It is not sex or color, she said, but "the principle formed in the soul" that makes men and women.[44]

Intraracial class, sex, color, and status conflicts gained their sharpest expression in New Orleans and Charleston, where mixed-race free people of color diligently built bridges and connections to slaveholding white elites. The governor of Louisiana, for instance, met with success when he built upon French and Spanish traditions of employing free people of color to put down slave revolts. In January 1811, slaves rebelled on the Andry plantation in St. John, the Baptist parish some forty miles north of New Orleans. They killed several whites and marched toward the city. The state armed free people of color, placed them under white officers, and engaged the enslaved rebels as they sought to advance on New Orleans. Following two weeks of warfare, free people of color who joined the local militia had helped to put down what turned out to be the "largest slave revolt in United States history." Governor William C. C. Claiborne praised the troops for performing with "great exactitude and propriety."

According to historian Amrita Myers, Charleston's free people of color also defined their interests narrowly. "Realizing they had little time, money, or power with which to help the larger black community, they worked instead to shore up their own precarious positions and protect their families from encroachments on their always contingent freedom." Such circumstances led some of the city's free black women as well as men "to buy and sell other black people for profit, use forced labor to grow their businesses, ally themselves with white persons of stature, and distance themselves from people who could jeopardize their position in society."[45]

Finally, across early nineteenth-century urban America, a small handful of well-educated black elites (some with deep family roots in slavery and the wage-earning working class) gradually sought to impose notions of "moral uplift," "respectability," and public decorum, as well as specific forms of worship, behavior, and values, on poor and working-class blacks, slave and free. They suggested that the natural character and self-expression of black workers were holding back the project of freedom and full citizenship. As early as 1784, New York's acclaimed African American poet Jupiter Hammon exhorted free people of color to set a "moral" example of "honest" work for their enslaved brothers and sisters. Free blacks, he said, "who allow bad courses, and who do not take care to get an honest living by your labour and industry, are doing more to prevent our being free, than anybody else." Bishop Richard Allen and Daniel Coker of the AME Church urged free blacks to contain the emotional outcry that characterized tent meetings, where "shouting, ring-dancing, and groaning" gained free expression in Methodist revival services.[46] Elites also condemned emerging forms of working-class music, dance, drinking, gaming, and leisure-time activities, particularly the illegal "cookshops" and "groggeries," as dens of sin.

Under the impact of the militant white colonization movement and increasing pressure of "moral uplift" ideas, both working-class and elite African Americans gradually increased emphasis on the "American" side of their identity as African people. But working-class blacks retained a consistent and enduring commitment to a class-inflected African American movement for liberation, full citizenship, and human rights.[47]

CONCLUSION

Despite the emergence of significant internal social conflicts and tensions within the preindustrial black community, antebellum African American workers helped to forge broad social movements to combat class and racial inequality. Against extraordinary odds and informed by their own history and culture as African people, they joined forces to build fraternal, religious, labor, and entrepreneurial organizations that not only served their spiritual and material needs but also provided a springboard for the development of militant campaigns for the emancipation of enslaved blacks and full citizenship rights for free people of color. By the eve of the Civil War, the predominantly enslaved black proletariat had given way to a predominantly free wage-earning working class in the urban North and most of the urban upper South. While rising numbers of antebellum urban blacks considered the utility of emigration and resettlement on land outside the United States as a route to freedom, the advent of the Civil War changed the dynamics of both class formation and the black freedom movement. Giving up any plans to leave the United States, African Americans resolved to transform the escalating war between the states into a fight for their full equality as workers and citizens of African descent. Their efforts would not only result in the emancipation of their enslaved brothers and sisters but also set the stage for the rise of the urban industrial working class during the late nineteenth and early twentieth centuries.

THREE

Prelude to the Modern Age

THE CIVIL WAR RESULTED IN THE EMANCIPATION OF some four million African American men, women, and children. In a complicated and drawn-out process that began during the war, a large wage-earning working class grew dramatically in rural areas through the emancipation and early Jim Crow years. At first, emancipated rural blacks aspired foremost to landownership as the road to independence and full citizenship in the republic. In their view and unfolding postwar experience, capitalist, market-driven, free-labor contracts robbed them of their freedom and access to the land of their birth. Besides unequal wage-labor agreements, however, a variety of other forces—including state-sanctioned violence, lynch law, disfranchisement, and unequal sharecropping contracts—derailed their dreams for landownership in the countryside. As living and working conditions deteriorated in the agricultural South, the prospect of leaving southern plantations and farms for life and labor in the expanding urban centers of late nineteenth- and early twentieth-century America took hold among rising numbers of young black workers and their families. Ultimately, then, the emergence of the large postbellum free black agricultural proletariat fueled the growth of the black urban industrial working class.

WARTIME: REHEARSAL FOR FREE WAGE LABOR

During the antebellum era, Frederick Douglass had offered the most forceful ongoing opposition to African American emigration, whether white- or black-led. His biographer Waldo Martin underscores that Douglass consistently opposed "massive black colonization, emigration, or migration in a domestic or foreign context," even during most of the turbulent years follow-ing the Fugitive Slave Law of 1850. Douglass adamantly believed that emigra-tion "tends to throw over the Negro a mantle of despair. It leads him to doubt the possibility of his progress as an American citizen. It also encourages popular prejudice with the hope that by persecution or by persuasion the Negro can finally be dislodged and driven from his natural home." In early 1861, however, even Douglass shifted course and declared his intention to explore an alternative homeland for black Americans in Haiti. Acknowl-edging increasing restrictions on enslaved and free people of color in the United States, he planned to visit Haiti in early spring to assess "prospects for emigration." There could have been no more dramatic illustration of the dete-riorating situation for African Americans.

Just before Douglass's planned journey, however, fighting broke out between North and South. For Douglass and others, the hostilities gave new hope that African Americans and their white allies might transform an impending war between the states into a fight for African American libera-tion and full citizenship. Long before Lincoln issued the Emancipation Proclamation, African Americans envisioned the war as a means to complete the unfinished work of the American Revolution, which they also had helped to set in motion, and bring their own freedom to full fruition. Within a month of the clash at Fort Sumter, Douglass urged the Union to carry the war into the heart of the slave South and vigorously recruit troops among fugitive slaves and free blacks. Furthermore, he said, "Any attempt to secure peace to the whites while leaving the blacks in chains . . . will be labor lost."[1]

Douglass's bold vision stood against what was a far more ambiguous set of opportunities and challenges that grew along with the war. At first, for exam-ple, Union authorities did not heed Douglass's call to incorporate blacks as troops. Though rising numbers of urban black workers and their communi-ties offered their services to the Union forces as hostilities increased with the South, these overtures from free people of color were routinely rejected. In New York, Philadelphia, Boston, and other northern cities, black men orga-nized their own military companies, drilled, and presented themselves for combat on behalf of the Union. In the spring of 1861, black Bostonians met at the Twelfth Street Baptist Church to urge repeal of racial restrictions on military service. Only in 1862 did labor shortages and military reverses com-pel Congress to enlist blacks in the construction of entrenchments and provi-sion of camp services "or any war service for which they may be found competent."

Even then, war authorities barred blacks from military service until issuance of the Emancipation Proclamation in 1863. African Americans were ready: following Lincoln's Proclamation, some eight thousand black Pennsylvanians (including fugitive slaves) eventually enlisted in the Union forces, with the hope that the City of Brotherly Love would finally fulfill its promise of freedom for blacks no less than for white citizens. In Boston, by early 1863, blacks had filled five companies of the Fifth Massachusetts Regiment. Meanwhile, housed in a training facility just outside the city, the Fifty-Fourth reported "recruits coming in at a rate of one hundred a week."[2]

While northern blacks provided labor and later troops for the Union army, their southern counterparts swelled the ranks of the Union forces as fugitives, refugees, labor "contraband," and eventually soldiers. Having first been compelled to support the Confederate war effort with their labor, rising numbers of southern blacks soon took advantage of the advancing Union army to desert southern plantations, encampments, and cities. They built upon historic patterns of resistance to slave labor and staged what W. E. B. Du Bois later described as labor's largest "general strike" in the nation's history. "Arrest that hoe in the hands of the negro," he said, "and you smite the [Confederate rebellion] in the very seat of its life." In Charleston, when Confederate troops deserted the city near war's end, the *Charleston Daily Courier* reported, "The [Union] recruiting officers in Charleston are head over heels in business. The Colored men are flocking to the United States flag by the dozens and the score." In Savannah, following the Union army's capture of Fort Pulaski in April 1862, the slave stevedore and river pilot March Haynes smuggled fugitive slaves into the Union camp in a boat that he concealed "in a creek among the marshes below the city." Indeed, Savannah city officials stepped up their surveillance of black churches and religious gatherings for possible signs of "sedition" or support for the Union cause in the interest of black liberation. When African Americans convened at one church and sang a hymn with the refrain "Yes we shall all be free," Savannah police stormed the church and arrested congregants for "planning freedom."

New Orleans blacks also prepared to strike a blow for their own liberty when the Union navy captured the city in 1862. Initially, the Louisiana Native Guard, composed of the city's free people of color, had offered its services to the Confederacy, but it was rebuffed and denied access to weapons and supplies. Thus, according to historian Rebecca Scott, long before the Union occupation of the city, "the free population of color in New Orleans was waiting in the wings, its most vocal members armed with a resolute

French inflected ideology of immediate abolition and universal manhood suffrage."[3]

In the meantime, on the edges of the New Orleans war zone, the number of black refugees from the sugar plantations escalated. They greatly enhanced Union recruitment of African Americans for the new black regiments. They also helped to forge "a pattern of collaboration and communications between the city and countryside" that would persist through the postbellum years. Similarly, from the outset of the Civil War, Washington, DC, became a haven for fugitives from plantations and farms in Maryland, Virginia, and Kentucky. By late 1864, some fifty thousand black refugees, defined by historian Stanley Harrold as "self-emancipated African Americans called *contraband* and later *freedmen*," moved to a cluster of forts in and near the nation's capital. Between the outbreak of the Civil War and war's end, the District's black population increased from about 21 to 44 percent of the total. As historian Kate Masur concludes, existing black District residents and fugitives joined forces and made "upstart claims" for full citizenship rights "in advance of the laws" of the land, mandating an end to human bondage and the incorporation of blacks into the body politic as citizens.[4]

At the same time that the war enabled many African Americans to escape their agricultural labor, federal authorities played a major role in the emergence of a larger black wage-earning workforce even on farms and plantations. As the Civil War gradually undermined and then demolished the institution of slavery, it also established precedents for the rise of a free, predominantly rural black proletariat. Some historians call this early process a "rehearsal for reconstruction" or emancipation. It was also a rehearsal for the widespread and forcible incorporation of previously enslaved agricultural workers into the free capitalist wage labor system. And while northern whites aimed to impose free-market capitalist labor relations on the South, former slaveowners fought to imbue labor contracts with as many of the coercive features of enslavement as northerners would tolerate and African Americans would bear. Thus, the state facilitated the transformation of enslaved people into workers and of slaveowners into employers on highly unequal terms, subverting the liberating and democratic potential of this new working class.

For their part, wartime southern blacks repeatedly articulated their desire for landownership. African Americans believed that they were entitled to the land by virtue of their labor to date, which had enriched and given value to that land. In 1864, for example, at Port Royal, South Carolina, a church elder told a northern visitor to tell President Abraham Lincoln that "we want land . . . that is rich with the sweat of we face and the blood of we back. We born here, we parents graves here; this here our home." Similarly, in January 1865, Garrison Frazier of Savannah spoke for legions of ex-slaves when he declared that the best way that black people could take care of themselves "is to have land, and turn it and till it by our own labor . . . until we are able to buy it and make it our own."[5]

The Union bureaucracy, however, saw things otherwise. In February 1862, the federal government initiated the cultivation of cotton with free black labor on the Sea Islands of South Carolina. When African Americans resisted growing cotton instead of raising their own subsistence crops, the government enlisted the aid of the military, northern white benevolent associations, and even the church to devise ways to coerce blacks back into the cotton fields as free wage earners. Specifically, the new free labor experiment replaced the whip with the withholding of food, clothing, and other products and services to drive blacks into exploitative labor contracts. In the face of these deprivations, Sea Island blacks gradually took work as wage earners on cotton plantations. Another tactic was employed in southern Louisiana, where Union general Nathaniel Banks promised planters use of the U.S. military to control wage-earning black workers in exchange for pledges of loyalty to the Union. Many slaveowners declared "loyalty" in order to reap the benefits of forced wage labor, backed up by the Union army. By war's end nearly a half million southern black workers had participated in these "experiments" with free wage labor.[6]

Meanwhile, wartime conditions unleashed another round of assaults and limitations on the lives of urban black workers. For one thing, President Lincoln himself revitalized the old ACS African recolonization program to address the fate of the free black population. By the summer of 1862, Congress had appropriated $600,000 to advance Lincoln's plan, with $100,000 targeted for the removal of free people of color from the District of Columbia to a place outside the continental United States. And for another, once the Union embraced emancipation of enslaved blacks as a cause of the Civil War, black enlistment in the Union forces was not always voluntary. Between 1863 and the end of hostilities, according to historian Jacqueline Jones, white officials "engaged in strong arm conscription tactics" to fill the ranks of all-black units. Military recruitment efforts sometimes resembled "the methods of slavecatchers, press gangs, and man-stealers." One Florida army officer reported in April 1863 that his black recruits *"have not been drafted. They have been kidnapped in the night"* (italics in original).[7]

U.S. Military Railroad Construction Corps in northern Virginia during the Civil War. Black railroad men alternately built, repaired, or destroyed rail lines under the exigencies of war. Here, they twist rails so that Confederate forces cannot possibly use them again. Andrew J. Russell photo. Courtesy, E. L. DeGolyer, Jr., Photograph Collection, DeGolyer Library, Southern Methodist University.

African Americans firmly rejected Lincoln's new iteration of the ACS African colonization project.[8] But Lincoln's plan reflected popular white opposition to full citizenship rights for black people even as African American labor and military contributions to the Union cause intensified. As the war escalated, violent conflict broke out between blacks and whites in the streets, on streetcars, and along the docks of Cincinnati, New York, Boston, Philadelphia, and other wartime cities.[9]

The New York City Draft Riots of 1863 were the most violent nineteenth-century assault on black workers and their communities. Despite persistent nativist sentiment against Irish people, both within and outside the Democratic party, Irish Americans identified with white Americans and developed little sympathy for African Americans; they firmly opposed the abolition of slavery. New York bishop John J. Hughes, highly regarded as the most influential Irishman in antebellum America, considered the "naturalized Irishmen" as "in no wise distinct or different" from "native born [white]

Americans." The pro-slavery *New York Herald* declared, in a ringing appeal to Irish and German workers, the emancipation of four million slaves would flood the North "with free Negroes, and the labor of the white man will be depreciated."[10]

Between July 13 and July 17, Irish immigrants and other working-class white mobs not only assaulted black men, women, and children on the streets of the city, but also burned their homes and institutions. Historian Judith Giesberg shows how such mob attacks on black people called attention to the ways "the war drew away [white] male wage earners" and "drove working-class and immigrant women to destitution."[11] When the violence ceased on the fifth day, over a hundred African Americans had died, mainly general laborers, domestics, and artisans, and property damage had reached millions of dollars.

RURAL, RURAL-INDUSTRIAL, AND CONVICT LABOR

Despite attacks both at home and on the battlefield, African Americans, against all odds, helped to defeat the Confederacy and emancipate enslaved workers. Enactment of the Thirteenth, Fourteenth, and Fifteenth Amendments to the U.S. Constitution extended full citizenship rights to blacks under the law. The federal Civil Rights Acts of 1866 and 1875 also strengthened African American claims to equal rights before the bar. Moreover, when the U.S. Supreme Court pronounced the Civil Rights Act of 1875 unconstitutional in the Civil Rights Cases of 1883, northern states gradually enacted new civil rights laws to ensure full citizenship for "all persons," "without regard to color or previous condition of servitude." But if anything, the search for fair working conditions became even more elusive in the aftermath of war, as white Americans used a variety of means to underpay black workers.

Following the general emancipation, as during the Civil War years, many southern African Americans continued to resist wage labor in favor of access to land that they could cultivate on their own terms. A South Carolinian commented, "I mean to own my own manhood . . . and I'm goin' on to my own land, just as soon as when I git dis crop in." A federal Reconstruction officer in the district of West Tennessee captured this widespread sentiment among ex-slaves when he reported, "Says the newly emancipated black, toil was the chief misery of my former condition. I am now free . . . and if I am compelled to work for wages to support me where fore is my condition bettered?" Similarly, North Carolinians, a local police chief reported, "intend to have lands, even if they shed blood to obtain them." In a letter to Abraham Lincoln, another ex-slave expressed the desires of many when he said, "I had rather work for myself and raise my own cotton than work for a gentleman for wages." A Virginia freedman, Bayley Wyat, declared in no uncertain terms, "We has a right to [that] land. . . . Didn't we clear the land and raise de crops. . . . And den didn't dem large cities in de North grow up on de cotton and de sugars and de rice dat we made."[12]

Postbellum African American dreams for landownership soon faltered. They collapsed under the weight of stubborn white resistance to black landownership as well as the pressures of a variety of abusive and unjust labor and sharecropping arrangements and contracts that made it impossible for agricultural workers to get ahead, let alone to purchase land. Former slaveholding whites abhorred the idea of treating ex-slaves as free workers under new and more equitable northern-inspired and -directed contractual arrangements. Planters repeatedly affirmed their conviction that "labor must be commanded completely, or the production of the cotton crop must be abandoned." Southern landowning elites, the *Augustus Transcript* reported, believed that their own class interests and the interests of the South required only "one single condition—the ability of the planter to command [black] labor." A Louisiana sugar planter declared, "The great secret of our success [as slaveholders] was the great motive power contained in that little instrument [the whip]." To keep the white landed elite in control, all eleven former Confederate states passed legislation to prevent black laborers from leaving farms and plantations without the approval of their employers or landlords. In addition, the early post–Civil War South saw a plethora of anti-enticement laws, which made it a crime to hire a worker still under contract with another employer, while vagrancy laws made unemployment (even temporary unemployment) a criminal offense.[13] In other words, "free" rural workers possessed virtually no freedom at all.

Some early postbellum planters and elite households sought to replace black men and women with American-born whites or immigrants from Europe or China. An Alabama planter explained his preference for Chinese over African American workers. He could bring over "millions of [Chinese] coolies," he said, "for a song. . . . It will take three of 'em to do the work of two [blacks]; but they'll live on next to nothing and clothe themselves." According to a South Carolina rice planter, "If white labor is generally introduced . . . it will drive the Negro down, and then the competition for labor will oblige them to work for little."[14] Some southern employers defined newly freed black women as unfit and advertised for white replacements: "Wanted: a white girl to do general housework"; "Wanted, a good white woman as a housekeeper"; "Wanted: A white girl for cook and housework. [Irish or] German preferred." But while labor recruiters attracted small numbers of Chinese, Dutch, Irish, and German immigrants to the South, few immigrants considered the South an attractive destination for work and a viable livelihood.[15]

Rather than enhancing the bargaining power of black workers, this failure to attract and retain an immigrant work force only intensified planters' determination to keep black workers on the land by depriving them of citizenship rights and removing them from the body politic. Beginning with Virginia in 1870, legislators passed stringent emigrant-agent laws, covering Alabama, Georgia, North Carolina, and South Carolina over the next twenty years. Emigrant agents paid the outstanding debts of prospective recruits, provided transportation to a new location, and guaranteed a job at the new site. In 1875, rather than a flat fee to recruit workers in the state, a new Georgia statute imposed a $100 fee for each county in the state where emigrant agents sought to recruit black labor. Later Georgia raised the fee to $500 per county. North Carolina imposed a fee of $1,000 per county. Some agents, such as Robert A. "Peg Leg" Williams, regularly defied emigrant-agent laws and even fought for their repeal in court. But in 1900, after agents like Williams challenged these laws, the U.S. Supreme Court upheld such statutes in *Williams v. Fears*. In the wake of the Supreme Court's decision and a narrow escape from a lynch mob, even Williams terminated his recruitment activities in Georgia. "All Colored Farm Hands," he said, "should settle down and go to work and stop the agitation that now prevails." The coercion of southern black farm workers persisted through World War I and beyond.[16]

From the outset of the emancipation years, federal officials, entrepreneurs, and other supposed northern allies of African Americans reinforced discriminatory policies against black workers in the rural South. Rising numbers of northern entrepreneurs moved into the rural South to take advantage of low-wage, newly emancipated African American labor. Even before war's end, the northern engineer Edward Philbrick joined with twelve other northern investors to form a joint stock company that would eventually purchase eleven plantations and lease two others on the South Carolina Sea Islands. Philbrick and his colleagues immediately discontinued the earlier plantation practice of distributing an allotment of food, clothing, and other necessities to enslaved workers. He agreed with the proposition that in slavery, "not only are natural rights denied, but what is quite as injurious, necessary wants are supplied." Even the liberal *New York Times* opined that black freedmen and freedwomen required strict discipline and, what's more, perhaps "new masters." U.S. military officers and the Freedmen's Bureau informed planters that they could no longer use "bodily coercion" against ex-slaves, but they nonetheless tilted their support toward the planter class, vigorously enforcing vagrancy laws and supporting the curtailment of food supplies, clothing, and other social services as a method of coercing black workers into postbellum labor contracts. One early postbellum northern officer of the Union army himself inflicted "twenty lashes" on one ex-slave and "rubbed him down right smart with salt, for having no visible means of support." Another northern commander stationed in Columbia, South Carolina, reported that "the liberty given" to freedpeople "simply means liberty to work, *work or starve*." General O. O. Howard, director of the Freedmen's Bureau, repeatedly impressed upon emancipated people that they must enter into labor contracts because any man "who can work has no right to support by the government."[17]

During a short interlude between the late 1860s and early 1870s, radical Republicans passed a series of measures that weighted the scale of labor law toward the protection of rural black workers' rights. This legislation supported the rights of black workers to change employers, move from place to place, and lay legal "claim" to a portion of the crops that they produced on sharecropping units. But these measures did not hold. The resurgence of the Democratic Party to power resulted in reinstatement of the harshest features of earlier vagrancy, wage contract, and sharecropping laws.

Moreover, aided and abetted by the Thirteenth Amendment's approval of "involuntary servitude" as "a punishment for crime," southern states established a new punitive criminal justice system that aimed not only to control recently freed people but also to meet the labor demands of the region's ex-slaveowners and their northern capitalist collaborators. In the years before the Civil War, few enslaved black workers faced incarceration for violations of southern laws and social practices. Slaveowners exercised almost exclusive authority over the disciplining of bondsmen and bondswomen. Invariably, slave offenses were punished by the whip or by sale from one plantation to another to avoid interruptions in the profitable employment of slave labor. As one ex-slave later recalled, jails were "built for the white folks. . . . When they [slaves] done wrong they was whipped and let go."[18]

By contrast, between the end of the Civil War and the beginning of World War I, southern states erected a new prison system that ensnared an escalating number of black workers. However, in order to sidestep responsibility for the cost of housing and supervision of a huge black convict population, Georgia, Mississippi, and Alabama, among others, established a "convict leasing system" that allowed prison authorities to lease black prisoners to a variety of private employers at huge profit to the state.[19] Owners of cotton plantations, lumber mills, coal mines, and railroads hired rising numbers of incarcerated black men and to some extent black women. Convict labor camps and chain gangs proliferated. As early as 1886, in Georgia, prison officials reported that one of every two hundred black workers was a convict, the vast majority working under the supervision of private employers. Black prisoners labored from sunup to sundown under armed guards and sometimes vicious prison guard dogs. Moreover, employers of convict workers regularly employed the whip.[20]

Alabama employed prison labor almost exclusively in the coal mines. In 1877, two major coal companies—the Tennessee Coal and Iron Company (TCI) and the Sloss Iron and Steel Company—claimed all of the state's incarcerated workers. Under the close surveillance and control of wardens, mine bosses, and guards, convict coal miners such as Green Cottenham "toiled under the lash" for nearly a half century after emancipation from human bondage. Under these exceedingly harsh and inhumane conditions, as historian Mary Ellen Curtin succinctly notes, "while on his knees, the average convict miner shoveled 8,000 to 12,000 pounds of dead weight" daily and helped to fuel the industrialization of the New South. Although some of these men acquired skills as convicts and returned to the mines as free wage earners upon release, the high mortality rate among convict workers, as well as long sentences, undercut this path into the free industrial workforce. At one Alabama mine, between 1893 and 1895, the death rate reached 90 per 1,000 workers, while the state's average death rate for miners stood at 64 per 1,000 workers—already the highest in the nation, including other southern convict labor states. Despite the gradual institution of prison reforms by the late nineteenth and early twentieth centuries, the state's convict mines and miners persisted until 1928. As one mine inspector admitted, the convict system remained intact to squeeze "all the revenue out of the convicts which can be had. That is the whole truth."[21]

While Alabama segregated men and women convicts into male and female jobs, Georgia officials placed women prisoners alongside men in traditionally male work on railroads, in lumber mills, and on road projects. Historian Talitha LeFlouria notes in her prize-winning book on the subject, "Within

ONLY WOMAN BLACKSMITH
IN AMERICA IS A CONVICT

MATTIE CRAWFORD.
She Is a Blacksmith at the State Prison Farm and Wears Man's
Clothing.

This photo of Mattie Crawford, a skilled African American woman prisoner at the state prison farm, appeared in the *Atlanta Constitution,* August 19, 1903. Courtesy, Newspaper Archive, Wilmington, DE.

the cavernous hold of Georgia's state penitentiary system, black women's laboring bodies were tossed to and fro. Some landed on the northwest side of the 'Empire State of the South' in the Dade coal mines, while others were set adrift in 'flying' railroad camps and mobile chain gangs. A sizable cluster was crammed into Atlanta's already overcrowded brickyards, while the remainder soldiered through the sprawling pine forests and cotton fields of the Northeast. Everywhere they landed terror and violence pursued them."[22]

Though some poor and working-class whites were also enmeshed in the new system of forced labor, it was largely a racialized system of labor control focused almost exclusively on the black workforce for the benefit of government officials, industrialists, and staple-crop farmers. By the early 1880s, according to available statistics, the ratio of black to white convicts leased to private employers stood at about 13:1 in North Carolina, 11:1 in Georgia, and 7:1 in South Carolina. In Georgia, African Americans made up between 90 and 95 percent of all convict workers between 1878 and 1902. When southern states gradually repealed the convict lease laws and placed black workers under the direct supervision of state-run penitentiaries during the early twentieth century, the old forms of coerced labor persisted on large state-run plantations and especially massive road-building projects. The latter resuscitated and expanded the chain gang, which persisted deep into the interwar years of the twentieth century. Mississippi's infamous Parchman Farm emerged as a violent symbol of how the reform of the southern prison labor system failed to improve conditions for black workers caught in the new system of coerced labor. The first generation of southern blacks born in freedom faced declining prospects for social justice as the new century got under way.[23]

TOWARD THE URBAN INDUSTRIAL WORKING CLASS

By the turn of the twentieth century, the African American search for land-ownership and a livelihood in southern agriculture increasingly dissipated, especially for those young African American men and women who had been born in freedom some twenty to thirty years earlier. They faced mounting racial barriers and hostility from rural landowners and the machinery of the state. Looking back, late nineteenth- and early twentieth-century white landowners now viewed the slave-born generation of black men and women as imbued with "habits of diligence, order, [and] faithfulness," while the new generation developed what they called "a migratory disposition." In 1881, the

Nashville Banner praised older agricultural laborers as dependable assets but complained that their children preferred to spend "most of their time in town." In testimony before the U.S. Industrial Commission in 1899–1901, southern farmers reinforced a stark comparison of new versus old black labor: "The older class of colored labor . . . are a first rate class of labor. The younger class . . . are . . . very trifling."[24]

As suggested by the pejorative references to young black men and women and their attraction to town life, increasing numbers of rural blacks were moving into cities seeking alternatives to work in southern agriculture. As noted above, beginning during the Civil War, rising numbers of blacks moved into southern towns and cities as well as to the urban North as fugitives from southern plantations and farms. This was no straightforward proposition. From the beginning of the emancipation years, as planters moved to restrict black agricultural workers to the land, southern cities enacted legislation and policies designed to limit the influx of blacks into their borders. As early as September 1865, southern officers of the Freedmen's Bureau issued orders to prevent black people from "crowding into cities and towns." Any blacks "found sleeping in the streets, or in excessively crowded rooms," or who were otherwise considered vagrants would be sent to special work farms. In February 1866, Freedmen's Bureau head O. O. Howard instructed local officials to "continue to use every possible effort . . . to reduce . . . any accumulations of [black] people in the different cities and villages." Like their rural counterparts, southern municipalities regularly fined black men for vagrancy and placed them in workhouses to generate revenue. Moreover, New Orleans and other southern cities also instituted new pass policies, modeled on the old plantation system, that prevented black people from walking the streets day or night of their own volition or in the regular conduct of their business and affairs. Even passes, blacks protested, "do not in all cases protect us from arrest, abuse, violence and imprisonment by military authorities, local police and civilians."[25]

The movement of black workers into cities occurred against a backdrop of growing discrimination across the country. Over the emancipation period, northern and southern whites gradually developed a new consensus on questions of race and labor. This racial consensus slowly bridged differences between regions and paved the way for the emergence of a white supremacist social order during the closing years of the nineteenth century. Growing numbers of white Americans, including former allies of newly emancipated black people, adopted new notions of social Darwinism and proclaimed blacks "inherently" or "genetically" inferior to white people and sanctioned the emergence of new formal and informal policies of racial violence, disfranchisement, and economic inequality.[26]

The Democratic Party, calling itself "the White Man's Party," pledged to remove black people as a viable force from the political economy of the nation. The party's program of racial terror blended seamlessly with ascendant white supremacist groups like the Ku Klux Klan. Both groups waged violent campaigns against African Americans across urban America. In New Orleans alone, race riots erupted in 1866, 1868, 1873, 1874, and 1877. In 1866, shortly after his return to New Orleans following the fall of the Confederacy, a rebel soldier declared, "It is hard to get back home after four years of hardships and find [blacks] with arms in hand doing guard duty in the city and to see a white man taken under Guard." The race riot of that year left over 50 blacks dead and another 150 people injured. The U.S. Army stationed in New Orleans and other federal authorities ignored pleas for help. A riot in Memphis the same year raged over a three-day period and resulted in 46 deaths, over 70 injuries, 5 recorded sexual assaults on black women, and the demolition of 4 African American churches, 12 schools, and 91 homes.[27] Nor were northern cities more welcoming: in 1871, when Philadelphia's white Republicans allied with blacks to dislodge the Democratic Party from power, a race riot broke out on Election Day, October 10. Before the conflict subsided, four black people had died. The *Philadelphia Tribune,* the local black newspaper, blamed the violence on the predominantly working-class white mobs, along with the actions of the police force and the city's Democratic mayor.[28]

As the white supremacist system increased its hold during the late nineteenth and early twentieth centuries, yet another cycle of racial violence erupted against predominantly working-class black communities in the urban North and South. In addition to the well-known Springfield, Illinois, Riots of 1904 and 1908 and the Wilmington, North Carolina, Riot of 1898, resort to mob violence emerged most prominently in the New York Riot of 1900 and the Atlanta Race Riot of 1906. In 1900, a New York City plainclothes policeman, Robert J. Thorpe, charged a young black woman with prostitution. When her boyfriend, Arthur J. Harris, a recent migrant from Richmond, Virginia, questioned the officer regarding his accusation and treatment of his friend, Thorpe clubbed Harris with his nightstick, and Harris pulled a knife and stabbed the officer. When Thorpe died from his wounds the following day, crowds of whites, including members of Thorpe's station-house comrades, attacked New York's black community. According to the *New York Daily Tribune,* "men and women poured by the hundreds from the neighboring tenements. Negroes were set upon wherever they could be found and brutally beaten." The *New York Times* also reported, "Every car passing up or down Eighth Avenue . . . was stopped by the crowds and every negro on board dragged out. . . . The police made little or no attempt to arrest any of [the] assailants." Although there were no reported deaths, some eighty black men and women filed affidavits describing their injuries. Published affidavits provided eyewitness accounts of the role of both police and the mobs in carrying out violence against black people. "It was said freely by witnesses," the *New York Times* reported, "the police had done as much as anybody to encourage and promote the abuse of inoffensive negroes." A writer for *Harper's Weekly* concluded there was little sympathy for blacks during or after the violence: "I heard many Native American [whites] . . . say after the riot . . . that they would have been glad if many of the negroes had been killed."[29]

Throughout the summer leading up to the Atlanta riot six years later, influential politicians and journalists had been fomenting a climate of racial hostility. Hoke Smith, a Georgia journalist and politician, repeatedly declared, "We will control the Negro peacefully if we can, but with guns if we must." In the weeks just before the outbreak of violence, whites circulated reports of four cases of black men sexually assaulting white women. The black man, the *Atlanta Journal* exclaimed, acts like a "barbarian" and destroys "what he cannot attain . . . [namely,] the fair young girlhood of the South." Some ten thousand white people poured into the streets of Atlanta, killing over two dozen black people, destroying homes, and demolishing churches, schools, and places of business. Mobs entered one popular barbershop with "heavy clubs, canes, revolvers," and rifles; they killed two black barbers and dragged their bodies through the streets and dumped them in an alley. When the violence spread outward to the upper-class black suburb of Brownsville, police disarmed black people in the area, while permitting growing numbers of white people to take up arms and assault black people and their communities, both within and outside the city limits.[30]

Nonetheless, despite the spread of the Jim Crow order, racial violence, and disfranchisement of black citizens, the postbellum period set in motion an enormous shifting of African Americans from farm to city. Although the Great Migration would pick up steam and run its course during the twentieth century, it had deep roots in both the transformation of black agricultural life and labor and the urban industrial transformation of the larger U.S.

economy before World War I. Hardly surprisingly, black migrants to the urban North repeatedly remarked that they were "tired of the South," "wanted to make a change," and were "willing to live anywhere, if the wages were good." Between 1890 and 1910, the black population increased from about 10,000 in New York and 22,000 in Philadelphia to, respectively, 92,000 and 85,000 by 1910. At about the same time, black residents in both Chicago and Pittsburgh rose from under 4,000 to over 25,000 and 44,000, respectively.[31]

The proportion of all blacks living in cities rose from under 10 percent in 1865 to over 25 percent in 1910. While the Old South cities of New Orleans, Baltimore, and Charleston continued to attract black population from surrounding farms and plantations, Washington, DC, Atlanta, and Birmingham became major new targets of black migration from the rural and small-town South. Black women made up over 55 percent of Washington's black population as it increased from about 32,000 to over 94,000 between 1870 and 1910. The vast majority of black men and women Washingtonians worked in household and general labor jobs, including employment in the expanding federal bureaucracy as well as in all-black institutions such as Howard University, though some African Americans worked in the Washington Navy Yard, particularly the anchor shop. About 30 percent black over the entire period, Washington became the site of the nation's largest African American urban community by World War I.[32] By 1880, however, as historian Kate Masur notes, lawmakers had defined the District's blacks as a problematic and divisive element in the body politic and demolished local self-government in the District of Columbia. Thus, beginning the postbellum years as a promising example of biracial democracy, Washington had reversed course ahead of the nation.[33]

African Americans increased to over 40 percent of the total population in the expanding New South cities of Birmingham and Atlanta. Both cities attracted increasing numbers of black women domestic and personal service workers. While women significantly outnumbered men in Atlanta, making up well over 50 percent of the total, the sex ratio reached near parity in Birmingham, as employers recruited growing numbers of black men to work in the area's expanding iron, coal, and steel industries. In 1881 and again less than ten years later, *Iron Age,* an employer journal, described the skills and capabilities of southern black workers—including skilled boilers, heaters, and rollers—and their capacity to meet the diverse labor demands of the steel industry. After a visit to the South in 1889, Andrew Carnegie described

Birmingham as "Pennsylvania's most formidable enemy." Furthermore, black workers made up nearly 90 percent of all workers classified as unskilled in the iron and steel industry. And between 1880 and 1910, African Americans increased from 42 percent to over 50 percent of Alabama's coal-mining labor force.[34]

Black workers found it more difficult to penetrate Atlanta's textile industry, except as general laborers and custodial workers. When the Atlanta Fulton Bag and Cotton textile company sought to employ black workers, it was less successful than the iron industry in overcoming the opposition of white employees. In 1897, the company employed black women to fill 20 to 25 positions as "bag folders," heretofore a job reserved for white women. Some 50 black men had already gained jobs at the firm, but they occupied the cellar of the company's workforce as "sweepers, scrubbers, yard hands, and roustabouts." When the company employed black women bag folders, 200 white women in the folding department walked off the job. The following day, an estimated 1,200 white men, women, and children joined the strikers. While white women framed their strike in economic terms as a threat to their wages and livelihood, white union men advanced a racialized gender interpretation of the strike as a gallant fight to prevent an action that would presumably "degrade [white] manhood, prostitute [white] womanhood and debauch [white] childhood" by placing black women on an equal footing with white women. After four days of strikes, the Fulton Bag and Cotton Company relented and discharged the black women employees. The white working men of Atlanta lauded the striking women as heroes and placed them at the front of the annual Labor Day parade in September.[35]

As was true in Washington and Atlanta, black women dominated the early black migration to Philadelphia, New York, and to a lesser degree Boston. (The newly emerging industrial cities of Chicago and Pittsburgh attracted significant numbers of male workers, and black men there slightly outnumbered black women.) Across the urban North, industrialization spurred the growth of the white middle class and created a substantial demand for household workers. As white women gained middle-class jobs as teachers, clerks, and nurses, the number of white domestic and personal service employees declined and opened the door to the employment of black women in northern urban and suburban households. By the same token, black women found few alternatives for making a living outside the realms of domestic and personal service. In Philadelphia, for example, at the turn of the twentieth century, an estimated 46 percent of all working women labored in manufacturing jobs, while another 38 percent worked in domestic and personal service; but 90 percent of black women took jobs in the household sector. Between 1880 and 1910, poorly educated, single or widowed black women represented "the lowest paid workers in the city." Black household workers figured prominently in arrest and conviction records for the period. In Philadelphia, "theft and other crimes against property" accounted for an estimated 70 percent of their offenses against the law. As one "servant thief" put it, "Unless I am willing to engage in a few menial occupations, in which the pay for my services would be very poor, there is no way I can earn an honest living."[36]

As black workers increased their presence in urban centers, African American men gradually gained access to northern manufacturing jobs as strikebreakers. By the late nineteenth century, the predominantly white organized labor movement was escalating and making increasing demands for higher wages, shorter hours, and better working conditions. As early as 1894, Birmingham's black workers helped to defeat the national railway strike and boycott of the Pullman Company. As the Louisville and Nashville Railroad hired increasing numbers of black brakemen and firemen, company officials soon declared "the backbone of the strike . . . practically broken." And Andrew Carnegie recognized the iron and steel industry in Birmingham as a weapon in his struggle with the demands of white workers.[37] Over time, all sorts of industrialists hired African Americans to defeat striking white workers in the steel, meatpacking, railroad, and other industries. Philadelphia's Midvale Steel Works employed black men during the early 1890s as "strike insurance" ahead of the walkout of white workers. By decade's end, the company reported some 200 African Americans in a total work force of 1,200 men. "Some of this work is [skilled labor]," the manager of the firm told researcher Isabel Eaton. "We have 100 colored men doing that skilled work now, and they do it as well as any of the others." The attraction of these jobs is not hard to fathom: in 1896, black domestics (and some general laborer jobs) averaged a high of just over $3.00 to $4.00 per week, but blacks working at the Midvale company started out at a wage of $1.20 per day.[38]

In New York City, blacks broke a variety of labor strikes in the years 1895, 1904, 1907, 1910, 1911, and 1912. They replaced striking longshoremen, general laborers, municipal street cleaners, baggagemen, hod carriers, waiters, and garment workers. After the 1895 New York longshoremen's strike, the Ward Line Company of Brooklyn relied on black labor "to the exclusion of all other races." Between 1902 and 1904, the number of regular gangs of black longshoremen increased from ten to thirty-five. The Stockyards Strike of 1904

and the Teamster Strike of 1905 brought significant numbers of black workers into Chicago's industrial workforce,[39] while the steel strikes of 1875,
1887–89, 1892 (the famous Homestead Strike), and 1909 brought successive
contingents of southern black workers to Pittsburgh and Allegheny County.
Despite these gains, black workers still represented only a tiny proportion of
industrial workers. For instance, before World War I, African Americans
made up only about 3 percent of the total steel industry work force of 300,000
in western Pennsylvania, compared to 29 percent who were American-born
whites and 68 percent who were immigrants.[40]

As the number of black workers in urban areas expanded, they looked for
ways to organize themselves to better their working and living conditions.
Labor organizing represented an important route to challenging the practices of mostly white employers and labor unions. But working-class blacks
also faced questionable treatment and exclusion by African American elites.
Over the postbellum period, their efforts to improve their lives resulted
sometimes in solidarity, sometimes in community fragmentation.

LABOR ORGANIZATIONS, CLASS CONFLICT, AND
COMMUNITY FRAGMENTATION

White workers often justified their assaults on black urban communities by
asserting that African Americans were antilabor strikebreakers. According
to rank-and-file white workers and their leaders, African Americans failed to
support organized white labor and protect the interest of working people
against the destructive labor policies of industrialists and other economic
and political elites. On the contrary, African American workers viewed
strikebreaking as a strategy to protect the interests of their own working
people against discriminatory and exclusionary white trade union policies
and practices. Meanwhile, urban black workers in the postbellum period
intensified their own labor organizing activities and challenged employers on
their own behalf. They resolved to strengthen their hand in negotiations with
employers and reap higher wages for their work.

In July 1869, some thirty black men met at Douglass Institute in Baltimore
"to organize the colored mechanics of Maryland, where white mechanics had
refused to permit black mechanics to work with or join their unions." The
convention set up a statewide labor organization for black workers and agreed
to serve as a dynamic center for organizing black workers on a national scale.[41]

The organized black labor movement focused on uniting a diverse mixture of skilled craftsworkers, and domestic and general laborers, including carpenters, barbers, masons, teamsters, longshoremen, and household, bar, restaurant, and hotel employees. On December 6, 1869, under the leadership of ship caulker Isaac Meyers, representatives of black workers from eighteen states met in Washington, DC, and formed the Colored National Labor Union (CNLU) for the "amelioration and advancement of the condition of those who labor for a living." The labor convention of 1869 endorsed the call for government-funded forty-acre lots for ex-slaves, the right of workers to organize and bargain collectively, and the acquisition of full political and citizenship rights for formerly enslaved people. The convention concluded that "our mottoes are liberty and labor, enfranchisement and education. The spelling-book and the hoe, the hammer and the vote, the opportunity to work and to rise ... we ask for ourselves and our children." Although the CNLU failed to meet again after about 1871, subsequent efforts to build a black labor movement would draw inspiration from this early beginning.[42]

By the late nineteenth and early twentieth centuries, black workers had formed unions in a wide range of skilled, semiskilled, general labor, and household service occupations. Among those who organized formally were carpenters, brick masons, and barbers; diverse day laborers; semiskilled longshoremen and teamsters as well as hotel, bar, and restaurant employees; and, gradually, industrial workers at shipyards, railroads, and iron and steel companies. And these independent black labor organizations and strike activities were not confined to black men. Between 1866 and 1881, African American washerwomen organized unions and launched strikes against their employers in Jackson, Mississippi; Galveston, Texas; and most notably Atlanta, Georgia. Atlanta's Association of Washer Women, formed in 1881, soon established a strike fund and struck for higher wages. As soiled laundry accumulated in elite households, the *Atlanta Constitution* reported rising discomfort and "inconvenience" among the city's white citizens. Though the strike eventually collapsed under the combined repressive activities of local police, the city council, and landlords who confronted the women with eviction from rental properties, it first helped to mobilize a broad range of other black household workers, cooks, and nurses, who advanced their own militant demands for better working conditions and higher pay.[43]

Where possible, black workers also launched interracial or biracial union strikes, closing ranks with their white counterparts against employers. Interracial and biracial labor cooperation emerged on the docks of New

Orleans, in the Birmingham industrial district, and in the Pittsburgh iron and steel mills. In 1881–82, for example, when the African American Garfield Lodge struck the Black Diamond Steel Works in Pittsburgh, white union men supported the effort by opening the way for black workers to gain employment in other mills during the duration of the walk out. Moreover, when the company sought to recruit replacement workers in Richmond, Virginia, that city's black Sumner Lodge squashed the company's effort.

Some of the most significant episodes of interracial labor struggle took place within the context of the Knights of Labor, the United Mine Workers of America (an interracial constituent of the otherwise racially exclusionary locals of the American Federation of Labor), and later the Industrial Workers of the World. Local assemblies and unions of these organizations staged remarkable struggles to bridge the racial gap in the labor movement as the Jim Crow system escalated. In 1886, during the Knights of Labor's General Assembly meeting in Richmond, the black organizer Frank Ferrell of District Assembly 49 of New York City followed Governor Fitzhugh Lee to the podium to address the audience on labor rights and the need for interracial unity in the organized labor movement. Before the turn of the century, black and white dockworkers collaborated on the division of jobs on the New Orleans waterfront.[44]

These interracial efforts, though few at best, found rhetorical support among certain emerging elite black leaders. Former slave Frederick Douglass, Congressman John R. Lynch of Mississippi, and T. Thomas Fortune of the *New York Age* all criticized "wage slavery" and emphasized the unity of interest between black and white workers. Douglass urged white labor organizations to accept black workers into their ranks. "The labor unions of the country," he said in 1883, "should not throw away this colored element of strength . . . [and] weaken the bond of brotherhood between those on whom the burden and hardships of labor fall."[45] Lynch appealed to the Democratic Party to change its racial policies because African Americans were closer to Democrats than Republicans on fundamental economic issues. And during the 1880s, Fortune adopted the "land monopoly" ideas of reformer Henry George, offering a scathing critique of what he called "*industrial slavery,* a slavery more excruciating in its exactions, more irresponsible in its machinations than any other slavery." Fortune held that "the black man who arrays himself on the side of capitalism as against labor would be like a black man before the war taking sides with the pro-slavery as against the anti-slavery advocates."[46]

Nonetheless, interracial labor organizing largely foundered on the shoals of racial conflict before the interwar rise of the Congress of Industrial Organizations. Meanwhile, class differences within the African American community affected the conditions and outlook of black workers. When diverse African American business and professional people gradually reached out to their poor and working-class counterparts, they did so with profoundly class-biased programs of racial "uplift." These programs were based on assumptions that allowed middle-class and elite blacks to distinguish and also distance themselves from the culture of working-class blacks as they migrated to cities in rising numbers. Even so, their attitudes toward newcomers stopped far short of endorsing the ideas of white supremacists. In particular, old black elites (mostly in the North) insisted that "slavery" and not "race" or "color" accounted for the socioeconomic and political difficulties confronting rural black Southerners.

Poor and working-class black women were a particular target for "uplift." In 1890, T. Thomas Fortune, Rev. Alexander Walters, and other influential black New Yorkers pushed for the organization of new "societies" and "homes" for "reclaiming fallen women." Meanwhile, middle-class black women residents took the lead in organizing programs to aid black female migrants to the city. In 1897, for instance, under the leadership of Victoria Earle Matthews, black women spearheaded the formation of New York's White Rose Mission (later White Rose Industrial Association) on East Ninety-Seventh Street. By 1905, the White Rose organization had worked with over five thousand women, including meeting with migrants at southern ports like Norfolk as well as the busy New York port. In her study of this generation of black professional women, historian Stephanie Shaw coined the insightful term "socially responsible individualism" to describe their racial uplift work, which also led to the formation of the National League for the Protection of Colored Women (NLPCW), one of the early parent organizations of the National Urban League.[47]

Sometimes the unstated goal of black elites was not only to "lift up" poor and working-class blacks who were entering northern cities in accelerating numbers but to expand clientele for their own enterprises. In 1900, under the leadership of Booker T. Washington, head of Tuskegee Institute in Alabama, African Americans met in Boston and founded the National Negro Business League (NNBL) to promote the expansion of black business and professional organizations. Emphasizing self-help, business development, and racial solidarity, local chapters of the NNBL soon spread throughout the nation, encouraging all blacks to patronize black-owned establishments.[48] Poor and working-class black migrants, women as well as men, not only promised a widening clientele for black business and professional people, but also buoyed this process through their own entrepreneurial efforts. In 1901, when the teenaged Lillian Harris left Mississippi, she landed in Boston and from there hitched her way to New York City (on hay, milk, and vegetable wagons), where she became one of Harlem's wealthiest street vendors. More widely known is the story of Louisiana-born Madam C. J. Walker, who was orphaned at 7 years of age; married at 14; and widowed with a daughter at 20. By World War I, in addition to having migrated to St. Louis, Indianapolis, and finally to New York, Walker had also built her own hair-products manufacturing company and employed over five thousand agents.[49]

Scholars and popular writers have produced volumes of commentary on the ideological conflicts between Booker T. Washington's notions of self-help and W. E. B. Du Bois's uncompromising call for the full integration of African Americans into all facets of the nation's life. Whether Washingtonian or Du Boisian, however, the class and gender biases of middle-class reformers undercut the efficacy of their efforts to aid the poorest black residents of the cities.[50] The activist churchwoman Nannie Helen Burroughs repeatedly urged her middle-class counterparts to erase their class biases against their poor and working-class sisters, including domestic service and household workers, and embrace them as equals: "The women who wash for a living have as much right, as much business, to be leaders in our churches, if they are spiritually, morally, [and] intellectually fitted, as the women who are mistresses of their own homes." In a volume of essays titled *A Voice of the South* (1892), Anna Julia Cooper, a graduate of Oberlin College and a teacher in the schools of Washington, DC, cited an 1899 Atlanta University publication showing that black women, mostly working class, "supported wholly or in part" 57 percent of the city's 1,137 black families. Thus, in her view, women had "a right to claim at least . . . fair play and all the rights of wage-earners in general."[51]

While all blacks faced discrimination as the Jim Crow order spread, working-class blacks carried the heaviest burden of proving their claim to respectability. Following the New York Riot of 1900, African American affidavits highlighted how both middle- and working-class black men and women articulated their own notions of respectability and roundly decried such blatant attacks and violations of their rights. But, according to historian Cheryl Hicks, more than African American doctors, lawyers, ministers, teachers, and businessmen, working-class blacks "felt compelled to emphasize the respectability of their labor as well as their appropriate and law-abiding behavior, insisting that those factors were important components of their identity."[52]

Meanwhile, in addition to questioning of their character, working-class black newcomers to urban areas often confronted stiff barriers to their full participation in some established black institutions. In 1884, black New Yorkers institutionalized the division between old and new Knickerbockers with the formation of the Society of the Sons of New York. In 1886, the organization formed a Daughters of New York female auxiliary and rein-forced social class and gender distinctions within the black community. Both units restricted membership to New York–born African Americans— though they developed a special "honorary" membership category for south-ern-born black elites like T. Thomas Fortune and the social welfare activist Victoria Earl Matthews.[53]

The pull toward elite "distinction" was not limited to New York. When the Englishman Arthur Shadwell visited Philadelphia at the turn of the twentieth century, he soon declared that he had discovered the home of the nation's "coloured aristocracy." Shadwell based his assessment on observa-tions of services at the African Methodist Episcopal churches. In his view, such services were nearly "indistinguishable from a high church (not ritual-istic) Anglican one in England, except that the surpliced choir was formed of women." Philadelphia's founding AME church had moved a long distance from its roots in the early nineteenth-century black working class. Calling themselves the "upper tens," elite families included what historian Willard Gatewood has described as "three distinct components": Philadelphia-born blacks (the Forten family, for example); light-skinned descendants of West Indian blacks from San Domingo and Haiti (the Austins, Appos, de Baptists, and Le Counts); and a final group of "fair-complexioned, free-born mulat-toes" from such Southern states as South Carolina, Virginia, and Maryland.[54]

For their part, however, blacks born in the southern United States and the Caribbean formed a plethora of new religious, fraternal, and social service organizations to address class and cultural biases within the expanding black urban community. In New York, these organizations included the Sons of Virginia, Sons of the South, Sons and Daughters of South Carolina, the Bermuda Benevolent Association, the Cubans' Society of Thirty, the Montserrat Progressive Society, and the Danish West Indian Ladies Aid Society, to name a few. New "down home" storefront churches also emerged before World War I. The city's Union Baptist Church epitomized the growth of these churches, with its gospel style of preaching, singing, and music. According to contemporary observers of the black church movement, organizations like Union Baptist Church brought together the most "recent residents of this new, disturbing city." These churches also enabled Christianity to gain a new birth of life on Sunday morning for large numbers of poor and working-class newcomers neglected by the established mainstream denominations.[55]

It is worth noting that despite the tensions between established middle-class and elite blacks and the poor and working-class blacks moving to the cities—tensions that threatened a fragmentation of the African American community—African Americans in the late nineteenth and early twentieth centuries also formed cross-class (if often elite-led) national organizations to intensify their push for full recognition of their rights as citizens. In relatively rapid succession, between the 1880s and 1910, African Americans formed the Afro-American League, the National Afro-American Council, the Constitution League, the Committee of Twelve, and the Niagara Movement. These early "New Negroes" established the ideological, tactical, and organizational foundation for the rise of the NAACP (formed in 1909) as the preeminent national civil rights organization in the nation. In her study of these organizations, historian Shawn Alexander convincingly argues that the emergence of the NAACP "represented a significant realignment or adjustment rather than a major paradigm shift."[56] Significantly, while the NAACP drew upon ideas from earlier organizations, it gained greater support among the masses of poor and working-class blacks than its predecessors, partly because of a more affordable membership fee and the *Crisis* magazine's effective articulation of the organization's goals to a national audience.[57] These and similar organizations would make their most significant contributions to black urban, labor, and working-class life during the acceleration of the Great Migration.

CONCLUSION

By the turn of the twentieth century, increasing numbers of southern black workers had departed plantations and farms for life and work in the nation's expanding urban-industrial centers—a movement accelerated by disfranchisement, lynching, unequal labor contracts, and the racialized carceral state. Wherever they landed, they contributed to the growth of the changing economy; even those arrested spurred the industrialization of the South as convict labor. North or South, blacks confronted an onslaught of violent repression. However, during the same period, class divisions between white workers and industrial elites persisted and even intensified, creating a breach in the armor of white supremacy. Thus, a door was opened for significant numbers of African Americans to enter the industrial workforce as strike-breakers, and, to some extent, sparked moments of interracial solidarity between black and white workers.

From these beginnings, the industrial working class would form in the early twentieth century as the Great Migration picked up steam. The inter-war years would see both tremendous progress by the black labor force and tremendous opposition from white supremacist culture and politics, setting the conditions for the social movements of the mid-twentieth century.

PART TWO

The Twentieth Century

FOUR

The Industrial Working Class

BEGINNING SLOWLY DURING THE FIRST HALF CENTURY after the Civil War, the Great Migration of black people accelerated under the impact of two world wars and the Great Depression. Expanding employment opportunities in the urban industrial economy opened an exciting and hopeful new chapter in the history of the black working class. While large numbers of black men and women would continue to work as general laborers and domestic servants in private households as well as a growing number of trade and transportation enterprises, manufacturing employment gradually emerged at the dynamic center of the new black workforce. Compared to labor in the agricultural South, jobs in the industrial sector represented higher wages, better working conditions, and increasing access to previously all-white unions.

Although black workers celebrated their movement into the industrial city as evidence of upward mobility and progress outside southern agriculture, several overlapping developments soon undercut the promise of the "promised land." Employers, white workers, and the state collaborated to erect a racial job ceiling in the workplace and a racially segregated housing market across the urban landscape. Black workers challenged deepening forms of racial inequality in the economic, institutional, and political life of the city, holding their ground whenever possible in the face of mob violence and recurring day-to-day assaults on their persons in public spaces. But as the Great Migration brought more and more African Americans north, their social struggles helped to gradually reshape the institutions and culture of the industrial city.

The numbers are staggering. An estimated three million African Americans moved from the rural and urban South to the North and West during the interwar years of the Great Migration. Another five million black people left the South for the urban North and West between 1940 and 1980.[1] Rising numbers of rural blacks also moved into the urban industrial South. During World War II alone, over two million migrants moved from one southern state to another. In search of a better life, organized their own movement from farm to city and from South to North and West, writing letters of inquiry to local branches of the National Urban League, to northern black newspapers like the *Chicago Defender,* and most of all to relatives and friends who had already moved to industrial cities. They also organized "migration clubs," pooled their resources, and purchased railroad tickets at reduced rates. In addition, some took the transportation, job, and housing offers of industrial labor recruiters to help with their moves.[2]

The industrial sector offered a significant incentive to blacks in southern agriculture. African Americans who moved directly from a southern farm labor job to the urban North may have increased their earnings by as much as 300 percent in some cases. Even after adjustments for the higher cost of living in their new homes, a recent econometric study suggests that increases in migrant earnings ranged from a low of about 56 percent to a possible high of 130 percent. Based partly upon expanding employment in the industrial sector, black workers often described northern, western, and to some extent southern cities in glowing terms as the "Promised Land," "New Jerusalem," "Land of Liberty," "Land of Hope," or simply the "land of milk and honey."[3]

Industrialists focused the bulk of their labor recruitment efforts on blacks in the Deep South states of Alabama, Georgia, Mississippi, Louisiana, and Texas.[4] One employer sprinkled handbills across the wartime Alabama sharecropping region. The broadside queried prospective black migrants: "Would you like to go North where the laboring man shares the profit with the Boss? ... Will advance you money if necessary. Go now. While you have the chance."[5] The Pennsylvania Railroad; the New York Central; the New Haven, Delaware, and Hudson; the Illinois Central; and other railroad companies recruited black labor for a wide range of manufacturing companies as well as their own extensive rail operations.

As a result, African Americans gained increasing access to jobs in the nation's railroad, shipbuilding, meatpacking, steel, rubber, and automobile manufacturing firms. Nationwide, the percentage of black men employed in "skilled," "semiskilled," and "unskilled" jobs other than domestic service increased from about 34 percent on the eve of World War I to an estimated 43 percent in 1930. Over the same period, the number of black workers jumped from under 600 in the auto industry to nearly 26,000; from 17,400 to 45,500 in steel; and from 5,800 to 20,400 in the meatpacking industry. By the end of World War II, although blacks continued to work disproportionately in household and general labor jobs compared to their white counterparts, nearly 75 percent of all African Americans (predominantly men) worked in nonfarm jobs defined as "unskilled" or "skilled" segments of the black working class.[6]

Each region and each industry had its own unique features or flavor as well as similarities. Some railroad, steel, and meatpacking firms had employed southern black workers as strikebreakers before World War I. In these industries, interwar black newcomers reinforced earlier concentrations of blacks in the industrial workforce. As discussed in chapter 3, the nationwide railway strike and boycott of the Pullman Company, the Chicago-based manufacturer of the popular "sleeping cars," and the New York longshoremen's strike the next year had opened both of those jobs to black workers. Some Philadelphia firms also built upon their pre–World War I experiences with black workers. As early as the 1890s, for example, the city's Midvale Steel Works employed African Americans in skilled as well as general labor positions. Under manager Frederick Winslow Taylor, a pioneering time-management specialist, the company attacked white-worker solidarity and undercut efforts to unionize the plant. "Now our gangs have, say, one Negro, one or two Americans, an Englishman, etc. The result has been favorable both for the men and for the works. Things run smoothly, and the output is noticeably greater."[7]

The U.S. Steel Homestead works, the Jones and Laughlin Steel Company, and Carnegie Steel built upon their prewar history and expanded their black labor force in Pittsburgh and western Pennsylvania. African Americans rose from only about 3 percent of workers in the steel industry in 1910 to nearly 15–20 percent during the height of the interwar years. Some companies—Oliver Iron and Steel, Pittsburgh Forge and Iron, and A.M. Byers among others—hired black workers for the first time, while other Pittsburgh iron and steel men had employed black strikebreakers during a series of steel strikes between 1875 and 1909. At the city's Black Diamond Steel Works and the Clark Mills, African Americans also gained access to such skilled jobs as roller, rougher, finisher, puddler, millwright, and heater.[8] In some cases, they even supervised some of their less skilled white counterparts.[9]

Chicago employers also built upon a coterie of black workers from prewar strikebreaking activities. Such manufacturing firms as Swift, Armour, Pullman, and International Harvester added increasing numbers of blacks to their payrolls. The Teamster strike of 1905 had resulted in a few jobs for blacks when the strike ended and white workers returned to their routes, but the stockyards strike of 1904 had brought over 360 black workers into the meatpacking industry. Soon after the stockyards strike, the segregationist governor of South Carolina, Ben Tillman, visited the city. The black workers, Tillman said, seeking to stir northern white working-class racial hatred, "whipped you in line. They were the club with which your brains were beaten out."[10]

In other industries, blacks made their first inroads. The Detroit auto industry had hired few blacks before World War I, but the Ford Motor Company emerged as the nation's foremost employer of industrial black workers during the interwar years.[11] Ford's black workforce rose from only 50 employees in 1916 to nearly 1,700 by the end of World War I. The company also offered blacks a broader range of production and supervisory opportunities than any other industrial firm within or outside the auto industry. A reporter for the Associated Negro Press later recalled, "Back in those days [1920s and early 1930s] Negro Ford workers almost established class distinctions here. . . . The men began to feel themselves a little superior to workers in other plants. . . . 'I work for Henry Ford' was a boastful expression."[12] In South Philadelphia, black workers made up over 50 percent of the workforce at some of the Sun Shipyard facilities. They also worked in smaller numbers at Philadelphia's Franklin Sugar, Atlantic Refinery, Westinghouse, and Disston Saw companies.[13]

Black men and women found fewer industrial opportunities in West Coast cities than they did in the urban North. By 1930, the percentage of black men working in the industrial sector reached well over 50 percent in major cities of the urban Northeast and Midwest; by contrast, West Coast blacks reported no more than about 30 percent of their numbers holding such jobs before the Great Depression got under way. In addition to the West Coast petroleum industry's exclusion of African Americans from both the drilling and refining ends of the business, the Los Angeles movie industry largely barred African Americans from jobs as actors and actresses during the interwar years. To make things worse, when northeastern and midwestern firms like Ford and Firestone opened plants in Los Angeles, they located in or near places like South Gate, a white working-class town that openly excluded blacks. In 1928, firms located near South Gate reported paying out wages of $4.7 million, almost exclusively to white workers.[14] Still, during World War II, San Francisco Bay Area shipyards recruited increasing numbers of southern black men. By 1942, in addition to advertising in southern newspapers, the Kaiser Shipyards "distributed brightly colored circulars throughout southern cities. The circulars extolled California's mild climate, its recreational facilities, and shipyard pay benefits and appealed to patriotism" as well. Located primarily in Richmond, California, the shipyards included African Americans as 20 percent of the total labor force at the peak of wartime production. The city of Richmond itself mushroomed from a "quiet town" of only 23,000 in 1940 to 100,000 by 1943.[15]

More than the urban West and North, southern cities built upon an extensive prewar history of employing black men and to some extent black women in the industrial sector. Under the impact of the Great Migration, southern employers, much like their northern counterparts, advertised widely for black workers in rural sharecropping areas, promising "steady work, high wages and a good time." When blacks migrated into the Birmingham industrial district from sharecropping homes, they often returned to rural areas to recruit relatives and friends for work in coal, iron mining, and milling firms surrounding the city. Through newspapers like the *Christian Hope,* blacks in Birmingham informed relatives of life and industrial labor in the city. They also set up "information bureaus" to assist migrants to find jobs and housing.[16]

In Houston, historian Bernadette Pruitt notes, the black weekly *Houston Informer* regularly printed job advertisements from such industrial firms as the Southern Oil Refining Company. The paper's editor, Clifton Frederick Richardson, also promoted Houston as a desirable site for prospective black migrants seeking relief from racial violence in rural East Texas towns. Richardson told readers that Houston provided a viable alternative to oppressive conditions elsewhere in Texas and the Deep South. On one occasion, he reported that the "colored citizens of Huntsville are all excited and many are anxious to sell out their little belongings and holdings and migrate to more civilized" areas like Houston.[17] Houston's black men gained increasing employment as "oil refinery workers, steelworkers, construction crews, cotton compress laborers, and railroad track repairmen." The city's black male industrial workforce increased most dramatically from about 5,200 in 1920 to nearly 8,800 in 1930, and to about 14,000 in 1940. Black men constituted an estimated 70 percent of all the city's work classified as "unskilled labor."[18]

Throughout the South, the Great Migration caused turmoil for employers. Rural planters resisted the labor recruitment activities of industrializing southern and northern cities. Alabama's "Black Belt" planters complained that labor recruiters "siphoned off" rural blacks for both the "northern industrial centers" and for the mines and mills "around Birmingham." As black labor slipped away from the Georgia countryside, the *Macon Telegraph* spoke bluntly for rural landowners and employers of black workers: "We must have the Negro in the South. . . . He has been with us so long that our whole industrial, commercial and agricultural structure has been built on a black foundation. It is the only labor we have; it is the best we have if we lost it we [would] go bankrupt." The regional newspaper *Southwestern Christian Advocate* warned black workers that industrial labor recruitment campaigns were long on promise and short on delivery.[19]

Even as southern industrial employers searched the countryside for black workers, heightening conflict with employers of farm labor, they protested the outmigration of their own black employees to the North and West. In 1918, a New Orleans official of the Atlantic Pacific Docks lamented that it had become "almost impossible to get workers." A contemporary newspaper also reported on the dearth of labor along the docks: "Where negro labor is much depended on, workmen are becoming more scarce every day. . . . Steamship men find it a considerable problem to facilitate the loading and unloading of cargoes." In December 1916, one Birmingham district mine supervisor, Milton Fies, observed that increasing numbers of black workers had left the area for the urban North. Northern "manufacturers of war munitions, machinery, [and] automobiles," he said, "are making very attractive offers to southern labor."[20]

Alex D. Pitts, the U.S. attorney for the Birmingham district, reported that black workers from the rural South were entering the city and region in rising numbers. In another twist, these newcomers worked for lower wages than resident black workers, who in turn accepted opportunities to move north. According to Pitts, this process had started on the eve of World War I, when "the great bulk" of some seventy thousand blacks from "Cotton Belt" Dallas County gained employment in the northern Alabama industrial district "because they could be employed cheaper than the negroes who were already there and that forced the negroes who were already there to leave." During the World War I years and in the war's early aftermath, according to historian Georgina Hickey, Atlanta's leading newspaper, the *Atlanta Constitution,* urged "better treatment of African Americans—improved wages and schools, and a crackdown on lynching, and so on—as an inducement for blacks to stay in the South."[21]

Black migration to jobs in the urban Upper South also accelerated. The Norfolkian George W. Bennett later recalled how his father left an Edenton, North Carolina, lumberyard for the shipyards of Norfolk, Virginia, during World War I. The escalating demand for labor transformed "the once sleepy seaport . . . into the foremost naval base of the Atlantic coast." While such jobs dissipated during the early 1920s and again during the Great Depression, they resurfaced under the production demands of World War II. James Wright left the small town of Russellville, Kentucky, for Louisville in September 1941. After three or more earlier trips to the city in search of work, he finally landed his first regular industrial job at International Harvester.[22]

Some contemporary analysts viewed the increasing movement of black men into the urban industrial economy as a "second emancipation" for black women as well. Presumably for the first time, large numbers of black men earned wages that were high enough to enable women to withdraw from the workforce and maintain the homefront. According to the National Urban League economist George Edmund Haynes, "thousands of Negro men for the first time found it possible to secure sufficient wages to provide for their families so that their wives remained at home, free from the necessity of having to earn the daily bread in addition to performing the duties of housekeeper, wife, and mother." Similarly, statistician Joseph Hill noted how, nationwide, the proportion of black women gainfully employed declined from 58 percent in 1910 to 44 percent by the end of World War I. Much like Haynes, Hill also concluded that "it is not improbable that the Negroes may have experienced some improvement in their economic position, making it less imperative for the women to contribute to the support of the family."[23]

In fact, most African American women continued to work, largely in household service occupations. Their employment supplemented the seasonal and often inadequate earnings of black male industrial workers. At the same time, rather than withdrawing from the workforce, black women gradually moved into manufacturing jobs. In Chicago, between 1910 and 1920, black women factory operatives increased from about 10 to 15 percent of all black women workers. In New York, the number of black apparel workers rose to an estimated 3,000 in 1925 and to 6,000 in 1927. In the wake of World War I, New York's black working women often expressed their desire to obtain factory work to avoid the "long hours, the confinement, and the friction of a personal boss."[24]

After Detroit's A. Krolik Garment Company hired its first black women, it soon developed an all-black female workforce. Working closely with the Urban League of Detroit, the company advertised openings at the plant in African American newspapers and in black churches, where ministers made "appeals for girls from their pulpits." The Krolik Company employed black women in all categories of labor except management; it also built a gymnasium, clubroom, and restaurant for African American employees. Following the lead of the Krolik Company, the Buhl Malleable Iron Company trained and employed black women in several skilled and semiskilled jobs, including coremaking. A few other black women worked in the city's automobile factories, auto parts plants, and machine shops. In Pittsburgh and western Pennsylvania domestic and personal service workers dropped only slightly from about 88 to about 86 percent of the black female workforce, but a handful of black women nonetheless became power machine operators at the National Shirt Factory, while another few worked at the mills of the Lockhart Iron and Steel Company. Hired to perform exceedingly exhaustive jobs, African American women employees, according to a later report by the Lockhart Company, had "done their work remarkably well."[25]

African American women used industrial work not only as an alternative to domestic service work but also as a mechanism for bidding up the price of their labor in household employment. Some black women migrated to the North from southern cities like Atlanta, where they had urged their sisters to leave household jobs for work in the industrial sector. One woman, a domestic service worker from Georgia, declared, "I'll never work in nobody's kitchen but my own anymore, no indeed!" Household employers soon complained that the gradual opening of industrial job opportunities for black women deprived them of low-wage domestic help. According to one Urban League report, some 80 percent of applicants for household work wanted "days work at $3.50 or $5.00 per day." In the past, widowed women with children performed most of the "day" work as opposed to "live-in" domestic service, but increasing numbers of young black women "refused to be strapped down to regular housework." Some of these women would soon adopt the motto "W.W.T.K. (White Women to the Kitchen)" and urge their sisters to leave domestic service employment for new manufacturing jobs.[26]

Women occupied an even broader range of manufacturing jobs in the South than in the urban industrial North and West. Durham, North

Carolina, represented an exceptional case. In 1930, at a time when domestic and personal service dominated the occupational structure of black urban women, 48 percent of Durham's black women worked in factories. Household labor represented under half of the city's black women workers. When Blanche Scott's family moved to Durham, both her mother and father found work in the tobacco industry, at the American Tobacco Company and Liggett and Myers, respectively.[27] In Norfolk, black women not only worked as dressmakers within and outside the factory setting but also took jobs as tobacco stemmers at the American Cigar Company. In Houston, between 1920 and 1930, black women increased from 38 to 40 percent of the total black workforce. In 1920, nearly 800 black women worked in Houston's industrial sector. Most of these women occupied low-end jobs at commercial laundries and as cotton-compress and warehouse workers along the city's ship channel.[28] And African Americans made up nearly 50 percent of all women in the industrial workforce of Memphis, Tennessee. By 1930, an estimated 1,600 black women worked mainly as dressmakers, garment workers, general laborers, and operatives in the city's chemical, clothing, and food plants.

World Wars I and II offered particular opportunities for black women as well as white women. During the first world war, Atlanta's economic and political elites praised women, especially black women, for the "capable manner in which they filled the men's jobs." One black war worker, Chaddie Wertham, left her job as a laundress and cook and found a position at the Union Box Company. Her job entailed "stacking boxes," a position previously reserved for men. Following the war, in an unusual move, the Union Box Company retained black women as part of a nearly all-female department.[29] Near the end of World War II, Rebecca Smith, a rural Cumberland County–born single mother, arrived in Louisville via Toledo, Ohio. She obtained her first industrial job on a "rivet gang" at the Louisville and Nashville Railroad (L&N). Black women's work at L&N "was dirty and dangerous but ultimately rewarding." It enabled Smith to support her family better than prior employment in domestic service jobs in Toledo.[30]

Despite their enthusiastic movement into the manufacturing economy, African Americans soon confronted deepening "color lines" in the workforce, housing, and community life of the industrial city. The outbreak of mob violence and the increasing urbanization of white supremacist groups like the Ku Klux Klan further exposed the limits of the industrial order for rising numbers of black workers and their communities. But it was the racial job ceiling in auto, steel, meatpacking, and other mass-production firms,

alongside the racist stranglehold on the housing market, that posed the greatest threat to African American hopes for a better life in the industrial city.

ERECTING THE RACIAL JOB CEILING

Even as African Americans made great gains in industrial jobs during the
interwar years, managerial and labor policies insured the racial stratification
of the urban workforce. Mill foremen hired their own men, arranged levels
of pay, and exercised control over firing. Ford employed black workers mainly
at the company's River Rouge complex and steadfastly refused to employ
blacks above the general laborer category at its plants outside of metropolitan
Detroit. Black autoworkers labored almost exclusively in paint spraying, steel
grinding, and hot and heavy foundry jobs. One Detroit automaker declared,
"We hired them for this hot dirty work and we want them [to stay] there. If
we let a few rise, all the rest will become dissatisfied." When "we can get all
the white workers we need," another Detroit employer declared, "why should
we take a chance on Negroes!" In the Pittsburgh steel industry, the prewar
generation of skilled black workers plummeted. Among twelve major steel
employers in Pittsburgh and western Pennsylvania, five classified all of their
black employees as "unskilled workers." The "unskilled" made up 90–95 percent at three other firms, and the remainder listed 50–75 percent of African
Americans in "unskilled" categories of work.[31]

Steel industry supervisors arbitrarily fired black workers and replaced
them with whites. Black workers sometimes noted specifically that some of
these bosses were from Alabama and Mississippi as well as southern, central,
and eastern Europe. When foremen obtained "power to hire and fire their
men," a contemporary sociologist concluded, "the negro often suffers."
Extraordinary employment opportunities for blacks in the auto industry
notwithstanding, African American workers reported mistreatment even
there. One auto foundry worker later recalled how one foreman would
repeatedly "curse and holler" at the men under his supervision. Another
employee recalled that foremen "never mentioned a wound serious enough to
go to First Aid." At the Armour Company in Chicago, managers placed an
asterisk or star on the time cards of black employees. Herbert March, a white
union organizer, remembered that white foremen "would look over the time
cards, and they would pick out the cards where there was a star. Those were
the [black] fellows who got laid off." In the city's stockyards, employers

A black packinghouse worker, called a "splitter," uses a large cleaver to separate a carcass into halves, ca. 1920s. Splitters exercised considerable skill as well as strength; a "poor cut could reduce the value of the meat." Burke and Dean Photographers. Courtesy, State Historical Society of Wisconsin, WHI (X3) 50369.

systematically excluded blacks from jobs as foremen. While some black men gained appointments as subforemen over all-black work crews, they were almost never given supervisory positions over white workers or even mixed gangs of black and white employees. In the meatpacking houses, according to Elmer Thomas, a black packinghouse worker, employers reserved the "clean, easy, light" jobs for white workers. Sam Parks, an employee at the Wilson Company, made the same point: "No Negroes worked in them clean, good departments. Where Negroes worked was the hog offal—that's where the guts and bowels all spill down. Hog kill, beef kill, beef offal, fertilizer department—those were the black jobs in that plant."[32] And, of course, some companies still refused to hire blacks at all: throughout the interwar years, such leading Philadelphia firms as the Budd Company, Bendix, Cramps Shipyard, and Baldwin Locomotive excluded African Americans from all categories of work, including jobs at the bottom of the workforce.[33]

Blacks faced even greater inequality in the urban industrial South. In the Birmingham district, Will Battle, a veteran black employee of the Tennessee Coal and Iron Company (TCI), later recalled that "the negro had his job, what he was doing, and the white man had his." White workers dominated the "better-paying" semiskilled and skilled positions and took most of the supervisory posts. These patterns also prevailed at U.S. Steel's subsidiary American Steel and Wire Company as well as U.S. Steel's Ensley and Fairfield operations. Some firms, like American Cast Iron and Pipe Company, reported all skilled workers as white.[34] In the Birmingham district, U.S. Steel's aggressive "modernization program" largely eliminated the "unskilled" categories of work occupied by blacks, while quadrupling the number of semiskilled jobs for whites. Southern employers also established racial wage differentials by categorizing skilled black workers as "helpers"—for example, "boilermaker's helper" rather than "boilermaker" or "plumber's helper" rather than "plumber," and so on.[35]

In Memphis and Houston, when employers classified African Americans performing identical work as whites as "helpers," they paid them uniformly lower wages than their white fellow workers. At the Firestone Company's Memphis plant, one black employee, Fred Higgins, described the process of racially stratifying the labor force: "You'd be classified as a 'helper,' but you'd be doing all the work. The white man would get the high wage . . . [but] he'd just be sittin' there watchin'." Another Firestone employee, Matthew Davis, declared, "All you had to do was have your face be white, and you'd move up the ladder." But blacks would remain "stuck" in a low-wage classification. In the Norfolk naval yards, some 83 percent of black workers earned $21–$25 per week, compared to 19 percent of whites at this level. An estimated 60 percent of whites earned $35 per week.[36]

No region was free of racial discrimination. In 1941, the writer Chester Himes arrived in Los Angeles from Mississippi via Cleveland. Himes later recalled that Los Angeles "hurt me racially as much as any city I have ever known—much more than I remember from the South. Black people were treated much the same as they were in any industrial city of the South." Himes lamented that, though he arrived in Los Angeles with a range of skills in carpentry, plumbing, electric wiring, brick masonry, and roofing, only two of his twenty-three different wartime posts allowed him to use his skills and training. The industrializing West offered another obstacle to black workers: unlike other parts of the country, in the West blacks competed for jobs and housing with Asian and Latino/Latina Americans.

In general, the urban West and Southwest presented a more complicated racial and ethnic environment than the urban North and South. In a contemporary study, "Negro Workers in Los Angeles Industries" (ca. 1927), Charles S. Johnson, director of the National Urban League's Department of Research, reported that some employers regarded Mexicans as white and prohibited their interaction and mixing with African Americans.[37] Other West Coast employers defined Latinos/Latinas as "colored" or "Negro" and not only placed them in work crews with African Americans but sometimes gave blacks "positions over them." In Houston, Texas, where African Americans also worked with rising numbers of Latino/Latina Americans and immigrants, competition for available work was sometimes quite fierce, but the racial rather than ethnic stratification of work presented the greatest obstacles to the city's black workers. The major barrier to the workplace advancement of African American workers, Pruitt convincingly argues, "was not the influx of Mexican American workers, but rather [white] racial hatred." As Johnson summed up, "In certain plants Mexicans and whites worked together; in some others white workers accepted Negroes and object[ed] to Mexicans; still in others white workers accepted Mexicans and object[ed] to Japanese. White women worked with Mexicans and Italian women, but refused to work with Negroes."[38]

Throughout the country, all-white labor unions as well as rank-and-file white workers reinforced the racially stratified urban workforce. The Chicago Stockyards Labor Council (SLC), formed in 1917, enacted a nondiscrimination membership policy but quickly established two racially segregated locals on the city's South Side: No. 65 for black men and No. 213 for black women. Moreover, the SLC tolerated the racially exclusionary policies of constituent locals, including the Machinists, who restricted membership to "white free-born male citizens of some civilized country," and the Railway Carmen's union, which allowed only "a white person, male or female, of good character" to obtain membership. Similarly, the unions of the electrical workers, black-smiths, and other craftsmen excluded blacks by constitutional clauses, provisions for local options on membership, or informal agreement.[39]

Racially biased labor policies had deep roots in the pre–World War I era. As discussed in chapter 3, black workers, excluded from white unions, regularly crossed the picket lines of striking white workers to gain access to better jobs. Later, in 1923, Eugene Debs, president of the American Railway Union, expressed remorse over his union's neglect of black workers during the national railway strike of 1894. In a speech before a Harlem audience, Debs said that "there would have been a different story of the strike" and "it would have had a different result" had the union brought black workers into the fold.[40] Instead, in case after case, white workers organized mob assaults on strikebreakers to prevent their entry into striking plants. In the Chicago stockyards strike of 1904, an estimated two thousand to five thousand striking white workers and their supporters attacked a group of about two hundred black strikebreakers at the Hammond Company plant. Similarly, in the 1905 Teamsters Union strike at Montgomery Ward's department store, a race riot broke out when black drivers appeared on the streets as replacement workers. When a black driver fought back against harassment by firing into a crowd and shooting an 8-year-old boy, whites retaliated by shooting a black man at a local club, and blacks in turn killed two white men and injured a dozen others before authorities brought the violence under control.[41]

Limits on African American access to labor unions, skilled jobs, and managerial positions reinforced their high concentration in general labor, domestic, and household service occupations. Most black women continued to cook, clean, and wash for white families, hotels, and a variety of business establishments, and more black men than white men worked as porters, janitors, teamsters, chauffeurs, waiters, and "general laborers of all kinds" across the urban North, South, and West. The African American Pullman porter emerged as a widespread symbol of black men's continued employment in the personal service field. At the height of railroad mileage and passenger travel during the early 1920s, the Pullman Company employed over 9,000 black porters. These men served some 31 million travelers a year. Another 11,000 mostly African American men worked for other companies on the railroads as coach porters or train porters. Porters remained on call day and night. Porters also expended a significant number of unpaid hours preparing their cars for travel. In oral recollections of their careers, African American porters often described their job as "a cross between a concierge, bellhop, valet, house-

A railroad porter's job was wide-ranging and never ending. This porter cleans outside the station along the tracks, Central Railroad of New Jersey Terminal, ca. 1920s–1930s. Courtesy, Reading Railroad Collection, Hagley Museum and Library, Wilmington, DE.

keeper, mechanic, baby sitter, and security guard." In some cases, attendants got no rest. "If you got any sleep at all," one porter, Leon Long, recalled, "that would be in the smoking room. . . . They put on an extra car, so they say I don't get any sleep [for three or four nights]. So I had to set up and do the best I could." The Pullman Company also equipped each coach with a bell to give passengers easy and continuous access to the porter's services.[42]

While working-class black men and women both encountered racial restrictions on their employment opportunities, black women faced the brunt of such practices. In the urban North and South, black female labor participation rates doubled those of American-born white women and tripled those of immigrant women. African American women nonetheless occupied the cellar of the gender- and racially divided workforce. During the 1920s, some 65–85 percent of black women worked in household and personal service jobs in New York, Chicago, Cleveland, Seattle, San Francisco, and other northern and western cities. During the first half of the twentieth century, the number of white female domestic service workers declined from a high of 1.3 million to a low of 542,000. At the same time, black women rose from about 30 percent of all household workers at the turn of the century to about 60 percent by the end of World War II. Employers devalued African American women's labor through low pay, lack of benefits, and the perpetuation of aspects of the old "master-servant" relationship governing domestic work. Indeed, during the mid-1920s, the United Daughters of the Confederacy moved to enshrine the "black mammy" in a monument on the mall of the nation's capital.[43]

When black women gained industrial jobs, they endured special racial and gender limits inside the factory gates. In New York, a black female garment worker complained, "Over where I work in the dye factory, they expect more from a colored girl if she is to keep her job. They won't give a colored girl a break." Philadelphia and eastern Pennsylvania glass manufacturers hired black women workers presumably because of "their ability to stand the heat without suffering." These women glassworkers confronted a hazardous work environment "where at times bits of broken glass were flying in all directions," exposing workers to serious cuts from shards of glass. Cleveland industrialists hired some black women in the garment industry as "pressers" in accord with the racial stereotype that black women could "stand heat better than a white girl." Other black women worked for the wartime railroad industry as "truckers, shearers, and yard workers sorting and hauling scrap and freight." They also earned on average less than their white counterparts performing similar work. In New York City, in 1922, for example, black women workers earned an average of nearly $2 less per week than their white counterparts.[44]

Southern black women occupied an even broader range of heavy, hot, and hazardous industrial workplaces than their northern and western sisters. In 1919, Norfolk's Mar-Hof textile company included a workforce of 53: 5 white men, 2 black men, 35 white women, and 11 black women. White men cut fabrics and maintained the machinery; black men worked as custodians; white women operated the power machines, inspected finished products, and supervised other women; but black women occupied "the hot and arduous job of standing over the pressing machines day after day." African American women examined bales of cotton in Houston's cotton compresses and warehouses. They inspected the "dirty or burnt cotton and removed the bad cotton from the bale." "Cotton pickers," as they were called, earned the lowest pay of all compress employees. And in Memphis, black women took "hot, heavy, dirty," and low-wage jobs in the city's chemical, clothing, and food plants.[45]

Tobacco factories claimed the largest number of black female industrial workers in Durham, North Carolina. "If there was a job that represented Jim Crow's intent to debase African American women, it was working tobacco," historian Leslie Brown concudes. Tobacco work duplicated slavery in many ways. Male hiring managers treated prospective black women employees as "as though they were on the auction block." At the beginning of the proverbial "green season," when employers hired seasonal stemmers, "hundreds of black women gathered in groups at the front steps of the factory. Foremen appeared periodically to select the workers they wanted, choosing the ones who presented the physical characteristics of strength and growth." One foreman told an investigator, "I rate them by their muscles.... The stronger they are the better they are." Once selected, the women encountered another round of persistent "verbal, physical, and sexual abuse" and surveillance. Dora Scott Miller, a black tobacco worker, later recalled supervision by "a one-eyed" white manager, George Hill. "He'd get on top of the machines and watch you to see if you were working alright and holler down and curse. Curse and we working. That's what we had to undergo."[46]

Urban industrial workers suffered economic inequality as a class, but black men and women shouldered special burdens during both boom and bust segments of the business cycle. The confinement of African American men to the most difficult, dirty, and hazardous jobs, described by some historians as the "occupational ghetto," also undermined the health and well-being of black workers and their communities. Across the industrial landscape, black men dominated jobs in foundries that entailed some of the most dangerous, life- and health-threatening responsibilities. African Americans worked in such positions "as shakeout, where dust, dirt and sand were cleaned from the molten metal. Coremaking was an even more dangerous and dirty job where many black workers died of gas explosions. If they survived occupational hazards, they often contracted occupational diseases such as silicosis, bronchitis, pneumonia, heart disease, and various stomach ailments." Historian Richard Walter Thomas notes that although Ford offered blacks their greatest employment opportunities, "its foundry was a deathtrap for many black workers. The lack of safety equipment, poor ventilation, and speed-ups all contributed in one way or another to the deaths of many black workers."[47] One foundry worker later recalled that after men emerged from some jobs in the foundry, "they were so matted and covered with oil and dirt that no skin showed.... The job was very rugged.... [We] couldn't recognize him by his clothes or looks. The men working in his section would tell us where he was or we could tell a friend by his voice."[48]

The precarious labor market position of poor and working-class black women reinforced the informal sex-work economy. In New York City, in 1917, a 29-year-old female underscored the disparity in the income of prostitutes and regular household service workers. A prostitute often earned $3 or $4 "from every man," while a laundress made $6 for an entire week of hard labor. Contrary to many historical accounts of prostitution, most of these women did not work "primarily on the streets." They were "inmates of houses of prostitution," some under the control of black madams. Some newcomers from the South also found themselves "forced" into a life of prostitution by unscrupulous employment agencies. Either way, as historian Cynthia Blair concludes, "the growing numbers of black women of working age who could find no suitable employment in Chicago's wage economy explains why more black women worked in the sex industry in the 1920s than in earlier decades."[49] And African American women paid for this discrimination in their disproportionately higher rates of arrests than white women—because of aggressive policing of the city's "Black Belt sex industry" and the ongoing historic "criminalization of black women" as a group. African American women made up over half of all women arrested for prostitution in Chicago during the mid-1920s. This figure jumped to 78 percent as the Great Depression got under way.[50]

During the Great Depression, as unemployment increased, rising numbers of black women gathered on the sidewalks of major cities and took work in what some contemporaries described as the "slave market." Not unlike white men seeking black women as prostitutes, white women drove up in their cars and offered these women work at the lowest possible wages, usually less than $5 per week for long hours and arduous work.[51]

Despite the discriminatory challenges, most urban black workers during the Great Migration experienced significant improvement in their living conditions as compared to those in rural southern homes. But, predictably, as the Great Depression deepened, African American men and women reported disproportionately higher rates of unemployment and requests for emergency public relief than their white counterparts across the urban North and South. By 1933, African American unemployment had increased to nearly three times the rate of whites in St. Louis, Detroit, Chicago, Los Angeles, Norfolk, and other northern, western, and southern cities.

Leah Boustan's economic history of the Great Migration suggests the importance of the racial job ceiling in shaping the experiences of both

During the Depression, many black artists supported themselves through work in the household service sector. A fellow artist was the inspiration for Palmer Hayden's *The Janitor Who Paints,* 1937. Courtesy, Smithsonian American Art Museum, Washington, DC/Art Resource, NY.

northern- and southern-born blacks—and the black community as a whole. Boustan highlights modes of economic competition between southern- and northern-born blacks as a possible explanation for the often hostile response that greeted migrants as they moved into established northern and western communities. Based upon a close comparative examination of wage, occupational, and educational data, she convincingly concludes that although migrants and northern blacks experienced parity in their access to industrial jobs and higher wages at the outset of the Great Migration, northern blacks increasingly lost ground during World War II and its aftermath—primarily because African Americans had to compete directly with each other for a limited number of jobs defined by the erection of the racial job ceiling. And Boustan reminds us, "Even if southern migration had been entirely reversed, blacks would not have reached parity" with their white counterparts in the urban North.[52]

The challenges of industrial life and labor included how African American workers and their families could safely navigate the social, cultural, and physical geography of the city. Restricted in the jobs that they could hold at work, African Americans also faced growing limits on where they were able to live. Poor and working-class black urban communities existed in a socio-economic, political, and cultural vortex created by residential segregation of the urban landscape.

SEGREGATING THE URBAN WORKER

Over two decades of scholarship on the dynamics of residential segregation has exploded the notion that de facto and informal modes of racially dividing urban space characterized the North, while state mandated and enforced forms of segregation divided black and white communities in the South. In the urban North as well as the South, as Richard Rothstein persuasively argues in his recent study, "public policy that explicitly segregated every metropolitan area in the United States . . . was so systematic and forceful" that "it is what courts call de jure: segregation by law and public policy."[53] The era of the Great Migration was crucial in the separation of black and white residential areas. In his influential book, *Ghetto: The Invention of a Place, the History of an Idea,* historical sociologist Mitchell Duneier shows how images of the ghetto as a segregated, enclosed, and exploited Jewish community increasingly gave way by the end of World War II to visions of the ghetto as a predominantly African American experience. Yet another recent innovative study of the ghetto, employing new digital humanities technology, documents the widespread use of such phrases as *black ghetto* and *ghetto systems* to denote the deepening color line in the residential life of the industrial city as early as the mid-1920s.[54]

As whites attempted to enshrine segregation, they first looked to—but refused to be limited by—the law. Beginning with Baltimore in 1910, several southern cities enacted municipal housing segregation ordinances prohibiting blacks and whites from occupying houses on the same streets. But the U.S. Supreme Court struck down these laws in *Buchanan v. Warley* (1917), declaring that they deprived citizens of "income without due process of law" by restricting property sales by race and thus violated the Fourteenth Amendment to the Constitution. At the same time, in the urban North, however, the court deemed "restrictive covenants" against prospective African American residents "private agreements," and thus immune from the court's injunction against municipal housing segregation policies. In 1926, in the case of *Corrigan v. Buckle,* the U.S. Supreme Court upheld the legality of restrictive covenants as private contracts that did not violate the "due process clause."[55] Following the high court's decision, white supremacist real estate dealers, homeowners, attorneys, and municipal officials were emboldened to employ a variety of other legal and extralegal measures in addition to restrictive covenants—zoning legislation, routes of public highways and roads, siting of commercial and public buildings, intimidation, and physical violence—to circumvent the law and maintain the color line in housing and other aspects of New York's geography.[56]

In 1926, the Indianapolis city council boldly defied the high court and passed a new municipal racial segregation ordinance. Proponents of the measure hoped that their new law would gain the approval of the courts because, unlike earlier statutes, it only "prohibited occupancy" of the same neighborhoods by black and whites, rather than restricting the "sale of property" by color. Moreover, the new ordinance permitted movement between neighborhoods by the "written consent of a majority" of black or white residents. When the courts again rejected this bold effort to entrench a racially segregated housing market in law, white homeowners formed numerous property-owners' associations and swore to uphold restrictive covenants against the rental, lease, or sale of property to black people. Should a property owner violate such an agreement, the home automatically reverted to the previous owner's "estate," and this covenant was "binding on the heirs, administration, successors and assigns of the purchaser."[57]

In Los Angeles, the courts ordered some black families to vacate homes that they owned in neighborhoods covered by restrictive covenants.[58] In 1919, in *Los Angeles Investment Co. v. Gary,* the California Supreme Court ruled that racially restrictive covenants against "purchasing" property were "illegal," but such covenants against African Americans "actually" occupying their own homes in previously all-white neighborhoods were "legal." Hence, in 1926, another black family, headed by William and Eunice Long, described by one historian as "an ordinary, hardworking couple," could not legally occupy a home that they had purchased at 771 East 41st Street. When the court finally settled the matter after a two-year battle, Eunice Long, now a widow, was evicted from her home.[59]

Realtors and white housing activists justified their segregation efforts throughout this period by repeatedly linking lower property values to areas inhabited by people of African descent. One civic association spoke for many when claiming its chief goal was to "prevent members of the colored race from moving into our midst, thereby depreciating property values fifty percent, or more." The true concerns of such groups were visible in their rhetoric. Active between the years 1910 and 1915, the Harlem Property Owners' Improvement Corporation (HPOIC), perhaps the most influential of these associations, defined black migration as "a crisis" and a "question of whether the white man will rule Harlem or the negro." Similarly, the Hyde Park Improvement Protective Club of Chicago, formed in 1908, had exclaimed, "The districts which are now white . . . must remain white. There will be no compromise."

When a group of hostile whites gathered to form a property-owners' association in Louisville, Kentucky, one speaker declared the goal of the association should be to make "a Negro living in the West End . . . as comfortable as if he was living in Hell." In Baltimore toward the end of the interwar years, white neighborhoods increasingly "ringed" the city's three principal black neighborhoods. In 1940, a spokesman for the city's white Mount Royal Home Improvement Association reported that restrictive covenants covered 2,800 of the 3,000 homes in the area that bordered the black community in northwestern Baltimore. Similarly, the Tolson Spring Improvement Association celebrated the nearly 100 percent of properties under covenant "sealing off" the black neighborhood on its west side.[60]

Homeowners' associations used teams of attorneys to craft legal tactics to prevent African Americans from occupying homes in previously all-white or nearly all-white neighborhoods. Following the high court's 1917 ruling against residential segregation laws, Atlanta passed new racially biased zoning laws in 1922, 1929, and 1931. These ordinances aimed to limit movement of African Americans into white areas. Whereas the city's 1913 and 1916 ordinances had designated certain blocks as black or white, subsequent zoning legislation pursued racial segregation through terminology around "land uses, building types, and tenant categories." Historian Ronald Bayor notes,

"Atlanta was divided into white and black single- and two-family dwelling sections, apartment-house areas, and racially undetermined commercial and industrial districts. . . . Invariably, blacks were given less land than whites for residential dwellings, and a number of their neighborhoods were classified as industrial."[61]

Atlanta not only reinforced residential segregation through zoning laws but also used highways, roads, and the location of large commercial or public building projects to maximize the separation of blacks and whites. Although a variety of factors, including African American resistance, thwarted the precise implementation of these plans, in 1917, 1941, and 1947, city planners vigorously promoted the use of highway construction projects to erect barriers to residential mobility between black and white neighborhoods.

White people in other cities took other measures to, as one black Louisville resident explained, "make it absolutely clear where the black folks' neighborhood stopped and theirs began." In Louisville, after about 1917, the municipality renamed streets that extended through both black and white neighborhoods. At the transition between the two communities, Walnut Street became Michigan, Madison became Vermont, Jefferson became Lockwood, and so on. During World War I, the city of Miami built a fence to demarcate the dividing line between predominantly white Highland Park and Miami's black downtown neighborhood. Moreover, when city workers finished work on the wall, they painted one side with "black tar" to denote "Black Town," with the unpainted side dubbed "White Town." [62] When blacks moved into a previously all-white neighborhood in Indianapolis, some neighbors erected so-called spite fences—"high walls" that surrounded African American homes on "three sides" to more or less quarantine the black population. Finally, in cities across the country, as historian Richard Pierce notes, certain streets became known as "white supremacy deadline" streets. Any blacks venturing beyond the line into white neighborhoods could expect violent reactions.

Intimidation and violence were deployed even more forcefully when African Americans defied white communities' forms of "persuasion" and insisted on occupying new homes in the face of lawsuits and offers to buy them out. In turn, black residents sometimes developed armed responses to efforts to forcibly remove them from their homes. In Louisville, in October 1925, a porter employed at the L&N Railroad bought a house at 1051 South 32nd Street; a short while later another black home buyer moved into a house on the opposite side of the street. Whites deluged both families with letters threatening to burn them out unless they moved. Both families refused to vacate their homes, despite the use of dynamite by their attackers. After dynamite damaged their homes a second time, one of the homeowners retaliated by firing "five shots at his fleeing assailants." The local NAACP branch rushed to the defense of the families. Eventually the mayor of the city ordered police to protect the families against mob attacks on their homes.[63]

Unfortunately, this instance of protection under the law was all too rare. During the mid-1920s, when a mob attacked the home of dentist Henry Ossian Sweet in a previously all-white neighborhood of Detroit, the Sweets returned fire, killing one white man and wounding another. Born in Orlando, Florida, Sweet had received his medical degree from Howard University. He moved to Detroit in 1922 and married Gladys Mitchell the same year. Sweet set up a successful practice in the section of Detroit's working-class black community called Black Bottom and quickly saved enough money to purchase and move into his own home. On the night of the shooting, authorities swiftly moved in and arrested ten occupants of the Sweet household, including Gladys, and placed them on trial for murder. Though an outpouring of national support for the Sweets resulted in their acquittal, Gladys contracted tuberculosis during her incarceration in the Wayne County Jail, which affected the couple's 1-year-old baby. Both Gladys and the baby died within four years after her exoneration and release from jail.[64] A short time later, on Stoepel Avenue, also on the northwest side, an estimated four thousand whites blocked the streets around the home of another black family for some seven blocks. The shouting, jeering, and rock-throwing mob soon shattered nearly every window in the house and dispersed only after the family opened fire on the crowd, injuring a white youth. In a recurring pattern, police then rushed the house and arrested all its occupants.[65]

The armed defense of black-owned homes often entailed substantial collaboration across class lines within the black urban community. In April 1919, for example, George Graham, a middle-class black Philadelphian, and his family purchased and moved into a home a few blocks north of the city's African American Seventh Ward. When Graham insisted on staying in his home amid efforts to discourage and block his occupancy, he and his family awakened one morning after 1:00 A.M. to the "sounds of windows shattering in the front room" and a "crowd of more than thirty whites, mostly men, screaming a 'shoot to kill' slogan with many guns in hand." Graham had already armed himself with a shotgun and held the mob at bay with gunshots, but when word of the embattled homeowner reached the Seventh Ward black community, a contingent of armed poor, working-class, and middle-class blacks arrived at the home and engaged the mob in a street battle. At that point, however, the police moved in and arrested all the African Americans involved in the confrontation, including homeowner George Graham and his family, along with a mere token of four white youths.[66]

The career of Jesse Binga, Chicago's renowned black banker and realtor, reveals another aspect of the cross-class dynamics of the African American search for homes during the interwar years. Born in Detroit, Binga became a Pullman porter and moved to Chicago as a young man during the 1890s. He soon invested his earnings in real estate, becoming a pioneer black homeowner in all-white neighborhoods. During the interwar years, he became known for providing much-needed rental properties for poor and working-class black residents. But some renters also complained that he gouged them "for ten to fifteen dollars per month more than white renters" who had previously occupied the same property. Nonetheless, Binga confronted and resisted racial violence and multiple incidents of fire bombings of both his home and his rental properties.

The violence in Chicago was particularly widespread. Between 1917 and 1921, an estimated fifty-eight racially motivated fire bombings shook the homes of black Chicagoans who had moved into all-white neighborhoods. These incidents resulted in two deaths, scores of injuries, and over $100,000 in property damage. In 1918, the Kenwood and Hyde Park Property Owners Association not only mobilized to bar blacks from their neighborhoods but also sought to remove some black families who had lived at their addresses for years. Black residents sometimes received warnings of impending violence. "We are going to BLOW these FLATS TO HELL and if you don't want to go with them you had better move at once." As part of its strategy for removing black residents, the organization also launched a boycott of white businesses that served black residents in the community.[67]

For their part, as early as 1920, African Americans formed the Protective Circle of Chicago to fight white terrorism in the housing market. "In every legitimate and legal way," the organization's constitution stated, blacks would combat "lawlessness . . . intimidation, bombing, threatening and coercion of Colored and white citizens of Chicago."[68]

Under the impact of New Deal social programs of the 1930s, white residents gained a federal ally in the pursuit of their racially exclusionary housing goals. FDR's Home Owners Loan Corporation (HOLC), established in 1933, helped large numbers of middle- and working-class whites avoid foreclosures on their homes during the Great Depression. But the federal government established a pattern of federally funded housing segregation in the process. The HOLC, in close collaboration with local municipalities and bank officials, created a system of secret Security Maps (color-coded rankings of neighborhoods popularly known as "redlining") to simplify decisions about who would or would not receive government-insured home loans. The HOLC Security Maps classified neighborhoods by a variety of characteristics, including race and ethnicity, and dubbed neighborhoods ranked A and B loan-worthy, while neighborhoods ranked C and D were considered high-risk areas and thus unlikely to qualify for home loans. Areas with high concentrations of blacks, regardless of quality of dwellings, routinely received the lowest grade, D. Meanwhile neighborhoods that contained large numbers of Latinos/Latinas, Asians, and to some extent Jews were ranked C, also nearly off-limits for such loans.[69] In 1934, when the U.S. Housing Act created the Federal Housing Administration (FHA), the FHA adopted the HOLC's classification system as a guide and perpetuated the racially divided housing market through the Depression and beyond.

Throughout the period of the Great Migration, as discriminatory real estate and homeowner practices closed much of the urban housing market to black residents, inner city property owners doubled and even tripled their revenue by subdividing large single-family homes into small single-room, small-kitchenette apartments for newcomers. Real estate speculators took over large mansions in older sections of cities, subdivided them into small one- or two-room apartments, charged black tenants exorbitant rents, and allowed the properties to deteriorate. Harlem property owners, for example, rapidly converted large apartment houses and brownstones of five, six, and seven rooms into rooming houses for single as well as married men and women with few children. After one Harlem landlord transformed nine houses into one-room flats, the buildings' gross receipts rose from $40 to $100–$125 per month. In Chicago, Timuel D. Black, Jr., later recalled how the rapid subdivision of large homes made it difficult for even blacks who could afford more space to find it: "The landlords cut up all the larger apartments and converted them into smaller units so they could make a lot more money. We lived in one of those huge apartments at 5000 Grand Boulevard. . . . But we had to move." The landlord planned to subdivide Black's unit and reopen with the prospect of increasing income on the property. In some cases, when Chicago's white homeowners converted previously all-white units to all-black ones, they also increased the rent 10–15 percent as blacks moved in.[70]

The increasing conversion of single-family homes into rental flats rein-forced the racially divided housing market and reduced the quality of hous-ing available for African American occupancy. Between World War I and 1930, the index of residential segregation by race rose across the urban North, from 67 to 85 percent in Chicago; from 64 to 78 percent in Boston; and from 46 to 63 percent in Philadelphia. This was accompanied by massive over-crowding in black neighborhoods. While the average density of white neigh-borhoods of Manhattan stood at 223 persons per acre in 1925, the figure for black Harlem was 336 persons per acre. In 1930, one Harlem block reported 671 people per acre, and another, 620 people per acre.[71] Philadelphia's pre-dominantly black wards reported a density of 150 persons per acre compared to the city's average of 111 persons per acre. In Detroit, some 12,000 blacks soon crowded into an area that had previously housed only half that number. One contemporary observer reported seeing rooms so crowded that "the most convenient way to dress was to stand in the middle of the bed."[72] Some migrants shared beds, which were called "hot beds." As many as three people on different shifts used the same bed on a daily basis. And the situation per-sisted through decades: in testimony before the U.S. House Investigation of Congested Areas Committee, a Richmond resident told the committee dur-ing the World War II years, "I can take you to see numerous families where 14 people live in one room."[73]

Inside a broad range of diverse but highly congested living quarters, African Americans pressed every conceivable space, including bathtubs and pool tables, into service for sleeping purposes. African Americans took up residence in makeshift bunkhouses, railroad boxcars, boathouses, and shan-ties in the steel towns of Pittsburgh and western Pennsylvania and elsewhere. As historian Carter Woodson noted at the time, as blacks overflowed hous-ing in existing black urban neighborhoods, movement into previously all-white areas did not necessarily mean better housing. According to Woodson, "the overflow of black population scattered throughout the city among white people. Old warehouses, store rooms, churches, railroad cars and tents have been used to meet these demands." Other migrants lived in neighborhoods that abutted outlying rural areas and sometimes "squatted on vacant land," living in tents, shacks, trailers, automobiles, and even "chicken coops" with-out "running water, electricity, sanitation facilities, paved roads," garbage collection, or street lights. For some migrants, particularly in southern cities, these conditions blurred the lines between rural and urban life and labor. A migrant from Greenwood, Mississippi, later recalled moving to Memphis in

1936 and living with her brother in a "shanty." The place was little more than "a shack on a rural plantation."[74]

In order to alleviate overcrowding, in 1926–27 the city of Detroit opened new temporary all-black subdivisions on outlying land within and outside the city limits. Described by historian Richard Walter Thomas as "satellite ghettos," these subdivisions included Eight Mile Road (four thousand families), Inkster (two thousand families), and Quinn Road (five hundred families). While these outlying settlements offered more space and less polluted air, such benefits were offset by inadequate water and sewerage services.

In December 1936, Philadelphia became the scene of a major tenement house disaster. The collapse of an old building at 517–519 South 15th Street killed nearly a dozen working-class black women and children and seriously injured as many others. The city's mayor, S. Davis Wilson, expressed his disbelief at the wreckage and carnage. In an interview with reporters, he said, "This is an emergency of public safety. . . . I saw sights yesterday which I would not have believed possible." The liberal Jewish editor of the *Philadelphia Record* declared his hope that this tragedy would sensitize the community to the lives of "thousands of our fellow citizens" whose "home is the place where the sun doesn't shine; the place where they contract tuberculosis; the place where there isn't any running water; the place that may fall down in the dead of night, smothering, burning—'Home, Sweet Home.'"[75]

Tenants had repeatedly complained about the poor and inadequate upkeep of the building. Just before its collapse, one tenant, Raymond Blackwell, had pleaded with the landlord, Abraham Samson, to repair the building, describing how "the walls on the second floor front room [are] bulging at least a foot and a half [and] the paper in the kitchen [is] falling off and the walls [have] begun to crack." In 1935, the *Philadelphia Tribune* developed a series of articles on housing among black Philadelphians, emphasizing "the neglect of city inspectors, price-gouging by white landlords, and substandard facilities within which Black Seventh Warders lived." Calling the area "Hell's Acre," the *Tribune* declared the African American housing stock "no accident," but rather "planned slums." By 1940, over 75 percent of all white homes in Philadelphia met the city's "minimum standards" of sanitation and safety, but only 46 percent of African American dwellings met these standards. Historian James Wolfinger describes how Philadelphia's blacks "found themselves boxed in. . . . They were forced to live in the city's oldest, most overcrowded areas." Arthur Faucet, an African American activist during the interwar years, made the same point, recalling how

Philadelphia had earlier prided itself as the "City of Homes." "Today," he said, "it would be more nearly correct to point to it as the city of slums."[76]

Interwar urban blacks not only occupied the most dilapidated, unhealthy, and unsafe housing in the city but also paid higher rents for similar or lower quality housing than their white counterparts. In 1917, in Pittsburgh, a boardinghouse room averaged about $1.50 to $1.75 per week; blacks paid between $10 and $15 per month to rent one or two of these rooms of usually poor quality. When one migrant woman from Petersburg, Virginia, witnessed the new home her husband had prepared for her, she could only mutter words from the Old Testament Book of Ruth: "Where you go, I will go, and where you lodge I will lodge." In 1925, a Harlem Municipal Court judge testified before the Mayor's Committee on Rent Profiteering that it was common for black tenants in Harlem "to pay twice as much as white tenants for the same apartment." As early as 1915, the National Urban League reported that Harlem's black families paid $4.71 per month per room compared to $4.03 for German Jews in the same community.[77] In 1927, New York City African Americans paid $8, $10, and $7 more, respectively, for three-, four-, and five-room houses or apartments than their white counterparts. Norfolk, San Francisco, and other cities reported similar levels of inequality among black and white rental properties. The Bureau of Labor Statistics concluded that African Americans generally occupied a few limited spaces where rents were "unduly high in comparison with the facilities furnished."[78]

And poor housing and living conditions exposed black neighborhoods to disproportionately higher rates of disease, crime, and delinquency. As historian Earl Lewis put it, "Whereas middle-class blacks found living conditions a discomfort, working-class blacks found them deadly." In Norfolk, the white death rate reached nearly 9 per 1,000 population, but the figure for blacks was 20 per 1,000 in 1920. Tuberculosis was a major killer of urban blacks during the era of the Great Migration. Between roughly 1915 and 1920 alone, Detroit's African American TB deaths increased from about 208 to 237 per 1,000 people; the white rate went down, from 97 in 1915 to 77 in 1920. During the entire interwar period, TB accounted for the highest number of deaths among the city's black residents. A significant racial gap also characterized the city's infant mortality rate: 118 deaths per 1,000 births among blacks compared to 76 per 1,000 among whites. During the mid-1930s, health officials reported 14 African American deaths in Central Harlem per 1,000 people, as compared to the average of 10 per 1,000 for the city. Harlem's infant mortality rate was twice the city's rate, while tuberculosis rates were over four times greater among blacks than whites. In Pittsburgh, between 1918 and 1928, the African American infant mortality rate dropped—from 215 to 113 per 1,000 births—but remained significantly higher than the rate among whites, which decreased from 136 to about 75 per 1,000 births in the same period.[79]

In addition to higher death rates from illness and infant mortality, urban blacks also dealt with more than their share of arrests, convictions, and incarceration for certain crimes. Between about 1913 and 1919, in Detroit, authorities arrested black men at a rate of 4,008 per 10,000 population compared to a white rate of 1,544 per 10,000 population. In its annual reports for the 1920s, the New York anti-vice Committee of Fourteen described Harlem as "the leading or near-leading prostitution center of Manhattan." At about the same time, in Chicago, black women accounted for an estimated 16 to 20 percent of all women convicted for prostitution, though they made up only 2 percent of the total population. In 1928 the Chicago Morals Court reported, "In former years the percentage of prostitutes were 85 percent white, 15 percent colored, but now 20 percent white and 80 percent colored."

As historian Khalil Muhammad notes, law enforcement officials viewed African Americans as people with "inherent criminal traits." Accordingly, while they favored social service programs for the rehabilitation of white criminals, they insisted on incarceration or removal of black women and men accused of crimes from the general population. In New York State, for example, prison officials frequently delayed the release of qualified women parolees, arguing that it was "better for . . . colored girls to be [transported back South] away from New York City." Whites repeatedly targeted blacks as the source of "crime waves" that presumably followed in the wake of the Great Migration. A white Los Angeles resident reported during the World War II years that "negroes are getting all the guns they can and are having their old ones fixed up."[80] On the contrary, African Americans reported growing incidents of police brutality and crimes against black residents. The NAACP not only regularly protested vicious police assaults on black residents and pressed charges, but also assailed biased police commission investigations that invariably returned decisions declaring "NO REASON FOR DISCIPLINARY ACTION" against police officers.[81]

Racial inequality was not limited to the job and housing markets. Throughout the country, the Great Migration resulted in efforts to nationalize the Jim Crow order. In the urban North and West, as in the South, municipalities established racially segregated playgrounds, parks, swimming pools, and beaches.[82] Although some northern and western restaurants, hotels, theaters, amusement parks, and other public accommodations served blacks and whites on an equal basis, most either excluded black patrons or served them on a segregated and unequal basis. In 1916, when African American alderman Oscar DePriest of Chicago proposed a municipal ordinance giving the mayor authority to revoke the licenses of discriminatory businesses, the *Chicago Tribune* ridiculed the measure. "It is a fiction that a Negro has full social rights in any American community," the paper declared.[83]

Furthermore, the color line confronted blacks in the media. During World War I, despite widespread efforts to recruit black workers to northern cities, white daily newspapers often expressed fear and even opposition to the increasing movement of blacks under such headlines as "Half a Million Darkies Swarm to the North to Better Themselves" and "Negroes Incited by German Spies: Federal Agents Confirm Reports of New Conspiracy in South." They also broadcast the "Peril to Health" that black newcomers presumably posed to white residents. Further, the Chicago Commission on Race Relations concluded that over 50 percent of all articles in that city's leading daily newspapers, including the *Tribune, Daily News,* and *Herald Examiner,* represented blacks in relation to criminal "violence and vice."[84]

In addition, the early twentieth century saw the revival of white supremacist organizations like the Ku Klux Klan. Following the wartime renaissance of the KKK in Georgia, with headquarters in Atlanta between 1916 and 1925, the Klan moved away from its rural southern roots to a predominantly urban setting. By 1921, under the impact of southern and northern urban membership drives, the organization's membership reached an estimated half million people. Perhaps even more so than the first Klan, the modern KKK was a product of growing white women's activism. Many Klanswomen, historian Kathleen Blee argues, like many other white women of their day, "brought a women's rights politics into the 1920s Klan from earlier suffrage, temperance, or moral reform movements but reshaped and recontextualized that politics in the service of racism and nativism."[85]

Some of the most significant local chapters of the Ku Klux Klan emerged in industrial cities of the Great Migration. In August 1921, an estimated ten thousand Klansmen attended initiation ceremonies on Chicago's North Central Avenue; the imperial wizard travelled to the city from Atlanta to help preside over the occasion. Instead of one chapter for the entire city, the usual practice, the Klan set up over twenty neighborhood units in Chicago. Not surprisingly, some of the earliest and most active chapters emerged in areas of increasing African American presence on the South Side: Englewood Klan No. 2, Woodlawn Klan No. 4, and Kenwood Klan No. 33. The Detroit Klan, founded in 1921, enrolled twenty-two thousand members over the next two years. In May 1921, the Klan also established offices in Philadelphia. Klan units in the City of Brotherly Love took such titles as Liberty Bell Klan No. 1, Old Glory Klan No. 5, and the William Penn Klan. When Seattle's Klan Unit No. 4 received its charter in 1922, it had reached a membership of two thousand. And when the national order staged a huge parade in the nation's capital in 1925, the Pittsburgh unit sent the largest delegation to the event.[86]

Finally, the eruption of urban race riots evidenced the refusal of whites in the North to embrace the influx of black workers. Between 1917 and 1921, violence broke out in East St. Louis, Tulsa, Chicago, and other major cities. The Chicago riot exploded following an interracial confrontation over a restricted area of beach along Lake Michigan for "whites only." When a black youth, Eugene Williams, drowned after being hit by a stone, the violence spread into the larger community. Local police refused to arrest any whites for the drowning of Williams; violence continued over the next week as blacks fought against white mobs and gangs, some calling themselves "athletic clubs"—including the Ragen Colts, the Dirty Dozen, and similar groups. Police openly supported mob attacks on the black community and added to the number of deaths, injuries, and loss of property. The Chicago riot resulted in the death of 23 blacks and 15 whites. The riot also left 1,000 people homeless and another 500, mostly blacks, seriously wounded.[87]

CONCLUSION

Following their very hopeful access to the industrial workforce, African Americans soon encountered the limits of their "Land of Hope." Both organized trade union and company policies reinforced the color bar in the industrial workplace during the early interwar years, leaving African Americans at the bottom of the occupational hierarchy and most vulnerable to unemployment in recurring cycles of boom and bust. Residential segregation meant black industrial workers and their families faced major obstacles to health and well-being as they strove to enjoy their leisure time and safely navigate the social and cultural geography of the city. Predominantly poor and working-class African American neighborhoods became targets of mob violence, institutional segregation, and discrimination as the Great Migration and industrial working-class formation accelerated.

But urban black workers and their communities did not despair. They gradually forged vibrant new social movements to meet the demands of life and labor in the industrial age, movements that insisted on full citizenship, equality before the bar, and social justice. Similar to the transformation of the nation during and following the Civil War, their struggles would help gradually to reshape the political culture and institutions of the industrial age.

FIVE

African American Workers Organize

AFRICAN AMERICAN WORKERS DEPLORED THEIR TENUOUS HOLD
on urban industrial jobs, homes, social services, and justice before the law
during the years of the Great Migration. Some considered moving back to the
rural and small-town South. But most stayed and resolved to strengthen their
footing in the labor force, neighborhoods, and politics of the city. They
forged new alliances with middle-class and elite blacks and their white allies
on the one hand and with organized white labor and radical social justice and
political movements on the other. These efforts spurred the rise of the
Modern Black Freedom Movement during the interwar years and the fall of
the segregationist system during the 1950s and 1960s.

At the same time, the class, racial, and gendered politics of the industrial
city were deeply rooted in the growth of a broader and more comprehensive
"Black Metropolis," or what recent historians describe as the fluorescence of a
dynamic new "black public sphere"—one that emerged from "the ashes of
denied citizenship" and advanced the emergence of "a modern black identity
that looked outward to the world beyond the United States, especially Africa."[1]

INTERRACIAL AND INDEPENDENT
LABOR ORGANIZING

During the later part of the interwar years, for the first time in the nation's
history, large numbers of black workers joined predominantly white labor
organizations on an equal footing with their white counterparts. Under the
impact of the Great Depression, New Deal labor legislation, and the militant
activities of the U.S. Communist Party (CP), the Congress of Industrial

Organizations (CIO) broke from the American Federation of Labor (AFL) in 1935 and energized the movement to organize workers across craft, color, and ethnic lines. The CIO employed African American organizers to recruit black workers for the new unions and soon challenged the hegemony of the racially exclusionary and craft-based AFL in each major manufacturing group.[2]

Working for the Packinghouse Workers Organizing Committee (PWOC), the United Automobile Workers (UAW), and the new Steel Workers Organizing Committee (SWOC), African American organizers helped to bring black workers from the periphery into the center of the industrial labor movement. Philip Weightman, LeRoy Johnson, James C. Harris, and other African Americans helped to unionize meatpackers for PWOC in Chicago and other cities. Philip Weightman later recalled how he made the transition from being a loyal company man to organizer and later president of Local 28 in Chicago. "One day one of the guys in our plant [Swift], Hank Schoestein, said to me, 'Hey Phil, why don't you come with me. We're going to have a meeting—we want to start a union.' I said, 'I don't want anything to do with a goddamn union.'" After witnessing the increasing firing and mistreatment of men associated with the union campaign, however, Weightman attended a few union meetings and then decided to join. He soon frightened company foremen when he arrived with multiple buttons pinned to his work hat: "The next morning the six buttons were put all around my cap! And my foreman walked up to that bench where I was working, and he saw that and he broke and run like a scared jackass!"[3]

Joseph Billups, Walter Hardin, Paul Kirk, Frank Evans, William Nowell, and others spearheaded the recruitment of black workers for the UAW in the Detroit area. In April 1937, the UAW employed Paul Kirk as the union's first paid black organizer. A crane operator at the Michigan Steel Casting Company, Kirk had migrated to Detroit from Alabama in 1929. He later became recording secretary of his racially integrated local, #281. Tennessee-born Walter Hardin soon emerged as perhaps the most well-known and effective organizer for the UAW. A coworker later recalled Hardin as an inspired public speaker and courageous fighter for worker rights: "He was the most convincing speaker I've ever seen in my life. He could move white union audiences because they respected his long fight for working people."

By July 1937, SWOC had hired fifteen black organizers to carry out recruitment of African American workers in Chicago, Pittsburgh, and Birmingham, among other steel centers. African American organizers included prominent communists like Ben Carreathers and Ernest Rice McKinney in the

Pittsburgh district and Henry "Hank" Johnson in Gary. In the Pittsburgh district, Carreathers would later estimate signing up some two thousand black workers for the Steel Workers Organizing Committee.[4]

As the CIO intensified its drive to reach black workers, large mass-production firms gradually relented and signed contracts with the new unions. Following militant sit-down strikes in 1936–37, General Motors, the nation's largest manufacturer, signed an agreement with the UAW in February 1937. Covering black and white workers alike, the new contract established formal grievance procedures to govern a broad range of day-to-day workplace issues; increased wages; and provided for an eight-hour workday, a forty-hour work-week, and a week of paid vacation time. The agreement also brought black workers into the seniority system, which would help alter the entrenched system of arbitrary color-based hiring and firing decisions, heretofore aided and abetted by rank-and-file white workers and their unions. In March 1937, U.S. Steel signed a collective bargaining agreement with SWOC. Hundreds of thousands of steelworkers, including African Americans, gained access to higher wages and better working conditions. Still, there were holdouts: unlike GM, Ford Motors, the largest employer of black workers, resisted recognition of the UAW until May 1941, and the "Little Steel" companies would not sign contracts until 1942, well into World War II.[5]

The interracial labor movement gained ground only gradually in the urban West, partly because few blacks had obtained industrial jobs in the San Francisco Bay Area, Los Angeles, or Seattle before the onset of World War II. Thus, as the CIO organized L.A.'s white industrial workers in steel, auto, and rubber plants during the 1930s, African American workers "were mostly shut out of the action." Even so, the massive Maritime Strike of 1934 underscored the gradual emergence of interracial organizing in the urban West that would escalate during World War II. According to a contemporary dissertation by African American economist Robert Francis, before the "Big Strike," all along the entire western waterfront, there were no more than two dozen black members of the International Longshoremen's Association (ILA). In the wake of the Great Maritime Strike, however, the situation "changed dramatically" under the leadership and growing influence of Harry Bridges and the radical left. Bridges went into black churches to plead with black workers to support the strike, promising them that this movement "means a new deal for Negroes. Stick with us and we'll stand for your inclusion in [the] industry." Three years after the strike, in 1937, longshoremen formed the International Longshoremen's and Warehousemen's Union

African American members of the United Automobile Workers of America, including these picket captains, rallied behind the union's strike at Ford's River Rouge plant in Dearborn, MI, in 1941. Courtesy, Walter P. Reuther Library, Wayne State University.

(ILWU) and affiliated with the CIO. By the end of World War II, African Americans made up an estimated 25 percent of the ILWU's membership. Numerous studies of the West Coast labor movement credit Bridges and the CP for paving the way for the rise of interracial unionism in San Francisco and other West Coast cities. African Americans often praised the ILWU as the most racially egalitarian labor union in the United States. At the same time, also in 1937, Ferdinand Smith, a Jamaican-born Communist Party member, became "second in command" of the newly formed, predominantly white National Maritime Union (NMU). Headquartered in New York City, the NMU was closely connected to waterfronts across the nation.[6]

But this egalitarianism was by no means evenly distributed across the waterfront. In Los Angeles, Local 13 of the ILWU maintained a firm color line against African Americans even as the San Francisco Bay Area emerged as a "haven of racial equality" along the docks. Still, by the end of World War II, growing numbers of black workers moved into the West Coast locals of the CIO, particularly in the shipyards of the Bay Area.[7] In Seattle, in 1933–34, the previously segregated Colored Marine Employees Benevolent Association (CMEBA) joined forces with the all-white Marine Cooks and Stewards Association of the Pacific (MCSAP) and launched an eighty-three-day strike that closed the city's waterfront. White maritime cooks called for unity with black stewards and union men, while black workers for their part implored African Americans to reject strikebreaking and walk the picket line with white workers.[8]

Compared to the urban North and West, the new labor movement encountered major obstacles in the South. While the Brotherhood of Sleeping Car Porters made substantial progress, discussed below, southern black railroad workers, particularly firemen and brakemen, fared poorly. Southern black railroad men, labor historian Eric Arnesen concludes, "found no salvation in New Deal labor legislation, which for them represented not labor's Magna Carta but rather a major setback to their organizational aspirations and even livelihood." Even so, a significant core of black CIO organizers risked life, limb, and livelihood to help build bridges between southern black and white workers.

On the docks of Memphis, Tennessee, Thomas Watkins spearheaded the organization of black workers during the Great Riverfront Strike of 1939.[9] The Memphis strike resulted in the Federal Barge Line's recognition of the combined majority black AFL and interracial CIO unions and negotiation of a contract with them. Nonetheless, Watkins and his family became the target of violent attacks both during and after the strike. Following a brutal beating by local police, which nearly killed him, Watkins soon left the city.

In the Birmingham district, where black workers made up over 50 percent of all steelworkers, a cadre of experienced black communists—Ebb Cox, Joe Howard, C. Dave Smith, and Hosea Hudson—led an interracial strike at the American Casting Company. Within less than a week, the company signed an agreement increasing wages by 20 percent and providing time and a half for overtime work. Despite this success, the black organizers endured both reprisals from management and municipal police and blowback from white union leadership. Birmingham's top SWOC leadership removed Joe Howard and C. Dave Smith from the payroll "for acting without authorization."[10]

While black workers crafted new movements and strategies for social change, they also built upon the lessons of earlier generations of labor struggles, using the segregated environment "as a vehicle for the organization of black workers" into autonomous all-black unions. The organized black labor movement had roots stretching back to the antebellum and immediate postbellum years. As noted in chapter 3, in 1869, under the leadership of Isaac Myers, African Americans met in Washington, DC, and formed the Colored National Labor Union and pushed for equal labor and citizenship rights regardless of color or previous condition of servitude. In the interwar years, black labor unions gained their greatest expression in the militant campaign to organize black porters on the nation's major rail lines in 1925. Under the leadership of A. Philip Randolph, the emergence of the Brotherhood of Sleeping Car Porters and Maids (BSCP), with headquarters in New York and locals in the Bay Area, Pittsburgh, Chicago, and other cities, reflected the growing class as well as race consciousness of black workers.[11]

From its inception through the remainder of the interwar years, the BSCP became the most prominent symbol of the organized black labor movement. Adopting the motto Service not Servitude, the union organized black porters and maids at the Chicago-based Pullman Company, the largest single employer of African Americans in the nation. According to a report in the *New Leader,* "The fight of the Pullman porters is the all absorbing topic wherever two or more Negroes gather in Harlem." Milton P. Webster became the principal organizer for the Chicago district, the largest employer of black porters, while other black organizers spearheaded the drive for membership in other cities: E. J. Bradley (St. Louis), Benjamin "Bennie" Smith (Detroit and Pittsburgh), and Morris Moore and later C. L. Dellums (Oakland). Wives and other female relatives of sleeping car porters and maids formed "ladies auxiliaries" in Philadelphia, Chicago, Los Angeles, and other cities. Women raised money to finance union halls, nationwide organizing campaigns, and media coverage of the grievances of the porters and maids. The words of the "Marching Song of the Fighting Brotherhood" were widely known among porters and non-porters alike: "Organize! Oh Porters come organize your might, / Then we'll sing one song of our Big Brotherhood, / Full of beauty, full of love and light."[12]

As the BSCP increased pressure on the company to dismantle its Pullman Porters and Maids Protective Association (PPMA) and bargain directly with the BSCP, the U.S. Labor Mediation Board ordered an election between the PPMA and the BSCP to settle the matter. Following the election on 1 July 1935, the mediation board declared the BSCP the legitimate labor representative of Pullman employees. The BSCP won by a vote of 5,931 to 1,422 out of 8,313 eligible voters, gaining sole jurisdiction over the work of porters, a key segment of the nation's transportation labor force. Only then did the AFL relent and issue an international charter to the union in August 1935. BSCP membership soared from a low of 658 during the early Depression years to 5,000 in 1936 and to 6,581 in 1938. Major northeastern, midwestern, and western cities—New York, Chicago, and San Francisco, among others—accounted for most of this rise in membership.[13]

The Brotherhood of Sleeping Car Porters Annual Convention, ca. 1940. A. Philip Randolph and Milton Webster of the Chicago district are seated near the center. The BSCP became the most prominent symbol of the organized black labor movement. Courtesy, Chicago Historical Society.

The BSCP soon entered formal negotiations with Pullman officials. Two years later, after stiff company resistance to BSCP demands, the Pullman Company signed its first agreement with Pullman Porters. After twelve years of struggle, the BSCP had finally achieved victory, which A. Philip Randolph described as "one of the most significant events" in his life. Not long thereafter, the mayor of New York received a delegation of porters at city hall, where he praised Randolph as "one of the foremost progressive labor leaders in America."[14]

Notably, despite the significant work of the BSCP's women's auxiliary, the organization not only failed to include Pullman's black women workers in its agreement, but it removed "and Maids" from the official name of the organization. While the BSCP gained a substantial victory for working men, it failed to address unequal employment practices along gender lines.[15]

Under the impact of New Deal labor legislation, however, some black women did gradually enter the ranks of the organized labor movement. Similar to their white counterparts, black women gained substantial access to membership in the International Ladies' Garment Workers' Union (ILGWU). In May 1933, New York garment worker Maida Springer joined Local 22 of the ILGWU. The local's black membership, predominantly women, rapidly increased to twelve thousand in 1938, about a third of the total membership. By the onset of World War II, Maida Springer had not only become a member of the local's executive board but also chaired its education committee. According to Springer's biographer, historian Yevette Richards Jordan, Springer had also served as a bridge between such labor and civil rights leaders as David Dubinsky, president of the ILGWU, A. Philip Randolph of the BSCP, and Lester Granger of the NAACP.[16]

New Deal labor legislation excluded household service workers—the group that included most black working women—from "minimum wage" and collective bargaining rights. Still, during the interwar years, dozens of household-service-workers unions emerged in cities across the country. Perhaps most notably, in 1934, under the leadership of Dora Jones, a domestic worker, African American women formed the New York-based Domestic Workers Union. This organization pushed for higher wages and improved conditions for household workers. Two years later, the union affiliated with the AFL's Building Service Employees International Union (BSEIU) and lobbied for passage of state-level minimum wage and workers' compensation laws for domestic workers.

The organizing efforts of African American women both as workers and as consumers attracted attention. In June 1935, under the "charismatic" leadership of Caribbean-born, working-class Communist Party member Bonita Williams, scores of black women took to the streets of Harlem to protest the high prices of food in their neighborhood. Following their march, described in Communist-affiliated newspapers as the "revolt of the housewives," some fifty Harlem stores reduced the price of meat by 25 percent. Williams explained that "unemployment and misery" rallied rising numbers of poor and working-class women to the "fight against the high prices." These organizing efforts gained the notice of other radical black women, some of them middle-class members of the Communist Party. In Birmingham, Alabama, the social worker and activist Esther Cooper Jackson later recalled how the struggles of the city's black domestic service workers underlay her decision to join the Community Party. Their suffering, she said, "helped to steer me to radical politics ... [to] really advance the people who were the most oppressed." For their part, professional black women and activists like Marvel Cooke (member of the Communist Party) and Ella Baker produced widely disseminated essays on the destructive impact of the Depression-era "slave market" on working-class black women.[17]

In addition to interracial and independent labor organizing, black workers in the interwar years continued to forge their own day-to-day resistance to unequal pay, hazardous working conditions, and mistreatment by supervisors. While employers repeatedly lamented the extent of turnover among the new industrial workers as evidence of their improvidence and unwillingness to work on a regular basis, in reality black workers moved from job to job to combat speedups, overwork, and restrictions on their occupational mobility. In Detroit in 1918, nearly 365 black workers out of 1,000 quit their auto jobs. The following year, an estimated 870 black workers out of 1,600 left their jobs. During the same period, one Pittsburgh-area company employed over 1,000 black workers in order to maintain a steady workforce of about 225 men. In 1919, interviews with nearly 200 black female newcomers to Pittsburgh revealed that 90 percent had already moved from one job to another "in an effort to increase their wages."[18]

Partly because African Americans gained increasing access to previously all-white labor unions, particularly in the meatpacking and steel industries, the incidence of strikebreaking dramatically declined during the interwar years. Still, strikebreaking activities persisted as a strategy for some black workers to breach remaining racial barriers in the labor force, as in the movement of black women into Philadelphia's wartime garment industry, the Great Steel Strike of 1919, the strike of maritime workers in Seattle in 1921, and the 1927 coal miners' strike in the Pittsburgh district. Each of these revealed the frustration of black workers with the limits they confronted. In the Steel Strike of 1919, one black worker bitterly declared, "All I am interested in is to make a living . . . and no 'hunky' has a right to keep me from working." In 1927, an African American strikebreaker in the Pittsburgh coal district similarly spoke for many when he said, "You would not work with me before the strike. Now I have your job and I am going to keep it." In Seattle, an atypical case, black men broke the strike of white women workers, waitresses and stewardesses at the Alaska Steamship Company and the Pacific Steamship Company. Organized by the International Seamen's Union and its all-white Marine Cooks and Stewards Association of the Pacific, this strike, according to historian Quintard Taylor, gave black men an opportunity to work "the boats" for the first time since the opening decade of the twentieth century. Black shipyard workers had lost their jobs following the war and only gained reemployment as ship stewards when they crossed the picket line of striking white workers.[19]

Both strikebreaking and extensive job turnover declined as strategies under the impact of the Great Depression and the rise of the New Deal state. During the 1930s, urban black workers and their communities leveraged the

New Deal coalition to broaden their footing in the labor movement and improve their condition through collective bargaining. They also used their support of FDR to expand their access to government-funded jobs under such programs as the Public Works Administration (PWA) and its low-income housing projects, particularly those earmarked for African American occupancy. In 1936, a coalition of Chicago social service, labor, and political organizations formed the Brotherhood Club of Black Bricklayers and pushed for African American employment on the construction of the city's PWA Ida B. Wells Homes, which were targeted for low-income African American families. The struggle for jobs on PWA projects resulted in the employment of over forty black bricklayers, among other skilled craftsmen. In Philadelphia, activist Crystal Bird Fauset gained appointment as head of the Works Progress Administration's (WPA) Division of Women's and Professional Projects. Under her leadership, some three thousand black women gained jobs on the WPA sewing project, representing over 50 percent of the workforce. Nationwide, following local struggles to secure greater access to WPA jobs, blacks increased to about 20 percent of all workers on WPA projects, with New York and Pennsylvania emerging as the top two states in terms of WPA jobs going to black workers.[20]

The Great Depression and FDR's New Deal programs changed the socioeconomic and political context of the African American struggle for equal access to the urban housing market. While poor and working-class blacks joined black professional and business people to protest the discriminatory housing policies of the HOLC and FHA, which redlined their neighborhoods and excluded them from federally insured loans, the fight for equal access to public housing programs emerged at the center of interwar efforts to improve the living conditions of poor and working-class blacks. In 1937, following FDR's reelection, Congress passed a new housing act that established the U.S. Housing Authority and empowered the federal government to distribute public funds to localities for clearing land of old homes and constructing low-income public housing. In Chicago, the fight for the Ida B. Wells Homes, the city's first public housing project for African Americans, spanned a period of eight years. The Chicago Council of Negro Organizations (CCNO), an alliance of some fifty-seven affiliate organizations, spearheaded the movement for low-income public housing in the city. Under the leadership of A. L. Foster, executive director of the Chicago Urban League, the CCNO filed a series of lawsuits, staged street protests, and entered "closed door negotiations" with municipal authorities to secure a commitment to the building of low-cost, government-financed housing for the city's poor and working-class black community.[21]

As early as November 1933, African Americans had joined the new interracial Citizens' Housing Committee and proposed the building of a low-income housing project on "a one-hundred-acre site bounded by 35th Street, Cottage Grove Avenue, Pershing Road, and Rhodes Avenue." Initially named the South Park Garden Homes, activists succeeded in renaming the project the Ida B. Wells Homes in honor of the antilynching activist. But stiff opposition from influential economic and political elites stymied the project's realization. In 1935, for example, the Sixth District U.S. Court of Appeals in Cincinnati ruled against the federal government condemning "private land for public housing." Thereafter, African Americans intensified their fight for public housing, achieving support from all sectors of the community, including churches and diverse labor, social service, and political organizations. CCNO director Foster soon reported to federal officials that "there was practically unanimous cooperation in a fight which meant everything to them." Only in 1938, however, did the Illinois State Senate smooth the way for the construction of the city's first black public housing project by permitting necessary tax exemptions for investors. In the meantime, and by contrast, the city had moved forward with the construction of three federal housing projects for white workers.[22]

Black Philadelphians in the 1930s built a strong chapter of the National Negro Congress (NNC), an umbrella organization designed to enhance the liberation of black workers and remove all vestiges of racial and class discrimination from the urban political economy. Coordinated by Arthur Huff, an activist school teacher and principal, the Philadelphia NNC helped to create the Tenants League in the wake of the tragic collapse of the Philadelphia tenement house that had killed nearly a dozen people and hospitalized over a dozen others in 1936. Building upon the tremendous outpouring of grassroots sentiment decrying the deaths as "a very serious situation," "a terrible thing," and "criminal" and charging city officials with responsibility, African Americans channeled their anger and grief into "protest marches, rent strikes, and neighborhood meetings against bad housing across the city." Under the leadership of its executive secretary Bernard Childs, the Tenants League helped bring about not only the establishment of the city's new public housing agency, the Philadelphia Housing Authority (PHA), but also the building of the first two of three low-income housing projects, the James Weldon Johnson Homes and the Richard Allen Homes, "to supply affordable housing to poor and working-class black residents."[23]

Black Baltimore waged an equally energetic campaign for a federal public housing project. African Americans joined the interracial Baltimore Citizens Housing Committee (BCHA) and pushed for federal funds to build low-income housing for the black and white poor. Under increasing pressure from African Americans and their white allies, the city established the Baltimore Housing Authority and soon sought federal funds to construct nine public housing projects, three designated for African Americans and the remainder for whites. The NAACP and representatives of the Baltimore CIO intensified grassroots community organizing to translate these plans into reality. As wartime production escalated, the city opened its first public housing project for African Americans, Edgar Allan Poe Homes, in 1940. The project proved a mixed blessing. Some three thousand tenants had been displaced by the project's construction, but only 47 residents of the old neighborhood entered the new facility. Furthermore, over 50 percent of project residents paid higher rents than they had previously paid for private rental housing.[24]

The fight for public housing throughout the country was a complicated one. For one thing, white families resisted sharing residential projects with black families. For another, the cross-class and interracial alliances that made African American access to public housing possible involved a difficult give and take. Even after municipalities designated certain projects for black occupancy, African Americans had to continue their struggle to prevent such projects from falling back into the hands of white residents. For example, in Philadelphia, the government promised and then withdrew its promise to open the Allen Homes primarily to poor and working-class black families; only after a fight was the plan reinstated. At the same time, the city largely barred African Americans from such housing projects as Tasker Homes, opened on the city's South Side, and later Shipyard Homes. In addition, as Marcus Hunter notes, Philadelphia's middle-class and elite blacks privileged their own quest for single-family homeownership over the quest for low-rent properties and public housing for poor residents.

Urban black workers repeatedly articulated their desire to inhabit solidly built, less crowded, and properly maintained and serviced housing units. When Philadelphia's mayor, Davis S. Wilson—with new federal money in hand—abruptly started to condemn property in the Seventh Ward without sufficient consultation with residents, Seventh Ward residents staged street protests to halt the process. Poor and working-class residents, with a degree of cross-class support, vehemently protested that, "the Mayor had no plan for rehousing displaced residents, and was instead focused on the superficial aspects of the [housing] problem, expending his energies solely on removing properties that looked bad."[25] When the city suggested housing displaced residents in a local armory, residents rejected the proposal. A group of black tenants declared, "We positively will not live like pigs in an armory. If they want us out of here, they'll have to come and drag us out." One young woman asserted her own and her neighbors' "right to a home" and to their "household furnishings, children and pets. What would we do with them in an armory." The mayor soon changed his policy on "slum clearance," ordering police to condemn properties but not to evict tenants who refused to move. Similarly, in Chicago, once housing activists settled on a particular location for public housing for black residents, they had to fight an ongoing battle to hold the line against less desirable proposals. In conversations with federal PWA officials, one South Side black resident captured residents' opposition to changes in the proposed location of the city's first black public housing project: "We are not going to accept a proposition over there west of State Street and along the railroad tracks. We don't care to have smoke and soot from trains blowing on us—we have had enough of that. What we have been promised, and what we want is to be over there, where the lake can blow on us."[26]

By the beginning of World War II, African Americans claimed about 30 percent of all PWA housing for low-income families. But such units not only unfolded on a segregated and unequal basis but also reinforced certain internal class distinctions and fragmentation within the African American community itself. In Atlanta, the government's University Homes housing project housed none of the poor and working-class residents uprooted by "slum clearance" to make way for the project. Instead, the tenant selection process favored higher-income groups. During her visit to the homes, First Lady Eleanor Roosevelt expressed disappointment that the rents were not "sufficiently low" for "average black families" and that none of the earlier poor and working-class residents had found a place in the new units.[27]

By the late 1930s, the east side of Atlanta had become associated with what historians have described as the "disreputable 'masses' left behind," while the West Side offered single-family dwellings for the black middle class, "bungalow and two-story homes" with suburban yards. Still, the West Side also housed many working-class African Americans of some means—"construction craftsmen and unskilled workers and better-paid service and domestic workers"—who "wished to escape the east side and live in respectable surroundings as homeowners." Historian Karen Ferguson concludes, "State incorporation thus divided the black community physically and politically into those chosen to move into full-fledged citizenship and those who were consigned to remain at the margins of civic life." Nonetheless, poor and working-class tenants embraced this hard road to mobility as one of the few viable options for improving their living conditions.[28]

As black workers and their allies fought for public housing, poor and working-class blacks frequently moved from house to house in a quest for better living quarters in the private housing market. In Pittsburgh, within a relatively short period of time, one family of newcomers moved thirteen times, searching for better housing with affordable rents. In 1920, the executive director of the Urban League of Pittsburgh located a section of Second Avenue where there was "a complete family turnover" nearly every two months. In Harlem, a New York Urban League study reported that half of the area's population had lived at their current addresses for less than a year, and the "most frequent reason" for moving "was the constant search for adequate housing."

Other families devised a range of strategies for paying the rent on over-priced and inadequate housing. Large numbers of newcomers took in lodgers, held house parties, and sold bootleg whiskey to raise money. By the mid-1920s, the *New York Age* reported that the "rent party" had become "a recognized means of meeting the demands of extortionate landlords."[29]

The entrepreneurial efforts of still other, mostly middle-class African Americans both alleviated and reinforced some of the challenges confronting blacks in the racially segmented urban political economy. Commercial, leisure-time, sports, and cultural organizations proliferated under the increasing stimulus of industrial work and residential concentration to harness the buying power of working- and middle-class black urban communities. In particular, black realtors sought ways to earn a living while addressing the housing crisis. In Richmond, California, Katherine Clark recalled how her father "bought up property and converted it into apartments [for rental to black people] . . . all down in West Oakland. He would buy them at low cost and fix them up" and rent them out to newcomers. While such ventures helped to meet the housing and even employment needs of black migrants, they sometimes entailed significant levels of rent gouging and exploitation of low-income black residents. Further, black and white realtors developed working relationships that reinforced residential segregation and allowed both (but particularly whites) to exploit poor and working-class residents' desperate need for low-rent housing. Yet tensions arose there too. In an "Open Letter to City Council," Miami's Colored Board of Trade insisted on a strictly segregated housing market—one that insured the incomes of black realtors and other business people: "We insist ... upon a segregation that really does segregate, absolute and inviolate. . . . If we are to be shut in, simple justice demands that the white people be shut out."[30]

FORGING A NEW BLACK METROPOLIS, PUBLIC SPACE, AND SACRED ORDER

Despite the racism that enforced segregation, the expansion of the black "city within the city" during the industrial era buoyed middle- and working-class hopes for a better life. African American workers, business, and professional people envisioned the development of the Black Metropolis not only as a site for essential social, religious, cultural, medical, and legal services but also as a source of opportunities for entrepreneurship, employment, and property ownership for themselves and their families. By the onset of the Great Depression, the black urban community included vibrant black business districts in major cities across the country.

Atlanta's Auburn Avenue and Decatur Street emerged as perhaps the most well-known of the new black business and cultural districts in the urban South. Adjoining the elite Peachtree Street area of exclusive white shops and cultural institutions just north of Five Points, Auburn Avenue provided what one historian has described as "much of the same cross-class entertainment and civic pride" that characterized its nearby white counterpart. Popularly known as Sweet Auburn by African Americans, this street housed such institutions as the Prince Hall Masonic Temple as well as numerous churches, stores, and nightclubs. One domestic worker later recalled, "We just enjoyed Auburn Avenue. That's why you dressed up and put [on] good clothes and go to the show on Auburn Avenue and you were going places." While Auburn catered to a heavily if not exclusively middle-class and elite clientele, Decatur Street, located near the train station, housed a plethora of "saloons, brothels, and gambling houses" serving primarily working-class and poor patrons.[31]

Birmingham, Norfolk, Louisville, Durham, Houston, Memphis, and other southern cities also developed their own black business districts (BBDs). And even the rise of northern BBDs had deep roots in southern black culture, politics, and business development. When southern blacks moved to the urban industrial North and West, they brought their own notions about entrepreneurship with them to Pittsburgh, Detroit, New York, Chicago, Los Angeles, and other cities. A broad cross-section of northern- and southern-born African American entrepreneurs, workers, artists, intellectuals, and political, civil, and human rights activists built the new black public sphere. The famous Stroll emerged in "a section of State Street on the South Side of Chicago that formed the heart of the Black Belt." Meanwhile, Seventh Avenue became the hub of black life in both Harlem and New York City generally. In 1928, renaissance writer and observer Wallace Thurman offered this description: "Seventh Avenue is a stream of dark people going to churches, theaters, restaurants, billiard halls, business offices, food markets, barbershops and apartment houses. . . . From five o'clock in the evening until way past midnight, Seventh Avenue is one electrifying line of brilliance and activity."[32]

Hastings Street in Detroit represented the equivalent to the young Rev. C.L. Franklin, father of the renowned rhythm and blues singer Aretha Franklin, when he arrived in Michigan via Buffalo during the interwar years. The bluesman John Lee Hooker vividly recalled Detroit's Hastings Street at the time: "Oh, that was *the street.* . . . Anything you wanted was on that street. Anything you *didn't* want was on that street." Contemporary residents often referred to Pittsburgh's Wylie Avenue as a "dynamic," "thriving," and "bustling" area, "the crossroads of the World," where there was "never a dull moment" and where "people never went to bed." And the editor of the California *Eagle* newspaper, Joe Bass, identified Central Avenue in Los Angeles, from 8th to 20th Streets, as "one of the most remarkable Negro business sections anywhere in the country," following the opening of a new theater owned by African Americans.[33]

As the black business and professional infrastructure expanded to include everything from restaurants to Negro League baseball teams, a variety of discriminatory municipal ordinances, licensing laws, building code enforcement policies, and bank lending practices forced black entrepreneurs into financing strategies that blurred the line between legitimate and illegitimate businesses. In addition to cabarets and nightclubs, the policy game (also called numbers and defined succinctly by one recent historian as a form of "illegal gambling" now legalized as "state lottery") financed grocery stores, restaurants, banks, and insurance companies and provided jobs for workers as well as some black professional people. In Chicago, John "Mushmouth" Johnson's Emporium Saloon on State Street; Robert T. Motts's Pekin Theater, also on State Street; and Elijah Johnson's Dreamland Ballroom (later Dreamland Café) all developed in part out of earnings from the numbers game and other forms of gambling. Policy income also supported the growth of Jesse Binga's bank, the Chicago American Giants professional baseball team, and the formation of the National Negro Baseball League in 1920.[34]

In Pittsburgh, when the city's black Steel City Bank failed in 1925, the numbers men emerged as the city's principal lenders. Sports historian Rob Ruck documents how Pittsburgh's numbers kings Gus Greenlee and Woogie Harris not only underwrote the development of professional baseball in the city but also provided "college tuition loans and start-up money for hotels, bars, restaurants, and legal and medical practices. Gus acted as an informal patron to black musicians and even set up 'Old Hot Sauce'" Williams in the barbeque business. In Detroit, some storefront churches became well-known sites of illegal policy stations. Members of some churches later cited the policy game as an incentive for joining and maintaining their membership. "Before I joined this church," one member related, "I used to play as big as fifty cents almost every day . . . and never hit. I went to this church, got a private reading. She told me to fast. I did three days; and one day I played fifty cents and won."

Black families with professional aspirations for their children, particularly their daughters, often decried the "policy racket," yet they conceded its benefits for young black women with few opportunities to work in the clerical fields. One black woman lamented that her daughter, trained for the music profession, "isn't working in her field now and I hope soon she will get back to [her] own interest in music." It was often these women who figured among the young female policy employees who made "between fifteen and twenty-five dollars a week and . . . seemed to be satisfied with their jobs."[35]

The rise of the Black Metropolis, including the policy game, was closely intertwined with the emergence of what historian Wallace Best describes as a "new sacred order" that bridged the spiritual and secular missions of the church. Baptist and Pentecostal churches spearheaded the growth of this new movement, expanding in multiple cities. In Chicago, migrants founded at least 5 new storefront or home-based Baptist churches between 1916 and 1919: Pilgrim, Progressive, Providence, Liberty, and Monumental. At the same time, other migrants initiated and sustained nearly 20 Holiness churches. In Harlem, a contemporary report (1926) identified 140 black churches in a 150-block area. Women like Ida B. Robinson and Lucy Smith headed the most successful of these new churches. Robinson moved to Philadelphia in 1917 and soon affiliated with the United Holy Church of America (UHCA). In 1924, she broke from the United Holy Church over limitations on female ministers and formed the Mount Sinai Holy Church of America. Mt. Sinai held its first national convention in 1925 and later became one of the largest Pentecostal organizations in the country, with branches in the Caribbean. Likewise, in 1916, Elder Lucy Smith, a Georgia-born migrant, organized All Nations Pentecostal Church in a one-room prayer meeting in her Chicago home. For ten years, the church moved from storefront to storefront until Smith initiated the building of a new edifice.[36]

While new Baptist and Pentecostal churches formed the center of the emerging new sacred order, established Baptist and AME churches also modified their programs in the wake of the Great Migration, creating new church-based social service organizations. Pittsburgh's Hill District Ebenezer Missionary Baptist Church, formed in 1875, created a Home Finder's League during the early 1920s, while the nearby Homestead AME Church formed a real estate agency and sold or rented homes to African Americans "on low monthly installments." Chicago's Olivet Baptist Church, under the pastorship of Lacey Kirk Williams, set up an employment bureau, a housing assistance program, and a letter-writing service to help newcomers. Moreover, the church organized volunteers to meet migrants at the train station to assist them in finding housing and settling in their new homes. As a result of such services and the increasing numbers of black migrants in the city, Olivet's membership increased from an estimated four thousand in 1915 to nearly nine thousand in 1920. Detroit's Bethel AME Church also created specialized social service, labor, and housing departments. The church's labor exchange distributed work cards to prospective employees and used its publication the *Voice of Missions* to advertise "good paying positions" in the city's automobile and other manufacturing plants.[37]

And the list goes on. In Philadelphia, a new Interdenominational Ministerial Alliance established a free employment and housing information bureau at East Calvary Baptist Church to direct people "to places of employment and places where they may find good homes to live in." In 1920, at the General Conference of the AME Church Meeting in St. Louis, black Methodists pledged to carry out a program to improve the economic opportunities of black workers. As a foundation for its work, the conference promised to systematically "collect data and facts as to labor conditions in general, and that of negro labor in particular, also a list of industrial plants employing negro labor and those who do not."[38]

But while churches organized significant employment and housing programs, local branches of the National Urban League (NUL) developed the broadest and most systematic range of programs and services to meet the economic needs of urban black workers and their families. Formed in 1910, the NUL operated some fifty-one branch offices in the urban North and parts of the South by the mid-1920s and was the premier interracial social service organization during the period. Local branches conducted numerous social scientific surveys of nonindustrial and industrial workplaces and used these quantitative data to set up job placement, vocational training, housing, and advocacy programs for black workers. In 1919 alone, according to the Chicago Commission on Race Relations, the Chicago Urban League placed over fourteen thousand blacks in area plants. In 1923, following the economic downturn of 1921–22, the Detroit Urban League, formed in 1916, reported receiving "more calls for workers than it could fill." Between January and June 1925, some 70 percent of New York Urban League job applicants found work in household, general labor, and personal service jobs. Beginning during the mid-1920s, however, the New York body discontinued its domestic-service placement activities and concentrated on what it described as "the better types of positions which have been denied to Negro workers." By the end of 1926, the league placed only fifty-nine applicants in domestic service positions, while the number of African Americans placed in industrial and clerical or public service jobs increased to over one thousand. Local offices of the NUL carried out similar works in cities across industrial America.[39]

The NUL also connected migrants to much-needed housing during the early stages of their migration to northern and western cities. Local branch housing departments inspected buildings to certify their fitness for human habitation; represented tenants before municipal authorities (particularly health code officers), real estate agents, and homeowners; encouraged migrants to challenge landlord violations of lease agreements; and educated tenants on the "practical knowledge of the sanitation and upkeep of properties" they occupied. In order to relieve the pressures of lodging large numbers of people in available housing, the NUL also urged landlords to combat what it called the "lodger evil"—that is, an increasing incidence of subletting among tenants to help meet exorbitant rent payments. Rather than extorting the highest rents for dilapidated dwellings, however, the Urban League encouraged owners to "manage and rent" their properties at "reasonable fees." The New York Urban League persuaded John D. Rockefeller, Jr., to establish the five-hundred-unit Dunbar Apartment Complex in Harlem to help stimulate new housing development for black tenants. Completed in 1927 and opened to tenants in 1928, the Dunbar Apartments received the American Institute of Architecture Award for the best design for 1927. Similarly, in Detroit, the league persuaded two firms that employed large numbers of black workers to construct low-rent houses for black employees. On one occasion, when the Detroit Police Department closed several houses of prostitution, the Detroit Urban League arranged for industrialists to assume the leases and transform the facilities into rental properties for black workers.[40]

TRANSFORMATION OF IDEOLOGY AND POLITICS

Industrial labor, the Great Migration, and the growth of the Black Metropolis underlay the emergence of new movements for social change. A plethora of interracial, nationalist, and labor organizations transformed the ideology and politics of the black community as it expanded across urban America. Unlike the National Urban League, which was largely a middle-class organization, the Brotherhood of Sleeping Car Porters and Maids (discussed earlier), the NAACP, and the Garvey Movement claimed grassroots working-class memberships and leadership, particularly at the local level. By the early 1920s, the NAACP reported three hundred branches and more than ninety thousand members.[41] Similarly, Marcus Garvey's Universal Improvement Association (UNIA) reached astounding membership in the early 1920s. Formed in Jamaica as World War I got under way, the UNIA spread to Harlem during the war years and soon established chapters throughout the United States and parts of the West Indies, Latin America, and Africa. At its peak, the organization claimed over a half million members and listed seven hundred branches in the United States and another two hundred abroad.[42]

These organizations intensified assaults on the social, cultural, and political structures of the Jim Crow edifice. The Chicago NAACP chapter defended African Americans against criminal charges when they resisted mob attacks on their homes during the Chicago Riot of 1919, protested segregation of blacks in public schools on the South Side, and adamantly opposed the discriminatory practices of restaurants in the Loop and the separation of black and white passengers in interstate travel. The Detroit branch emerged at the center of the national fight against housing segregation and mob violence during the mid-1920s, when the dentist Henry Ossian Sweet, his wife, and others faced trial for murder in the shooting death of a white man during a mob attack on their home. As noted in chapter 4, the Detroit NAACP immediately mobilized local and national support for the case, which resulted in acquittal for all the accused.[43]

In San Francisco and Oakland, despite the small size of black communities, the Bay Area NAACP branch challenged racial discrimination at the Presidio, a local military base, and in Chinese restaurants and a delicatessen at the San Francisco Civic Center. The organization also monitored the San Francisco *Call* and the *Chronicle* for evidence of racially biased reporting. In Los Angeles, meanwhile, the NAACP branch informed the national office in January 1918 that it occupied a strategic place in the heart of the film industry. The local office pledged to play a key role in "detecting and reporting many of the pictures which by design or otherwise, would injure our interests." Three years after release of *The Birth of a Nation* (1916), the Los Angeles NAACP spearheaded passage of City Council Ordinance 37778, prohibiting the screening of another racially inflammatory film, *Free and Equal*. During the first five years of its existence, the Los Angeles NAACP also won significant victories against racial discrimination in public accommodations and educational institutions, including most notably the admission of black women into the Los Angeles County nurses training program.[44]

Southern blacks also established a growing number of NAACP chapters, supported the national assault on Jim Crow, and forged their own local civil rights and political agenda. In 1920, for the first time since its founding in 1909, the NAACP reported more members in the South (42,588) than in the North and West (38,420). Established in 1917, the Atlanta branch became the first southern city to host the national meeting of the organization three years later. In his pioneering history of the NAACP, historian Charles F. Kellogg declared, "It took courage to call an interracial conference south of the Mason Dixon line, where ... lynching and mob violence had reached a peak rather than abated." W. E. B. Du Bois, editor of the NAACP's *Crisis* magazine, remarked that the Atlanta conference underscored that there was "no difference of aim and desire" among northern and southern blacks.[45]

Notwithstanding the dramatic rise of the NAACP as the country's premier civil rights organization, radicals such as A. Philip Randolph, Chandler Owen, Hubert Harrison, and Cyril Briggs underscored its shortcomings as a movement for social justice. During World War I, Randolph, Owen, and other southern- and Caribbean-born black radicals joined the Harlem unit of the Socialist Party and soon advanced strong class analyses of the "race problem." In 1917, as southern migrants to New York City, Randolph and Owen established the *Messenger* magazine and intensified their efforts to bring black workers into the Socialist Party. They described the *Messenger* as "the only magazine of scientific radicalism in the world published by Negroes"; in its pages Randolph and Owen openly opposed the war as a product of both white supremacist and capitalist ideology.[46] Urged forward by radical black activists, the American Communist Party (CP) initiated the formation of the American Negro Labor Congress (ANLC) in 1925. At the founding meeting, held in Chicago in October, the new organization declared its solidarity with white workers and challenged the NAACP and Urban League to take a more militant stand in defense of workers' rights. Although the ANLC would prove short-lived—despite some forty-five local chapters by 1927, membership remained small—the CP continued its influence by launching the new League of Struggle for Negro Rights (LSNR) in 1930.[47]

Despite their commitment to a class analysis of racial injustices, black socialists and communists nonetheless decried the parties' efforts to reduce all facets of the "race problem" to issues of class inequity. In 1917, in order to give voice to their concerns, West Indian–born Cyril Briggs and a cadre of other New Yorkers broke from the Socialist Party and formed the African Blood Brotherhood (ABB). In the columns of the *Crusader,* the official organ of the ABB, Briggs called for a concerted struggle against colonialism abroad and racism at home. Like Briggs, the West Indian socialist Hubert Harrison also abandoned the Socialist Party and spearheaded the formation of a new organization, the Liberty League, and its publication, the *Voice,* to address the neglect of race issues by members of the radical left. Harrison's break with the Socialist Party became even more pronounced when he became a contributing editor of Marcus Garvey's widely disseminated *Negro World* newspaper. Harrison then declared, "The roots of class-consciousness ... inhere in a temporary economic order; whereas the roots of race-consciousness must of necessity survive any and all changes in the economic order."[48]

Radical black print media like the *Crusader,* the *Messenger,* the *Voice,* and *Negro World* played a major role in the critique of racial liberalism as well as the shortcomings of international communism. Lara Putnam concludes, "It is simply impossible to find an influential Caribbean activist or intellectual in this era who did not found a newspaper, edit a newspaper, or earn a living writing for newspapers for at least a part of his or her life."[49]

But the black radical critique of the Communist Party did not emanate from African American men only. As black men challenged the racial limitations of the party, a small group of black women communists contested its gender biases among black and white men. Historian Erik S. McDuffie shows how black women gradually entered the ranks of the CP when the Harlem social worker Grace P. Campbell officially joined in 1923. Black women party members not only spearheaded street protests and participated in other forms of party activities but also challenged the party to recognize the black woman's "triple oppression" under class, racial, and gender forms of inequality. In 1936, the well-known Harlem writer and party member Louise Thompson Patterson sharply articulated this notion in an article published in the party's organ, *Woman Today*. "Over the whole land," Thompson Patterson wrote, "Negro women meet this triple exploitation—as workers, as women, and as Negroes."[50]

Meanwhile, Marcus Garvey and the UNIA identified crucial gaps in both radical and liberal movements designed to address issues of racial inequality. Garvey repeatedly underscored the persistence of entrenched patterns of racial hostility among rank-and-file white workers even as their local and national leaders articulated the goals of class solidarity across the color line. He described as "folly" efforts to forge alliances with reluctant and racially exclusionary white workers.[51] Emphasizing "race first" and a very positive identification with blackness and the continent of Africa, the Garvey movement, before its demise by the mid-1920s, had helped to transform the cultural and political landscape of urban industrial America. Great masses of black people expressed increasing pride in their African heritage, challenged the color hierarchy within the black community, and staunchly resisted the tenets of white supremacy in U.S. society more generally. And as the BSCP moved to organize black workers, it soon echoed some of the black-consciousness tenets of the Garvey movement.[52] Thus Randolph and the BSCP synthesized elements of black nationalism, radical class analysis, and trade unionism as the principal vehicles for the economic emancipation of black workers as well the completion of the unfinished work of extending full citizenship rights to black people.[53]

Alongside the proliferation of new interracial, nationalist, and radical social movements, the growth of the Black Metropolis and the black industrial working class also fueled the spread of new African American Republican and Democratic Party organizations across the urban North and West. On the ground, it was black women who provided the organizational backbone for the rise of twentieth-century black electoral politics. Following World War I and the advent of woman's suffrage, black women intensified their participation in the electoral process and mediated the transformation of black politics during the period.[54] They built upon their extensive network of local and national organizations to enable a new generation of black political leaders to build influential "submachines" within the established two-party system and increasingly challenge white control in predominantly working-class black voting districts.[55]

On the eve of World War I, a young cohort of black Republicans— including Edward H. Wright, Oscar DePriest, Robert R. Jackson, and Beauregard Moseley—had already forged an independent black Republican organization in Chicago. Their efforts resulted in the election of Oscar DePriest as Chicago's first black alderman in 1915 and a second one in 1918. In 1924, Chicagoans elected their first black state senator and four years later sent DePriest to the U.S. Congress. The latter office not only symbolized the growth of black power at the local level but also signaled the resurgence of African Americans in national politics following the disfranchisement of southern blacks and the ascendancy of Jim Crow. By 1930, African Americans controlled the Republican Party on Chicago's South Side, where they made up majorities of the Second, Third, and Fourth Wards.

Moreover, from World War I through the interwar period, African Americans in northern and western cities sought to control not only votes and elections but patronage appointments in predominantly black electoral districts. These efforts led directly to black job growth. Despite the relatively small size of Seattle's black population as World War I got underway, blacks formed the King County Colored Republican Club (KCCRC) and gradually secured such positions as deputy U.S. marshal and county sheriff, as well as numerous jobs for janitors, elevator operators, and groundskeepers at municipal and state buildings. In Detroit, following his election in 1924, Mayor Smith expanded the number of African American employees in the post office as well as the Sanitary Division of the Public Works Department. In the wake of increasing political mobilization during the same period, hundreds of black Chicagoans took positions as teachers, clerks, policemen, and postal workers as well as the customary jobs as custodial employees and general laborers. Blacks made up about 7 percent of the city's total population as the Great Depression got under way but accounted for some 25 percent of all postal service workers. At city hall, an African American held the position of assistant corporation counsel and trial lawyer for property damage litigation totaling millions of dollars. Twenty other blacks worked as legal investigators for the department. Moreover, in addition to municipal jobs, some African Americans gained police "protection for activities within the underground economy."[56]

During the Great Depression, African Americans joined the Democratic Party coalition both to expand the scope of social and labor programs available for poor and working-class people in general and to strengthen their own hand in the fight to eliminate racial inequities in the administration of such programs. While African Americans forged a growing alliance with the liberal New Deal labor coalition, segregationists not only hampered their efforts to eliminate Jim Crow from programs funded through federal contracts but also thwarted the reemployment of black workers in the private sector as the economy recovered from the Great Depression and unemployed whites returned to work.

Frustrated by the limits of the ballot and support for FDR's New Deal coalition, by the late 1930s black workers and their communities organized nonviolent direct-action Don't Buy Where You Can't Work protests in Philadelphia, New York, and Washington, DC. Closely aligned with the organized labor movement, these militant boycotts targeted businesses serving but not employing members of the African American community. In Philadelphia, in addition to its protests against exploitive and hazardous housing conditions, discussed above, the NNC boycotted businesses and pushed for the equal employment of African Americans on an equal basis. The Citizen's League for Fair Play in New York and the New Negro Alliance in Washington, DC, also spearheaded boycotts and picketing of stores that either refused to hire blacks or confined them to the lowest rungs of the workforce. Some firms, such as Blumenstein's Department Store in New York and the A&P chain grocer, signed agreements to employ and upgrade black workers. These agreements represented some of the first "affirmative action" programs for improving the status of black workers. Don't Buy Where You Can't Work campaigns set the stage for the March on Washington Movement during World War II.[57]

MARCH ON WASHINGTON MOVEMENT (MOWM)

Before the United States declared war on the Axis powers and entered World War II, a broad cross-section of African American and interracial social justice organizations rallied behind militant calls for defense industry jobs. This coalition included the NAACP, BSCP, NUL, and the National Council of Negro Women, among numerous church-based organizations. In early 1941, following a meeting of civil rights organizations in Chicago, African Americans forged the March on Washington Movement to achieve their goals of desegregating the industrial workplace and the armed forces. Under the leadership of A. Philip Randolph and the BSCP, the March on

Washington Movement developed into a national grassroots working-class movement for social change. By early 1942, it also coalesced with the spirited Double-V campaign, popularized by the *Pittsburgh Courier,* for victory at home and victory abroad. Moreover, following Gandhi's initiation of the Quit India movement in the late summer of 1942, Randolph, the Double-V campaign, and the MOWM moved increasingly toward the Indian independence movement for inspiration. As historian Nico Slate puts it, the Quit India movement reinforced connections between the Black Freedom Movement, Indian independence, and "racial equality as necessary components of a global double victory."[58]

Within less than six months, the MOWM had established headquarters in cities across the urban North and West, from New York and Washington, DC, in the east to San Francisco and Seattle on the West Coast. At the same time, both the leadership and rank-and-file members of the BSCP spread word of the march into the South. As early as December 1940, Randolph and Webster had advanced the march idea in meetings in Savannah, Tampa, and Miami. In May 1941, the official organ of the movement, *The Black Worker,* issued the call to march: "We call upon you to fight for jobs in National Defense. We call upon you to struggle for the integration of Negroes in the armed forces. . . . The Federal Government cannot with clear conscience call upon private industry and labor unions to abolish discrimination based upon race and color so long as it practices discrimination itself against Negro Americans."[59]

By early June, the leading black weeklies predicted that some fifty thousand to one hundred thousand black people would march on the nation's capital. In its headline, the *Chicago Defender* declared "50,000" blacks were preparing to "march for jobs and justice," while the *Amsterdam News* enthusiastically reported "100,000 in March to Capital." In a survey to determine the extent of pro-march sentiment among black people, the *Pittsburgh Courier* reported that an overwhelming majority of blacks in Detroit, New York, Chicago, and St. Louis expressed strong support for the march. Convinced that thousands of black people would march on the nation's capital during a time of war emergency, FDR issued Executive Order 8802 on 24 June 1941. Executive Order 8802 not only banned racial discrimination in government employment, defense industries, and training programs but also established the Fair Employment Practices Committee (FEPC) to receive, investigate, and address complaints of racial discrimination in the defense program.[60]

With this early success, the march itself was called off, but the MOWM persisted, facing perhaps its greatest challenge: generating enough consistent pressure to transform the president's order—which carried almost no power of enforcement—into real jobs and economic opportunities for black workers. Across the country, in the wake of the FEPC, African Americans mobilized to bring the fruits of wartime production to black workers. In St. Louis, for example, the BSCP field organizer Theodore D. McNeal declared in the newspaper the *Argus*, "The chief crisis of the Negro people is the crisis of the Negro worker, for in the main, the Negro workers are the Negro people. . . . We intend to organize the Negro in the poolroom, on the street corner, in the church and every place else he is found." The St. Louis MOWM soon claimed a series of victories, including the reinstatement of nearly two hundred black workers arbitrarily terminated by the U.S. Cartridge and Small Arms plant, wage increases, access to skilled job training programs, and increased hiring of black women, even if initially mainly in domestic capacities. Moreover, in addition to escalating the filing of complaints with the FEPC and justifying the establishment of a regional office to handle the grievances of black workers in the St. Louis area, the organization staged mass rallies to generate broad-based grassroots support under the very powerful rubric "Winning Democracy for the Negro Is Winning the War for Democracy."[61]

Under the impact of the FEPC and the MOWM, blacks employed in war-production jobs rose from under 3 percent as late as March 1942 to over 8 percent in 1944. The FEPC "integrated thousands of Negroes as skilled laborers in the electrical and light manufacturing industries, from which they had been barred by custom, and in the vast new airplane-engine factories. . . . They also began to filter into minor managerial and clerical positions in increasing numbers."

But the fruits of the FEPC were not evenly distributed from city to city, across regions, or by gender. In the urban South, African Americans confronted the formal segregationist order. Birmingham, New Orleans, and Atlanta public officials and employers insisted on providing defense industry employment on a racially segregated basis. Frank Dixon, governor of Alabama, articulated the views of segregationists when he declared support for the training and employment of black war workers only "within the bounds of the segregationist system established by law and social custom in the southern states."[62]

And civil rights and labor organizations themselves prioritized placement of black men over women, reinforcing the barriers that confronted African

Defense Worker   — . THRASH

Following the demands of the militant March on Washington Movement and FDR's Executive Order 8802 mandating an end to racial discrimination in firms with government contracts, African Americans expanded their footing in defense industry jobs. While employed by Philadelphia's WPA project, artist Dox Thrash produced this iconic New Deal image of the black worker as an integral part of the nation's industrial workforce, *Defense Worker* (ca. 1942). Courtesy, Works Progress Administration, Free Library of Philadelphia.

American women. But this did not stop black women from using the FEPC. In Detroit, black women filed over 170 employment discrimination complaints, many of them resulting from white women's firm opposition to working alongside black women. In February 1942, at a UAW Women's Conference, one white female union representative spoke for the majority of her constituents when she declared, "I don't think we should consider bringing them [African American women] into the shops—If we bring them in even in this crisis we'd always have them to contend with. And you know what that means—We'd be working right beside them, we'd be using the same rest rooms, etc. I'm against it." When black women finally broke the barrier and moved into defense industry jobs in large numbers, they invariably entered segregated all-black or predominantly black departments. In the Los Angeles aircraft industry, Videll Drake, a migrant from Dallas, Texas, later recalled that North American Aviation "didn't let the [black and white women] work together; the colored mostly worked together. There always been a kind of discrimination in that plant."[63]

As the MOWM opened up new job markets to black people, albeit on a segregated and unequal basis, class and racial conflict intensified on the homefront. In Detroit, a struggle over the Sojourner Truth public housing project fueled the outbreak of racial violence in 1943. In the months leading up to the violence, authorities had designated the Sojourner Truth project for African American occupancy. For a brief moment, however, grassroots white resistance turned the project over to poor and working-class whites. This struggle inflamed race relations in the city and helped to ignite the outbreak of violence between blacks and whites at Detroit's Belle Isle Amusement Park. The violence soon spread into the African American Paradise Valley neighborhood. Before federal troops helped to put down the fighting, authorities reported thirty-four deaths, nearly two thousand arrests, and $2 million in property damage. Racial violence also broke out in Harlem in 1943. Unlike earlier outbreaks of urban violence, when white mobs invaded black neighborhoods and left scores of black fatalities and the destruction of black homes, businesses, churches, and other institutions in their wake, wartime violence revealed rising numbers of white casualties as well as damage to white-owned property. In the New York and Detroit riots, significant numbers of poor and working-class blacks took up arms, looted stores, burned buildings, and sometimes maimed, injured, and killed whites in defense of their homes and communities and as modes of protest against long-standing and persistent injustices within their neighborhoods.[64]

As World War II ended, black workers complained that some CIO as well as AFL unions continued to drag their feet on equal treatment of and opportunities for black workers. Increasingly frustrated, some staged wildcat strikes to call attention to the persistence of racial inequality in the workplace—while some white workers struck to protest the progress that had been made. In 1944, over three hundred black workers walked off the job at the Monsanto Chemical Company in St. Louis to call attention to the persistence of racial segregation at the firm. On the other hand, when federal officials forced the hiring of black workers as drivers at the Philadelphia Transportation Company in 1944–45, white workers struck the firm, demanding the release of all black employees assigned as drivers. Only the use of federal troops forced white employees back to work.

As the war neared an end, African Americans experienced the early edges of the ubiquitous last-hired-first-fired phenomenon. Philadelphia's segregated Sun Shipyards closed down its operation, resulting in the layoff of 80 percent of its black workforce during 1945–46. In the meantime, A. Philip Randolph and supporters of the MOWM initiated the National Council for a Permanent FEPC and worked to deepen liberal white support for a postwar struggle for economic and political rights for black people. As mixed as the results of these efforts may have been, together, interwar and wartime initiatives established the foundation for the postwar spread of the Modern Black Freedom Movement.[65]

CONCLUSION

Compared to the labor politics of the preindustrial era, the strategies of the black working class during the industrial era—including an interracial labor movement, engagement with the New Deal social welfare state, and different expressions of black nationalism—emerged as roads to empowerment for the twentieth-century black working class. Programs that developed in the Black Metropolis during the interwar period—from the "new sacred order" to new entrepreneurial, housing, and employment initiatives—helped to offset some of the most destructive aspects of the racially stratified industrial order. Meanwhile, momentum for change continued to build. In the years after World War II, these overlapping, entangled, and complicated local and global movements would energize new grassroots assaults on the old white supremacist order.

SIX

Demolition of
the Old Jim Crow Order

FOR A BRIEF MOMENT DURING WORLD WAR II, the March on Washington Movement (MOWM) placed Jim Crow employment policies and practices on the defensive. Although the Fair Employment Practices Committee (FEPC) lacked enforcement powers, its public hearings exposed the glaring contradiction between the nation's claim to be the dependable "arsenal of democracy" overseas and its practice of racial discrimination at home by firms holding lucrative government contracts. Even so, the government rejected grassroots appeals to transform the FEPC into a permanent agency to oversee racial equity issues in the postwar years. Consequently, postwar blacks built upon the lessons and momentum of the March on Washington Movement for "jobs and justice" and intensified challenges to the segregationist system. By 1970, the Modern Black Freedom struggle had demolished the Jim Crow order, established a new equal opportunity regime, and opened the door for significant changes in the lives of poor and working-class black families.

JIM CROW'S ADVANCE INTO THE POSTWAR ERA

Without the counterweight of the FEPC and the emergency of wartime mobilization, Jim Crow advanced into the postwar era and deepened the racially divided job and housing markets. In the mass production industries, where the interracial organized labor movement had gained its strongest foothold during the interwar years, collective bargaining agreements instituted departmental rather than plant-wide seniority systems. These labor-management agreements reinforced the racial job ceiling and concentrated black industrial workers in "dead-end job classifications" with little or no room for promotions into skilled, managerial, and professional occupations.[1]

Postwar technological changes and labor and race relations exposed black workers to the sharpest edges of downturns in the business cycle and the resulting harsh retrenchments of the workforce. The Ford Motor Company shifted all engine production from its River Rouge plant, the largest employer of black workers in the Detroit area, to its new automated facility in suburban Brook Park, near Cleveland, Ohio, and its new Dearborn plant outside Detroit. Employment at River Rouge plunged from eighty-five thousand workers at the end of World War II to only thirty thousand workers in 1960. The Michigan *Labor Market Letter* lamented the "creation of a very large and alarmingly consistent list of long-term unemployed" blacks in the city and state.[2]

Meatpacking firms, another huge employer of black industrial workers, closed dozens of old multistory plants in central cities across the urban Midwest. Meatpacking companies moved to large, modernized, single-story facilities in the all-white suburbs and surrounding countryside. The big four meat packers—Swift, Armour, Wilson, and Cudahy—eliminated twenty-one major plants between 1956 and 1965. In New York and other seaport cities, "containerization," a new mode of packing and shipping bulk goods, reduced the demand for manual labor and undercut black employment and union strength on the waterfront. Whereas during World War II, Brooklyn's all-black Local 968 had gained pier jurisdiction and improved the position of black longshoremen, the union now lost such jurisdiction, and by 1949, only about one hundred of its one thousand members reported regular jobs. "Negroes aren't hired to work until all white longshoremen are shaped up," Cleophus L. Jacobs, head of Local 968, reported.[3]

Thus, in the postwar years, for the first time in the nation's history, the unemployment of black men and women increased to double the rate of their white counterparts. In urban America, however, black unemployment nearly trebled the white rate, especially for teens and entry-level young workers 19–24 years of age. By the mid-1960s, in New York's Bedford-Stuyvesant neighborhood, black male unemployment reached 17 percent compared to 5 percent citywide.[4] Working-class black women found it even more difficult than black men to maintain wartime gains in the urban industrial economy. In June 1945, Josephine McCloudy, the only custodian on night shift at a Detroit-area Packard automobile plant, lost her job for seeking to use the company's white-only restroom; her UAW Local 190 representative refused to take up her case with management. In 1946, the R. Gesell Company, a cosmetics manufacturer in lower Manhattan, not only housed black and white women in two different buildings but systematically paid white women four or more dollars per week more than black women doing the same work. As noted by historian Jacqueline Jones, in 1950, 41 percent of black women worked in household jobs without the benefit of minimum wage and hours legislation, unemployment compensation, and social security benefits that prevailed in the unionized sector of the economy.[5]

The explosion of postwar government-funded housing, health, education, and transportation projects created a "golden age" for building and construction workers, bankers, and contractors, but black workers received few of the employment benefits of this expansive economic growth. The building trades were one of the most racially exclusionary sectors of the nation's postwar economy. By 1960, although blacks accounted for over 65 percent of all the nation's building trades laborers, plasterers, and cement finishers, few African Americans gained access to the skilled crafts as electricians, carpenters, brickmasons, and plumbers. In 1961, young African Americans made up less than 1 percent of all apprentices in New York City's extensive construction industry. Two years later, Philadelphia reported only one black craftsman, an electrician, among 7,300 members of local plumbers, electricians, and steamfitters' unions.[6]

The same story prevailed in other cities. One white Democratic Party leader explained to the *Pittsburgh Courier* the exclusion of blacks from skilled jobs on municipal projects: "No politician," he said, "wants [white] labor against him." In 1964, Pittsburgh recorded only one black apprentice bricklayer, operating engineer, and lather; two sheet-metal workers; three painters; and four carpenters. The *American Federationist,* the principal organ of the AFL-CIO after the two unions merged in 1955, concurred that white union–dominated apprenticeship programs discriminated against black workers and locked them out of "the income elite of manual labor."[7] In New York, Philadelphia, Pittsburgh, Chicago, Detroit, Los Angeles, and San Francisco, leading department stores—Kaufmann's; Sears, Roebuck; Gimbels; Horne's; and others—hired blacks primarily as stock room employees, cargo handlers, elevator operators, janitors, maids, and maintenance workers, arguing that white customers would not conduct business with black salespeople.[8]

The hardships and social struggles of urban black workers also continued to include racial barriers to where they could live, raise their families, and build institutions to serve their own needs. In 1948, when the U.S. Supreme Court outlawed restrictive housing covenants in the case of *Shelley v. Kraemer,* proponents of residential segregation swiftly created new racially exclusive private homeowner associations, repeating a process that had followed the earlier outlawing of residential segregation ordinances in 1917. Reaching about five hundred by 1962, homeowners associations mushroomed to twenty thousand a decade later.[9] Meanwhile, by the mid-1950s, according to the National Committee Against Discrimination in Housing, half of all new housing construction benefitted from government finances, but only 2 percent of such projects accepted African American residents. Abraham Levitt of Long Island, New York, and his sons William and Alfred transformed the housing market by applying mass-production techniques to new home construction projects in Pennsylvania, New Jersey, and New York. In Levitt lease contracts, tenants agreed "not to permit the premises to be used or occupied by any person other than members of the Caucasian race." The original leases not only barred blacks from buying or leasing but from visiting Levittown homes as guests.[10] The largest government-aided low-cost housing development in the nation, the Levittown development skillfully used legal agreements and binding contracts to build a racial wall around the housing market.

When such obstacles were insufficient to keep black families out, they were reinforced by intimidation and violence. In 1956, a spokesman for a Seattle neighborhood association appeared on the front lawn of a newly arrived black family. He boldly announced his instructions "to buy you people out." White residents of this community, he said, would not tolerate black neighbors.[11] When African Americans ignored such threats, most often they faced an escalating barrage of attacks on their homes and their families. In Philadelphia, historian John Bauman documented 213 housing-related racial incidents in the first six months of 1955 alone. These conflicts "reinforced an anti-black climate" that heightened the segregation of North Philadelphia's black community. New York City blacks reported violent reactions to their quests for housing in Flatbush, Greenwich Village, the Bronx, and Long Island. In Detroit, the most violent encounters occurred in the city's predominantly working-class neighborhoods on the Northeast Side, the Wyoming Corridor, and the Lower West Side. Similarly, according to the Chicago Commission on Race Relations, in the half decade after World War II, housing conflicts accounted for nearly three-fourths of all reported racial incidents, including the violent Park Manor Riots (1946), Airport Homes Riot (1946), Fernwood Riot (1947), Englewood Riot (1949), and Trumbull Park Homes Riots (1949–1954). In 1966, the Southern Christian Leadership Conference (SCLC) shifted its civil rights campaign to Chicago's segregated housing market; the Reverend Martin Luther King, Jr., later said of violent encounters on the city's west side, "I have never seen—even in Mississippi and Alabama—mobs as hostile and as hate-filled as I've seen in Chicago."[12]

Despite such widespread hostility against urban black neighborhoods, recent studies of Cleveland and Philadelphia suggest that violence was not an inevitable response to African American efforts to occupy homes in previously all-white communities. Based upon a systematic examination of housing policies and practices in Glenville, Mt. Pleasant, and Lee-Harvard, neighborhoods on the periphery but within the municipal boundaries of Cleveland, Ohio, historian Todd Michney concludes that African Americans confronted far less violence as they moved into these neighborhoods than they did in Chicago or Detroit. On the contrary, some of the neighborhoods' first southern-born middle- and working-class blacks purchased land through established federal mortgage financing arrangements with the aid of their white neighbors. Moreover, in one prominent case, when a group of whites organized a racially exclusionary homeowners association during the 1940s, another group of whites sided with African Americans and countered the movement. Still, each of these three communities became a predominantly black neighborhood during the 1950s and 1960s. In her recent study of the Mt. Airy neighborhood in Philadelphia's northwest side, historian Abigail Perkiss makes a similar point. She underscores how white Mt. Airy residents welcomed their new black neighbors and launched a vigorous movement to build a racially integrated community.[13]

While the hostility of white homeowners no doubt varied somewhat from place to place within and between cities, the African American encounter with the postwar housing market was on the whole an exceedingly violent process, partly because of the destructive impact of federal urban renewal programs on poor and working-class African American neighborhoods. By 1973, federal urban renewal programs had demolished some 2,500 neighborhoods and extended housing segregation in nearly 1,000 U.S. municipalities. Dubbed "Negro removal" by African American communities, these projects included Paradise Valley in Detroit; the Lower Hill District in Pittsburgh; the Chavez Ravine community in Los Angeles; and the historic West Oakland neighborhood in the Bay Area, to name only a few. As early as August 1949, black Bay Area resident Lola Bell Sims wrote to President Harry Truman expressing fear of displacement. "Just now here in Oakland," she said, "the colored people are much confused and very unhappy . . . thinking that they are going to lose their all and all by the U.S. government taking their property by force whether or not they want to give it up." Her fears were fully justified. In 1959, the Oakland Redevelopment Agency defined all of the predominantly black West Oakland neighborhood as blighted. The city council approved the plan for renewal and listed the African American community among the first sites scheduled for the bulldozer.[14]

Despite protests from black residents and civil rights organizations such as the NAACP, the city of Oakland demolished the West Oakland area to make way for commercial and industrial development. Twenty new industrial firms—including Mack Trucks, United States Plywood Corporation, and the California Packing Corporation—opened plants in the area. While a handful of former black residents gained entry level jobs in the new industries, the city had not erected a single new housing unit on the property by as late as 1969.[15] Similarly, in Pittsburgh, from the third-floor window of his building in the Hill District, artist Carlos Peterson later recalled the sight of the bulldozers moving into his neighborhood: "I was young and did not fully understand what was happening. I only knew this process was coming towards us. Coupled with the sense of personal loss of friends and neighborhood, this event had quite an influence on my life." Taminika Howze and other Hill District residents remembered "so well what was going on. I saw chunks of the Hill taken, destroyed, and in some places replaced with other structures."[16]

As old black neighborhoods were bulldozed, poor and working-class African Americans moved into public housing projects in rising numbers. Title II of the federal Housing Act of 1949 authorized the construction of 800,000 public housing units, but this and subsequent allotments proved insufficient to meet the needs of the increasing numbers of displaced residents. Nonetheless, by 1970, low-income public housing projects had become nationally known as symbols of residence for poor and working-class black communities: Cabrini-Green and Robert Taylor Homes in Chicago; Richard Allen and Johnson Homes in Philadelphia; Jeffries, Brewster, and Douglass Homes in Detroit; Bedford Dwellings, Addison Terrace, and Allequippa Terrace in Pittsburgh; and Pruitt-Igoe in St. Louis, to name a few. In the urban West, African Americans constituted the majority of public housing residents in the Bay Area cities of Oakland, Richmond, Vallejo, and Berkeley, while working-class whites moved increasingly into industrial suburbs like Milpitas, Fremont, and San Leandro. Before the end of World War II, public housing authorities had instituted racially integrated policies and moved African Americans, European Americans, and Latino/Latina Americans into such low-income housing projects as Hacienda Terrace in Los Angeles and Yesler Terrace in Seattle. These policies persisted into the postwar years in Seattle, while the Watts community in Los Angeles, one historian concludes, "became a dumping ground for public housing developments that were not welcome in other parts of Los Angeles."

Not everything about these housing projects was negative. In her recollections of Pittsburgh, Gail Austin remembered how her family had once occupied a building without hot running water. When Bedford Dwellings opened, she recalled, "We were happy to move there." Likewise, the Hill resident and later city councilman Sala Udin recalled how delighted his family was to move into the new public housing that contrasted greatly with his second-floor apartment at Fullerton and Epiphany Streets, which was "very old. . . . We were constantly having to turn out the lights because the light bill was too high. We would only turn up the heat just enough . . . to prevent frostbite because the heating bill was too high." African Americans expressed similar appreciation and praise for the new units elsewhere, but patterns of neglect soon emerged: lack of repairs, dysfunctional elevators, and inadequate garbage pickup and police protection.[17]

As urban renewal plans progressed, large numbers of uprooted black families also moved into previously all-white or predominantly white communities. While white flight certainly accounted for opening up spaces for the growing black population, African Americans also took a hand in gradually transforming increasing numbers of these neighborhoods into nearly all-black communities. In Chicago, South Side black residents gained access to new housing in "areas of transition" along the boundaries of Oakland, Kenwood, Hyde Park, and Woodlawn in the Cottage Grove Avenue area to the east, Park Manor and Englewood to the south and southwest, and North Lawndale on the west side. In Pittsburgh, black families moved from Lower Hill to the Upper Hill near downtown and to Homewood-Brushton and East Liberty in the city's East Side. In New York City, blacks spread out from Harlem into South Jamaica, Bedford-Stuyvesant, Brownsville, and other areas. In 1950, in Brownsville, African Americans made up 22 percent of the total population; by 1970, Brownsville's population had increased to 77 percent black and 19 percent Puerto Rican. The white population had decreased to only 4 percent of the total. At about the same time, African Americans gradually moved out of their neighborhoods in South Central Los Angeles and Watts into better housing in West Adams, Compton, and Leimert Park.[18]

As Jim Crow strengthened its hold on the postwar job and housing markets, urban black workers and their communities intensified their assaults on all aspects of the larger segregationist edifice. Although inspired by the national March on Washington Movement, postwar social struggles emerged out of the economy, politics, and history of labor and class relations at the local level. In December 1946, for example, the NAACP, the Urban League, the CIO, and the Pittsburgh Interracial Action Council (PIAC) converged on downtown Pittsburgh to protest the color line in department stores. After nearly two years of protests, the city's Retail Merchants Association (RMA) issued a nondiscrimination statement and promised to employ and upgrade black workers. A year later, black New Yorkers boycotted the White Tower restaurant chain in the Bedford-Stuyvesant area of Brooklyn. White Tower soon reversed its policy and hired African Americans, declaring that it no longer believed "Negroes aren't capable of being good countermen [and women]."[19]

Founded in 1948, a local chapter of the Congress of Racial Equality (CORE) transformed the border city of St. Louis with one of the earliest and most energetic interracial campaigns to end segregation in downtown restaurants. Although the organization nationally included veteran trade union activists who "regarded labor organizations as vehicles for social change beyond the workplace, including the area of race relations," the St. Louis chapter had a majority of middle-class "professionals with high educational and occupational status." Together they launched a militant movement to desegregate downtown restaurants and drugstore soda fountains in such establishments as the Stix, Baer, and Fuller Department Store; the Woolworth five and dime store; Sears and Roebuck; the Greyhound Bus terminal; and both the YMCA and YWCA. During the sit-ins at Stix, Baer, and Fuller in early 1949, urban and labor historian Clarence Lang notes, "the smartly dressed demonstrators often sat quietly the length of the day, occupying the silences with knitting, academic studies, or the Bible. These quiet hobbies and pursuits, much like the crisp, elegant clothes they wore, were part of a carefully orchestrated pageantry that asserted the demonstrators' middle class 'respectability' and cleverly aimed to shame white patrons. The silent protesters attracted onlookers from the shopping floor, and made the pages of the *American* and *Argus*."[20] Though the city's white dailies and newly elected mayor largely ignored these early efforts, which dissipated without achieving substantial results, they provided a model that would later inform the Greensboro, North Carolina, student sit-ins of 1960.

Other groups took on employment discrimination. In the spring of 1960, black Philadelphians launched renewed Don't Buy Where You Can't Work boycotts to force discriminatory companies to change their racial hiring policies and practices. Under the leadership of the Baptist minister Rev. Leon Sullivan, Philadelphians formed a new organization, called 400 [Black] Ministers, and demanded jobs at such disparate firms as Tastykake Baking Company, Gulf Oil, and Sun Oil, as well as local ice cream parlors, supermarkets, and newspaper companies. By mid-June, the organization identified the popular Philadelphia-based Tastykake Baking Company as its first target and presented Tastykake with a straightforward list of five demands: the upgrade of three black substitute drivers to full-time salesmen-drivers, employment of additional salesmen-drivers "in the near future," placement of two black women on the company's clerical and professional staff, equal promotion opportunities for black women in the production department and termination of racially segregated locker rooms for female employees, and "a written policy of nondiscrimination in employment assignments in all departments."[21]

After nearly three months of "selective patronage," as they called their boycott to elude antiboycott laws, 400 Ministers announced victory on Sunday, August 7. Tastykake met all their demands, and the boycott was over. Rev. Leon Sullivan later recalled that "black people were walking ten feet tall in the streets of Philadelphia." In the fall of 1962, SCLC invited Sullivan to Atlanta to explain his program of corporate boycotts in Philadelphia, which inspired the formation of SCLC's Operation Breadbasket. Sullivan told the ministers "how to select target firms, request statistics on black employment statistics from them, and recommend specific improvements to the companies if their opportunities for blacks were inadequate. He also stressed that the ministers should ask their constituents to boycott the firm if those recommendations were not accepted." Under the leadership of Ralph Abernathy, Atlanta ministers immediately launched boycotts against two food-processing firms before year's end.[22]

Postwar social justice movements included ongoing efforts to merge labor struggles with the broader, multifaceted goals of the modern civil rights movement. Meeting in Chicago in 1951, black workers had formed the National Negro Labor Council (NNLC) under the leadership of radical labor activist William R. Hood. Inspired by the internationalist labor and class ideology of the Communist Party but disenchanted with the growing conservatism of the CIO in light of Cold War repression of radical ideas and social movements, the NNLC soon opened thirty-five branches in cities across the urban North and West. The organization insisted that black people, particularly black workers, define and lead the movement for the economic and political emancipation of African Americans and people of African descent. Hood and the NNLC nonetheless repeatedly articulated unity with white workers as well as "freedom for the darker people of America and independence for the darker people of the world."[23]

At the same time, a small group of radical black communist and noncommunist women—Claudia Jones, Louise Thompson Patterson, and others—both challenged and reinforced the early postwar agenda of the Communist Party. In 1951, they formed the militant Sojourners for Truth and Justice organization. Sent out in September, "A Call to Negro Women" urged black women to meet in Washington, DC, to demand "unconditional redress of grievances" by the president, the Justice Department, the State Department, and Congress. The organization underscored its particular concerns with the interests of working-class black women when it met in the facilities of the CIO-affiliated Cafeteria Workers Union between September 29 and October 1.

Both the Sojourners and the NNLC collapsed by 1956 under a barrage of Cold War–inspired attacks, including the vigorous opposition of black anti-Communist labor leader A. Philip Randolph, the CIO, and the FBI. Along with black men like W. E. B. Du Bois, Paul Robeson, and others, radical black women activists were victims of McCarthy-era suppression of human and civil rights, including the deportation of Caribbean-born Claudia Jones from the country in 1955. The FBI compiled over 450 pages of surveillance notes on the Sojourners within a year of initiating a watch on the group.[24]

The Negro American Labor Council (NALC), formed in 1961, succeeded the NNLC. Under Randolph's leadership, the new organization helped to bridge African American labor struggles and the nonviolent direct action movement for equal rights in all aspects of American and African American life. The NALC also advanced its own transnational agenda for black workers' struggles. As early as 1952, Randolph and other anti-communist black labor leaders, including the influential international black labor activist Maida Springer, had articulated the need for a "world congress of Negro workers" that would combat "both colonialism and communism" at home and abroad. Maida Springer played a major role in these efforts. In 1945, as a participant in a "labor exchange trip to England," Springer became known as the "first Negro woman to represent American labor abroad." During the

1950s, she travelled widely across Europe and Africa as a spokesperson for the AFL and later the AFL-CIO. She built extensive connections with labor movements in the United States, Europe, and Africa. In 1960, her international labor activism on behalf of black and white workers in the United States and abroad culminated in her appointment as the AFL-CIO international affairs representative. Springer had a profound impact on AFL-CIO policy toward the labor movement in decolonizing Africa and in Cold War America.[25]

Springer's career was emblematic of black women's growing leadership role in the labor movement. In Chicago, for example, working-class black women like Mississippi-born Addie Wyatt shaped the city's labor and municipal politics. Wyatt, an ordained minister and cofounder of the city's Vernon Park Church of God, took her first job as a canner in the city's meatpacking industry during World War II. She also moved into the city's Altgeld Gardens public housing project with her husband and became the first black woman elected president of Local 56 of the United Packinghouse Workers of America during the 1950s.[26]

Under the growing impact of local activism as well as the emergence of national labor and civil rights organizations, African American workers and their communities marched on banks, utility companies, government agencies, and building and construction firms as well as hotel, restaurant, and grocery chains. On a national scale, these movements converged at the nation's capital during the famous March on Washington for Jobs and Freedom, which produced Martin Luther King's renowned "I Have a Dream" speech. In his recent study of the 1963 march and the struggle for economic equality, historian Will Jones accents the abiding connection between the earlier MOWM fight for both labor and civil rights and the 1960s march for jobs and freedom.[27]

While the groundswell of popular support for the March on Washington sprang from local conditions, the national march in turn reinforced activism at the municipal level. In the wake of the 1963 march, activists in San Diego, San Francisco, Los Angeles, Pittsburgh, New York, St. Louis, and other cities intensified pressure on downtown and neighborhood banks, public utilities, grocery chains, retail outlets, and public schools, among numerous other public and private institutions pursuing racially discriminatory employment, training, and education policies.[28] Within days of the March on Washington for Jobs and Freedom, the St. Louis chapter of CORE spearheaded a grassroots boycott of the city's chief financial institution, the Jefferson Bank and

This young protester was participating in a mass demonstration for equal employment opportunities at Pittsburgh's new downtown Civic Arena during the 1960s. Courtesy, Charles "Tennie" Harris Collection, Carnegie Museum of Art, Pittsburgh, PA, photo #2001.35.7071.

Trust Company. Predominantly working-class activists urged Jefferson Bank to hire no fewer than thirty-one African Americans in sales, clerk, and teller jobs within a two-week period. When bank spokesmen rejected the ultimatum, CORE leaders authorized pickets at the bank and resolved to defy any court injunction on their activities and go to jail if necessary. Authorities soon arrested nineteen activists for their role in organizing the campaign, which developed into a broad "general strike" against the major corporate employers in the city. Demonstrators converged on the St. Louis Land Clearance and Housing Authority, conducted a sit-in at the office of the city treasurer, and staged a mass rally at City Hall to halt bank deposits. Protesters carried signs urging municipal authorities to "remove city money from Jim Crow banks." In November, the protest picked up cross-class support when a coalition of ministers declared, "This fight is no longer CORE's fight" and supported a two-day consumer boycott of downtown stores. Unlike its early postwar effort, this time CORE emerged victorious: in March 1964, the Jefferson Bank and fourteen other financial institutions finally conceded and hired over thirty-five black employees.[29]

By the mid-1960s, the black freedom struggle underwent another transformation. The escalating influence of the Nation of Islam, the outbreak of violence in the streets of poor and working-class black neighborhoods, and the spread of the antiwar movement fueled the increasing movement of Black Power from the periphery to the center of the Modern Black Freedom Movement. In her recent synthesis of scholarship on the Black Power struggle, historian Rhonda Williams not only excavates what she calls "the era of expansive Black Power" from the mid-1960s through the late 1970s but also underscores the deep roots of this movement for "self-determination" and "nationhood" in the politics of the early twentieth century: "race pride, militant cultural aesthetics, assertions of dignity that brooked no white counsel, black economic radicalism, self-defense, expressions of black manhood, proto-black feminism, and black nationalism and internationalism were all there" before the end of World War II.[30]

Founded during the 1930s under the leadership of Elijah Muhammad, the Nation of Islam emphasized liberating the minds, culture, and bodies of black people for the new black nation. Beginning with only four temples at the end of World War II, the Nation grew to fifty temples in twenty-eight cities across twenty-two states and the District of Columbia by the early 1960s. Following his release from prison in 1952, Malcolm X emerged as the Nation's most forceful and persuasive young minister. He not only helped to organize temples in Boston and Philadelphia but also spearheaded the transformation of New York City's small Temple No. 7 into a major force in the Nation and the city. Membership at the Harlem Temple jumped from one thousand in 1946 to ten thousand before Malcom's death in 1965.[31]

Before his assassination in New York City's Audubon Ballroom in February 1965, Malcolm had inspired the movement toward black pride, armed self-defense, and unity with African people around the globe. Following his lead, rising numbers of activists and intellectuals conceptual-

Women stood firmly behind the sanitation strikers at a mass rally at Clayborn Temple on 28 March 1968, who would take to the streets bearing the slogan "I Am a Man" the next day. Courtesy, Sanitation Strike, Special Collections, University of Memphis.

ized the black urban community as an occupied colony of the imperialist United States and, as historians Donna Murch and Robert Self note, they turned to the "global uprisings against colonial rule, from Algiers to Prague, Luanda to Hanoi" and to Cuba, China, and Vietnam as fresh new models for advancing the African American freedom struggle beyond the confines of the earlier nonviolent direct action movement.[32] In the months and years after Malcolm's death, the outbreaks of violence in black urban communities reinforced the black nationalist agenda. Between 1964 and 1968, violence erupted in over one hundred cities, including New York, Los Angeles, Chicago, Cleveland, Newark, Detroit, Pittsburgh, and Washington, DC.[33] Moreover, by the late 1960s and early 1970s, as historian Kimberley Phillips shows, a determined group of black war resisters had helped to shape and reshape the civil rights struggle into an "antiwar freedom movement."[34] Before his death in 1968, partly under the increasing influence of the emerging Black Power and antiwar movements, Martin Luther King had also sharpened his focus on the interrelationship between poverty, the fate of black workers, and the Vietnam War. In his 1967 speech at the Riverside Church in New York, King declared, "I have watched the [poverty] program broken and eviscerated as if it were some idle political plaything of a society

On 29 March 1968, following the eruption of violence the previous day, sanitation strikers and a white sympathizer march through downtown Memphis in the face of National Guardsmen. Courtesy, Sanitation Strike, Special Collections, University of Memphis.

gone mad on war". A year later, King was assassinated in Memphis before leading a march of striking sanitation workers, while he was in the midst of organizing the Poor People's Campaign.[35]

Even more than the earlier phase of the Modern Black Freedom struggle, the Black Power movement was deeply anchored in poor and working-class black urban communities. Historian Robyn C. Spencer describes the movement for Black Power simply as "a response to the crises and opportunities in working-class black America in the 1960s and 1970s." In 1966, Huey P. Newton and Bobby Seale, students at Oakland's Merritt College, founded the Black Panther Party (BPP) for Self Defense. The BPP incorporated the Nation of Islam's Wants and Beliefs into the party's Ten-Point Program for the attainment of armed self-defense, political control of the black community, economic independence, and institutional and cultural autonomy, but it was fundamentally rooted in the culture, economy, and politics of the Bay Area black community. West Coast cities like Oakland had experienced their most explosive black population growth during the second wave of the Great Migration. Increasing numbers of Oakland blacks gained jobs in the shipbuilding industry, but they occupied jobs with few opportunities for upward mobility. At the same time, like blacks in other major metropolitan areas, Bay Area blacks confronted increasing residential segregation, inequality in the schools, displacement by urban renewal, and police brutality.[36]

Although the BPP recruited across class lines within the black community and expressed a commitment to building interracial alliances with "progressive" or "radical" white organizations, it emphasized recruitment among poor and working-class urbanites, including what party members called the "lumpenproletariat," the most dispossessed segment of the black working class, such as long-term unemployed blacks and participants in the informal or illegal economy of prostitution, drug dealing, and fencing of stolen goods. In addition to launching armed community patrols to monitor interactions between blacks and police and prevent police brutality, the BPP established liberation schools, free health clinics, and free breakfast programs. In early 1967, the Black Panther Party gained national attention when an armed contingent of members arrived at the state capitol in Sacramento to protest both the recent killing of a black youth by Richmond police and a proposed California gun-control law. Following this episode, young recruits swelled the ranks of the party over the next three years to over forty chapters and five thousand members in the major metropolitan areas of the nation.[37]

Though it began as a local organization, inspired by broader currents of political thought and action, by decade's end the BPP had become a national and international force, and its militant call for Black Power could be heard around the globe. Along with influencing Latino, Puerto Rican, and Native American groups like the Brown Berets, the Young Lords, and the American Indian Movement,[38] the Black Panther Party inspired similar movements in such diverse countries as the United Kingdom, Israel, Australia, and India. The Dalit Panthers, formed by a group of young Dalits in Bombay in 1972, declared its connection to the U.S. party in its manifesto: "Due to the hideous plot of American imperialism ... the Black Panther movement grew. From the Black Panthers, Black Power emerged. ... We claim a close relationship with this struggle." In New Zealand, the Polynesian Panther Party adopted the U.S. Black Panther Party's Ten-Point Program and clearly articulated the ideas of Huey Newton and Malcolm X: "We cannot have black and white unity until we have black unity." For a brief moment in Israel as well, a U.S.-inspired Panther movement emerged during the early 1970s. Targeting discrimination and inequality at the hands of Ashkenazi elites, the Israeli Panthers aimed to mobilize Israelis of North African or Middle Eastern descent. According to historian Oz Frankel, poor and unemployed second-generation immigrants from Morocco dominated the ranks of the short-lived Israeli Panthers.[39]

Although the Oakland-based BPP emerged as the most prominent symbol of the revolutionary Black Power movement during the 1960s and 1970s, numerous grassroots black nationalist organizations and movements emerged in other industrial cities with slightly different but overlapping labor and working-class histories. In Detroit, the auto industry would become an organizing base for the city's most radical and popular expression of Black Power. Beginning in 1967, a cohort of black radicals (most notably John Williams, Luke Tripp, and Mike Hamlin) established a new publication, the *Inner City Voice,* following the outbreak of violence in the city. The editors immediately sought contacts with black autoworkers and encouraged their organization in conjunction with ongoing community-based organizing. When Chrysler fired activist General Baker, four other black men, and two white women for participating in a wildcat strike, Baker joined Marian Kramer, Chuck Wooten, and eight other black men and formed the Dodge Revolutionary Union Movement (DRUM) in May 1968. Within a short period of time, according to historian Heather Thompson notes, "DRUM-like groups sprang up almost overnight: JARUM, FORUM, ELRUM, CADRUM, CHRYRUM, FRUM, and UP-RUM."[40]

The revolutionary black union movement also spread to auto plants in New Jersey and Georgia, as well as into sectors outside the auto industry, including transit workers in Chicago and New York, the United Steelworkers union, the Building Service Employees International union, and the American Federation of Teachers. In 1969, revolutionary black unionists formed the League of Revolutionary Black Workers (LRBW) to coordinate their activities. While the league acknowledged the significance of working-class unity across racial lines, it proclaimed the primacy of organizing black workers into a united front with each other and with "students, intellectuals, and community residents." In its constitution, black workers declared their "sole objective is to break the bonds of white racist control over the lives and destiny of black workers. . . . Membership is denied to all honkies due to the fact that said honky has been the historical enemy, betrayer, and exploiter of black people. Any relationship that we enter into with honkies will be only on the basis of coalition over [specific] issues." The LRBW also supported the employment of armed force if necessary. At a DRUM fund-raising raffle in November 1968, the "first prize offered was a new M-1 rifle, the second prize was a new shotgun, while the third prize was a bag of groceries and a turkey."[41]

The success of these Black Power groups was perceived as a major threat by the U.S. government. In the wake of the Detroit Riot of 1967, the FBI launched more intense investigations and intimidation of black activists, particularly those associated with the emerging Black Power movement. In August 1967, according to the new counterintelligence program known as COINTELPRO, the FBI aimed "to expose, disrupt, misdirect, discredit, or otherwise neutralize the activities of black nationalist, hate-type organizations and groupings, their leadership, spokesmen, membership, and supporters, and to counter their propensity for violence and civil disorder." In March 1968, the FBI instructed agents to "prevent the rise of a 'messiah' who would unify, and electrify, the militant black nationalist movement." Among all black nationalist groups, the FBI defined the Black Panther Party as "the greatest threat to the internal security of the country." The BPP soon became the target of 233 of the agency's aggressive actions against radical groups. It was the object of more raids than any other organization defined as "subversive" in the bureau's history. Deborah Johnson (now known as Akua Njeri), the girlfriend of slain Chicago party leader Fred Hampton, later recalled, "I think everyone that was in the Black Panther Party kind of understood—it was a given—that you would have wiretaps, that we would be followed, that we would be harassed, locked up, even beaten [or killed] by the police."[42]

As the government stepped up surveillance of activist black civil rights and Black Power organizations, inter- and intraracial conflicts increasingly fragmented the Modern Black Freedom Movement. The FBI claimed credit for the growing friction between Oakland headquarters of the BPP and its Southern California, New York, and overseas units. In Los Angeles, violence broke out between the black nationalist organization US and the Black Panther Party in 1969 and 1970, resulting in the shooting deaths of two BPP members. During the spread of internal dissension among black nationalist groups, the FBI enthusiastically reported that "the chaotic conditions of the Black Panther Party leaders Huey P. Newton and Eldridge Cleaver is possibly a direct result of our intensive counterintelligence efforts."[43]

Apart from assaults by the FBI, the nonviolent direct action and Black Power phases of the Modern Black Freedom Movement also faced internal conflicts. A substantial body of scholarship underscores the emergence of deep ideological, class, and gender divisions in the movement.[44] Though the widely disseminated sexist ideas of Eldridge Cleaver and Stokely Carmichael have invigorated a large body of critical writings on the Black Power movement in general and the Black Panther Party in particular, a more complicated portrait of gender dynamics within the Black Power movement has emerged in recent years. Studies by Rhonda Williams, Tracye Matthews, Kimberly Springer, and others show that gender relations evolved over time within black nationalist organizations. "Ideas about gender and gender roles," Matthews writes, "were far from static within the BPP. . . . Some women and men in the Party challenged characterization of the struggle as one solely for the redemption of Black manhood and worked within its constraints to serve the interests of the entire community." Across all facets of the Modern Black Freedom Movement, black women mobilized their numbers, created new organizations, and demanded a viable voice in the ongoing work of African American liberation.[45] Moreover, black women activists such as Ella Baker not only helped to bridge the generational and ideological divides within the movement but also facilitated the rise of a more radical interracial alliance of black and white activists. When Baker returned to New York City following an extensive stay in the South, she soon helped to organize a National Committee to Free Angela Davis and All Political Prisoners as the Black Power movement accelerated.[46]

Despite internal fragmentation, and government surveillance and suppression of militant black political organizations, the Modern Black Freedom Movement demolished the Jim Crow order and improved the material, social, and political position of black workers and their communities. As sociologist Bart Landry noted, the gains of the Modern Black Freedom struggle reached "far down into the neighborhoods and homes" of the black working class as well as the middle class.[47] Between 1954 and 1968, the U.S. Supreme Court's *Brown v. Board of Education* decision and the Civil Rights Acts of 1964, 1965, and 1968 established the foundation for the emergence of a new equal opportunity regime. By the early 1970s, the high court sanctioned "color consciousness–affirmative action" in employment and education programs, mandated steps to dismantle separate and unequal schools for black children, and demanded timetables for achieving proportional representation of blacks in skilled, white collar, and professional jobs in firms with government contracts.[48]

In 1972, the federal government approved the Philadelphia Plan, which established "numerical goals and timetables" for the integration of blacks and other minorities into the building and construction trades. Federal courts not only upheld the plan but sanctioned its application to "government contractors in all areas of service and supply throughout the country." The U.S. Justice Department also spearheaded the landmark AT&T and U.S. Steel consent decrees, which paid punitive monetary damages to women and minorities for past discrimination. According to one study, the AT&T case "marked a new stage in EEO enforcement and induced the EEOC and other government agencies in the equal employment field not only to adopt a more aggressive attitude but also to seek punitive money damages as a regular course of action." The Bell system increased its black workforce, mainly in New York City, Philadelphia, Detroit, Chicago, and Los Angeles, from 4.3 percent of all employees in 1963 to nearly 10 percent in 1970.

In the South, African Americans also finally gained access to the heretofore almost exclusively white textile industry. Until the 1960s, those few African Americans who worked in the southern textile industry had occupied only the lowest-paid general laborer or household service occupations rather than production, supervisory, or clerical positions. In the case of *Sledge v. J. P. Stevens* (1978), a federal court found the firm, the South's second-largest textile manufacturer, "guilty of systematic [racial] discrimination in its hiring practices" and ordered the equal employment and promotion of black workers. Under the impact of such rulings, African Americans increased from only about 5 percent of southern textile workers during the 1960s to about a quarter of the labor force by the early 1980s. In the state of South Carolina alone, the number of black women in textile jobs increased from only about 250 to over 8,000.[49]

In 1960, only 13 percent of all African Americans occupied middle-class positions. Ten years later, the percentage had nearly doubled, rising to nearly 26 percent. Between 1964 and 1969, black median family income rose from $5,921 to $8,074, which represented a gain in the ratio of black to white income from 54 to 61 percent. The percentage of black people living below the poverty line dropped from 48 to about 28 percent in the decade 1959 to 1969, and the unemployment rate of nonwhite men, primarily African Americans, also declined from 7.2 percent during the early 1960s to 2.5 percent by decade's end. Meanwhile, increasing black suburbanization signaled the opening of new and better housing for some black residents. Between World War II and 1960, the number of black suburbanites rose from 1.5 to 2.0 million people. Another 3.5 million blacks moved to the suburbs during the 1960s and 1970s. Suburbanization of blacks now proceeded at a faster rate than that of whites.[50]

CONCLUSION

By the late 1960s and early 1970s, the Modern Black Freedom struggle had dismantled the segregationist system. Significant numbers of blacks from poor and working-class families moved into middle-class, business, and professional occupations as well as skilled and supervisory jobs in the industrial sector. Fueled by the increasing grassroots mobilization of African American workers and their communities, the struggle against Jim Crow inspired a host of other liberation movements among diverse ethnic and nationality groups as well as women at home and abroad. Yet, the collapse of the white supremacist edifice coincided with the decline of the manufacturing economy, the resurgence of conservatism in U.S. politics, and the fall of the black urban industrial working class by the turn of the twenty-first century. Government repression of social justice movements, grassroots white opposition to equal opportunity programs, and rising levels of unemployment and poverty unraveled the lives and livelihoods of industrial black workers and their families. As we will see in chapter 7, these destructive social processes would also precipitate a spirited search for new and more effective strategies for social change as the twentieth century slipped away.

SEVEN

Demise of the Industrial Working Class

THE MODERN BLACK FREEDOM MOVEMENT dismantled the segregationist system. But a relentless long-term process of deindustrialization and
resistance to the democratization of American society unraveled the socioeconomic and political foundation of the new equal-opportunity regime. By
the turn of the new century, these global changes had eclipsed the black
urban industrial working class and precipitated a growing shift from grassroots social movements to electoral politics as the most promising mode of
political struggle in the wake of Jim Crow's demise.

Deindustrialization had deep roots in the years after World War II, but the
loss of manufacturing jobs accelerated and played out during the final decades
of the twentieth century, when plant closings and layoffs dominated headline
news on the health and welfare of the city, state, and nation. On Thanksgiving
Day 1979, the *New York Times* reported U.S. Steel Corporation's plans to
close fourteen steel facilities in eight states. But it was not only steel that was
laying off rising numbers of workers. Meatpacking, automobile, and other
mass-production industries were also hastening the demise of the manufacturing economy. As joblessness spread, increasing numbers of workers registered the painful impact of deindustrialization on their lives.

During the early 1980s, in Chicago, an employed 25-year-old, unmarried
father sympathized with the city's unemployed young men: "I know a lot of
guys that's my age, they don't work and I know some that works temporary,
but wanna work, they just can't get the jobs. You know, they got a high school
diploma." Later in the same decade, Ottie Davis, a resident of Chicago's
Robert Taylor Homes, discussed the paucity of jobs in the Windy City:
"People was messed up, wasn't no work.... I remember because a lot of us
couldn't find nothing, I mean nothing, and we ain't even had no families."[1]

Against this painful backdrop of economic decline, black workers and their communities forged a new politics that would profoundly shape city, state, and nation as the twentieth century came to a close.

DECLINE OF THE MANUFACTURING SECTOR

From New York to Los Angeles, the black urban industrial working class nearly disappeared by the early 1990s. Between 1967 and 1987, the manufacturing sector declined by 64 percent in Philadelphia, 60 percent in Chicago, 58 percent in New York, and 51 percent in Detroit. In other words, Philadelphia lost 160,000 manufacturing jobs; Chicago, 326,000; New York, over 500,000; and Detroit, 108,000. These losses took their most destructive toll on the lives of black workers. Further, both established U.S. manufacturing firms and foreign-affiliated companies selected job sites far from large urban black communities for new production facilities. The proportion of jobs in inner-city Detroit decreased from nearly 60 percent of all metropolitan-area employment during the 1970s to only 21 percent by 1990. In the brief period between 1978 and 1981, a cluster of eight companies accounted for the loss of 18,000 jobs in Los Angeles. Uniroyal, U.S. Steel, Ford, and Pabst Brewing, among other Southern California employers, not only closed significant numbers of manufacturing plants but transferred over three hundred firms from South Central Los Angeles to new suburban locations such as South Bay and northern Orange County. In Chicago, according to sociologist William J. Wilson, none of the city's other ethnic group men endured such a steep decline in manufacturing employment as did African American men. Altogether, black workers dropped from a peak of about 25 percent of the nation's workforce in 1980 to just over 10 percent as the new century got under way.[2]

Although the story of deindustrialization is told almost exclusively from the vantage point of the urban North and West, it was also partly a southern story as well. Similar to steel and other mass-production industries employing large numbers of black workers, the predominantly southern textile industry lost over 500,000 jobs between 1980 and 1994. Thousands of black workers lost jobs in the wake of the textile industry's collapse.

The impact of deindustrialization on African American communities did vary somewhat from city to city. As manufacturing jobs dissipated in Chicago, New York, and Los Angeles, significant numbers of young black men and women found employment in new, largely low-wage retail trade and service occupations, along with Euro-Americans, Latinos/Latinas, and Asian American workers. In metropolitan Detroit, however, large suburban shopping malls like the Northland Shopping Center in Oakland County deprived Motor City residents of a large and vibrant retail base, capable of employing an expanding number of low-wage service workers. Meanwhile, African Americans in Boston benefitted from that city's early economic turnaround, in contrast to their counterparts in other cities undergoing deindustrialization and economic restructuring. Starting the decade of the 1980s with family incomes below the national average for blacks, Boston's African Americans— nearly a third of whom were immigrants from Caribbean and African countries—increased their household incomes by 40.2 percent (slightly higher than the growth in all Boston incomes) between 1980 and 1990. Boston registered the nation's largest increase in income for blacks during that period, while black family income dropped by 15 percent in such major industrial cities as Detroit and Pittsburgh. In the Greater Boston Social Survey, economists Barry Bluestone and Mary Stevenson also found that 86.2 percent of Boston's black men with only a high school education reported being in the labor force, a slightly higher proportion than that of white men (82.7 percent), though somewhat lower than that of Hispanic men (87.2 percent). Thus, according to Bluestone and Stevenson, Boston did not have the "jobless ghetto" that scholars had documented in other deindustrializing cities.[3]

Still, despite significant differences from city to city, high rates of unemployment and low and inadequate incomes in new service-sector jobs underlay the spread of poverty across black urban America. In the central city, African American poverty increased by 74 percent, rising from 3.1 million to 5.4 million people between 1969 and 1982, while inner-city whites living in poverty rose by 52 percent (from 9.7 to 14.5 million). In 1990, according to a massive study of urban inequality in four major U.S. cities, African Americans in Detroit had the highest poverty rate at 33 percent, compared to 20 percent in Los Angeles, Boston, and Atlanta.[4] Predominantly black urban public housing projects—Broadhead Manor, Northview Heights, and St. Clair Village in Pittsburgh; Columbia Point (later Harbor Point) and Franklin Field in Boston; and Cabrini-Green and Robert Taylor Homes in Chicago—reported the highest incidence of poverty, crack cocaine, and gang- and drug-related street violence. The Robert Taylor Homes, Chicago's single largest housing project, housed only 0.5 percent of the city's total population but accounted for an estimated 9–11 percent of reported aggravated assaults, rapes, and murders. Similarly, according to Chicago Police Department reports, "In a nine-week period beginning in early January 1981, ten Cabrini-Green residents were murdered; thirty-five were wounded by gunshots, including random sniping; and more than fifty firearms were confiscated, 'the tip of an immense illegal arsenal.'"[5]

Older public housing residents repeatedly contrasted the late twentieth century with earlier, more hopeful times in the projects. One resident underscored the changing social environment of Robert Taylor Homes after she had raised thirteen children and sent them to college: "Things are different now, things are tense now. The young people have nothing to do. No jobs. No recreation. So they are rowdy. They don't go to school. They make trouble." Another resident tired of the emphasis on gangs, violence, and drugs given the general deterioration of project living: "Everything was about gangs, that's all you heard about.... There were people ain't had no sink or hot water for months. What about that?" Such conditions were not limited to housing projects. In Groveland, a middle-class black neighborhood on Chicago's South Side, Anna Morris lamented the toll the changing environment took on her 19-year-old daughter, Neisha, and her boyfriends: "She lost two boyfriends. And she really took this last one hard.... This last one, Sugar, we just buried.... They done lost ten friends already. Close friends too."[6]

Meanwhile, new forms of intraracial class conflict emerged. One substantial symbolic expression of these conflicts was the ongoing fight over the lyrics of the new rap and hip-hop music (particularly images of violence against women) and its cultural impact on a young generation of urban blacks. When a federal appellate judge ruled that rap lyrics were not obscene and therefore not subject to governmental censure, middle-class black leaders like C. Delores Tucker of Philadelphia, Carol Mosley Braun of Chicago, and Jesse Jackson demanded a U.S. congressional hearing to look into the matter and take steps to curtail such music. During the congressional hearings in 1994, Ed Lover, a cohost of *Yo, MTV Raps,* underscored the class divide it illustrated. In his view, leading political and civil rights leaders were out of touch with the urban poor. Lover praised hip-hop artist Luther Campbell for "being on the ground level and grassroots of this community," while sharply criticizing middle-class black leaders. "You're never in the projects, you're never in the hood," Lover said. For their part, black women rappers and other women involved with hip-hop culture resented their portrayal in the media as well as in the lyrics of some hip-hop music, but they were largely silent during the public controversy over lyrics in rap music. According to Tricia Rose, a leading scholar of black popular culture, these women did not want the sexism against black women to become a weapon in unjust racist attacks on black men.[7]

At the same time, black urban neighborhoods became increasingly targeted by well-coordinated and aggressive campaigns against crime. Spurred by passage of the federal Comprehensive Crime Control Act of 1985, national, state, and local authorities soon employed new legal mechanisms such as mandatory sentencing for certain offenses, particularly those involving the use and sale of illegal substances. The government's war on crime resulted in the arrest, conviction, and incarceration of increasing numbers of young black men between the ages of 18 and 30. Driven by the war on drugs and the fear of violence within African American urban communities, the prison-industrial complex expanded to accommodate growing numbers of poor and working-class black inmates. By 1990, a Washington, DC–based National Sentencing Project study revealed that the number of young black men ages 20–29 "under the control of the criminal justice system" was greater than the number of all African American men enrolled in the nation's colleges and universities. In 1999, for example, in Illinois, just under a thousand black men received bachelor's degrees from state institutions of higher education, while the following year the state released some seven thousand young African American men from prison for drug offenses alone.[8]

The war on drugs took a huge toll on the lives of young black men, their families, and their communities. In her analysis of early twenty-first-century black life, Michelle Alexander emphasized the escalating problems of the criminalized black youth and young adults as the linchpin of a new Jim Crow. But this trend unfolded in conjunction with broader social and political movements that undercut the livelihood of the gradually expanding black middle class as well as poor and working-class blacks. Nationwide, grassroots white opposition to equal-opportunity employment, housing, and education programs for black people intensified. As numerous policy analysts have noted, by the late 1990s, public policy makers "increasingly devolved, privatized, and dismantled" the national welfare state. Government agencies, employers, realtors, and school officials developed new, more subtle and not-so-subtle mechanisms for sidestepping equal-opportunity initiatives in employment, housing, education, and social welfare programs. As early as 1978, white workers and middle-class property owners joined forces to pass Proposition 13 in California. This measure cut taxes that supported social welfare services and stimulated the rapid spread of the "tax revolt" across the country. In 1996, California voters again helped to lead the fight against the civil rights agenda when voters approved Proposition 209. Known as the California Civil Rights Initiative, Proposition 209 aimed to completely dismantle the state's affirmative action programs for minorities and women.[9]

Dual attacks on affirmative action programs and social welfare services continued through the turn of the century, increasingly restricting the opportunities for poor and working-class blacks. In 1981, the U.S. Congress passed the Omnibus Budgetary Reconciliation Act, which curtailed eligibility for federal programs and cut federal support for local social welfare services, including health care. Later, in 1996, Democratic president Bill Clinton signed into law the Republican-sponsored Personal Responsibility and Work Opportunity Reconciliation Act (PRWORA). The new welfare law emphasized "personal self-sufficiency" over the "entitlements and income maintenance" approaches sanctioned by the earlier New Deal order. Beginning during Ronald Reagan's first administration during the early 1980s, the federal government had also cut the affirmative action enforcement powers of the Office of Federal Contract Compliance (OFCC) and the Equal Employment Opportunity Commission (EEOC). Although some large corporate employers expressed support for the federal affirmative action mandate, they welcomed and took advantage of the latitude to craft their own largely voluntary diversity initiatives. In Philadelphia, the welfare rights activist Roxanne Jones decried the welfare cuts as "human genocide," coming as they did on the heels of the "cold winter we went through, people freezing to death, and not having enough money to pay their fuel bills." In his analysis of changes in social services, political scientist David O. Sears concluded, "Racial prejudice, along with general political ideology, had the largest total effect on support for the tax revolt and was also a strong predictor of preferences for smaller government."[10]

Closely aligned with deindustrialization and the dismantling of the social service state was the end of the great African American south-to-north labor migration. During the 1970s, after nearly a century of steady movement out of the rural South, the tide of black population movement turned southward again.[11] Rather than returning to the rural South, however, most northern and western returnees, their children, and grandchildren moved to the expanding urban South. During the 1970s alone, southern nonagricultural employment jumped by 46 percent. This growth reflected over a million manufacturing jobs added at the same time that many northeastern and midwestern industries closed their doors—some of them, of course, relocating to the sunbelt South and Southwest. In his epic synthesis of black population movements, historian Ira Berlin notes that the new southern migrants and returnees worked in offices, shops, and factories of the urban South and "navigated the streets and alleys of the inner city." In February 1978, for the first time, *Ebony*, the black monthly magazine, listed five southern cities among the "ten best cities for blacks" seeking upward mobility in the U.S. economy.[12]

As the Great Migration came to a close, another change to the urban black working class was the acceleration of new waves of immigrants from overseas. In 1965, the U.S. Congress had passed the Immigration and Nationality Act, known as the Hart-Celler Act, which supplanted the restrictionist Johnson-Reed Act of 1924. Whereas the earlier law privileged immigrants from northern and western European countries, the new law not only emphasized the recruitment of immigrants based on "needed skills and the unification of families" but established the principle of first come, first served. Thus, it opened the door to immigrants from Asia and Latin America, as well as blacks from Africa, the Caribbean, and other parts of the globe. Between 1970 and 2000, in the top twenty U.S. cities, the proportion of nonwhites, Hispanics included, rose from just under 40 percent to 60 percent of the total population. Among the ten largest cities in the nation, nine had a majority of minorities. And by the end of the twentieth century, an estimated 1.3 million people of African descent had entered the United States. As the new century got under way, nearly one-tenth of the African American population was an immigrant or the child of an immigrant. In New York, immigrants and their children made up over 50 percent of the total black population.[13]

The new immigrants and their children not only gradually transformed the ethnic composition of black urban communities and the black working class but also signaled important changes in class and race relations. It was during this period that white Americans began to see previously despised Asian Americans as "model minorities." At the same time, inside the African American urban community, as black immigration escalated, according to New York's *Amsterdam News*, black New Yorkers directed "discrimination, both verbal and physical" toward some 4,400 Africans who lived in Central Harlem. These recent black immigrants soon countered with the development of their own political, civil rights, and cultural organizations, including the Organization for the Advancement of Nigerians, the National Association of Yoruba Descendants in North America, and the West Indian Carnival in Chicago, New York, and other cities. Moreover, Haitian and other black immigrants sometimes prominently displayed the flags of their ancestral countries, signaling to white Americans "that they expect to be treated differently because they are not African American." Still, other powerful forces—including African American engagement in the Southern African anti-apartheid movement and racially discriminatory policing practices—brought U.S.-, African-, and Caribbean-born blacks closer together and helped to temper cultural and nationality differences among them. In 1999, after New York policemen killed the unarmed West African student Amadou Diallo, Manthia Diawara, a New York University professor of African descent, declared, "Little do the Amadou Diallos of the world know that the black man in America bears the curse of Cain, and that in America they, too, are considered black men, not Fulanis, Mandigos, or Wolofs. They cut Amadou Diallo down like a black American, even though he belonged to the Fulani tribe in his native Guinea. There is a lesson here for all of us to learn."[14]

Meanwhile, by century's end, poor and working-class black women and men had formed such labor organizations as Atlanta's National Domestic Workers Union of America; Cleveland's Domestic Workers of America; Detroit's Household Workers Organization; the Bronx Household Technicians; the New York State Household Technicians; and the Household Technicians of America. As recently as 2007, thirteen local domestic workers' organizations formed the National Domestic Workers Alliance and launched a spirited campaign to establish national and "global standards for household labor."[15] They also launched radical grassroots protests against hazardous living conditions, environmental injustice, unemployment, and police brutality. These late twentieth-century social struggles were built on earlier battles for civil rights and Black Power that had intensified rather than abated following the assassinations of Malcom X and Martin Luther King and the outbreak of street violence. While they sometimes succeeded in achieving needed change and sometimes failed, the efforts were extraordinary.

Among the earliest issues addressed were lead poisoning and neighborhood-destroying highway construction projects. In St. Louis, activist Ivory Perry and the People's Coalition Against Lead Poisoning (formed in 1970) fought for and secured the city's first municipal ordinance mandating testing of children for lead poisoning, thereby acknowledging the problem as more widespread than heretofore admitted by public health officials and policy makers. Through the mid-1970s, Baltimore's anti–highway construction activists waged a spirited struggle against the building of new highways through established African American and other working-class neighborhoods in the city, led by the Relocation Action Movement (RAM, formed in 1967) and the Movement Against Destruction (MAD, formed in 1968).

As the industrial economy collapsed, some African American women continued to labor as household workers, and they formed new organizations, such as Cleveland's Domestic Workers of America, to demand "pride, respect, and dignity." Courtesy, Michael Schwartz Library, Cleveland State University.

Despite some successes, these movements had collapsed by the late 1970s as the city devised different and more subtle strategies for building "the highway piece by piece."[16]

During the late 1970s and early 1980s, under the leadership of Harvey Adams, the Pittsburgh branch of the NAACP forged a broad interracial coalition of civil rights and social justice organizations and demanded jobs for African Americans on the city's highly touted Renaissance II building and construction projects. Should corporate and public officials fail to provide such work for the rising numbers of unemployed black workers in the city, Adams announced, the coalition was determined "to essentially close the multi-million-dollar Oxford project down." Activists also staged an "affirmative action" rally at Market Square, a prominent center of the Renaissance II building effort. Rather than face ongoing massive picketing, marches, and protests, municipal and corporate elites relented and signed an affirmative action agreement promising new jobs for blacks at such diverse firms as Pittsburgh Plate Glass company, USX, and the Oxford Development Corporation.[17]

Single black women with children, including recipients of public housing and welfare programs like Aid to Families with Dependent Children (AFDC), exerted increasing influence in the political struggles of the late twentieth century. In her pioneering study of Baltimore, historian Rhonda Williams shows how the struggles of diverse groups of poor and working-class women converged around fights for tenants' rights, welfare rights, and basic recognition as full "citizens" in a democratic polity. AFDC recipient Margaret "Peggy" McCarty, also the first chair of an activist group called Mother Rescuers, believed that nobody could "tell her that being on welfare meant that she can't speak out and hold her head up high." McCarty emphatically declared, "I'm a citizen who has a job to do, instead of a poor forgotten colored woman, like some of our people feel." In 1978, Baltimore's black public-housing residents staged a rent strike to protest and demand rectification of the dilapidated and rat-infested O'Donnell Heights housing project. Although the movement stopped short of majority support from residents, it underscored the ongoing struggle of poor and working-class women to change the conditions under which they and their families lived. The protestors enlisted the help of legal-aid lawyers, exposed the hazardous conditions at the complex, and set the groundwork for the city's receipt of a $30.1 million federal grant in 1981 to improve its dilapidated public housing stock.[18] In 1983, under the leadership of Roxanne Jones, poor and working-class black Philadelphians staged a sit-in at the Philadelphia Gas Works to protest the rising termination of service to poor families unable to pay their fuel bills. And in Watts, Brooklyn, and Philadelphia, grassroots activist women fueled the development of government- and foundation-funded Community Development Corporations. For a brief moment, these organizations creatively addressed the challenges of unhealthy and unsafe living conditions in black neighborhoods, not by flight but by rebuilding. As such, they advanced an agenda that historian Brian Purnell describes as the "unmaking" of the ghetto.[19]

In 1986, following the shooting death of her 16-year-old son in Detroit, Clementine Barfield founded SOSAD (Save Our Sons and Daughters) "to go beyond mourning" and "create positive alternatives to violence throughout the community." In Los Angeles, black women formed Mothers ROC (Reclaiming Our Children) and Mothers of East Los Angeles (MELA). These organizations not only aimed to curb black-on-black violence but also worked to find jobs for young men and help those caught in the throes of the racially biased criminal justice system. When the state of California proposed to build a prison in East Los Angeles, MELA, founded in 1984, joined forces with the Latino community and blocked the project. MELA also thwarted plans to build a hazardous-waste incinerator in the area.[20]

The grassroots social organizing that persisted across the final decades of the twentieth century inspired the emergence of a new African American urban politics. By century's end, people of African descent had emerged as the most consistent supporters of the waning liberal-labor political coalition in U.S. politics. In city after city, African Americans built multiracial coalitions with liberal whites as well as Latino/Latina Americans and Asian Americans. They articulated a clear vision for building a fairer urban social order than existed under the leadership of white Democratic and Republican political elites. Across the late twentieth-century urban landscape, African Americans won the mayor's office in such diverse cities as Detroit, New Orleans, Philadelphia, Atlanta, Los Angeles, New York, and Chicago. But the expansion of electoral politics built upon rather than supplanted earlier grassroots social movements that had developed during the heyday of the industrial working class.[21]

THE NEW URBAN POLITICS

As early as 1972, a broad cross section of African American political, civic, religious, and cultural organizations met in Gary, Indiana, to establish a permanent National Black Political Assembly. Convening over a three-day period, between March 10 and 12, the National Black Political Convention attracted three thousand official delegates from forty-four states under the slogan Unity Without Uniformity. Black elected officials and established new and old civil rights organizations like the Southern Christian Leadership Conference, People United to Save [later Serve] Humanity, and the National Urban League joined forces with a host of black nationalist groups, including the Black Panther Party, the Republic of New Africa, and the Nation of Islam. Among major civil rights and political organizations, only the NAACP, citing the all-black composition of the convention as intolerable, refused to send official delegates to the meeting.[22] Working from a previously prepared document, "Outline for a Black Agenda," delegates agreed that "the American system does not work for the masses of our people and it cannot be made to work without radical fundamental change."[23]

The Gary convention rejected proposals to create a third, all-black political party. Instead, the gathering urged urban communities to mobilize the predominantly working-class black electorate, build multiracial alliances where possible, and wrest control of municipal government from old white political and economic elites. Affiliated mainly with the Democratic Party, such efforts involved sharp conflicts with the declining organized labor movement. When the AFL-CIO refused to endorse either the Republican or Democratic Party candidate for president in 1972, African American trade unionists met in Chicago and formed a new national labor organization: the Coalition of Black Trade Unionists (CBTU). Supported partly by funds from the AFL-CIO, the new organization reached out to other minorities and to women and vigorously mobilized voters for candidates deemed supportive of "the needs and aspirations of black and poor workers." By the first decade of the new century, however, the AFL-CIO withdrew funding from constituent groups like the CBTU.[24]

Nonetheless, African Americans forged political alliances with a wide variety of community-based labor, ethnic, and racial groups. Campaigns for the election of black mayors intensified in cities with large percentages of blacks and other minorities. In Los Angeles, as the percentage of non-Hispanic whites dipped from 61 to 30 percent of the total, the door opened for African Americans and other minorities to seek the mayor's office. After losing his first bid to unseat conservative mayor Sam Yorty in 1969, Tom Bradley built a stronger multiracial coalition and defeated Yorty in the mayor's race of 1973 to become the city's first black mayor.[25]

That same year, African American Detroit mobilized behind the mayoral candidacy of labor organizer and political militant Coleman Young. Young not only pushed for reforms that would improve housing, jobs, education, and social services for blacks, but he also accented the need to reform the Detroit Police Department—specifically, to create what he called a "people's police department." In November 1973, Young became Detroit's first African American mayor, defeating his opponent by the slim margin of 233,674 votes to 216,933. Although the mobilization of large numbers of new black voters fueled Young's victory, his success also rested on the strength of "a coalition of blacks, unions, and white liberals." Unlike several other cities with rising numbers of new immigrants, there were few Asian or Latino/Latina voters in Detroit at the time. Over the next four election cycles (1977, 1981, 1985, and 1989), Young beat his closest rivals by wide margins. Upon taking office, however, Young sought to address the fears of his most conservative, law-and-order white critics as well as blacks who hoped for a new era of police-community relations and the prosecution of officers in "blue suits with silver badges" for abusive policing of African American neighborhoods.[26]

Meanwhile, the 1983 election of Harold Washington as Chicago's first African American mayor underscored the difficulties of building alliances across the color line. Despite Washington's victory in the Democratic primary, most white regular party members opposed him either by sitting out the general election or by crossing over to his Republican opponent. Some supporters of the Republican candidate wore T-shirts with the slogan Vote Right, Vote White.[27] Washington nonetheless prevailed in the general election, winning over Bernard Epton by a margin of 46,250 votes out of a 1.29 million total. African Americans gave Washington 95 percent of their votes. He also received the majority of Latino votes, but the turnout was low. About 87.6 percent of whites voted for Epton, and only about 12.3 percent voted for Washington. In his election-night address, despite the racialized voting returns, Washington accented what he believed was the promise of a broad-based multiracial political coalition. "Out of the crucible of this city's most trying election," he said, "blacks, whites, Hispanics, Jews, gentiles, Protestants, and Catholics of all stripes have joined hands to form a new Democratic movement." Washington then invited his opponents to come together "to heal the divisions that have plagued us." "Together," he stated, "we will overcome our problems."[28]

Only in 1989 did New York City elect its first African American mayor: David Dinkins, the son of a barber who had migrated to the urban Northeast from Virginia. Dinkins sought election against the backdrop of strong white ethnic domination of the regular party organization, the persistence of residential and neighborhood segregation, and increasing competition between blacks, Latinos, immigrants, and white ethnic groups over the city's resources. Nonetheless, Dinkins was able to build a significant alliance of African Americans, Latino/Latina Americans, Asian Americans, and non-Latino white liberals to defeat his conservative Republican opponent, Rudolph Giuliani.[29]

The rise of the new black politics was not limited to the urban North. Black majorities underlay the election of African American mayors in Atlanta, New Orleans, and, following the restoration of municipal elections, Washington, DC. In Atlanta, Maynard Jackson, son of a Baptist minister and migrant from Dallas, Texas, became the first African American mayor of a large southern city in 1973. He owed his election to Atlanta's transition to a majority black city as whites moved increasingly into the surrounding suburbs. Jackson bluntly told the Atlanta Chamber of Commerce, "I don't need you guys to get elected . . . but I've learned that I certainly need you to govern."[30]

Grassroots efforts to elect black mayors galvanized African American communities and created extraordinary unity across class, neighborhood, and ideological lines. In New York, when an interviewer asked Dr. George Lopez of Queens if the city's various elite black cliques had ever unified on a common goal, he replied yes: "One example when we all pulled together was when we got David Dinkins elected as mayor [of New York]. . . . When David was running for mayor in 1989, you saw blacks from all five boroughs as well as from Nassau County and Westchester, working together on fundraisers and voter drives." In Chicago, Washington's campaign organization, the Task Force for Black Political Empowerment, evolved out of an earlier grassroots political effort, the ChicagoFest boycott. Organized to protest mayor Jane Byrne's unequal and unfair policies toward Chicago's black community, the ChicagoFest boycott brought together a broad cross section of black organizations, registered hundreds of new voters, and prepared the groundwork for African Americans to capture city hall.[31]

Black mayors invariably highlighted their capacity to generate widespread grassroots poor and working-class support. Near his campaign's end, Washington declared, "This campaign started in the 'hood, and it will end in the 'hood."[32] Edna Ewell Watson, member of Detroit's League of Revolutionary Black Workers, later recalled how the league shaped the ideas and actions of "many of those who served as the backbone and linchpin of

Coleman Young's [election and] administration." Other observers also underscored the league's "invisible legacy [that] was realized through electoral politics."[33] In Philadelphia, earlier Black Power activists had gained significant victories in the movement for local control of schools, jobs, and social services within the African American community. As early as 1968, however, a group of "black independent Democrats" formed a new organization, the Black Political Forum (BPF), and pushed for the election of black public officials "who were accountable to black community and movement organizations, rather than to the city's white-led party organizations." Over the next decade and a half, in addition to helping to fuel Wilson Goode's successful mayoral bid in 1984, the Black Political Forum spurred the election of African American activists to the U.S. Congress, the Pennsylvania legislature, and the city council.[34]

Under the impact of black mayoral regimes, African Americans made important gains, though not enough to fully offset the destructive effects of deindustrialization on their lives. On the one hand, blacks increased their access to low-income public housing and a variety of professional and managerial jobs in the municipal workforce. In Chicago, by 1985, the city's black businesses received 17 percent of all city contracts, and the mayor's office announced plans to increase this number to 25 percent in subsequent years. Between 1983 and 1985, Chicago also added over 9,500 new residential units to the public housing stock. Attorney Jetta Norris Jones, director of External Affairs in Washington's administration, later recalled, "When Mayor Washington was in office, there were clearly black entrepreneurs and other professionals who were having their first chance at starting businesses because they had not had these chances with prior mayors." In Detroit, between Young's election in 1973 and 1977, black municipal administrators rose from 12 to 24 percent, professional staff from 23 to 41 percent, and members of the police force from 5 to 30 percent. Likewise, Philadelphia's Wilson Goode also awarded an estimated 17 percent of municipal contracts to African American businesses.[35] In Atlanta, following his election, Maynard Jackson quickly replaced the white police chief with an African American and instituted an aggressive affirmative action program that required one-third of all construction contracts to go to minority-owned firms.[36] In New Orleans, after Ernest "Dutch" Morial, a New Orleans–born member of an established "black creole" family, became mayor in 1977, he soon instituted a strong affirmative action program and considerably increased the proportion of African Americans hired at all levels of municipal government.[37]

On the other hand, as black mayors took over cities with a daunting series of problems, they adopted what policy analysts call "growth politics." Facing such challenges as the declining manufacturing base of the city; decreasing population and the loss of tax revenues, capital investments, and political representation; and the deterioration of the urban housing stock and infrastructure, they emphasized attracting large businesses and stimulating investment in inner cities and their downtown cores. While African American mayors roundly criticized corporate and financial leadership in their campaigns for office, in the days after obtaining office, they quickly convened meetings with corporate and financial elites and forged agreements to bring dollars into their cities. Such agreements usually came with a steep price tag for the city in the form of tax abatements and other subsidies. Moreover, in some cases white residents articulated their determination to refuse cooperation with the new black-led regimes. Before Coleman Young's bid for the mayor's office in Detroit, one resident expressed the sentiments of many whites then and later: "If by any fluke you become mayor of Detroit, you will be mayor of a dung heap because any WHITE who is able to do so will move out."[38]

Even Atlanta, self-advertised as the "city too busy to hate," was by no means ideal. The Multi-City Study of Urban Inequality employed the phrase "the Atlanta paradox." During the final decades of the twentieth century, though Atlanta appeared to be a land of opportunity, it remained divided by race and class. As the Multi-City Study put it, despite "phenomenal regional growth, mean real family income in the city between 1969 and 1989 declined, both absolutely and relative to the suburbs. . . . The poverty rate of blacks in the city in 1990 was 35 percent, an increase from 29 percent in 1970." Moreover, over 65 percent of the jobs were located in the northern part of the metropolitan region, but over 70 percent of African Americans lived in the southern portion of the region.[39]

Maynard Jackson's administration underscored the uneven class distribution of benefits under black municipal officials. In 1975, Atlanta fired hundreds of black sanitation workers when negotiations broke down and the workers walked out on strike. Similarly, in New Orleans, "Dutch" Morial offered few concessions to the city's sanitation workers. From the outset of his administration, he also angered some of the city's existing municipal employees, particularly noncreole blacks, when he undertook "the mass firings of black patronage appointees to upgrade government operations and secure the loyalty of his own staff." His political rivals soon assailed Morial for hiring only "Super Negroes."

In Washington, DC, Marion S. Barry confronted other limitations. A civil rights activist and migrant from the Mississippi Delta via Memphis, Tennessee, Barry won the mayor's office in 1978, but Congress's continuing control over the District's budget—coupled with his own drug abuse charges, rehabilitation treatment leaves, and jail time—stymied his efforts to implement policies designed to improve the lives of poor and working-class Washingtonians during his four terms as mayor over nearly two decades.[40] At the same time, Barry had to reconcile the often conflicting interests of the city's expanding white gay and lesbian community with the demands of the African American population. Historian Kwame Holmes notes in his research on the subject that the white gay and lesbian community defined itself as a predominantly white victimized minority and distanced itself from the social struggles of the predominantly poor and working-class black community.[41]

The new black urban politics also underlay the growing influence of blacks in national politics. As early as 1972, in New York City, congresswoman Shirley Chisholm rose to prominence in Brooklyn's predominantly working class, majority black Twelfth District. Her bold run for the Democratic Party's nomination in 1972 gained the endorsement of the Black Panther Party. Despite opposition to such endorsement from party leaders, Chisholm expressed her firm belief that the BPP's support would enhance rather than "alienate a broader voter base" for her campaign. Just over a decade later, inspired by Chisholm's vigorous challenge to party leadership, Jesse Jackson's Democratic presidential campaigns in 1984 and again in 1988 (headquartered in Chicago) set the stage for the election of Barack Obama as the first African American president of the United States.[42]

CONCLUSION

Despite the profound limits of the new politics for poor and working-class black people, their energy, enthusiasm, and support fueled the rise of black mayoral regimes during the late twentieth century. They achieved significant electoral victory in the face of extraordinary odds. The collapse of the segregationist system and the deindustrialization of the urban economy coincided with the fall of the black working class and the resurgence of conservatism in U.S. politics. Escalating opposition to the civil rights and Black Power agenda undercut the gains of grassroots social justice movements. Consequently, growing numbers of African Americans turned toward the electoral arena as the most promising strategy for combatting assaults on newly won affirmative action, equal opportunity, and poverty programs. Poor and working-class black communities were not only key to the rise of new African American mayoral regimes, as we will see, but they were also instrumental in the election and reelection of Barack H. Obama as the first United States president of African descent and most recently in the Black Lives Matter movement to address new but deeply rooted manifestations of white supremacy in the expanding postindustrial age of the twenty-first century.

Facing the New Global
Capitalist Economy

UNTIL THE MID-TWENTIETH CENTURY, the vast majority of black men, women, and to some extent children added to the wealth, culture, and politics of the nation as general laborers, factory hands, and household and domestic service workers. This portrait of the black working class, enslaved and later free, changed dramatically during the twentieth century, when the Modern Black Freedom Movement toppled the white supremacist order, expanded the scope of American democracy, and created a new equal opportunity regime. Men and women from a variety of ethnic and racial groups soon invoked the language and strategies of the African American freedom struggle to broaden their own access to the benefits or "perquisites" of American citizenship. But the late twentieth-century decline of the manufacturing sector and the intensification of grassroots white resistance to affirmative action programs reinforced the color line in the emerging postindustrial economy. At the turn of the new millennium, according to economist Doug Henwood, the largest single category of work for white men was salaried managers and administrators; for black men, truck drivers; for white women, secretaries; and for black women, nursing aides and orderlies.[1]

Thus, as the twenty-first century got under way, most poor and working-class blacks and their children occupied the bottom rungs of the evolving global capitalist workforce. As historian and activist Clarence Lang notes, during the closing years of the twentieth century, "the strong winds of neoliberalism" continued to sweep the nation politically to the right and established the foundation for a steady push against the gains of the earlier mid-century social welfare state. Specifically, the new liberalism included the increasing "transition from industrial production to an economy driven by financial capital; market deregulation and austerity; privatization; antiunion policies; [and] the erosion of working conditions and pay in order to generate greater productivity and higher corporate profits."[2]

Based upon these profound changes in recent U.S. and African American life, the notion of a "new Jim Crow" system gained increasing currency during the first and second decades of the twenty-first century. Fueled by the mass incarceration of young black men and women, the new Jim Crow reinstitutes the old white supremacist order under the legal rubric of "felon." As legal scholar Michelle Alexander explains, "Once you are labeled a felon, the old forms of discrimination—employment discrimination, denial of the vote, denial of educational opportunity, denial of food stamps and other public benefits, and exclusion from jury service—are perfectly legal."[3] *Blood in the Water,* historian Heather Ann Thompson's Pulitzer Prize–winning book on the Attica prison revolt of 1971, makes the same point. While significant prison reforms followed the violent state suppression of the Attica prison takeover (including better visitation procedures and the establishment of an inmate liaison committee to voice the grievances of prisoners), the rapid spread of a more hostile and punitive system of incarceration largely cancelled out the benefits of reform for the prisoners. In late twentieth-century New York and elsewhere, public officials were determined to "rein in 'those' black and brown people who had been so vocally challenging authority and pushing the civil rights envelope."

Mirroring as well as setting the tone for other states, New York's predominantly African American and Latino/Latina prison population mushroomed from 12,500 in 1971 to nearly 73,000 as the new century got under way. Sentenced due to criminalization of a host of heretofore minor or noncriminal acts, particularly involving the possession and use of drugs, these inmates were assigned to work in prison industries for the benefit of the state. During the final two years of the 1990s alone, New York State's Division of Correctional Industries (Corcraft) produced $70 million in income using disfranchised prison labor, reminiscent to some extent of the postemancipation years of the nineteenth century.[4]

Black working people are by no means occupying the bottom rungs of today's evolving transnational economy quietly. Labor organizing remains one strategy for improving working conditions. As manufacturing and other jobs dissipated, the balance of power within the labor movement shifted from the old blue-collar industrial, construction, and transport unions to new service and public-sector unions, including the Service Employees International Union (SEIU), the American Federation of State, County, and Municipal

Employees (AFSCME), and the American Postal Workers Union. These all cover occupations employing large numbers of African Americans. As noted above, local unions founded the National Domestic Workers Alliance and pushed for the adoption of equitable transnational labor policies designed to increase wages and working conditions for household workers.[5]

Many labor activists, white and black, see African Americans as the most promising prospects for rebuilding a vibrant labor movement in the twenty-first century. Historian Robert Zieger concluded in his synthesis of black labor history that "it was an article of faith among many African Americans, and many white supporters as well, that blacks and other people of color represented the only real hope of reviving and revitalizing a labor movement that had been in decline for a quarter century."[6]

Writing ahead of the 2016 election, historian Liz Faue also emphasized the potential for building a broader and more inclusive labor movement during the early twenty-first century. These efforts included not only the Black Lives Matter movement (BLM), but also the Occupy Wall Street movement, the struggle for LGBT rights, and the Fight for $15 movement for a higher minimum wage for all workers. In Faue's view, these movements energetically addressed "the challenges of young, undocumented, minority, and women workers" in a "new form and in a new language."[7] Labor scholar Michael Zweig and historian Robin Kelley both reinforce this perspective. In particular, Kelley urges activists to "stop referring to the South as a political backwater, a distinctive site of racist right wing reaction" and to build interracial working-class alliances across regional as well gender, racial, and sexuality lines.[8]

But the obstacles to a unified labor movement are exceedingly strong: some African American activists and their nonwhite allies as well as women from a variety of ethnic and racial groups have despaired at building alliances with white male workers. These activists detest the persistence of white male privilege in the workplace, white workers' anti–welfare state ideology, and, most of all, white workers' failure to embrace a variety of ethnic- and racial-group workers as comrades in arms against unjust postindustrial global capitalist labor policies and practices.[9] Hence, early twenty-first-century poor and working-class blacks continue to supplement their labor-organizing strategies with new forms of grassroots activism as well as cross-class, interracial, and interethnic electoral politics.

Recent urban black politics buoyed Barack Obama's two presidential bids as well as the emergence of the Black Lives Matter (BLM) movement during his second term.[10] By the time Obama had arrived in Chicago to work as a community organizer during the early 1980s, the city's black community had already carved out new and highly articulated patterns of multiclass and multiracial coalition politics. In 1973, for example, packinghouse worker and union leader Addie Wyatt and her husband Claude (an early packinghouse employee and later a postal service worker) had joined the Committee for a Black Mayor and helped to lay the groundwork for the election of Harold Washington as Chicago's first black mayor in 1983 and Jesse Jackson's 1984 and 1988 Rainbow Coalition campaigns for the Democratic Party's endorsement for president. In his analysis of Obama's election as the country's first African American president, historian Peniel Joseph concludes that Jackson's two presidential runs, which brought scores of new working-class black voters into the electoral process, "provided a blueprint for the Obama campaign."[11]

After Obama's reelection to a second term as president in 2012, the increasing incidents of police brutality underlay the groundswell of grassroots activism that launched the BLM in 2013. Following the acquittal of George Zimmerman in the shooting death of unarmed Trayvon Martin in Sanford, Florida, a gated suburban community, activist Alicia Garza and others used new internet technology, a pivotal factor in Obama's campaigns, to generate a movement that soon not only resulted in street protests against police brutality from coast to coast but also produced some twenty-five organized local BLM chapters across the country. As indicated by the case of Ferguson, Missouri, these efforts also reflected the social and political impact of the increasing suburbanization of African American working-class life and poverty in recent decades.[12]

Under the impact of the 2016 presidential election and the triumph of the most conservative wing of the Republican Party, massive street protests broke out in cities nationwide. Many Black Lives Matter activists called for deeper and more extensive local grassroots organizing as well as greater engagement in the established electoral system. Garza, a pioneer in the development of the BLM as well as an organizer for the National Domestic Workers Alliance, reported "doing a lot of work to build bridges between other movements and communities caught in the crosshairs of Trump's agenda. . . . It's a real opportunity for us to build a movement of movements. . . . Our futures are tied to each other."[13]

The discomfort and resistance of economic and power elites will no doubt intensify as working-class movements spread and escalate demands for social justice. Such movements as well as the resistance that they spawn are not new. The civil rights era, as historian Nathan Connolly reminds us, was another moment when many African Americans without property, jobs, and formal political influence "moved to kick open the door to the conference room and take a seat at the negotiating table."[14] Equally important, as suggested by four hundred years of black labor history in this book, slavery was another moment when masses of enslaved, poor, and working-class people of African descent moved to claim their freedom and redefine American democracy and the scope of citizenship. Early African Americans forged strong identities as workers, producers, citizens, and African people and laid powerful claim to both human and civil rights for themselves and for future generations.

From the ongoing issues of poverty, health, housing, and employment to the recent upsurge of lethal police-community relations, black people continue to stand at the intersection of class and racial conflict in twenty-first-century America. They also continue, as in the past, to contribute to the health and wealth of the nation in the face of extraordinary legal and extralegal barriers. Contemporary public policies, social movement strategies, educational programs, media campaigns, and philanthropic decisions—designed to address the persistent challenges of inequality in a democratic society—require deeper and more thoughtful historical perspectives on the dynamics of race and class relations in the economy, institutions, culture, and politics of the past. *Workers on Arrival* offers a place to start.

Interpreting the African American Working-Class Experience

AN ESSAY ON SOURCES

This book synthesizes research on black urban labor and working-class history since the early twentieth century. This scholarship not only illuminates regional, gender, and status differences in the experiences of black workers but also provides significant transnational and comparative perspectives on African American urban life and labor over time. Until the mid-twentieth century, however, scholars of black urban life confronted and challenged entrenched ideas about the inherent inferiority of black people compared to their white counterparts. Early twentieth-century black scholars and their small contingent of white allies emphasized the destructive impact of racial hostility and global capitalist development on the lives of African American workers. Even so, early twentieth-century pioneers questioned the capacity of black workers to fully understand and act in their own best interests as the Great Migration accelerated. During the second half of the twentieth century, scholars of African American urban, labor, and working-class history not only exposed these early class biases in research on workers, their families, and their communities but also uncovered the neglect of poor and working-class women, aspects of black popular culture, and certain transnational and global themes in grassroots black social movements. As such, this book and the twenty-first-century field of African American urban labor history is indebted to both the foundation laid by early twentieth-century scholars as well as the groundbreaking research of the past half century.[1]

ORIGINS OF BLACK LABOR HISTORIOGRAPHY

Whether African Americans lived and worked in town or country, U. B. Phillips, George T. Surface, A. H. Stone, and other early twentieth-century white scholars concluded that black people were "a product of old-world forces" and innately inferior by "nature." As such, according to white supremacist research, enslaved and later free black people were "hardly transformed by the requirements of European civilization." African people presumably enjoyed leisure, abhorred manual labor, and deplored steady and systematic work of any kind. Racist research both reflected and reinforced widespread stereotypes of African American workers as irregular in labor and "unstable in residence." According to these scholars, it was not "slave labor" or even free black labor "but Negro labor which was, at bottom, responsible" for the low productivity of southern farms and industry compared to their northern counterparts.[2]

W. E. B. Du Bois, Charles H. Wesley, Sterling D. Spero, Abram L. Harris, and other first-generation black labor and working-class historians rejected these racist portraits of African American workers. These pioneering African American scholars presented an image of black workers as productive participants in the urban political economy and placed the onus of racism squarely on the shoulders of white employers, workers, and the state. These studies indicted white workers for their racism as well as employers and their political allies for using the state to reinforce class and racial prejudices. They showed how black workers not only built houses, made clothing, and manufactured and repaired equipment in the rural and urban South but also fueled northern urban industrial development as well. As such, early black labor historians fathomed the intersections of race and class and exploded dangerous myths about the inferiority of black workers and established essential groundwork for placing the lives of black workers within the larger context of socioeconomic and political changes affecting workers across racial and ethnic lines. Interwar black scholars also pondered what, then, should be the black man's attitude toward white laborers and the labor movement. Invariably the answer was, as W. E. B. Du Bois and Augustus Dill put it, that "the salvation of all laborers, white and black, lies in the great movement of racial uplift known as the labor movement. . . . Let us black men fight prejudice and exclusion in the labor world and fight it hard; but do not fight the labor movement."[3]

Despite such significant contributions to early twentieth-century scholarship, the first generation developed blind spots of its own. First and perhaps most important, few of these studies analyzed the experiences of black workers (particularly unorganized or "unskilled" workers) from the vantage point of their own institutional, cultural, and political perspectives. As such, these studies failed to fully explore the interrelationship between the development of the black working class and the growth of the Black Metropolis. Second, in according agency to the lives of black workers, these studies overplayed the role of organized labor unions, particularly under the impact of the New Deal and the rise of the CIO. Third, closely interrelated labor, urban, and migration studies gave insufficient attention to the socioeconomic, political, and cultural resources that southern black migrants brought to the city under the impact of the Great Migration. Nonetheless, by treating black workers as energetic, competent, and efficient as their white counterparts, W. E. B.

Du Bois, Charles Wesley, and other activist scholars established the foundation for the fluorescence of antiracist research on African American urban, labor, and working-class history in the years after World War II.

TRANSFORMATION OF SCHOLARSHIP:
THE INDUSTRIAL ERA

Under the impact of the Modern Black Freedom Movement, an early wave of "ghetto-formation" studies carried the antiracist insights of early black labor studies into the postwar years. Urban historians Gilbert Osofsky, Allan Spear, Kenneth Kusmer, and others analyzed black workers' lives within the larger context of the "making" of racially segregated northern "ghettos," emphasizing the pre–World War I roots of the process.[4] While Osofsky and others documented the role of white hostility in the creation of segregated black urban communities on the one hand and the responses of emerging predominantly middle-class activists to the process on the other, the ghetto-formation scholarship muted the voices of black workers and downplayed their role in the making of black urban communities.[5]

Studies of the urban South and West largely avoided ghetto-formation approaches. Instead, John Blassingame, Howard Rabinowitz, Robert Perdue, George Wright, and other scholars of the urban South emphasized shifting patterns of black-white relations, community formation, and political engagement.[6] In the border city of Louisville, Kentucky, for example, historian George Wright focused on the issue of "race relations, black response to white discrimination, and black activities behind the walls of segregation," concluding that white Louisvillians crafted a "polite form" of racism that "would remain polite as long as Afro-Americans willingly accepted 'their place,' which, of course, was at the bottom."[7] Even more than research on the urban South, scholarship on blacks in the urban West challenged prevailing race, class, and ethnic interpretations of black urban life. Careful studies of the urban West by Douglas Daniels, Quintard Taylor, Albert Broussard, and more recently Douglas Flamming, Matthew Whitaker, and Scott Kurashige and others underscore how multiethnic nonwhite (Asian Americans and Latino/Latina Americans) as well as diverse white ethnic communities in the urban West shaped the experiences of African Americans in unique ways.[8] Building upon an expanding body of scholarship on blacks in the urban West, for example, Kurashige documents the unique "triangular" interaction of blacks, whites, and Japanese Americans under the impact of World War II. He shows not only how Los Angeles's "Little Tokyo" gave way to a predominantly black community in the wake of Japanese internment but also how the two groups forged a tenuous political alliance that collapsed in the postwar years as the notion of Japanese Americans as a "model minority" took hold.[9]

Proletarian Perspectives

By the early 1980s, scholars of black urban life broke ranks with the emerging historiography of the northern ghetto as well as persistent emphases on race-ethnic relations in some southern and western studies. James Grossman's, Peter Gottlieb's, Richard Walter Thomas's, and my own scholarship helped to shift the focus from the "making" of segregated spaces to the "making" of the black urban industrial working class in Chicago, Pittsburgh, Detroit, Milwaukee, and other northeastern and midwestern cities. Their numbers cresting during the late 1980s and early 1990s, these studies placed African American men in meatpacking, steel, automobile, and other manufacturing and industrial firms at center stage. This scholarship not only emphasized the role of black workers in shaping their own workplace experiences but also the creation of vibrant, predominantly proletarian cross-class communities. Unlike earlier studies, however, this generation of labor history also emphasized the many ways that black workers influenced the larger labor movement and politics of the city and nation.[10]

Informed by the emerging new labor and working-class history, historians Peter Rachleff, Robin D. G. Kelley, Michael Honey, Robert Korstad, Eric Arnesen, and Earl Lewis soon challenged the race-relations and community-formation model employed by such southern historians as Blassingame, Wright, Rabinowitz, and others. These scholars emphasized changing class as well as race relations in southern cities. This scholarship shows how working-class blacks—with few material resources and surrounded by hostile whites, workers, and elites from the end of the Civil War through the early twentieth century—created an "impressive community." Rachleff describes this community as weaving "together the formerly free and the formerly slave, the city native and the 'country negro,' dark-skinned and light-skinned, literate and illiterate, skilled and unskilled." These studies also stepped outside of the so-called C. Vann Woodward paradigm (which emphasized the rise and persistence of a racially "solid [white] South" following the Civil War) and documented interracial working-class alliances, particularly with the late nineteenth-century rise of the Knights of Labor, albeit short-lived, and later most notably with the emergence of the CIO during the interwar years.[11]

According to Robin Kelley, the movement of Alabama blacks into the Communist Party during the 1930s suggested that "racial divisions were far more fluid and Southern working-class consciousness far more complex" than most historians had realized. Whereas Kelley focused significant attention on community-based African American institutions that fueled black working-class consciousness, Arnesen emphasized the development of a biracial labor movement among New Orleans dockworkers, arguing that black and white workers forged complex identities based on their interactions in workplaces and labor unions. Similarly, in his study of Memphis, Michael Honey documented the development of a successful industrial union movement in the Jim Crow urban South, but he also showed how African Americans coupled their interracial unionizing activities with a vibrant civil rights movement. Nonetheless, Honey concludes that such efforts dissipated in the face of persistent antiradical and antiblack sentiment and practices after World War II. Focusing on the tobacco-manufacturing city of Winston-Salem, North Carolina, labor historian Robert Korstad offers an extraordinary account of what he describes as "civil rights unionism" during World War II and its early aftermath. Korstad shows how blacks and a small number of white tobacco workers formed Local 22 of the CIO's Food, Tobacco, Agricultural, and Allied Workers union. He convincingly argues that African Americans and their white comrades used Local 22 not only to address pressing workplace issues but also to challenge the principal pillars of the segregationist edifice: "economic exploitation, political disfranchisement, and discrimination . . . throughout the decade of the 1940s."[12]

Historian Earl Lewis not only incorporated proletarian perspectives into his study of Norfolk but also exposed the blind spots in proletarianization or working-class-formation scholarship. Specifically, he urged historians to acknowledge both the impact of the Great Migration on the urban South as well as certain biases (including the neglect of women workers and the privileging of manufacturing over the transport and service sectors of the economy) in research on black workers in the urban Northeast and Midwest. Rather than placing work or residence at the center of urban community studies, Lewis emphasized "the complex interplay between conditions at work and at home." He also coined the notion of "congregation" to underscore the ways that African Americans transformed segregated spaces into creative community environments that protected black families and provided a foundation for launching grassroots movements against the Jim Crow system. Moreover, by calling for more systematic attention to the lives of black urban women, Lewis also offered a bridge to the later rise of a new generation of research on working-class black women.[13]

Working-Class Women and Gender Dynamics

The emergence of African American urban history as a new field of scholarship gradually transformed our understanding of black workers and their communities in the North, South, and West. This scholarship illuminated numerous heretofore hidden or ignored dimensions of black workers' lives and labor, but it also, with few exceptions, treated working-class black women as marginal participants and players in class making and community formation. In 1985, historian Jacqueline Jones called attention to this significant gap in our knowledge in her book *Labor of Love, Labor of Sorrow*. She showed how working-class black women inhabited a unique culture, "one not shared entirely by either black men or white women, though these latter groups" had received the lion's share of attention from historians of African American and U.S. labor history at that time.[14]

Building upon the expanding insights of labor and women's history, African American women's urban working-class history gradually emerged during the 1990s and early twenty-first century. This scholarship—most notably Tera Hunter's study of Atlanta, Elizabeth Clark-Lewis's study of Washington, DC, and Darlene Clark Hine's seminal essay on black women and the migration process—placed the lives of black women workers at the center of a broader and more inclusive portrait of African American labor and working-class history. Studies by Hunter, Clark-Lewis, and Hine informed the subsequent research of twenty-first-century historians Victoria Wolcott, Georgina Hickey, Leslie Brown, and others.[15] In her groundbreaking study *Remaking Respectability: African American Women in Interwar Detroit,* Wolcott placed women at different class levels at the center of her analysis of "migration and urban growth." She broke new ground in her analysis of differences in the ideas and behaviors of middle-class and elite black women on the one hand and working-class black women on the other. She also shifted the locus of her study away from the industrial shop floor to the neighborhood, where women dominated the terrain as caretakers, supervisors of children's street play, and tenders of local institutions. In her view, "prostitutes, gamblers, and performers shaped black Detroit as vitally as club leaders, church founders and social workers did."[16]

Early twenty-first-century studies of the urban South also accented the role of black women in the history of the African American working-class. In her study of Atlanta's working-class women, black and white, Georgina Hickey reinforced emphases on the intersections of class, gender, and race in the lives of urban women, concluding that "race was not always the most salient feature of public discourse. . . . Sometimes, gender and class position mattered even more."[17] Leslie Brown placed black women, elite and working-class, at the core of her history of Durham, North Carolina. Set against the backdrop of emancipation and the rise of Durham as a New South industrial city, Brown demonstrates how African American women represented "the central constituency of black migration, urbanization, and prole-tarianization." Women dominated the Great Migration of African Americans to Durham nearly every decade between 1880 and 1950. As such, Brown shows how black women navigated the "work culture" of male-dominated black businesses on the one hand and the "work culture" of white-owned tobacco firms that employed a predominantly black female labor force on the other. Like Hunter's conclusion about an "Atlanta paradox," Brown also dubs Durham "a paradox." Black women, she says, were victims of both "racism and misogyny" but crafted notions of "respectability," emphasizing morality, thrift, piety, and restraint, that cut across class lines within the African American community and became a "hegemonic" idea. African Americans, particularly women, at different class levels "wore respectability like armor" and "carried" it like a "sword."[18]

A growing body of research probed questions of criminality and crime among urban black communities. Based mainly on the experiences of blacks in Philadelphia, New York, and Chicago, historian Khalil Muhammad describes his study of black criminality as "a biography of the idea of black criminality in the making of modern America." He shows how Progressive Era social scientists employed statistical data to create social programs for the "redemption and rehabilitation" of the "dangerous classes" of European immigrants, while defining the expanding urban black working class as "criminal" and prescribing incarceration and removal from networks of families and communities as the most effective mode of treatment.[19] For his part, Kevin Mumford explores the historical development of "interracial vice districts" (i.e., "interzones") as part of Chicago's and New York's larger racialized and sexualized urban landscape. In a telling analysis of the boxer Jack Johnson's persecution in the urban North, Mumford convincingly argues that Johnson's experience symbolized "the beginnings of a new gender-sexuality system": the tightening of restrictions on sexual relations between black men and white women, while permitting white men to cross the color line and gain sexual access to black women as prostitutes or sex workers.[20]

While Mumford and Muhammad offered significant insights into the class, race, space, and gendering of crime in the industrial city, an expanding closely related body of work on the lives of female prisoners and sex workers deepened our understanding of working-class black women and their relationship to middle-class black and white women, including especially their ideas about "respectability." Innovative studies by Kali Gross, Cheryl Hicks, and more recently Cynthia Blair, Talitha LeFlouria, and Sarah Haley illuminate the interconnected histories of sexuality, criminality, and class relations in African American urban life during the industrial era.[21] Focusing on the period 1870–1930, Blair documents how the African American prostitute in Chicago was "more than a contested symbol" of expanding middle-class notions of respectability; she was also "a worker" under the increasing pressures of black migration, industrial working-class formation, and "repeated shifts in the location of urban red-light districts, and the growth of commercialized leisure industries."[22]

Examining the lives of working-class black female prisoners in New York and Philadelphia, respectively, Hicks and Gross persuasively counter prevailing notions that imprisonment fundamentally meant "criminality" for these women. These scholars show how imprisoned women remained connected to a thick web of community-based kinship and friendship relations. As such, these studies employ black female criminality "as a vehicle for gaining insight into the lives of otherwise marginalized [working-class and poor] black women" and demonstrating how the lives of these women reflected "the complexity and contested character of class and gender relationships within black communities." According to Kali Gross, the self-activities of black women intersected with the discriminatory policies of the state, media organizations, and penal reformers in the historical construction of the black female as criminal, while Hicks underscores how these women interpreted their own lives "as African Americans and wage laborers." These women—some incarcerated for sex offenses (primarily prostitution/sex work), violent crimes against persons (murder), and crimes against property (theft)—were not representative of working-class black women in general, but Hicks nonetheless compares their ideas and beliefs (particularly notions of respectability and domesticity) with those of both black and white elite and middle-class reformers and concludes that working-class black women "forged their own distinct ideas about feminine dignity." As Hicks put it, working-class black women were by no means "mute" or "voiceless." On the contrary, their ideas influenced struggles for racial justice and social and economic development in early twentieth-century New York City.[23]

LeFlouria's recent award-winning study *Chained in Silence: Black Women and Convict Labor in the New South* counters a number of prevailing misconceptions about black women and the southern segregationist penal system. Although her book focuses on black women prisoners and chain gang laborers across the state of Georgia, LeFlouria's study also illuminates the experiences of black women from Savannah, Atlanta, and other cities. Specifically, *Chained in Silence* documents how the labor of black women convicts alongside that of black men reinforced the industrialization of the "New South." Whereas the state of Alabama sex-segregated men and women in the convict labor process, Georgia mixed men and women on work crews. "Whether working together or separately, bondswomen and bondsmen assembled railroads, mined clay, fired bricks, chopped down trees, sawed lumber, built roads, plowed fields, and raised crops."[24]

Whereas LeFlouria emphasizes the work and labor dimensions of black women convicts' lives, historian Sarah Haley covers essentially the same temporal and geographical ground but accents the racial construction of gender ideology as both a "discursive and material process." Specifically, her book *No Mercy Here: Gender, Punishment, and the Making of Jim Crow Modernity* contributes to what historians Kali Gross and Cheryl Hicks recently described as "the tangled dynamics of race, gender, enslavement, and the law" in black women's long history of incarceration. She convincingly argues that race and gender represented "mutually constitutive" and exceedingly "violent" forces not only in the construction of subordinate "subject positions" in law and practice but also in the production of knowledge, the southern penal regime itself, and ultimately the larger system of what she describes as "Jim Crow modernity." Whereas so much of working-class resistance and social movement scholarship emphasizes work stoppages and diverse forms of physical encounters, Haley documents these as well as the rhetoric of resistance as expressed by black prison women themselves as well as ideas advanced in black popular blues recordings of their nonprison sisters.[25]

As the African American urban field documented the complicated intersections of class, gender, and race across regions, groundbreaking studies by Davarian Baldwin, Adam Green, Wallace Best, Clare Corbould, Kevin Mumford, and others revamped our understanding of the "new Negro" phenomenon, development of a black "public sphere," consumer culture, the black church, community, and religious beliefs from the vantage point of poor and working-class black urbanites.[26] In his innovative study of consumer culture and intellectual life in 1920s Chicago, Baldwin adopts the notion of "marketplace intellectual" and places the newly arrived black migrant or "the folk" as "consumer patrons" at the core of his novel bottom-up analysis of the "interface between urban and migrant cultural practices and the mass consumer marketplace." In short, in the lives of many poor and working-class blacks, Baldwin persuasively argues that the power of expression "found on Chicago's city streets and in its cinemas, beauty salons, Sanctified churches, and sports stadiums, arguably loom[s] larger than the traditional mediums of pen, paint, and paper."[27]

Similar to Baldwin, Corbould underscores the making of a "black public sphere" that not only embraced formal "print culture" but also built upon live, recorded, and radio music as well as dynamic street-level interactions and performances of all kinds, including public oratory and debates on pressing contemporary issues. Above all, she concludes that this new public space enabled the masses of previously "enslaved or oppressed [black] working people to communicate with one another away from the ears of white people." "Black citizens" of these new public spaces "used style to distinguish themselves from white Americans and to link black America [and the diaspora] to Africa, a continent where oral cultures dominated." She also gives substantial attention to the transnational dimensions of this process, involving substantial ties of black New Yorkers to Haiti and African countries. As such, she concludes that African-descended people not only forged their own unique sense of peoplehood but offered a model for other ethnic and racial groups, including Europeans, to advance their own claims to distinctive ethnic identities and nationalities.[28] For his part, however, in his study of Newark, historian Kevin Mumford carefully underscores how the black public sphere emerged from the racially exclusionary and antidemocratic or "civic racism" of the white public sphere.[29]

Closely related to analyses by Mumford, Baldwin, and Corbould, historian Wallace Best documents the profound transformation of black religious culture under the impact of the Great Migration and class formation. He shows how black women emerged at the forefront of a new generation of working-class church leaders while an older "coterie of well-educated, middle class male minsters" declined in influence. Specifically, Best underscores how southern black working-class and poor migrants created "a new sacred order"—one that increasingly synthesized social services and spiritual support to meet their needs during the industrial era.[30]

Building upon the theoretical and methodological insights of twentieth-century literary, social, and political analysts (including Vernon Forrest, Raymond Williams, Clifford Geertz, and Benedict Anderson), historian Adam Green reinforces the basic claims of Best and Baldwin. He persuasively argues that Windy City blacks not only helped to create a synthesis of black sacred and secular music but also participated in both production and consumer markets as liberating processes. *Selling the Race: Culture, Community, and Black Chicago, 1940–1950* also demonstrates that black blues men and women were neither fully middle class nor wholly working class. Before gaining a foothold in their craft, however, aspiring black artists invariably held a variety of working-class jobs as general laborers, but they cultivated a kind of professionalism, ambition, and entrepreneurship that defied easy categorization as either working class or middle class in orientation.[31]

In addition to studies that treat African American workers within the larger framework of urban community formation and movements for social change, this book also incorporates a significant body of research on specific aspects of the labor force. This scholarship includes an expanding number of case studies of dockworkers, meatpackers, steelworkers, autoworkers, household service workers, and railroad workers, most notably porters and the Brotherhood of Sleeping Car Porters (BSCP). Studies by Eric Arnesen, Rick Halpern, John Hinshaw, David Lewis-Colman, and Dennis Dickerson, among others, illuminate the dynamics of interracial conflict and cooperation among black and white workers on the docks of the waterfront, in the railroad industry other than as porters, in automobile plants, on the killing floors of meatpacking plants, and in the blast furnaces and foundries of the steel industry, and, as alluded to above, studies by Elizabeth Clark-Lewis, Tera Hunter, and recently Premilla Nadasen, among others, focus attention on black women household workers.[32] Despite the substantial numbers of black workers who worked the rails as track laborers and maintenance-of-way employees, firemen, and brakemen, as Arnesen notes in *Brotherhoods of Color,* black Pullman car porters have received the lion's share of research on blacks in a particular industry. In their recent collection of essays, *Reframing Randolph,* historians Andrew E. Kersten and Clarence Lang highlight the dramatic transformation of scholarship on both Randolph (as a labor leader and social justice activist) and the struggles of the Brotherhood of Sleeping Car Porters over the past decades.[33] Whereas William H. Harris's groundbreaking study of Randolph and the BSCP, *Keeping the Faith,* had broadened our understanding of the union from the vantage point of lesser-known figures in the Brotherhood, two decades later, studies by Paula F. Pfeffer, Melinda Chateauvert, Beth Tompkins Bates, Cornelius L. Bynum, and Cynthia Taylor deepened our understanding of railroad porters by probing such questions as manhood and manhood rights, gender equity for the black women maids in the railroad workforce, and Randolph's religiosity as a component of his labor and social activism and leadership.[34]

While the bulk of scholarship on urban black workers and their communities focuses on the industrial era, this book also benefits from recent changes in our perspective on the preindustrial black urban working class. Unlike research on the industrial era, however, the first round of post–World War II research on the early black urban working class unfolded within the larger context of regional studies of free blacks and slaves in the North and South. In 1961, historian Leon Litwack published his pioneering study *North of Slavery: The Negro in the Free States, 1790–1860*. Litwack called attention to the many ways that "the more subtle forms of twentieth-century racial discrimination had their antecedents in the ante bellum North" before the onset of the segregationist system of the late nineteenth and early twentieth centuries. Yet, he concluded his analysis with an emphasis on the wider margins of freedom for blacks in the urban North compared to the predominantly rural South. "Above all," he said, "the northern Negro was a free [wage-earning] man; he was not subject to the whims and dictates of the master or overseer; he could not be bought and sold; he could not be arbitrarily separated from his family."[35]

A little over a decade later, historian Ira Berlin challenged Litwack's perspective on free people of color in antebellum America. In his influential study *Slaves without Masters: The Free Negro in the Antebellum South,* Berlin showed how the experiences of free blacks in the urban North were not entirely unique. In such southern cities as Charleston, New Orleans, Savannah, Richmond, and Baltimore, free blacks gained greater access to skilled jobs and property than most of their northern counterparts. Within the South, however, there were also important differences in the experiences of free people of color from region to region. By the late antebellum years, African Americans enjoyed greater access to freedom in Baltimore, situated in the declining tobacco region of the Chesapeake, than they did in Charleston, Savannah, and New Orleans, located in the booming cotton- and sugar-producing regions of the Deep South.[36]

Other regional studies of the colonial and early American South focused directly on the institution of urban slavery itself. Published in 1964, Richard Wade's *Slavery in the Cities* set the terms for an ongoing debate over the precise relationship between urbanization, cities, and the system of human bondage. Wade cast his net broadly across the entire border, Upper South, and Lower South, including large cities as well as small towns. With the notable exception of Richmond, Wade concluded that slavery had declined in the urban South because the city itself "had created its own kind of world, with a pace, sophistication, and environment that separated it from rural modes. In the process it transformed Negro no less than white, slave no less than free man." Furthermore, according to Wade, "It was the total environment rather than industrial or commercial employment which eroded slavery in the cities. The problem was not what happened in the factory or shop but what happened in the back street, the church, the grocery store, the rented room, and the out-of-the-way house. It was not contact with machines or an industrial process which broke the discipline, it was contact with people of all kinds in numerous ways which generated the corrosive acids."[37]

Over the next decade studies by Robert Starobin (1970), Ronald Lewis (1979), and Claudia Goldin (1976) contested Wade's thesis about the "corrosive" nature of the city and the trajectory of urban bondage. In *Urban Slavery in the American South,* economic historian Claudia Goldin concluded that cities and slavery were by no means "incompatible." Cities, she said, "were just subject to more dramatic shifts in slave populations due to the availability of substitute [free white] labor and to other factors which made the urban demand for slaves more elastic than for rural areas."[38]

Instead of privileging the city itself as a liberating force in rise of a free wage-earning black proletariat, however, recent studies emphasize the impact of working-class enslaved and free blacks on the urban environment itself. This scholarship emphasizes how enslaved people adapted "to urban environments to benefit from what they had to offer" and illuminates how African people "contributed to shaping an environment that could be beneficial to them." Mariana Dantas offers a comparative study of colonial Baltimore and Sabará, Brazil, emphasizing how black urbanites, enslaved and free, helped to craft and extend the system of living and working out, earn income, and purchase their own freedom. For her part, Nathalie Dessens documents the impact of Saint-Domingue migrants on the culture, economics, and politics of New Orleans in the wake of the Haitian Revolution. She illuminates what she describes as a process of continuing "creolization" or "re-creolization" of culture among migrants who were in effect "refugees" from diverse backgrounds, European and African, enslaved and free.[39]

But this issue is by no means settled. Based upon a close study of enslaved women in Bridgetown, Barbados, a recent prize-winning book by Marisa J. Fuentes, *Dispossessed Lives: Enslaved Women, Violence, and the Archive,* challenges scholars of slave societies in the Caribbean and North America to attend to sharp "continuities ... of violence from plantation to the urban complex." In her view, urban labor was by no means "necessarily easier and less constraining or violent" than plantation slavery.[40]

Community studies of preindustrial black urban life gradually gained a foothold during the late 1970s and 1980s and continued to expand over the next two decades. The initial outpouring of scholarship focused mainly on the antebellum North. Studies by James and Lois Horton, Robert J. Cottrol, Gary Nash, and Julie Winch uncovered the early dynamics of migration, work, and community formation among enslaved and free blacks.[41] During the final decade of the twentieth century and the first decade of the new century, historians Shane White, Harry Reed, Leslie Harris, Leslie Alexander, and Jane Dabel, to name a few, increasingly transformed our understanding of African American life and labor in colonial, revolutionary, and early American as well as antebellum northern cities.[42] Harris shows how Africans made the transition from enslaved to free workers and how African ideas and cultural practices influenced the process of class formation, while historian Dabel situates working-class black women even more squarely at the core of her study of mid-nineteenth-century New York City, arguing that the lives of poor and working-class black women "were not less influential than their middle-class counterparts."[43] Alexander focuses primarily on the elite or leadership dimensions of New York City's changing black culture. Rather than emphasizing the role of black workers and working-class dynamics, Alexander accents "the leadership's changing relationship to its African cultural heritage and the ideological battles among Black activists over questions of political strategy and racial identity as they responded to local, state, national and international movements."[44]

Recent research offers equally compelling insights into the development of African American life and labor in the eighteenth- and early nineteenth-century urban South. Unlike scholarship on the urban North, however, research on the urban South also explores the utility of the "three-tier" interpretation of class and race relations in early America. During the early nineteenth century, the argument goes, a significant free black population emerged in the urban Deep South. Although linked to their enslaved counterparts through kinship and the history of enslavement, precariously situated free people of color nonetheless allied with slave-owning white elites over their enslaved brothers and sisters, particularly in New Orleans and Charleston.[45]

Local case studies of slavery in the urban South reveal significant variation from city to city. In his analysis of antebellum Charleston, historian Bernard Powers demonstrates how all antebellum free blacks "suffered from the oppressive burdens" of slavery, "but, despite its strictures . . . a comparatively prosperous, cultured, mulatto elite developed." Some of these free people of color owned slaves, allied with white elites, received certain privileges, and served as a protective buffer between whites and the darker-skinned and "dangerous" black slave majority.[46] Conversely, in his illuminating study of Savannah, Georgia, Whittington Johnson challenges regional studies that treat Savannah as one of several three-tier cities in the antebellum South. In Savannah, according to Johnson, the lives of enslaved and free people of color remained tightly intertwined as they struggled together to build an independent black church. Thus, in his view, "Black Savannah was not a replica, therefore, of other communities in the Lower South."[47] In their collection of essays on Savannah's history from the colonial era through recent times, historians Leslie Harris and Daina Berry reinforce emphasis on the convergence of experiences among free and enslaved blacks during the preindustrial era.[48] For his part, Christopher Phillips concludes that antebellum Baltimore was more "inclusive of free Negroes as well as slaves" than elsewhere and therefore "less racked by class and intraracial divisions" than black communities in northern and Deep South cities like Philadelphia, Charleston, and New Orleans.[49]

Similar to researchers on the urban North, scholars of the urban South gradually brought the experiences of black women and gender relations under systematic investigation. Focusing on the experiences of free black women of Charleston, historian Amrita Myers places free black women's definition of freedom at the center of her story. Building upon the insights of historian Wilma King and others, Myers illuminates how "freedom meant more to persons of color than just an end to physical bondage." Among many other things, freedom also meant access to the legal apparatus of the state to certify emancipation and prevent reenslavement of one's self and loved ones. Freedom for preindustrial black female Charlestonians, Myers pointedly concludes, was nonetheless not "a fixed legal category" but an "experience." Similarly, in her study of "libres" in Spanish-occupied New Orleans, historian Kimberly Hanger underscores how preindustrial black women were substantially divided by their class and conditions. Free black women of substantial socioeconomic standing expressed their acceptance of the "barriers of slavery" so long as the boundaries remained fluid enough for them to purchase and liberate their own kin.[50]

Local community studies of black life and labor by no means exhaust the range of relevant studies on the preindustrial experience. A corpus of colonization and emigration studies offers insights into key dimensions of early nineteenth-century black working-class life and labor.[51] Similarly, the history of the early black working class is integral to the huge body of scholarship on the Underground Railroad, particularly the rising emphasis on the centrality of enslaved and free blacks in constructing this intricate network of resistance to slavery.[52]

CHANGING PERSPECTIVES ON THE LATE
TWENTIETH CENTURY

In relatively rapid succession over the past quarter century, studies of the long civil rights movement, deindustrialization, the underclass, the urban crisis, and, most recently, the carceral state have transformed our understanding of the late twentieth-century black working class. Sociologist William J. Wilson's body of scholarship set the terms of debate on African American life and labor in the emerging postindustrial phase of urbanization and U.S. capitalist development. In 1978, the University of Chicago published Wilson's influential book *The Declining Significance of Race: Blacks and Changing American Institutions.* Impressed by the successes of the Modern Black Freedom Movement in opening doors of opportunity for the expansion of a highly educated black middle class, Wilson suggested that the nation had turned the corner toward a much more class- as opposed to race- or caste-based society. Such white supremacist ideas and social practices were on the wane as the emerging new equal-opportunity regime took hold.[53]

A decade later, Wilson published his equally influential *The Truly Disadvantaged: The Inner City, the Underclass, and Public Policy*. Whereas a certain amount of optimism had animated his earlier work, this study sounded an alarm regarding the rapid and disproportionate spread of poverty across black urban America. In Wilson's view, this phenomenon was a product of the rapid deindustrialization of the nation's economy. It also took a toll on white poor and working-class families; in addition, it represented the emergence of a new "underclass" of long-term unemployed, disproportionately black female urbanites with children, which challenged liberal policy makers to acknowledge and take urgent steps to address the issue. Specifically, Wilson decried the rising chorus of conservative voices arguing that, rather than structural changes like deindustrialization, it was the social service and affirmative action programs of the civil rights era that had undermined the black work ethic and produced the crisis of the increasing long-term-unemployed, poor black population.[54]

Partly to counter conservative voices regarding the cultural deficiencies of poor and working-class blacks, Wilson advocated broad class-based employment and social welfare policies. Such policies, he believed, would improve the lives of poor blacks and whites and alleviate some of the unfolding conflicts over affirmative action and other programs that whites increasingly viewed as "reverse discrimination." Although Wilson would soon abandon his notion of underclass and give greater room to the persistence of racialized forms of inequality, it was Douglas Massey and Nancy Denton who offered an alternative that brought the persistence of race and racialized forms of discrimination back into the forefront of analysis. In 1993, adopting notions of "hypersegregation" and "apartheid," building on the worldwide human rights sanctions against the South African system of racial segregation, Massey and Denton underscored the persistence of racial practices and policies by real estate firms, banks, and government housing agencies that reinforced the color line in low-income public and private housing markets during the closing decades of the twentieth century.[55]

In his seminal study *Origins of the Urban Crisis: Race and Inequality in Postwar Detroit*, historian Thomas Sugrue responded primarily to arguments advanced by Wilson and other sociologists, economists, and policy analysts on the timing and impact of deindustrialization on employment, housing, and race relations in the late twentieth-century city. Informed partly by Arnold Hirsch's conceptualization of the "second ghetto," particularly its emphasis on violent grassroots white opposition to African American movement into white neighborhoods, Sugrue added an equally powerful focus on white opposition to equal employment for black workers and their families as the industrial economy declined in the years after World War II. Focusing on the city of Detroit between World War II and 1960, Sugrue analyzed the roots of what he called the "contemporary urban crisis," defined as the way the city's vibrant industrial economy gave way to a city "plagued by joblessness,

concentrated poverty, physical decay, and racial isolation" by the 1990s. He emphasized how, at the same time that blacks developed a civil rights movement and
demanded full access to the fruits of the industrial city, working- and middle-class
whites escalated their demands for social welfare services, job security, housing subsidies, and other benefits from the state, particularly jobs on new highway construction projects that fueled increasing movement to the suburbs. Sugrue offered few
insights into the role that blacks played in shaping their own experiences under the
impact of deindustrialization, rising unemployment, and poverty.[56]

Over the past decade, a growing volume of studies challenged Sugrue's limited
perspective on the role that poor and working-class blacks played in their own
deindustrializing experience. If deindustrialization had deep roots in the early
years after World War II, then, this scholarship suggests, the spread of the Modern
Black Freedom struggle was partly a response to the nascent "urban crisis." Research
by historians Donna Murch, Clarence Lang, Luther Adams, Rhonda Williams,
Kevin Mumford, Robert Self, Wendell Pritchett, Marcus Hunter, Martha Biondi,
Matthew Countryman, Heather Thompson, Lisa Levenstein, and others elucidates
African American class, gender, and cross-class labor, community, and worker activism during the era of increasing deindustrialization. Taken together, for example,
Countryman and Hunter show how black Philadelphians "constructed a vital and
effective social movement" that remade the city's "political and cultural landscape"
during the late 1960s and 1970s, and—as symbolized by the election of Wilson
Goode as the city's first black mayor in 1983—moved the African American community from the periphery to the center of municipal politics. African Americans
helped to "frame" their own understanding of urban social change; they forged
vibrant inter- and intra-racial alliances that allowed them to shape their own
migration from the old Seventh Ward into new black urban communities on
Philadelphia's North, West, and South sides. In varying degrees, these processes
played out elsewhere, but they also entailed significant fissures in cross-class alliances that characterized late twentieth-century black politics.[57]

In her stellar study of the Black Panther Party (BPP), *Living for the City,* Donna
Murch documents the impact of recurring waves of southern black newcomers on
the economy, culture, and politics of postwar Oakland, including the rise of the
Black Panther Party and numerous other radical black political organizations. She
demonstrates how young black men and women carried the "moral and spiritual
values of their parents," some grounded in the Pentecostal church, into the development of a plethora of black radical groups determined to challenge the persistence
of class and racial inequality in the Bay Area. These organizations included the West
Coast branch of the Revolutionary Action Movement (RAM) as well as the Black
Panther Party. *Living for the City* also shows how Oakland-based black radicalism
developed increasing connections with decolonization movements across the globe
in the wake of the Los Angeles Watts rebellion of 1965. Echoing Earl Lewis's earlier

suggestions about the significance of "home" and the "home sphere," historian Luther Adams reflects on the interrelationship between black power and the so-called urban crisis from the vantage point of a southern city, Louisville, Kentucky. He places the notion of home at the center of his study and persuasively argues that persistent patterns of class and racial inequality did not rob black people of their capacity to act in their own interests during the increasing deindustrialization of the black urban working class. As such, he illuminates black migration, urbanization, and class formation within the South as dynamic processes that brought poor, working-class, elite, and middle-class blacks together—through complicated networks of kin, friends, and community. These networks in turn fueled the rise of the modern civil rights and Black Power movements.[58]

Williams, Levenstein, and Mumford accent the need for better assessments of the role of working-class women, gender relations, and sexuality in late twentieth-century black urban politics and social movements. Focusing on the experiences of black women in the public housing projects of Baltimore, Williams shows how public housing residents not only fought for "daily subsistence" but also for societal recognition and human rights during Baltimore's gradual transformation into a postindustrial city. Although their actions failed to arrest the long-term racialized assault on social welfare provisions in the late twentieth-century urban political economy, the efforts of public housing tenants no less than those of their middle-class counterparts helped to influence policy at the local, state, and federal levels. Yet according to Williams, studies of black workers too often privilege the experiences of black men and the vagaries of wage labor, while studies of black women and the gender construction of social welfare policies emphasize the doings of middle-class women and their elite allies. Levenstein reinforces this point. She shows how Philadelphia's poor and working-class black women not only "worked" to secure essential welfare services from reluctant and very intrusive state bureaucracies but also devised a variety of stances toward the highly racialized system of welfare services itself. Some women used the welfare system to avoid or bid up the price of their labor as domestics or other low-paid service workers, while others opted to work in exceedingly low-wage jobs to avoid the surveillance of the welfare state.[59]

Building upon the extraordinary accomplishments of his first book, *Interzones,* Kevin Mumford offers an equally compelling perspective on the lives of black women in his second book, *Newark: A History of Race, Rights, and Riots in America.* This book illuminates the role of women and gender dynamics in the outbreak of violence and official responses to the 1967 Newark riot. Mumford shows how authorities camouflaged the identity of women in presenting lists of people killed at the hands of police brought in to put down the violence. He also documents the treatment of women as participants in the violence, noting how political and economic elites created the "criminal female" image alongside the "criminal male" image in descriptions of the rioters. Such portraits of young black women justified their rough treatment, along with black men, by police officers. In other words, Mumford urges us to consider how issues of racial as well as class and gender hierarchies shaped the politics of urban blacks during the second half of the twentieth century.[60]

In his forthcoming book on gay and lesbian experiences in late twentieth-century Washington, DC, historian Kwame Holmes adds the issue of sexuality to recent emphases on the interplay of class, race, and gender relations in black urban history. Treating the experiences of gay men and lesbians in the nation's capital as a case study of developments following Stonewall but before the onset of the HIV/AIDS epidemic, Holmes shows how, unlike their black gay and lesbian counterparts, white gay men and lesbians penetrated the power structure of DC and achieved major victories through the electoral process—including removal of prohibitions against the employment of gays in the public schools; inclusion of gays in human rights legislation; defunding of "morals squads" charged with monitoring the behavior and curtailing the freedom of gays and lesbians; and municipal sanction of Gay Pride Day celebrations. As Holmes puts it, DC's political geography "produced white gay ghettos and dissolved black gay residency into the broader black urban population."[61]

Some scholars not only addressed the urban crisis thesis but also engaged in debates about the "long civil rights movement." In March 2005, the *Journal of American History* published Jacquelyn Dowd Hall's presidential address to the Organization of American Historians, "The Long Civil Rights Movement and the Political Uses of the Past." Hall urged historians to extend the chronology of the Modern Black Freedom Movement back from the mid-1960s into the interwar years on the one hand and forward into the late twentieth century on the other. But historians Clarence Lang and Sundiata Keita Cha-Jua soon warned that such an effort risks ahistoricizing and homogenizing the Black Freedom struggle by blurring the line between what they consider distinct social conditions surrounding the black liberation movement at particular moments in time. In their view, the long civil rights movement notion threatened to give the movement a vampire-like quality by downplaying its distinctive historical dimensions.[62]

Clarence Lang and Heather Thompson offered somewhat different emphases on the import of the "long civil rights" thesis and the related argument about the decline of working-class activism and social justice struggles during the 1970s. In his book on St. Louis, Lang not only illuminates the pivotal role of working-class blacks in the development of the city's Modern Black Freedom Movement but also underscores its decline in the wake of "capitalist disinvestment and economic restructuring" during the late twentieth century. He concludes that St. Louis clearly emerged as "the patron saint of the national urban crisis" with black workers facing an uphill struggle to retain the vitality of their earlier grassroots movements. On a somewhat different note, Heather Thompson documents the emergence of Detroit as a "war zone" of labor and race conflicts by the mid-1970s but concludes that urban class and race relations were more complex than urban-crisis scholarship would lead us to believe. She shows how a vibrant urban-based, interracial, liberal movement persisted through the mid-1980s.[63]

Even as a growing body of scholarship successfully challenged the urban-crisis perspective on late twentieth- and early twenty-first-century African American urban life, a very recent cohort of studies also contests the victimization portrait of the urban-crisis school. But these scholars also urge us to acknowledge and account for a broader range of white reactions to the movement of middle- and working-class African Americans into certain previously all-white communities in the years after World War II; to reconceptualize aspects of the Modern Black Freedom Movement in environmental terms; and to move away from the making of racially stratified urban communities to the "unmaking" of the "ghetto" by the late twentieth century.[64] Based upon the systematic examination of several black neighborhoods on the periphery but inside the municipal boundaries of Cleveland (most notably Glenville, Mt. Pleasant, and Lee-Harvard), Todd Michney's new *Surrogate Suburbs: Black Upward Mobility and Neighborhood Change in Cleveland, 1900–1980* reinterprets the class and racial dynamics of black population movement from established to new neighborhoods within the city. Michney concludes that white hostility was not nearly as prominent in the process of new black neighborhood formation in Cleveland as scholars have found in Detroit and Chicago. Specifically, in the outlying areas, this study shows how black residents were not only predominantly southern-born black workers (men, women, and their children) who lived in husband-wife families, but they were also African Americans who purchased land through established mortgage financing arrangements with the aid of their white neighbors.[65]

A recent study by Robert R. Gioielli embraces aspects of the urban crisis argument but emphasizes modes of urban working-class activism and responses to inequality from the vantage point of environmental history. He persuasively argues that scholars of emerging postindustrial black urban life address but do not explicitly define environmental issues in the recurring social struggles over housing, jobs, and neighborhood conditions. In order to help close this gap in our knowledge of the interplay of civil rights and environmental struggles, Gioielli recasts much of the contents of these social movements into categories that fall squarely within what he defines as the purview of environmentalism. Focusing on Baltimore, St. Louis, and Chicago as case studies, Gioielli documents the grassroots movement of African Americans and working-class urbanites against childhood lead poisoning and destructive highway construction projects as part of a broader struggle to create a healthier and safer physical environment. At the same time, he laments how self-proclaimed environmental activists (mainly middle-class and elite white men and women) remain preoccupied with definitions of the environmental movement that privilege ideas about the "wilderness, animals, and the general health of the planet" rather than concerns of African Americans, the poor, and "civil rights, community, and/or housing activists." In short, he urges historians of urban class, race, and ethnic relations to avoid defining all questions of unequal power relations as "environmental justice" concerns and confining environmental issues to the doings of predominantly middle-class and elite white men and women.[66]

Focusing on Brooklyn's Bedford-Stuyvesant community from the 1960s through recent times, historian Brian Purnell introduces the notion of "unmaking the ghetto" as a novel concept for understanding the emergence of a new era in postindustrial America. In doing so, he flips the usual approach to ghetto formation on its head. Instead of documenting the "making" and/or "remaking" of the ghetto, the notion of "unmaking" allows him to uncover a process by which multiclass black activists launched a successful assault on a wide range of "structural causes" associated with an earlier pattern of ghetto making, including "redlining, blockbusting, realtor speculating, deindustrialization, and restricted access to bank credit." African American women spearheaded this movement, which ultimately failed, as the arrival of increasing numbers of young, white, "moneyed," and "creative classes" unmade the ghetto by nudging poor and working-class black residents out into inner ring, previously all-white suburbs that became blacker and poorer, while the old ghetto became whiter and richer.[67]

Similar to research on the industrial era, carceral state studies represent a rapidly developing field of study on late twentieth-century African American life. In *The New Jim Crow: Mass Incarceration in the Age of Colorblindness*, legal scholar Michelle Alexander set the terms of debate in this field. Focusing on the rise of the mass imprisonment of young black men in the wake of civil rights–era achievements in demolishing the old Jim Crow, Alexander persuasively argues that the lives of this group of black males and their families constitute the emergence of a "new Jim Crow," or "racial caste" system, defined much like the earlier Jim Crow and racial caste order: "Rather than rely on race, we use our criminal justice system to label people of color 'criminals' and then engage in all the [Jim Crow] practices we supposedly left behind. Today it is perfectly legal to discriminate against criminals in nearly all the ways that it was once legal to discriminate against African Americans." Specifically, Alexander underscores how the new Jim Crow embodies a new mechanism for "racial control." As she puts it, "Mass incarceration operates as a tightly knit system of laws, policies, customs, and institutions that operate collectively to ensure the subordinate status of a group defined largely by race."[68] Alexander's study dovetails with Nathan Connolly's emphasis on the persistence of the Jim Crow order under the feet of civil rights–era marchers, but Connolly underscores how blacks and whites of different class backgrounds reinforced Greater Miami's color line during the late twentieth century. Black tenants decried exploitive rental housing practices of black realtors and middle-class political leaders, but the various civil rights initiatives of black elites often blunted the force of their criticism and to some extent abetted the construction and reconstruction of the Jim Crow system.[69]

Since publication of Alexander's seminal critique of the criminal justice system a half decade ago, carceral-state studies of the black urban population have dramatically expanded. These studies both reinforce and challenge certain of Alexander's propositions. While Alexander focused almost exclusively on black men, recent efforts offer growing insights into the experiences of black women and the gendered as well as racial and class dimensions of incarceration. Other recent studies accent the connection between inner city and suburban aspects of the massive incarceration phenomenon, along with increasing attention given to the relationship between deindustrialization of the urban North and West and the expansion of the Sunbelt South and West as both sites of employment in the emerging new economy and the proliferating prison industrial complex.[70]

GLOBAL RESEARCH

This book also benefits from an expanding body of transnational and comparative research on African American urban life. In 1995, in his innovative assessment of scholarship on the black experience from enslavement through the closing decades of the twentieth century, historian Earl Lewis urged historians to "write African Americans" into what he called "a history of overlapping diasporas." In advancing this transnational agenda, he accented the special place of cities in such a project. Over the past two decades, scholars produced a growing number of global, transnational, or comparative histories of blacks in cities. In this book, my analysis of urban black workers from the transatlantic slave trade to recent times draws upon this scholarship to illuminate connections between black urban communities and people of color across national boundaries.[71]

A roster of studies by Jeffrey Bolster, Marcus Rediker, Peter Linebaugh, and others uncovers the myriad ways that flows of information back and forth across the Atlantic helped to forge a unique African identity and culture that historian Paul Gilroy defines as the "Black Atlantic." Centered on the experiences of black sailors and seafarers, these transatlantic networks also fueled grassroots social and political movements against the system of enslavement itself. As Jeffrey Bolster put it in his influential study *Black Jacks: African American Seamen in the Age of Sail,* enslaved sailors "linked far-flung black communities and united plantations with urban centers" across the Atlantic world. Notably, Linebaugh and Rediker pinpointed the global dimensions of the New York Conspiracy of 1741 and the multiracial "mobs" of Revolutionary America from Philadelphia and Boston to Charleston, South Carolina. The recent collection of essays *The Black Urban Atlantic in the Age of the Slave Trade* focuses directly on the making of the enslaved and free black urban working class within the broader context of the transatlantic slave trade. As editors Jorge Cañizares-Esguerra, Matt D. Childs, and James Sidbury make clear,

The Black Urban Atlantic not only accents similarities and differences in the rise of enslaved urban black populations on both sides of the Atlantic, but also underscores the need to revamp "long-standing debates about creolization and African cultural survivals" based mainly on staple-producing plantations rather than cities, which provided enslaved blacks with opportunities to live and labor in black communities that "dwarfed even very large plantations" in size, complexity, and access to resources that would facilitate the emancipation process.[72]

Studies by Mariana Dantas, Michael Gomez, Margaret Washington Creel, and Daniel Walker deepen our understanding of urban black workers during the transatlantic slave trade. Focusing on both colonial and early American Baltimore and Sabará, Minas Gerais, Brazil, Dantas shows how black urbanites used the city as a lever to renegotiate urban labor agreements, occupy land, and acquire their own property and freedom in these southern and northern Atlantic places. In these and other ways, enslaved people of African descent helped to define "the character" of urban centers. Although focusing mainly on the rural context, Gomez nonetheless underscores how the Anglicization of African religion was an exceedingly slow process even in early American cities. Furthermore, he persuasively argues that "even if it were true that the rapid replacement of the African-born by their American-born progeny occasioned a steady erosion in the coherence of African indigenous religions, it does not at all follow that, ipso facto, these people were becoming Christian." For her part, Washington Creel concludes that the failure of the Denmark Vesey rebellion of Charleston blacks reinforced rather than diminished the long-term impact of African-inspired Gullah culture and politics. As she puts it, "resistance against white power and hegemony was conspicuous in the Gullah's sense of cultural autonomy, authoritative, creative community-building, and their spiritual disengagement from the slavocracy's version of Christian teachings."[73]

For New Orleans, Walker compared another aspect of early black urban culture, the annual Day of the Kings festival in Havana, Cuba, to the weekly cultural activities of African Americans in "Congo Square" (later, the French Quarter) and concludes that African-descended people in both Havana and New Orleans used these cultural events "as counterstatements to the social-control designs of their respective slave societies." But their responses were products of local conditions in New World cities as well as Old World ideas and social practices. In her pioneering study of people of African descent in Louisiana and Cuba, *Degrees of Freedom,* historian Rebecca Scott shows not only how African people remained connected to each other through complicated channels of transatlantic travel and communication networks but that such connections persisted into the early postemancipation era of both societies. According to Scott, there were ongoing "crossings and recrossings of the Gulf of Mexico" of black men fighting to defeat Jim Crow in New Orleans on the one hand and their counterparts organizing independence movements on the island of Cuba on the other.[74]

As transnational research on the eighteenth and nineteenth centuries expanded, so did scholarship on the global dimensions of twentieth-century African American life and labor. As discussed above, global perspectives also characterized the work of local case studies by Donna Murch and others. But a growing body of studies— such as those by Carl Nightingale, Minkah Makalani, Nico Slate, Gerald Horne, Kevin Gaines, Yevette Richards Jordan, Erik McDuffie, and Keisha Blain—center the transnational and global components of twentieth-century class, race, space, and gender relations. Carl Nightingale's *Segregation: A Global History of Divided Cities* compares the connection between the racially divided housing markets in Baltimore, San Francisco, and Chicago to similar processes in Johannesburg, Calcutta, Nairobi, Hong Kong, and other places around the globe. By 1920, as "segregation reached its high-water mark," Nightingale underscores how African Americans responded by helping to organize "a massive social movement" to resist segregation. By World War II, this movement had forged tangible alliances with emerging liberation movements in Africa, Asia, and around the globe.[75]

A new volume of essays on the "global ghetto" suggests that transnational studies of racially divided cities will likely continue to expand into a very promising area for groundbreaking studies over the next several decades. Focusing on the city of Chicago during the late nineteenth and early twentieth centuries, historian Tobias Brinkmann offers a telling analysis of the ways that the first-generation of German Jews disdained and then embraced their counterparts from Eastern Europe. As their unity took hold, however, both groups distanced themselves from the massive in-migration of rural southern blacks, who increasingly inherited the label "ghetto residents." In his extraordinary contribution to this volume, Jeffrey Gonda illuminates how African Americans and their white allies defined the African American ghetto as a destructive form of human habitation that violated the United Nations charter on human rights. By treating the ghetto as "an international human rights crisis," civil rights attorneys astutely harnessed the increasing national and international condemnation of Nazi ghettos to their spirited and ultimately successful campaign to strike down restrictive covenants in the U.S. Supreme Court case *Shelley v. Kraemer* (1948).[76]

While much of the emerging research on the ghetto in transnational perspective addresses the problematic questions of race, space, structure, and agency in the African American quest for housing and decent living conditions, studies by Makalani, Slate, Horne, and Gaines accent the global dimensions of social movements to dismantle Jim Crow as a component of the worldwide system of European colonialism. Specifically, Makalani illuminates the relationships between African American radicals in New York and their African counterparts in London between the two world wars. Unlike most studies of black internationalism during the period, rather than riveting on the black-white left alliance, Makalani reveals fresh new insights into the way black radicals forged bonds with their Asian counterparts, who "opened up the Comintern so that it might be seen as a vehicle for pan-African liberation." Makalani also adopts what he describes as a "New Negro" perspective on black internationalism that transcends the usual focus on "Harlem and London or Harlem and Paris" and also looks at "Chicago and Paris, Lagos and Hamburg, Liverpool and Marseilles, Cardiff and Accra, Port-au-Prince and Dakar, and Port-of-Spain, Georgetown, and Bridgetown."[77]

Nico Slate's *Colored Cosmopolitanism* reinforces and expands upon the insights of Makalani. Slate explores Black-Indian relations within the larger context of international migration, overlapping diasporas, and the simultaneous spread of the segregationist system in the United States, the expansion of British imperialism, and the reinforcement of caste lines in India. Specifically, *Colored Cosmopolitanism* shows how African Americans and their Indian counterparts forged a dynamic movement against racism, caste, and imperialism on a global scale. They also exposed related intranational forms of oppression, including class and gender, among people of color themselves. African American and Indian activists like W. E. B. Du Bois and Cedric Dover forged a mode of transnational unity that Slate describes as "colored cosmopolitanism." Unlike their earlier "racial diplomacy" counterparts, "colored cosmopolitans," following the scholarly and political writings of W. E. B. Du Bois, recognized the existence of multiple oppressions (class, caste, gender) and sought to bridge social movements designed to deal with these forms of inequality as well as larger patterns of group or national inequality. The notion of colored cosmopolitanism, Slate concludes, gained its greatest expression during World War II as the grassroots March on Washington Movement (MOWM) took hold. Under the leadership of A. Philip Randolph, the MOWM increasingly looked toward Gandhi's Quit India struggle for inspiration.[78]

For his part, however, historian Gerald Horne illuminates the transnational role of the Communist Party member, sailor, and Jamaican-born labor leader Ferdinand Smith. In his groundbreaking book *Red Seas: Ferdinand Smith and Radical Black Sailors in the United States and Jamaica,* Horne documents the process by which Smith helped to found the predominantly white National Maritime Union in 1937 and became "second in command" before his deportation from the country in 1951. Before his departure from the country as an "alien Communist" and a threat to national security during the antiradical Cold War climate of the postwar years, Smith had played a major role in the movement to merge the labor movement and the civil rights movement in the interest of African American liberation. Some contemporary commentators on black labor leadership placed Smith and his union on a par with A. Philip Randolph and the Brotherhood of Sleeping Car Porters.

Kevin Gaines's *American Africans in Ghana: Black Expatriates and the Civil Rights Era* explores the transnational aspects of the nonviolent direct action phase of the Black Freedom Movement. He persuasively argues that Ghana became a desirable site of mid-twentieth-century migration for some African Americans because of U.S. foreign policy (designed to squash a radical black and white left) and changes in the social and political dynamics of the modern civil rights movement on U.S. soil. Conversely, Slate's edited volume *Black Power beyond Borders* illuminates the impact of the Black Panther Party on social movements in such widely dispersed places as Israel, New Zealand, and India.[79]

Similar to research on other aspects of African American urban, labor, and working-class history, until recently most transnational scholarship focused on the doings of black men and neglected the role of women and gender dynamics. But this picture is rapidly changing. At the turn of the twenty-first century, based upon a plethora of oral interviews and extensive manuscript collections on the international black female labor leader Maida Springer-Kemp, for example, historian Yevette Richards Jordan has focused on the intertwined questions of race, labor, gender, and the African American woman. *Maida Springer-Kemp: Pan-Africanist and International Labor Leader* not only addresses overemphasis on male activists, intellectuals, and labor leaders like A. Philip Randolph and W. E. B. Du Bois but also suggests the need to rethink the role of such national black leaders as Malcolm X and Martin Luther King, Jr., in national and international affairs. By carefully exploring Springer-Kemp's extensive interactions with white labor leaders in both the United States and Britain, Richards Jordan offers a stellar assessment of the interplay of race, sex, nationality, and union affiliation during the repressive cold war struggle of African Americans for social justice at home and overseas.[80]

Sojourning for Freedom: Black Women, American Communism, and the Making of Black Left Feminism, historian Erik McDuffie's innovative study, illuminates heretofore largely hidden dimensions of grassroots black politics. His study not only employs the notion of "black left feminism" to illustrate how black radical women developed the concept of "triple oppression" to explain the unique suffering of African American women in urban industrial society, but it also emphasizes how the ideas of black women communists seeded the postwar black feminist movement of the 1960s and 1970s. In addition, *Sojourning for Freedom* documents the community networks that these women built to support each other in their fight against male and racial bias within the party as well as capitalist oppression outside the party. But the activities of these women were not limited to the local or even the national level but embraced the struggles of women on a global scale. They forged their own "black women's international" to challenge the global dimensions of the "intersecting" gender, race, and class biases that they encountered within the economy and politics of the United States.[81]

Similar to McDuffie's contribution to knowledge of black women's class as well as gender politics in global perspective, historian Keisha N. Blain's new book *Set the World on Fire: Black Nationalist Women and the Global Struggle for Freedom* promises to revamp our understanding of the transnational dimensions of the Garvey movement. Unlike so many studies that treat Garvey and black nationalism as distant forces by the late 1920s, Blain shows how the movement persisted well into the post–World War II years and helped to animate the rise of black feminism. Most important, poor and working-class black women were key spearheads of the movement's longevity and impact on black politics during the era of the Modern Black Freedom Movement.[82]

CONCLUSION

As suggested by studies employed in this book, African American urban labor and working-class history is a dynamic and changing field of scholarship. Under the impact of the Modern Black Freedom Movement, African American urban history emerged as a vibrant professional enterprise during the years after World War II. But this research and writing had its genesis in the publication of a series of ground-breaking interdisciplinary social scientific investigations of African American urban life and labor during the early twentieth century. Building upon these pioneering efforts, in relatively rapid succession, a series of overlapping studies analyzed patterns of residential segregation and community formation during the 1960s and 1970s; class and labor relations during the 1980s; and the complicated intersections of race, class, and gender since the 1990s. While the initial phases of this scholarship focused primarily on the urban Northeast and Midwest, local case studies included a growing volume of research on the industrial, preindustrial, and emerging postindustrial urban North, West, and South as the new century got under way.

Comparative, global, and transnational research also gradually emerged and helped to reshape our perspective on African American labor and working-class history across regional and national boundaries. In the meantime, yet another generation of innovative research is already unfolding within the larger context of the mass incarceration of young black men and women during the closing decades of the twentieth century and the evolving twenty-first-century Black Lives Matter movement. This movement answers Michelle Alexander's ringing plea for an aggressive grassroots assault against the spread of the new Jim Crow into the contemporary social, economic, and political life of the nation. The dynamic interplay of these forces within and outside the academy will no doubt soon produce a dramatic reinterpretation of African America's long urban labor and working-class history. It is my hope that this synthesis will provide a helpful intellectual foundation for that effort.

NOTES

PROLOGUE

1. Michael Zweig, "White Working-Class Voters and the Future of Progressive Politics, *New Labor Forum Blog,* May 11, 2017, http://newlaborforum.cuny .edu/2017/05/11/white-working-class-voters-and-the-future-of-progressive-politics/; quote from Tyler Stovall, "Race, Class, and History in the Trump Era," *Perspectives on History: The Newsmagazine of the AHA,* May 2017, www.historians.org/publications-and-directories/perspectives-on-history/may-2017/race-class-and-history-in-the-trump-era; Justin Gest, *The New Minority: White Working Class in an Age of Immigration and Inequality* (New York: Oxford University Press, 2016), 20–23; Arlie R. Hochschild, *Strangers in Their Own Land: Anger and Mourning on the American Right* (New York: New Press, 2016), 3–23.

2. Seth Rockman, *Scraping By: Wage Labor, Slavery, and Survival in Early Baltimore* (Baltimore: John Hopkins University, 2009), 1–2. Cf. Peter Way, *Common Labour: Workers and the Digging of North American Canals, 1780–1860* (Cambridge: Cambridge University Press, 1993), 6.

3. Eric Foner and Lisa McGirr, *American History Now* (Philadelphia: Temple University Press, 2011); Peter Novick, *That Noble Dream: The "Objectivity Question" and the American Historical Profession* (Cambridge: Cambridge University Press, 1988); Julie Des Jardins, *Women and the Historical Enterprise in America: Gender, Race, and the Politics of Memory, 1880–1945* (Chapel Hill: University of North Carolina Press, 2003); Ellen Fitzpatrick, *History's Memory: Writing America's Past, 1880–1980* (Cambridge: Harvard University Press, 2002); Darlene Clark Hine, *The State of Afro-American History: Past, Present, and Future* (Baton Rouge: Louisiana State University Press, 1987). Popular social and political history accounts of U.S. history included initially Howard Zinn, *A People's History of the United States* (1980; repr. New York: Harper/Collins, 2005), followed by a plethora of diverse new syntheses on the subject, including Christopher Clark, Nancy Hewitt, Joshua Brown, and David Jaffee, *Who Built America? Working People and the Nation's History,* vols. 1 and 2, 3rd ed. (Boston: Bedford/St. Martin's, 2008). For a telling recent study of

negative popular and elite perceptions of the white poor and "the pervasiveness of a class hierarchy" in U.S. history, see Nancy Isenberg, *White Trash: The 400-Year Untold History of Class in America* (New York: Viking, 2016), xvii.

4. Kenneth Pomeranz, "Histories for a Less National Age" (Presidential Address, annual meeting of the American Historical Association, Washington, DC, January 3, 2014).

5. Jorge Cañizares-Esguerra, Matt D. Childs, and James Sidbury, eds., *The Black Urban Atlantic in the Age of the Slave Trade* (Philadelphia: University of Pennsylvania Press, 2013); Sven Beckert, *Empire of Cotton: A Global History* (New York: Knopf, 2014); Edward Baptist, *The Half Has Never Been Told: Slavery and the Making of American Capitalism* (New York: Basic Books, 2014); Walter Johnson, *River of Dark Dreams: Slavery and Empire in the Cotton Kingdom* (Cambridge: Belknap Press / Harvard University Press, 2013); Nico Slate, *Colored Cosmopolitanism: The Shared Struggle for Freedom in the United States and India* (Cambridge: Harvard University Press, 2012); Minkah Makalani, *In the Cause of Freedom: Radical Black Internationalism from Harlem to London, 1917–1939* (Chapel Hill: University of North Carolina Press, 2011); Lara Putnam, *Radical Moves: Caribbean Migrants and the Politics of the Jazz Age* (Chapel Hill: University of North Carolina Press, 2013). For a ringing early call for transnational scholarship on the black urban experience that is now in full bloom, see Earl Lewis's seminal essay, "'To Turn as on a Pivot': Writing African Americans into a History of Overlapping Diasporas," *American Historical Review* 100 (June 1995), 765–87. As Lewis put it, "It is in the nation's cities, after all, where African-descended immigrants encountered American blacks, creating in the encounter what has been called a transgeographical America" (786).

6. Johnson, *River of Dark Dreams,* 10. Also see Russell R. Menard, "Reckoning with Williams: Capitalism and Slavery and the Reconstruction of Early American History," *Callaloo* 20, no. 4 (1997), 791–99.

7. Beckert, *Empire of Cotton,* xvi.

8. Baptist, *The Half Has Never Been Told,* xxi–xxii.

9. For a detailed discussion of this scholarship, see the essay on sources at the end of this book, "Appendix: Interpreting the African American Working-Class Experience."

10. Jacqueline Jones, *American Work: Four Centuries of Black and White Labor* (New York: W. W. Norton, 1998), 13. See also her *Labor of Love, Labor of Sorrow: Black Women, Work and the Family from Slavery to Freedom* (New York: Basic Books, 1985).

11. Nancy Maclean, *Freedom Is Not Enough: The Opening of the American Workplace* (New York: Russell Sage; Cambridge: Harvard University Press, 2006), 3.

12. Ira Berlin, *The Making of African America: The Four Great Migrations* (New York: Viking, 2010), 11–12. Also see Steven A. Reich, *A Working People: A History of African American Workers since Emancipation* (Lanham, MD: Rowman and Littlefield, 2013); Robert H. Zieger, *For Jobs and Freedom: Race and Labor in America since 1865* (Lexington: University Press of Kentucky, 2007); Bruce Nelson, *Divided We Stand: American Workers and the Struggle for Black Equality* (Princeton, NJ:

Princeton University Press, 2001); William H. Harris, *The Harder We Run: Black Workers since the Civil War* (New York: Oxford University Press, 1982); Philip Foner, *Organized Labor and the Black Worker, 1619–1973* (New York: International Publishers, 1974).

CHAPTER ONE

1. African American urban life unfolded within the larger context of plantation slavery and the development of rural America. See Jorge Cañizares-Esguerra, Matt D. Childs, and James Sidbury, eds., *The Black Urban Atlantic in the Age of the Slave Trade* (Philadelphia: University of Pennsylvania Press, 2013); Ira Berlin, *The Making of African America: The Four Great Migrations* (New York: Viking 2010); Ira Berlin, *Many Thousands Gone: The First Two Centuries of Slavery in North America* (Cambridge: Belknap Press / Harvard University Press, 1998), 12, 83–84, 145; Ira Berlin, "From Creole to African: Atlantic Creoles and the Origins of African-American Society in Mainland North America," in *Origins of the Black Atlantic: Rewriting Histories,* ed. Laurent Dubois and Julius Scott (New York: Routledge, 2010), 116–18; Alexander X. Byrd, *Captives and Voyagers: Black Migrants across the Eighteenth Century British Atlantic World* (Baton Rouge: Louisiana State University Press, 2008), 32–85; Jacqueline Jones, *American Work: Four Centuries of Black and White Labor* (New York: W. W. Norton, 1998); W. Jeffrey Bolster, *Black Jacks: African American Seamen in the Age of Sail* (Cambridge: Harvard University Press, 1997); Marcus Rediker, *The Slave Ship: A Human History* (New York: Viking, Penguin Group [USA], 2007); Ras M. Brown, *African-Atlantic Cultures and the South Carolina Lowcountry* (New York: Cambridge University Press, 2012); James Horton and Lois Horton, *In Hope of Liberty: Culture, Community, and Protest among Northern Free Blacks, 1700–1860* (New York: Oxford University Press, 1997); William D. Piersen, *Black Yankees: The Development of an Afro-American Subculture in Eighteenth-Century New England* (Amherst, MA: University of Massachusetts Press, 1988); Edward Baptist, *The Half Has Never Been Told: Slavery and the Making of American Capitalism* (New York: Basic Books, 2014); Walter Johnson, *River of Dark Dreams: Slavery and Empire in the Cotton Kingdom* (Cambridge: Belknap Press / Harvard University Press, 2013); Sven Beckert, *Empire of Cotton: A Global History* (New York: Knopf, 2014); Christopher Clark, Nancy Hewitt, Joshua Brown, and David Jaffee, *Who Built America? Working People and the Nation's History, American Social History Project,* vol. 1, 3rd ed. (Boston: Bedford / St. Martin's, 2008). These African sources of Louisiana labor dissipated after about 1731. The French imperial government took the colony out of the hands of the Company of the Indies and disrupted its connections to the transatlantic slave trade. Under subsequent Spanish control, however, the traffic in enslaved Africans accelerated, creating what some scholars describe as the "re-Africanization" of Louisiana during the final decades of the eighteenth century.

2. Gary Nash, "The Social Evolution of Preindustrial American Cities, 1700–1820," in *The Making of Urban America,* ed. Raymond A. Mohl, 2nd ed.

(Wilmington, DE: Scholarly Resources, 1997), 18–20; Howard P. Chudacoff, Judith E. Smith, and Peter C. Baldwin, *The Evolution of American Society*, 7th ed. (Boston: Prentice Hall, 2010), 4, 7, 17–20; Reynolds Farley, "The Urbanization of Negroes in the United States," *Journal of Social History* 1 (1968): 242–44; Gary B. Nash, *Forging Freedom: The Formation of Philadelphia's Black Community 1720–1840* (Cambridge: Harvard University Press, 1988), 9–10; Horton and Horton, *In Hope of Liberty*, 13; James O. Horton and Lois E. Horton, *Black Bostonians: Family Life and Community Struggle in the Antebellum North* (New York: Holmes and Meier, 1979), xiii–xv; Robert J. Cottrol, *The Afro-Yankees: Providence's Black Community in the Antebellum Era* (Westport, CT: Greenwood Press, 1982), 14–16; Piersen, *Black Yankees*, 6–7; Leslie M. Harris, *In the Shadow of Slavery: African Americans in New York City, 1626–1863* (Chicago: University of Chicago Press, 2003), 18–19, 29–30; Thelma W. Foote, *Black and White Manhattan: The History of Racial Formation in Colonial New York City* (New York: Oxford University Press, 2004), 23–40, 65; Robert Olwell, *Masters, Slaves, and Subjects: South Carolina Low Country, 1740–1790* (Ithaca, NY: Cornell University Press, 1998), 1–2, 11, 27–29; Emma Hart, *Building Charleston: Town and Society in the Eighteenth-Century British Atlantic World* (Charlottesville: University of Virginia, 2010), 25, 32–33; James A. McMillin, "The Transatlantic Slave Trade Comes to Georgia," in Leslie M. Harris and Daina R. Berry, eds., *Slavery and Freedom in Savannah* (Athens: University of Georgia Press, 2014), 12–13; Phillip D. Morgan, *Slave Counterpoint: Black Culture in the Eighteenth-Century Chesapeake and Lowcountry* (Chapel Hill: University of North Carolina Press, 1998), 59–62; Shannon L. Dawdy, *Building the Devil's Empire: French Colonial New Orleans* (Chicago: University of Chicago Press, 2008), 83, 156–58, 175–76; Lawrence N. Powell, *The Accidental City: Improving New Orleans* (Cambridge: Harvard University Press, 2012), 53–54, 70–71; Daniel H. Usner, "Colonial Projects and Frontier Practices: The First Century of New Orleans History," in *Frontier Cities: Encounters at the Crossroads of Empire*, ed. Jay Gitlin, Barbara Berglund, and Adam Arenson (Philadelphia: University of Pennsylvania Press, 2013), 36–40; Daniel H. Usner, Jr., "From African Captivity to American Slavery: The Introduction of Black Laborers to Colonial Louisiana," *Louisiana History* 20 (1979), quote, 25, 25–29; Daniel H. Usner, Jr., *Indians, Settlers, and Slaves in a Frontier Exchange Economy: The Lower Mississippi Valley before 1783* (Chapel Hill: University of North Carolina Press, 1992), 25, 33, 41; Gwendolyn Midlo Hall, *Africans in Colonial Louisiana: The Development of Afro-Creole Culture in the Eighteenth Century* (Baton Rouge: Louisiana State University Press, 1992), 29, 57–60; Kimberly S. Hanger, *Bounded Lives, Bounded Places: Free Black Society in Colonial New Orleans, 1769–1803* (Durham, NC: Duke University Press, 1997), 10–11. For the notion of a "charter generation" among early African Americans, see Berlin, *Many Thousands Gone*, 12–13, 83–84; Berlin, *The Making of African America*, quote, 71.

3. Usner, "From African Captivity to American Slavery," 26; Hall, *Africans in Colonial Louisiana*, 29, 57–60, 127; Dawdy, *Building the Devil's Empire*, 157, 177–79.

4. Powell, *The Accidental City*, 73–74.

5. Olwell, *Masters, Slaves, and Subjects,* quote, 1–2, 11; Hart, *Building Charleston,* 32–33; Morgan, *Slave Counterpoint,* 75–76. For an innovative study of both the environmental and social construction of New Orleans over nearly two hundred years of its history, see Ari Kelman, *A River and Its City: The Nature of Landscape in New Orleans* (Berkeley: University of California Press, 2003), 1–17.

6. Harris, *In the Shadow of Slavery,* 14–31, 32; Foote, *Black and White Manhattan,* 36; Joyce Goodfriend, *Before the Melting Pot: Society and Culture in Colonial New York City, 1664–1730* (Princeton, NJ: Princeton University Press, 1992), 119, 124; Christopher Moore, "A World of Possibilities: Slavery and Freedom in Dutch New Amsterdam," in *Slavery in New York,* ed. Ira Berlin and Leslie M. Harris (New York: New Press, 2005), 35–45; Horton and Horton, *In Hope of Liberty,* 10.

7. Erica A. Dunbar, *A Fragile Freedom: African American Women and Emancipation in the Antebellum City* (New Haven, CT: Yale University Press, 2008), quote, 16; Nash, *Forging Freedom,* 10–12 (quote, 10); Gary B. Nash, "Slaves and Slave Owners in Colonial Philadelphia," *William and Mary Quarterly,* 3rd ser., 30 (1973): 223–56.

8. Horton and Horton, *Black Bostonians,* 74–75; Piersen, *Black Yankees,* 43–44; Lorenzo J. Greene, *The Negro in Colonial New England, 1620–1776* (1942; repr. New York: Atheneum, 1968), 34–35, 60, 150, 111.

9. Cañizares-Esguerra, Childs, and Sidbury, *Black Urban Atlantic,* 1–3; W. E. B. Du Bois, *The Philadelphia Negro: A Social Study* (1899; repr. Philadelphia: University of Pennsylvania, 1996), 17–18; W. E. B. Du Bois and Augustus Dill, eds., *The Negro Artisan* (Atlanta: Atlanta University Conference Publications no. 17, 1912): 35ff.; Leonard Stavisky, "The Origins of Negro Craftsmanship in Colonial America," *Journal of Negro History* 32, no. 4 (October 1947): 417–29; Philip S. Foner and Ronald L. Lewis, eds., *The Black Worker to 1869,* vol. 1 (Philadelphia: Temple University Press, 1978), 9; Moore, "A World of Possibilities," 35–38, 41–45; Nash, "Social Evolution of Preindustrial American Cities," 19; Goodfriend, *Before the Melting Pot,* 112–13, 119; Harris, *In the Shadow of Slavery,* 14, 16–17, 20, 28–31.

10. Catherine W. Bishir, *Crafting Lives: African American Artisans in New Bern, North Carolina, 1770–1900* (Chapel Hill: University of North Carolina Press, 2013), 6–18; L. Diane Barnes, *Artisan Workers in the Upper South: Petersburg, Virginia, 1820–1865* (Baton Rouge: Louisiana State University Press, 2008); Hart, *Building Charleston,* 102, 103; Usner, "From African Captivity to American Slavery," 31–35; Hanger, *Bounded Lives, Bounded Places,* 57–70; Dawdy, *Building the Devil's Empire,* 177–78.

11. Powell, *The Accidental City,* 70.

12. Christopher Phillips, *Freedom's Port: The African American Community of Baltimore, 1790–1860* (Urbana: University of Chicago Press, 1997), 16–17; Charles G. Steffen, *The Mechanics of Baltimore: Workers and Politics in the Age of Revolution, 1763–1812* (Urbana: University of Illinois Press, 1984), 36–44; T. Stephen Whitman, *The Price of Freedom: Slavery and Manumission in Baltimore and Early National Maryland* (Lexington: University Press of Kentucky, 1997), 16–28; Mariana L. R. Dantas, *Black Townsmen: Urban Slavery and Freedom in the Eighteenth-Century Americas* (New York: Palgrave/Macmillan, 2008), 75–80, 145–47; Powell, *The Accidental City,* 70.

13. Du Bois and Dill, *The Negro Artisan*, 35; Bolster, *Black Jacks*, 48–49; Hilary McD. Beckles, *White Servitude and Black Slavery in Barbados, 1627–1715* (Knoxville: University of Tennessee Press, 1989), 104, 108; Pedro L. V. Welch, *Slave Society in the City: Bridgetown, Barbados 1680–1834* (Kingston, Jam.: Ian Randle, 2003), 43. See also Constance M. Green, *American Cities in the Growth of the Nation* (New York: J. De Graff, 1957), 19; Peter H. Wood, *Black Majority: Negroes in Colonial South Carolina From 1670 Through the Stono Rebellion* (New York: W. W. Norton, 1974), xiv, 45–46, 132, 146–47, 219–21; Catherine Coquery-Vidrovitch, *The History of Cities South of the Sahara: From the Origins to Colonization* (Princeton, NJ: Markus Wiener, 2008), 1–26, 49–52, 155–69; Rebecca Shumway, *The Fante and the Transatlantic Slave Trade* (Rochester, NY: University of Rochester Press, 2011), 40–42; A. G. Hopkins, *An Economic History of West Africa* (New York: Columbia University Press, 1973), 4–8; Sandra Barnes, *Ogun: An Old God for a New Age* (Philadelphia: Institute for the Study of Human Issues, 1980).

14. Bolster, *Black Jacks*, 48–49; Bishir, *Crafting Lives*, 6, 9, 38, 51; Barnes, *Artisan Workers in the Upper South*, 143–46.

15. Cottrol, *The Afro-Yankees*, 37, 44; Harris, *In the Shadow of Slavery*, 14, 20, 30–31; Morgan, *Slave Counterpoint*, 494–95; Betty Wood, *Slavery in Colonial Georgia, 1730–1775* (Athens: University of Georgia Press, 1984), 84; Catherine Adams and Elizabeth H. Pleck, *Love of Freedom: Black Women in Colonial and Revolutionary New England* (New York: Oxford University Press, 2010), 32–35; Hanger, *Bounded Lives, Bounded Places*, 57–60, 63–66; Suzanne Lebsock, *The Free Women of Petersburg: Status and Culture in a Southern Town, 1784–1860* (New York: W. W. Norton, 1984), 97–98; Jacqueline Jones, *Labor of Love, Labor of Sorrow: Black Women, Work, and the Family from Slavery to the Present* (New York: Basic Books, 1985), 18; Bishir, *Crafting Lives*, 19 (on notion of an artisan "golden age").

16. Harris, *In the Shadow of Slavery*, 28–31; Goodfriend, *Before the Melting Pot*, 119, 124; Sharon B. Sundue, *Industrious in Their Stations: Young People at Work in Urban America, 1720–1810* (Charlottesville: University of Virginia Press, 2009), 112–14; Joanne P. Melish, *Disowning Slavery: Gradual Emancipation and "Race" in New England, 1780–1860* (Ithaca, NY: Cornell University Press, 1998), 8, 20–21.

17. See Robert E. Desrochers, Jr., "Slave-for-Sale Advertisements and Slavery in Massachusetts, 1704–1781," *William and Mary Quarterly*, 3rd ser., 59, no. 3 (July 2002): 623–64; Greene, *The Negro in Colonial New England*, 15, 23–50; Du Bois, *The Philadelphia Negro*, 14; Nash, *Forging Freedom*, 9–11; Baptist, *The Half Has Never Been Told*, 1–37; Walter Johnson, *Soul By Soul: Life Inside the Antebellum Slave Market* (Cambridge: Harvard University Press, 1999), quote, 19; Daniel E. Walker, *No More: Slavery and Cultural Resistance in Havana and New Orleans* (Minneapolis: University of Minnesota Press, 2004), quote, 85–86.

18. Goodfriend, *Before the Melting Pot*, 119, 124; Piersen, *Black Yankees*, 43–44; Harris, *In the Shadow of Slavery*, 14–31; Moore, "A World of Possibilities," 35–45; Nash, *Forging Freedom*, 36, 218; Shane White, *Somewhat More Independent: The End of Slavery in New York City, 1770–1810* (Athens: University of Georgia Press, 1991), 26–27; Leonard P. Curry, *The Free Black in Urban America, 1800–1850: The*

Shadow of the Dream (Chicago: University of Chicago Press, 1981), 250; Wood, *Black Majority*, 206; Ira Berlin, *Slaves without Masters: The Free Negro in the Antebellum South* (New York: Free Press, 1974), 55; Whitman, *Price of Freedom*, 50–58, 61, quote, 77–78; Seth Rockman, *Scraping By: Wage Labor, Slavery, and Survival in Early Baltimore* (Baltimore: Johns Hopkins University Press, 2009), 45–46, 62–67; Dantas, *Black Townsmen*, 87–89; Steffen, *The Mechanics of Baltimore*, 41–42; Phillips, *Freedom's Port*, 67; Dylan C. Penningroth, *The Claims of Kinfolk: African American Property and Community in the Nineteenth-Century South* (Chapel Hill: University of North Carolina Press, 2003), 53.

19. Bolster, *Black Jacks*, 69, 95, 101; Peter Linebaugh and Marcus Rediker, *The Many-Headed Hydra: Sailors, Slaves, Commoners, and the Hidden History of the Revolutionary Atlantic* (Boston: Beacon Press, 2000), 243; Rediker, *The Slave Ship*, 41–72; Morgan, *Slave Counterpoint*, 238–39.

20. Olaudah Equiano, *The Interesting Narrative of the Life of Olaudah Equiano, Written by Himself*, ed. and introduction, Robert J. Allison (1791; repr. Boston: Bedford Books / St. Martin's Press, 1995), 2–3; Vincent Caretta, "Olaudah Equiano or Gustavus Vassa?: New Light on an Eighteenth-Century Question of Identity," *Slavery and Abolition*, 20, no. 3 (1999): 96–105; Cañizares-Esguerra, Childs, and Sidbury, *Black Urban Atlantic*, 1–5; Julius Scott, "Negroes in Foreign Bottoms: Sailors, Slaves, and Communication," in Dubois and Scott, eds., *Origins of the Black Atlantic*, 69–70; J. William Harris, *The Hanging of Thomas Jeremiah: A Free Black Man's Encounter with Liberty* (New Haven, CT: Yale University Press, 2009), 61.

21. Kevin Dawson, "The Cultural Geography of Enslaved Ship Pilots," in Cañizares-Esguerra, Childs, and Sidbury, *Black Urban Atlantic*, 163–84, quotes, 164, 167; Bolster, *Black Jacks*, 49; Harris, *Hanging of Thomas Jeremiah*, 61.

22. Bolster, *Black Jacks*, 3–4, 16, 25–36, 131–57, 258–66; Cañizares-Esguerra, Childs, and Sidbury, *Black Urban Atlantic*, 1–5; Equiano, *Interesting Narrative of the Life*, 2–3; Dubois and Scott, *Origins of the Black Atlantic*, 43–71.

23. Morgan, *Slave Counterpoint*, 494–95.

24. Walker, *No More*, 2–3; Hanger, *Bounded Lives, Bounded Places*, 1–2, 11–12, 21–23, 145–47, 163; Dawdy, *Building the Devil's Empire*, 4–12, 146–54; Whittington B. Johnson, *Black Savannah, 1788–1864* (Fayetteville: University of Arkansas Press, 1996), 39, 59–65, 70–71, 81–82; Janice L. Sumler-Edmond, "Free Black Life in Savannah," in *Slavery and Freedom in Savannah*, ed. Harris and Berry, 130–31; Bernard E. Powers, Jr., *Black Charlestonians: A Social History, 1822–1885* (Fayetteville: University of Arkansas Press, 1994), 48–50; Amrita Chakrabarti Myers, *Forging Freedom: Black Women and the Pursuit of Liberty in Antebellum Charleston* (Chapel Hill: University of North Carolina Press, 2011), 122–35; Cynthia M. Kennedy, *Braided Relations, Entwined Lives: The Women of Charleston's Urban Slave Society* (Bloomington: Indiana University Press, 2005), 65–66.

25. Stephen Middleton, *The Black Laws: Race and the Legal Process in Early Ohio* (Athens: Ohio University Press, 2005), 7–41; Wilma King, *The Essence of Liberty: Free Black Women during the Slave Era* (Columbia: University of Missouri, 2006), 64–65; Berlin, *Slaves without Masters*, 21–23; Horton and Horton, *In Hope of*

Liberty, 71–76; Melish, *Disowning Slavery,* 86–88; Leon Litwack, *North of Slavery: The Negro in the Free States, 1790–1860* (Chicago: University of Chicago Press, 1961), 7–15; Arthur Zilversmit, *The First Emancipation: The Abolition of Slavery in the North* (Chicago: University of Chicago Press, 1975), 113–16, 124–37, 176–84, 208–14; Curry, *Free Black in Urban America,* 247–48, 250–55.

26. King, *Essence of Liberty,* 64–65; Walker, *No More,* 86–87; Curry, *Free Black in Urban America,* 252–53; Richard Wade, *Slavery in the Cities: The South, 1820–1860* (New York: Oxford University Press, 1964), 329–30; Jennifer Morgan, *Laboring Women: Reproduction and Gender in New World Slavery* (Philadelphia: University of Pennsylvania Press, 2004); Rockman, *Scraping By,* 101–3, 111; Horton and Horton, *Black Bostonians,* 25; Nash, *Forging Freedom,* 136–37, 142–43.

27. Adams and Pleck, *Love of Freedom,* 32–35, quote, 34; Rockman, *Scraping By,* 100–03; Jane E. Dabel, *A Respectable Woman: The Public Roles of African American Women in Nineteenth-Century New York* (New York: New York University Press, 2008), 6–7, 15–16, 78, 82–83; King, *Essence of Liberty,* 61–72; Lebsock, *Free Women of Petersburg,* 97–98; Kennedy, *Braided Relations, Entwined Lives,* 66.

28. Adams and Pleck, *Love of Freedom,* 32–35, 37; Kennedy, *Braided Relations, Entwined Lives,* 120–21; Dabel, *A Respectable Woman,* 6–7, 15–16, 78, 82–83; Lebsock, *Free Women of Petersburg,* 97–98; King, *Essence of Liberty,* 66–69; Rockman, *Scraping By,* 129–30.

29. Morgan, *Slave Counterpoint,* 352–53; Curry, *Free Black in Urban America,* 33–36, 260–66; Powers, *Black Charlestonians,* 41–43; Charles H. Wesley, *Negro Labor in the United States, 1850–1925: A Study in American Economic History* (1927; repr. New York: Russell and Russell, 1967), 13; Johnson, *Black Savannah,* 96–97; Wade, *Slavery in the Cities,* 37; Robert S. Starobin, *Industrial Slavery in the Old South* (New York: Oxford University Press, 1970), 10–18, 28–33, 63–65; Ronald L. Lewis, *Coal, Iron, and Slaves: Industrial Slavery in Maryland and Virginia, 1715–1865* (Westport, CT: Greenwood Press, 1979), 35, 88.

30. Powers, *Black Charlestonians,* 41–43; Myers, *Forging Freedom,* 57–63; Harris and Berry, *Slavery and Freedom in Savannah,* 45–46; Johnson, *Black Savannah,* 96–97.

31. Whitman, *Price of Freedom,* 33–39; Dantas, *Black Townsmen,* 81–88; Joe William Trotter, Jr., *River Jordan: African American Urban Life in the Ohio Valley* (Lexington: University Press of Kentucky, 1998), 27–29.

32. Midori Takagi, *"Rearing Wolves to Our Own Destruction": Slavery in Richmond, Virginia, 1782–1865"* (Charlottesville: University of Virginia Press, 1999), 16–36, 71–95; Wade, *Slavery in the Cities,* quote, 12–13, 32, 35, quote, 36, 37, 327; Gregg D. Kimball, *American City, Southern Place: A Cultural History of Antebellum Richmond* (Athens: University of Georgia Press, 2012), 161–62, quote; Peter Rachleff, *Black Labor in Richmond, 1865–1890* (1984; repr. Urbana: University of Illinois Press, 1989), 5–6; Starobin, *Industrial Slavery in the Old South,* 10–18, 28–33, 63–65; Claudia D. Goldin, *Urban Slavery in the American South, 1820–1860: A Quantitative History* (Chicago: University of Chicago Press, 1976), 26, 45–46, 52–54.

33. Takagi, *"Rearing Wolves to Our Own Destruction,"* 24–30; Rachleff, *Black Labor in Richmond,* 6–7; Joshua D. Rothman, *Notorious in the Neighborhood: Sex*

and *Families across the Color Line in Virginia, 1787–1861* (Chapel Hill: University of North Carolina Press, 2003), 92–94; Kimball, *American City, Southern Place,* quote, 65.

34. Kimball, *American City, Southern Place,* 23, quote, 65; Starobin, *Industrial Slavery in the Old South,* 148–49; Lewis, *Coal, Iron, and Slaves,* 179–80.

35. Wesley, *Negro Labor in the United States,* 62; Ira Berlin and Herbert G. Gutman, "Natives and Immigrants, Free Men and Slaves: Urban Workingmen in the Antebellum American South," *American Historical Review* 88, no. 5 (December 1983): 1178, 1180, 1181–82, quote, 1193; Phillips, *Freedom's Port,* 195–96; Wade, *Slavery in the Cities,* 29–30, 273–74; Starobin, *Industrial Slavery in the Old South,* 136–37; Curry, *Free Black in Urban America,* 25–26.

36. Paul Spickard, *Almost All Aliens: Immigration, Race, and Colonialism in American History and Identity* (New York: Routledge, 2007), 102, 481; Berlin and Gutman, "Natives and Immigrants, Free Men and Slaves," 1181–82; Aaron S. Fogleman, "From Slaves, Convicts, and Servants to Free Passengers: The Transformation of Immigration in the Era of the American Revolution," *Journal of American History,* 85, no. 1 (1998): 43–76; Christopher Clark, *Social Change in America: From the Revolution through the Civil War* (Chicago: Ivan R. Dee, 2006), 60–88, 110–19; Phillips, *Freedom's Port,* 195–96.

37. Curry, *Free Black in Urban America,* 260–61; Nikki M. Taylor, *Frontiers of Freedom: Cincinnati's Black Community, 1802–1868* (Athens: Ohio University Press, 2005), 16–18.

38. Curry, *Free Black in Urban America,* 260; Trotter, *River Jordan,* 14, quote, 27, 29; Gilbert Osofsky, "Enduring Ghetto," in *Harlem: The Making of a Ghetto: Negro New York, 1890–1930* (1963; repr., New York: Harper and Row, 1971), quote, 263n44.

39. Du Bois, *The Philadelphia Negro,* 33; Horton and Horton, *In Hope of Liberty,* 117; Sterling D. Spero and Abram L. Harris, *The Black Worker: The Negro and the Labor Movement* (1930; repr., New York: Atheneum, 1968) 11–15; Harris, *In the Shadow of Slavery,* 80; Cottrol, *The Afro-Yankees,* 151–53.

40. Horton and Horton, *In Hope of Liberty,* 117; Spero and Harris, *The Black Worker,* 11–15; Harris, *In the Shadow of Slavery,* 80; Cottrol, *The Afro-Yankees,* 151–53.

41. Curry, *Free Black in Urban America,* 260; Osofsky, "Enduring Ghetto," in *Harlem: The Making of a Ghetto,* quote, 263n44. See also Frederick Douglass, *Narrative of the Life of Frederick Douglass: An American Slave* (New York: New American Library, 1968), 117–18.

42. Horton and Horton, *In Hope of Liberty,* quote, 110; Bolster, *Black Jacks,* 161; Taylor, *Frontiers of Freedom,* 27–29; Nancy Bertaux, "Structural Economic Change among Black Workers in Nineteenth Century Cincinnati," in *Race and the City: Work, Community, and Protest in Cincinnati, 1820–1970,* ed. Henry Louis Taylor, Jr. (Urbana: University of Illinois Press, 1993), 132–41, 133, 134; Thomas Buchanan, *Black Life on the Mississippi: Slaves, Free Blacks, and the Western Steamboat World* (Chapel Hill: University of North Carolina Press, 2007), 53–86.

43. Taylor, *Frontiers of Freedom,* 16–18; Trotter, *River Jordan,* 14, 29.

44. Quoted in Bertaux, "Structural Economic Change," in Taylor, *Race and the City*, 133. See also Curry, *Free Black in Urban America*, 21–22, 25–26, 258–66; Wade, *Slavery in the Cities*, 30–33; Goldin, *Urban Slavery in the American South*, 42–47; Litwack, *North of Slavery*, 153–62; Lebsock, *Free Women of Petersburg*, 97–100; Wade, *Slavery in the Cities*, 31.

45. Nash, *Forging Freedom*, 121–25; Horton and Horton, *In Hope of Liberty*, 90–92.

46. Martin R. Delany, "A Black Nationalist Manifesto, 1852," in *Let Nobody Turn Us Around: An African American Anthology*, ed. Manning Marable and Leith Mullings (Lanham, MD: Rowman and Littlefield, 2000), 70–82; King, *Essence of Liberty*, 59.

47. Douglass, quoted in Wesley, *Negro Labor in the United States*, 54–55; Douglas W. Bristol, Jr., *Knights of the Razor: Black Barbers in Slavery and Freedom* (Baltimore: Johns Hopkins University Press. 2009), 114–15; Delany, "A Black Nationalist Manifesto, 1852," in Marable and Mullings, *Let Nobody Turn Us Around*, 70–82; King, *Essence of Liberty*, 59.

48. Bristol, *Knights of the Razor*, 4–5, 61–69, 204.

49. Frederick Douglass, "Learn Trades or Starve," quoted in Harris, *In the Shadow of Slavery*, 240–41; Graham R. Hodges, *New York City Cartmen, 1667–1850* (New York: New York University Press, 1986), 4–5, 157–59; George E. Walker, *The Afro-American in New York City, 1827–1860* (New York: Garland, 1993), 30–35, quote, 35n18; Curry, *Free Black in Urban America*, 18–19; Harris, *In the Shadow of Slavery*, 217–18; Wesley, *Negro Labor in the United States*, 62–63.

50. James M. Campbell, *Slavery on Trial: Race, Class, and Criminal Justice in Antebellum Richmond, Virginia* (Gainesville: University Press of Florida, 2007), 11–12; Trotter, *River Jordan*, 25; Powers, *Black Charleston*, 10–15; Johnson, *Black Savannah*, 40–41, 45, 52; Curry, *Free Black in Urban America*, 17.

51. Stephen Kantrowitz, *More Than Freedom: Fighting for Black Citizenship in a White Republic, 1829–1889* (New York: Penguin, 2012), 14–33; Middleton, *Black Laws*, 3–12; David A. Gerber, *Black Ohio and the Color Line, 1860–1915* (Urbana: University of Illinois Press, 1976), 3–12; Trotter, *River Jordan*, 24–26; Harris, *In the Shadow of Slavery*, 80, 116–19; Litwack, *North of Slavery*, 64–93; Taylor, *Frontiers of Freedom*, 63–64; Curry, *Free Black in Urban America*, quote, 87.

52. Ousmane K. Power-Greene, *Against Wind and Tide: The African American Struggle against the Colonization Movement* (New York: New York University Press, 2014), 1–2; Claude A. Clegg III, *The Price of Liberty: African Americans and the Making of Liberia* (Chapel Hill: University of North Carolina Press, 2004), 30–31; P.J. Staudenraus, *The African Colonization Movement, 1816–1865* (New York: Octagon Books, 1980), 234–39, 196–97; James Campbell, *Middle Passages: African American Journeys to Africa, 1787–2005* (New York: Penguin, 2006), 40–46; C. Peter Ripley, Roy E. Finkenbine, Michael F. Hembree, and Donald Yacavone, eds., *Witness for Freedom: African American Voices on Race, Slavery, and Emancipation* (Chapel Hill: University of North Carolina Press, 1993), quote, 2; Kantrowitz, *More Than Freedom*, 27.

53. Staudenraus, *African Colonization Movement*, 5–8; Nash, *Forging Freedom*, 101–3, 177–79, 246–47; Julie Winch, *Philadelphia's Black Elite: Activism, Accom-*

modation, and the Struggle for Autonomy, 1787–1848 (Philadelphia: Temple University Press, 1988), 176n11; Nicholas Guyatt, "'The Outskirts of Our Happiness': Race and the Lure of Colonization in the Early Republic," *Journal of American History*, 95, no. 4 (2009): 992–93.

54. Clare A. Lyons, *Sex among the Rabble: An Intimate History of Gender and Power in the Age of Revolution, Philadelphia, 1730–1830* (Chapel Hill: University of North Carolina Press, 2006), 356; Emily Clark, *The Strange History of the American Quadroon: Free Women of Color in the Revolutionary Atlantic World* (Chapel Hill: University of North Carolina Press, 2013), 6.

55. Harris, *In the Shadow of Slavery*, 134–35; Melish, *Disowning Slavery*, 76, 193; Clegg, *Price of Liberty*, 145–46; Staudenraus, *African Colonization Movement*, 234–38; Trotter, *River Jordan*, 34; Phillips, *Freedom's Port*, 185–86.

56. Middleton, *Black Laws*, 201–3; R. J. M. Blackett, *Making Freedom: The Underground Railroad and the Politics of Slavery* (Chapel Hill: University of North Carolina Press, 2013), 32, 51–53; Graham Russell G. Hodges, *David Ruggles: A Radical Black Abolitionist and the Underground Railroad in New York City* (Chapel Hill: University of North Carolina Press, 2010), 199–200; Fergus M. Bordewich, *The Underground Railroad and the War for the Soul of America* (New York: HarpersCollins, 2005), 169–72; Kantrowitz, *More Than Freedom*, 1–7, 176–98; Ari Kelman, *A River and Its City: The Nature of Landscape in New Orleans* (Berkeley: University of California Press, 2003), 82–84; Wilbur Siebert, *The Underground Railroad from Slavery to Freedom* (1898; repr. New York: Arno Press and *New York Times*, 1968), 17–40, 308–9; Clegg, *Price of Liberty*, 171–77; Ripley et al., *Witness for Freedom*, 179–84; Harris, *In the Shadow of Slavery*, 271–73.

57. Middleton, *Black Laws*, 215–16; Harris, *In the Shadow of Slavery*, 271–73; Curry, *Free Black in Urban America*, 244–51, 261; Wade, *Slavery in the Cities*, 325–30; Berlin, *Slaves without Masters*, 136–37; Goldin, *Urban Slavery in the American South*, 51–60; Powers, *Black Charlestonians*, 267–68; Johnson, *Black Savannah*, 151–52; Philips, *Freedom's Port*, 236–37; Barbara Jean Fields, *Slavery and Freedom on the Middle Ground: Maryland during the Nineteenth Century* (New Haven, CT: Yale University Press, 1985), 47–48, 62.

CHAPTER TWO

1. Nikki M. Taylor, *Frontiers of Freedom: Cincinnati's Black Community, 1802–1868* (Athens: Ohio University Press, 2005), quote, 63–64; Joe William Trotter, Jr., *River Jordan: African American Urban Life in the Ohio Valley* (Lexington: University Press of Kentucky, 1998), 35–36; Leonard P. Curry, *The Free Black in Urban America, 1800–1850: The Shadow of the Dream* (Chicago: University of Chicago Press, 1981), 100–101; Gary B. Nash, *Forging Freedom: The Formation of Philadelphia's Black Community 1720–1840* (Cambridge: Harvard University Press, 1988), 275–79; W. E. B. Du Bois, *The Philadelphia Negro: A Social Study* (1899; repr., Philadelphia: University of Pennsylvania, 1996), 27–29; Joanne P. Melish, *Disowning*

Slavery: Gradual Emancipation and "Race" in New England, 1780–1860 (Ithaca, NY: Cornell University Press, 1998), 204–5; Robert J. Cottrol, *The Afro-Yankees: Providence's Black Community in the Antebellum Era* (Westport, CT: Greenwood Press, 1982), 53–55, 57.

2. Martin V. Melosi, *The Sanitary City: Urban Infrastructure in America from Colonial Times to the Present* (2000; abr. ed., Pittsburgh: University of Pittsburgh Press, 2008), 22–25; Leslie M. Harris, *In the Shadow of Slavery: African Americans in New York City, 1626–1863* (Chicago: University of Chicago Press, 2003), 251–55, 266–67; Nash, *Forging Freedom,* 163, 165–69; Curry, *The Free Black in Urban America,* quotes, 49–52; George E. Walker, *The Afro-American in New York City, 1827–1860* (New York: Garland, 1993), 8–13; James O. Horton and Lois E. Horton, *Black Bostonians: Family Life and Community Struggle in the Antebellum North* (New York: Holmes and Meier, 1979), 16–19.

3. Curry, *The Free Black in Urban America,* 59–60; Amrita Chakrabarti Myers, *Forging Freedom: Black Women and the Pursuit of Liberty in Antebellum Charleston* (Chapel Hill: University of North Carolina Press, 2011), quote, 24; Christopher Phillips, *Freedom's Port: The African American Community of Baltimore, 1790–1860* (Urbana: University of Chicago Press, 1997), quote, 97–98, 99, 100–02.

4. Curry, *The Free Black in Urban America,* 49–57, 67–68, quote, 79; Horton and Horton, *Black Bostonians,* 2–4, quote, 5, 15–16; Harris, *In the Shadow of Slavery,* 251–55, 266–67; Nash, *Forging Freedom,* quote, 169–70.

5. Theda Skocpol, Ariane Liazos, and Marshall Ganz, *What a Mighty Power We Can Be: African American Fraternal Groups and the Struggle for Racial Equality* (Princeton, NJ: Princeton University Press, 2006), 2–3, 34; Julie Winch, *Between Slavery and Freedom: Free People of Color in America from Settlement to the Civil War* (Lanham, MD: Rowman and Littlefield, 2014), 54–56; Martin Sommers, *Manliness and Its Discontents: The Black Middle Class and the Transformation of Masculinity, 1900–1930* (Chapel Hill: University of North Carolina Press, 2004), 18–21; Adelaide Cromwell, *The Other Brahmins: Boston's Upper Class, 1750–1950* (Fayetteville: University of Arkansas Press, 1995), 31; Horton and Horton, *Black Bostonians,* 30–31. This chapter is indebted to Craig Wilder's conceptualization of the relationship between black fraternalism and the rise of early black churches. See Craig Steven Wilder, *In the Company of Black Men: The African Influence on African American Culture in New York City* (New York: New York University Press, 2005), 36–37.

6. Prince Hall, "Thus Doth Ethiopia Stretch Forth Her Hand from Slavery, to Freedom and Equality" (1797), in *Let Nobody Turn Us Around: Voices of Resistance, Reform, and Renewal,* ed. Manning Marable and Leith Mullings (Lanham, MD: Rowman and Littlefield, 2000), 16–23, quote, 17; Horton and Horton, *Black Bostonians,* 30–31; James Oliver Horton and Lois E. Horton, *In Hope of Liberty: Culture, Community, and Protest Among Northern Free Blacks, 1700–1860* (New York: Oxford University Press, 1997), 141–42; Curry, *The Free Black in Urban America,* 184–85; Harry Reed, *Platform for Change: The Foundations of the Northern Free Black Community, 1775–1865* (East Lansing: Michigan State University Press, 1994), 25–26. See also Richard S. Newman, *Freedom's Prophet: Bishop Richard Allen, the*

AME Church, and the Black Founding Fathers (New York: New York University Press, 2008).

7. Paul Harvey, *Through the Storm, Through the Night: A History of African American Christianity* (Lanham, MD: Roman and Littlefield, 2011), 146–48; Clarence E. Walker, *A Rock in a Weary Land: The African Methodist Episcopal Church during the Civil War and Reconstruction* (Baton Rouge: Louisiana State University Press, 1982), 4–11; Eric Lincoln and Lawrence H. Mamiya, *The Black Church in the African-American Experience* (Durham, NC: Duke University Press, 1990), 56–58; Curry, *The Free Black in Urban America,* 175–78; Reed, *Platform for Change,* 19–20, 29–30; Nash, *Forging Freedom,* 100–101, 109–33, 218–19, 227–33, 272–73; Julie Winch, *Philadelphia's Black Elite: Activism, Accommodation, and the Struggle for Autonomy, 1787–1848* (Philadelphia: Temple University Press, 1988), 4–15; Frederick V. Mills, "Richard Allen," in *African American National Biography,* vol. 1, ed. Henry Louis Gates, Jr., and Evelyn Brooks Higginbotham (New York: Oxford University Press, 2008), 93–95.

8. Wilder, *In the Company of Black Men,* 2, 42, 46–47; Leslie Alexander, *African or American?: Black Identity and Political Activism in New York City, 1784–1861* (Urbana: University of Illinois Press, 2008), 11, 188n46, n48; Harris, *In the Shadow of Slavery,* 120; Curry, *The Free Black in Urban America,* 179; Eddie Claude, *Exodus! Religion, Race, and Nation in Early Nineteenth-Century Black America* (Chicago: University of Chicago Press, 2000), 24–26; Lincoln and Mamiya, *The Black Church,* 56–60; Taylor, *Frontiers of Freedom,* 43–44; Trotter, *River Jordan,* 42–43.

9. Harvey, *Through the Storm,* 38–39; Walker, *Rock in a Weary Land,* 8–9; Lincoln and Mamiya, *The Black Church,* 50–56; Reed, *Platform for Change,* 32–33; Phillips, *Freedom's Port,* 131–43; Sylvia R. Frey, *Water from the Rock: Black Resistance in a Revolutionary Age* (Princeton, NJ: Princeton University Press, 1991), 294–97; Richard Wade, *Slavery in the Cities: The South, 1820–1860* (New York: Oxford University Press, 1964), 168–69, 240; Ira Berlin, *Slaves without Masters: The Free Negro in the Antebellum South* (New York: Free Press, 1974), 289–90; Curry, *The Free Black in Urban America,* 178.

10. Bernard E. Powers, Jr., *Black Charlestonians: A Social History, 1822–1885* (Fayetteville: University of Arkansas Press, 1994), 20–21, 61; Myers, *Forging Freedom,* 71; Douglas R. Egerton, *He Shall Go Out Free: The Lives of Denmark Vesey* (1999; rev. ed., New York: Rowman and Littlefield, 2004), 109–25; Edward A. Pearson, *Designs against Charleston: The Trial Record of the Denmark Vesey Slave Conspiracy of 1822* (Chapel Hill: University of North Carolina Press, 1999), 49–53; Margaret Washington Creel, *"A Peculiar People": Slave Religion and Community-Culture among the Gullahs* (New York: New York University Press, 1988), 131, 153–54, 162–63; Whittington B. Johnson, *Black Savannah, 1788–1864* (Fayetteville: University of Arkansas Press, 1996), 7–10. Whereas most black churches resulted from an irreconcilable "schism" between blacks and whites "within a biracial church," historian Whittington Johnson shows how Savannah's black church "was begun by African Americans, mainly slaves" but also free blacks who accepted slave leadership and desired the freedom of their own "church home."

11. Claude, *Exodus!*, 8–9, 24–26.

12. Wilder, *In the Company of Black Men*, 36–37; Alexander, *African or American?*, quotes 2, 8, and 11, (articles of incorporation) 68–69, 70–75, 211n66; Harris, *In the Shadow of Slavery*, 1. For West African influences on Southern black institutions, see Creel, *"A Peculiar People,"* 4–5; and Michael Gomez, *Exchanging Our Country Marks: The Transformation of African Identities in the Colonial and Antebellum South* (Chapel Hill: University of North Carolina Press, 1998), 128–29, 255–56.

13. Philip Foner, *Organized Labor and the Black Worker, 1619–1973* (New York: International Publishers, 1974), 10–11; Philip S. Foner and Ronald L. Lewis, eds., *The Black Worker to 1869*, vol. 1 (Philadelphia: Temple University Press, 1978), 236–41, 245–46; Phillips, *Freedom's Port*, 78, 172, 202; Charles H. Wesley, *Negro Labor in the United States, 1850–1925: A Study in American Economic History* (1927; repr., New York: Russell and Russell, 1967), 55–62; Juliet E. K. Walker, *The History of Black Business in America: The History of Capitalism, Race, Entrepreneurship*, vol. 1, *To 1865* (Chapel Hill: University of North Carolina Press, 2009), 116, 132.

14. Harris, *In the Shadow of Slavery*, 77–79, 239–40; Walker, *History of Black Business in America*, 116, 134, 135–36, 138–39; Du Bois, *The Philadelphia Negro*, quote, 33; Nash, *Forging Freedom*, 148–54; Douglas W. Bristol, Jr., *Knights of the Razor: Black Barbers in Slavery and Freedom* (Baltimore: Johns Hopkins University Press, 2009), 41–70; Trotter, *River Jordan*, 40.

15. Du Bois, *The Philadelphia Negro*, 33–34; Nash, *Forging Freedom*, 148–54; Harris, *In the Shadow of Slavery*, 77–79; Walker, *History of Black Business in America*, 134, 135–36.

16. Douglas W. Bristol, Jr., *Knights of the Razor: Black Barbers in Slavery and Freedom* (Baltimore: Johns Hopkins University Press, 2009), 41–70; Walker, *History of Black Business in America*, 138–39; Trotter, *River Jordan*, 40.

17. John N. Ingham and Lynne B. Feldman, *African-American Business Leaders: A Biographical Dictionary* (Westport, CT: Greenwood Press, 1994), 233–39; Nash, *Forging Freedom*, 51–52, 148–49; James Campbell, *Middle Passages: African American Journeys to Africa, 1787–2005* (New York: Penguin Press, 2006), 44; Walker, *History of Black Business in America*, 116, 132.

18. Ingham and Feldman, *African-American Business Leaders*, 233–39; Nash, *Forging Freedom*, 51–52, 148–49; James Campbell, *Middle Passages: African American Journeys to Africa, 1787–2005* (New York: Penguin, 2006), 44; Walker, *History of Black Business in America*, 116, 132.

19. Phillips, *Freedom's Port*, 95; Powers, *Black Charlestonians*, 43; Walker, *History of Black Business in America*, 136–37, 150.

20. Phillips, *Freedom's Port*, 95; Powers, *Black Charlestonians*, 43; Walker, *History of Black Business in America*, 113, Delany quote, 150; Tania Simmons, "Andrew Cox Marshall," in Harris and Berry, *Slavery and Freedom in Savannah*, 102–3; Ingham and Feldman, *African-American Business Leaders*, 410–11; Johnson, *Black Savannah*, 11–12, 46–47, 82.

21. Wilma King, *The Essence of Liberty: Free Black Women during the Slave Era* (Columbia: University of Missouri, 2006), 69–71, 73; Walker, *History of Black Business in America*, 178.

22. Johnson, *Black Savannah*, 72–73; Walker, *History of Black Business in America*, 178.

23. King, *The Essence of Liberty*, 12, 70–71, 73; Walker, *History of Black Business in America*, 178–79.

24. Kimberly S. Hanger, *Bounded Lives, Bounded Places: Free Black Society in Colonial New Orleans, 1769–1803* (Durham, NC: Duke University Press, 1997), 63–65; entry by Alisha Cromwell, in Harris and Berry, *Slavery and Freedom in Savannah*, 54–55; Myers, *Forging Freedom*, 95–96; Dylan C. Penningroth, *The Claims of Kinfolk: African American Property and Community in the Nineteenth-Century South* (Chapel Hill: University of North Carolina Press, 2003), 61–65; Johnson, *Black Savannah*, 69 (as early as 1812, the Savannah city council passed an ordinance to limit African American women selling such goods as "cakes" and "apples" without a license); entry by Tania Simmons, in Harris and Berry, *Slavery and Freedom in Savannah*, 102–3; Ingham and Feldman, *African-American Business Leaders*, 410–11; Walker, *History of Black Business in America*, 113; Johnson, *Black Savannah*, 11–12, 46–47, 82. Although little is known about the business beginnings of wealthy free black Thomy Lafon of New Orleans, popular accounts say that he began his career "selling cakes to the workmen along the wharves" of the city. This lore of Lafon's early business career underlines how enslaved and free black men also participated in the urban street-vending business in early nineteenth-century American cities.

25. Harris, *In the Shadow of Slavery*, 255–57; Johnson, *Black Savannah*, 67, 135; Alisha Cromwell, "Enslaved Women in the Savannah Marketplace," in Harris and Berry, *Slavery and Freedom in Savannah*, 54–55; Powers, *Black Charlestonians*, 23–24; Myers, *Forging Freedom*, 96–97; Phillips, *Freedom's Port*, 77.

26. Harris, *In the Shadow of Slavery*, 75–76, 266–67; Phillips, *Freedom's Port*, 97–98, 99, 100–102, includes comparative property-ownership rates for Baltimore, Philadelphia, and Charleston.

27. C. Peter Ripley, Roy E. Finkenbine, Michael F. Hembree, and Donald Yacavone, eds., *Witness for Freedom: African American Voices on Race, Slavery, and Emancipation* (Chapel Hill: University of North Carolina Press, 1993), quote, 2; Nash, *Forging Freedom*, 101–3, 237–38; P. J. Staudenraus, *The African Colonization Movement, 1816–1865* (New York: Octagon Books, 1980), 32–35; Ousmane K. Power-Greene, *Against Wind and Tide: The African American Struggle against the Colonization Movement* (New York: New York University Press, 2014), 48–49; Peter P. Hinks, *To Awaken My Afflicted Brethren: David Walker and the Problem of Antebellum Slave Resistance* (University Park: Pennsylvania State University Press, 1997), 184n30; Floyd J. Miller, *The Search for a Black Nationality: Black Emigration and Colonization, 1787–1863* (Urbana: University of Illinois Press, 1975), 47–53; Winch, *Philadelphia's Black Elite*, 35–36; Reed, *Platform for Change*, 133–35.

28. Alexander, *African or American?*, 68–69, 70–75, 211n66; Power-Greene, *Against Wind and Tide*, 48–49; Hinks, *To Awaken My Afflicted Brethren*, 184n30.

29. Alexander, *African or American?*, 68–69, 70–75, 211n66; Ripley et al., *Witness for Freedom*, 2–4; Constance M. Green, *The Secret City: A History of Race Relations in the Nation's Capital* (Princeton, NJ: Princeton University Press, 1967), 34; Phillips, *Freedom's Port*, 214, 220–26, quote, 225; H. E. Sterkx, *The Free Negro in Ante-Bellum Louisiana* (Rutherford, NJ: Associated University Press, 1972), 289–94, quote, 294; Staudenraus, *African Colonization Movement*, 146–49. Cf. Hinks, *To Awaken My Afflicted Brethren*, 184n30.

30. R. J. M. Blackett, *Building an Antislavery Wall* (Baton Rouge: Louisiana State University Press, 1983), 47–54, 77–88; Campbell, *Middle Passages*, 48–53; Nicholas Guyatt, "'The Outskirts of Our Happiness': Race and the Lure of Colonization in the Early Republic," *Journal of American History*, 95, no. 4 (2009), 992–94.

31. Horton and Horton, *Black Bostonians*, 28–29; Alexander, *African or American?*, xviii–ix, 68–69, 70–75, 211n66; Hinks, *To Awaken My Afflicted Brethren*, 91–115; Curry, *The Free Black in Urban America*, 226–27; Ripley et al., *Witness for Freedom*, 42–46; Shirley J. Yee, *Black Women Abolitionists: A Study in Activism, 1828–1860* (Knoxville: University of Tennessee Press, 1992), 95–96, 115–16, 125, 141–42.

32. Marilyn Richardson, *Maria W. Stewart: America's First Black Woman Political Writer* (Bloomington: Indiana University Press, 1987), xiii–xvii, 3–27; Yee, *Black Women Abolitionists*, 95–96, 115–16, 125, 141–42; Darlene Clark Hine and Kathleen Thompson, *A Shining Thread of Hope: The History of Black Women in America* (New York: Broadway Books, 1998), 106–7. Born in Hartford, Connecticut, around 1803, Stewart moved to Boston as a teenager and worked as a domestic for another decade. In the meantime, she learned to read and write informally through regular attendance at Sunday school, most likely at Boston's African Baptist Church, where she later married businessman James Stewart, a "shipping outfitter" who occupied a prominent spot on the Boston wharf. See also Nell Irvin Painter, *Sojourner Truth: A Life, A Symbol* (New York: W. W. Norton, 1996), quotes, 7–8, 167; Erlene Stetson and Linda David, *Glorying in Tribulation: The Lifework of Sojourner Truth* (East Lansing: Michigan State University Press, 1994), 57–80, 88–120.

33. Ripley et al., *Witness for Freedom*, 4–6, 49–51, 152–54; Harris, *In the Shadow of Slavery*, 171, 197–99; Nash, *Forging Freedom*, 276–79; Horton and Horton, *Black Bostonians*, 88–93; Daniel Feller, "A Brother in Arms: Benjamin Tappan and the Antislavery Democracy," *Journal of American History*, 88, no. 1 (2001), 48–74; Van Goose, "'As a Nation, the English Are Our Friends': The Emergence of African American Politics in the British Atlantic World," *American Historical Review*, 113, no. 1 (2008), 48–71; Paul A. Gilje, *Rioting in America* (Bloomington: Indiana University Press, 1996), 81–82; Stephen Kantrowitz, *More Than Freedom: Fighting for Black Citizenship in a White Republic, 1829–1889* (New York: Penguin, 2012), 50–58; Leonard L. Richards, *"Gentlemen of Property and Standing": Anti-Abolition Mobs in Jacksonian America* (New York: Oxford University Press, 1970), 155.

34. Harris, *In the Shadow of Slavery*, 219–21; Alexander, *African or American?*, 100–101, 213n10; Horton and Horton, *Black Bostonians*, 94–97; Kantrowitz, *More Than Freedom*, 99–101; Ripley et al., *Witness for Freedom*, 4–6, 49–51, 152–54.

35. R. J. M. Blackett, *Making Freedom: The Underground Railroad and the Politics of Slavery* (Chapel Hill: University of North Carolina Press, 2013), 2; Graham Russell G. Hodges, *David Ruggles: A Radical Black Abolitionist and the Underground Railroad in New York City* (Chapel Hill: University of North Carolina Press, 2010), 5; Fergus M. Bordewich, *The Underground Railroad and the War for the Soul of America* (New York: HarperCollins, 2005), 4, 167–78, 367; Keith Griffler, *Frontline of Freedom: African Americans and the Forging of the Underground Railroad in the Ohio Valley* (Lexington: University Press of Kentucky, 2004), 37–47.

36. Hodges, *David Ruggles*, 97–98, 167, 184; Kantrowitz, *More than Freedom*, 70–74; Horton and Horton, *Black Bostonians*, 108, 114.

37. Yee, *Black Women Abolitionists*, 95–96, 98–100, 115–16, 125, 141–42; Catherine Clinton, "'Slavery is War': Harriet Tubman and the Underground Railroad," in *Passages to Freedom: The Underground Railroad in History and Memory*, ed. David Blight (Washington, DC: Smithsonian, 2004), 195–209.

38. Thomas Buchanan, *Black Life on the Mississippi: Slaves, Free Blacks, and the Western Steamboat World* (Chapel Hill: University of North Carolina Press, 2007), 101, 102, 103–21; Bordewich, *Underground Railroad*, 167–78, 367; Griffler, *Frontline of Freedom*, 39, 42, 43–46; Blackett, *Making Freedom*, 68–71; Hodges, *David Ruggles*, 4–5.

39. For colonial era revolts, see Jill Lepore, *New York Burning: Liberty, Slavery, and Conspiracy in Eighteenth-Century Manhattan* (New York: Vintage Books, 2005), 170–71; Thomas J. Davis, *A Rumor of Revolt: "The Great Negro Plot" in Colonial New York* (Amherst: University of Massachusetts, 1990), ix–xiii, 1–97; Mat Johnson, *The Great Negro Plot: A Tale of Conspiracy and Murder in Eighteenth-Century New York* (New York: Bloomsbury USA, 2007); and Peter Hofer, *Cry Liberty: The Great Stono River Slave Rebellion of 1739* (New York: Oxford University Press, 2010). For postrevolutionary southern revolts and plots, see Daniel E. Walker, *No More: Slavery and Cultural Resistance in Havana and New Orleans* (Minneapolis: University of Minnesota Press, 2004); Nathalie Dessens, *From Saint-Domingue to New Orleans: Migration and Influences* (Gainesville: University of Florida Press, 2007); Hanger, *Bounded Lives, Bounded Places*.

40. Egerton, *He Shall Go Out Free*, 109–25; Pearson, *Designs against Charleston*, 49–53; Powers, *Black Charlestonians*, 20–21, 61; Creel, *"A Peculiar People,"* 131, 153–54, 162–63; Frey, *Water from the Rock*, 294–97; Wade, *Slavery in the Cities*, 168–69, 240; Berlin, *Slaves without Masters*, 289–90.

41. Alexander, *African or American?*, 24–26.

42. Power-Greene, *Against Wind and Tide*, 4–5, 19–45; Nash, *Forging Freedom*, 102–03, 184–85, 242–45; Horton and Horton, *Black Bostonians*, 97–98; Winch, *Philadelphia's Black Elite*, 35; Staudenraus, *African Colonization Movement*, 9–11; Miller, *The Search for a Black Nationality*, 47–50; Ashli White, *Encountering*

Revolution: Haiti and the Making of the Early Republic (Baltimore: Johns Hopkins University Press, 2010), 209–10; Alexander, *African or African Americans?* 24–26.

43. Power-Greene, *Against Wind and Tide*, 147–48, 163–66; Kantrowitz, *More Than Freedom*, 256–62.

44. Alexander, *African or American?*, 68–69, 70–75, 211n66; King, *Essence of Liberty*, 120; Rhodes, *Mary Ann Shadd Cary*, 74–75; Shirley J. Yee, *Black Women Abolitionists: A Study in Activism, 1828–1860* (Knoxville: University of Tennessee Press, 1992), 14, 116, 121–22, 126–27, 169n69; Hine and Thompson, *A Shining Thread of Light*, 106–7; Dorothy Sterling, ed., *We Are Your Sisters* (New York: Norton, 1997), 66–69, 151, 170–71; Bettye Collier-Thomas, *Daughters of Thunder: Black Women Preachers and Their Sermons, 1850–1979* (San Francisco: Jossey-Bass, 1998), 46–53; 57–68, Harris, *In the Shadow of Slavery*, 178–79; Deborah Gray White, "Simply Truths: Antebellum Slavery in Black and White," in Blight, *Passages to Freedom*, 59–60; Painter, *Sojourner Truth*, 7–8, 167; Jane E. Dabel, *A Respectable Woman: The Public Roles of African American Women in Nineteenth-Century New York* (New York: New York University Press, 2008), 140.

45. Walker, *No More*; Dessens, *From Saint-Domingue to New Orleans*; Hanger, *Bounded Lives, Bounded Places*, 166, 168; Powers, *Black Charlestonians*, 52–54; King, *Essence of Liberty*, 28–29; Myers, *Forging Freedom*, 11.

46. Alexander, *African or American?*, xviii–6, quote, 2, 68–69, 70–75, 211n66; Willard B. Gatewood, *Aristocrats of Color: The Black Elite, 1880–1920* (Fayetteville: University of Arkansas Press, 2000), 10–14; Adelaide Cromwell, *The Other Brahmins*, 19–44; Winch, *Philadelphia's Black Elite*, 1–25; Lincoln and Mamiya, *The Black Church*, 52–53.

47. Berlin, *Slaves without Masters*, 58, quote, 130; Powers, *Black Charlestonians*, 51–52; Lincoln and Mamiya, *The Black Church*, 52–53; Nash, *Forging Freedom*, 211–22; Curry, *The Free Black in Urban America*, 212–13, 234–38; Reed, *Platform for Change*, 104–5, 116–17.

CHAPTER THREE

1. Waldo Martin, *The Mind of Frederick Douglass* (Chapel Hill: University of North Carolina Press, 1984), 74; Steven Hahn, *A Nation under Our Feet: Black Political Struggles in the Rural South from Slavery to the Great Migration* (Cambridge: Harvard University Press, 2003), 341–42; James M. McPherson, ed., *The Negro's Civil War: How American Negroes Felt and Acted during the War for the Union* (New York: Vintage Books, 1965), quote, 17.

2. Leslie M. Harris, *In the Shadow of Slavery: African Americans in New York City, 1626–1863* (Chicago: University of Chicago Press, 2003), quote, 279; James O. Horton and Lois E. Horton, *Black Bostonians: Family Life and Community Struggle in the Antebellum North* (New York: Holmes and Meier, 1979), 135–36, quote, 137; Ira Berlin, "Slavery, Freedom, and Philadelphia's Struggle for Brotherly Love, 1685 to 1861," in *Antislavery and Abolition in Philadelphia: Emancipation and the Long*

Struggle for Racial Justice in the City of Brotherly Love, ed. Richard Newman and James Mueller (Baton Rouge: Louisiana State University Press, 2011), 38; Julie Winch, "Self-Help and Self-Determination: Black Philadelphians and the Dimension of Freedom," in Newman and Mueller, *Antislavery and Abolition in Philadelphia,* 85–86.

3. Steven A. Reich, *A Working People: A History of African American Workers since Emancipation* (Lanham, MD: Rowman and Littlefield, 2013), quote, 7–8; Bernard E. Powers, *Black Charlestonians: A Social History, 1822–1885* (Fayetteville: University of Arkansas Press, 1994), 70; Wilbert Jenkins, *Seizing the New Day: African Americans in Post–Civil War Charleston* (Bloomington: Indiana University Press, 1998), 30–37; Whittington B. Johnson, *Black Savannah, 1788–1864* (Fayetteville: University of Arkansas Press, 1996), quote, 163; Jacqueline Jones, *Saving Savannah: The City and the Civil War* (New York: Knopf, 2008), 135; Rebecca Scott, *Degrees of Freedom: Louisiana and Cuba after Slavery* (Cambridge: Harvard University Press, 2005), 34–35, 78; Frank Towers, *The Urban South and the Coming of the Civil War* (Charlottesville: University of Virginia Press, 2004), 203; Mark A. Lause, *Free Labor: The Civil War and the Making of an American Working Class* (Urbana: University of Illinois Press, 2015), 56–57.

4. Scott, *Degrees of Freedom,* 34–35, 78; Stanley Harrold, *Subversives: Antislavery Community in Washington, D.C., 1828–1865* (Baton Rouge: Louisiana State University Press, 2003), 225–26; Kate Masur, *An Example for All the Land: Emancipation and the Struggle over Equality in Washington, D.C.* (Chapel Hill: University of North Carolina Press, 2011), 7.

5. Willie Lee Rose, ed., *Rehearsal for Reconstruction: The Port Royal Experiment* (1964; repr., New York: Oxford University Press, 1976); Ira Berlin, Barbara J. Fields, Steven F. Miller, Joseph P. Reidy, and Leslie S. Rowland, eds., *Free At Last: A Documentary History of Slavery, Freedom, and the Civil War* (New York: New Press, 1992), 314; Hahn, *Nation under Our Feet,* 140.

6. Berlin et al., *Free At Last,* 241–43, 318–26; Joe William Trotter, Jr., *The African American Experience* (Boston: Houghton Mifflin, 2001), 266.

7. Jacqueline Jones, *American Work: Four Centuries of Black and White Labor* (New York: W. W. Norton, 1998), quote, 289; Masur, *Example for All the Land,* 13–15.

8. Masur, *Example for All the Land,* 13–15. On August 14, 1862, at Washington's Union Bethel African Methodist Episcopal Church, African Americans expressed their resolve to stay put in two resolutions, both approved by the gathering. One resolution declared that it was "inexpedient, inauspicious, and impolitic" to support the president's plan, and the other opposed efforts to use the District of Columbia's black population to set policy for the group and "to compromise the interests of over four-and-a-half millions of our race by precipitate action on our part."

9. Judith Giesberg, *Army at Home: Women and the Civil War on the North Home Front* (Chapel Hill: University of North Carolina Press, 2009), 127–30; Paul A. Gilje, *Rioting in America* (Bloomington: Indiana University Press, 1996), 92–94; Philip S. Foner, *Organized Labor and the Black Worker, 1619–1981* (1974; new ed., New York: International Publishers, 1981), 14–15; Philip S. Foner and Ronald L.

Lewis, eds., *The Black Worker to 1869*, vol. 1 (Philadelphia: Temple University Press, 1978), 275–76, 277–304; Roger Lane, *Roots of Violence in Black Philadelphia, 1860–1900* (Cambridge: Harvard University Press, 1986), 47–49; Herbert Aptheker, ed., *A Documentary History of the Negro People in the United States*, vol. 1, 6th ed. (1951; New York: Citadel Press, 1968), 505–6; McPherson, *The Negro's Civil War*, 257.

    10. Noel Ignatiev, *How the Irish Became White* (New York: Routledge, 1995), 12, 148–75; David R. Roediger, *The Wages of Whiteness: Race and Making of the American Working Class* (New York: Verso, 1991), 133–56; Harris, *In the Shadow of Slavery*, 280–85; Iver Bernstein, *The New York City Draft Riots: Their Significance for American Society and Politics in the Age of the Civil War* (New York, 1990), 1–42; Giesberg, *Army at Home*, 127–30.

    11. Giesberg, *Army at Home*, 127–30.

    12. Masur, *Example for All the Land*, 134–58, 214–17, 248–56; Hahn, *Nation under Our Feet*, quotes, 135–36; Eric Foner, *Reconstruction: America's Unfinished Revolution* (New York: Harper and Row, 1988), 421–22, 542–63, quote, 590; Howard N. Rabinowitz, *Race Relations in the Urban South, 1865–1890* (Urbana: University of Illinois Press, 1980), 259–77; Stephen Kantrowitz, *More Than Freedom: Fighting for Black Citizenship in a White Republic, 1829–1889* (New York: Penguin, 2012), 4, 8–9, 316–20, 375–76; Wilson Jeremiah Moses, *Alexander Crummell: A Study of Civilization and Discontent* (New York: Oxford University Press, 1989), quotes, 207–8; Roger Lane, *William Dorsey's Philadelphia and Ours: On the Past and Future of the Black City in America* (New York: Oxford University Press, 1991), 200–201, 205–6; Edwin G. Burrows and Mike Wallace, *Gotham: A History of New York City to 1898* (Oxford: Oxford University Press, 1999), 1034–35; Trotter, *African American Experience*, 299, 302.

    13. Edward Royce, *The Origins of Southern Sharecropping* (Philadelphia: Temple University Press, 1993), 115–18; David E. Bernstein, *Only One Place of Redress: African Americans, Labor Regulations, and the Courts from Reconstruction to the New Deal* (Durham, NC: Duke University Press, 2001), 10–16; Nan Woodruff, *American Congo: The American Freedom Struggle in the Delta* (Cambridge: Harvard University Press, 2003), 8–37; Rabinowitz, *Race Relations in the Urban South*, 20–21; Robert H. Zieger, *For Jobs and Freedom: Race and Labor in America since 1865* (Lexington: University Press of Kentucky, 2007), quote, 10.

    14. Leon F. Litwack, *Been in the Storm So Long: The Aftermath of Slavery* (New York: Vintage Books, 1979), quotes, 316, 319, 351–53.

    15. John W. Blassingame, *Black New Orleans, 1860–1880* (Chicago: University of Chicago Press, 1973), 61–62; Wilbert L. Jenkins, *Seizing the New Day: African Americans in Post–Civil War Charleston* (Bloomington: Indiana University Press, 1998), 61; Powers, *Black Charlestonians*, 110–11; Rabinowitz, *Race Relations in the Urban South*, quote, 66–69, 355n13.

    16. Bernstein, *Only One Place of Redress*, 8–27, quote, 19–20; Donald G. Nieman, *Promises to Keep: African-Americans and the Constitutional Order, 1776 to the Present* (New York: Oxford University Press, 1991), 126–27; Gilbert Osofsky, *Harlem: The Making of a Ghetto, Negro New York, 1890–1930*, 2nd ed. (1963; Chicago: Ivan R. Dee, 1996), 26–28.

17. Susan E. O'Donovan, *Becoming Free in the Cotton South* (Cambridge: Harvard University Press, 2007), 167; Julie Saville, *The Work of Reconstruction: From Slave to Wage Laborer in South Carolina, 1860–1870* (Cambridge: Cambridge University Press, 1994), quotes, 3–4, 47; Gerald David Jaynes, *Branches without Roots: Genesis of the Black Working Class in the American South, 1862–1882* (New York: Oxford University Press, 1986), 80–81; Trotter, *African American Experience,* 293–94.

18. Zieger, *For Jobs and Freedom,* 14.

19. For reviews of this extensive scholarship, see Kelly Lytle Hernandez, Khalil Gibran Muhammad, and Heather Ann Thompson, "Introduction: Constructing the Carceral State," *Journal of American History,* 102, no. 1 (June 2015): 18–24; Kali N. Gross and Cheryl D. Hicks, "Gendering the Carceral State: African American Women, History, and the Criminal Justice System," *Journal of African American History,* 100, no. 3 (Summer 2015): 357–65.

20. Reich, *A Working People,* 48–49; Zieger, *For Jobs and Freedom,* 44–51; William H. Harris, *The Harder We Run: Black Workers since the Civil War* (New York: Oxford University Press, 1982), 13, 20; Douglas A. Blackmon, *Slavery by Another Name: The Re-enslavement of Black Americans from the Civil War to World War II* (New York: Anchor Books, 2008), 1–5.

21. Blackmon, *Slavery by Another Name,* 1–5; Mary Ellen Curtin, *Black Prisoners and Their World: Alabama, 1865–1900* (Charlottesville: University Press of Virginia, 2000), 1–11, quote, 10, 155.

22. Talitha L. LeFlouria, *Chained in Silence: Black Women and Convict Labor in the New South* (Chapel Hill: University of North Carolina Press, 2015), quote, 5–6. See also Sarah Haley, *No Mercy Here: Gender, Punishment, and the Making of Jim Crow Modernity* (Chapel Hill: University of North Carolina Press, 2016), 3–4.

23. Harris, *The Harder We Run,* 192n13; Zieger, *For Jobs and Freedom,* 41–51; David M. Oshinsky, *"Worse Than Slavery": Parchman Farm and the Ordeal of Jim Crow Justice* (New York: Free Press, 1996).

24. Rabinowitz, *Race Relations in the Urban South,* 28–29; Osofsky, *Harlem,* quotes, 25–26.

25. Royce, *Origins of Southern Sharecropping,* 115–18; Bernstein, *Only One Place of Redress,* 10–16; Woodruff, *American Congo,* 8–37; Rabinowitz, *Race Relations in the Urban South,* 20–21.

26. Kantrowitz, *More Than Freedom,* 389–91, 412; Foner, *Reconstruction,* 587–90; Nieman, *Promises to Keep,* 103–4; Kevin K. Gaines, *Uplifting the Race: Black Leadership, Politics, and Culture in the Twentieth Century* (Chapel Hill: University of North Carolina Press, 1996), 21–31; Osofsky, *Harlem,* 46–52; August Meier, *Negro Thought in America, 1880–1915: Racial Ideologies in the Age of Booker T. Washington* (Ann Arbor: University of Michigan Press, 1973), 42–44; Audrey Smedley, *Race in North America: Origin and Evolution of a Worldview* (Boulder: Westview Press, 2007), 259–82; Mia Bey, *The White Image in the Black Mind: African-American Ideas about White People, 1830–1925* (Oxford: Oxford University Press, 2000), 189–202; Nell Irvin Painter, *The History of White People* (New York: W. W. Norton, 2010), 201–11; Kali N. Gross, *Colored Amazons: Crime, Violence, and Black Women*

in the City of Brotherly Love, 1880–1910 (Durham, NC: Duke University Press, 2006), quote, 121; Najia Aarim-Heriot, *Chinese Immigrants, African Americans, and Racial Anxiety, 1848–82* (Urbana: University of Illinois Press, 2003), 1–14.

27. Gilje, *Rioting in America,* 94–100, 108–10; Herbert Shapiro, *White Violence and Black Response: From Reconstruction to Montgomery* (Amherst: University of Massachusetts Press, 1988), 6–7, 13–14, 64–75, 96–103; Blassingame, *Black New Orleans,* 174–76; Litwack, *Been in the Storm So Long,* 281.

28. Shapiro, *White Violence and Black Response,* 17–19; eyewitness account of W. C. Bolivar, *Philadelphia Tribune,* in W. E. B. Du Bois, *The Philadelphia Negro: A Social Study* (1899; repr., Philadelphia: University of Pennsylvania, 1996), 40–42; Lane, *Roots of Violence in Black Philadelphia,* 45–46.

29. Published affidavits cited in Cheryl D. Hicks, *Talk with You Like a Woman: African American Women, Justice, and Reform in New York, 1890–1935* (Chapel Hill: University of North Carolina Press, 2010), 68–74. See also Osofsky, *Harlem,* 46–52, quotes, 48, 49, 51.

30. Gregory Mixon, *The Atlanta Riot: Race, Class, and Violence in a New South City* (Gainesville: University Press of Florida, 2005), 1, 85–100, 107–08; Edward L. Ayers, *The Promise of the New South: Life After Reconstruction* (New York: Oxford University Press, 1992), 436; Gilje, *Rioting in America,* 109–10; Shapiro, *White Violence and Black Response,* 100–01.

31. Osofsky, *Harlem,* quotes, 20, 21, 23; Lane, *Roots of Violence in Black Philadelphia,* 77; Carter G. Woodson, *A Century of Negro Migration* (1918; repr. New York: Russell and Russell, 1969), 2–7.

32. James N. Gregory, *The Southern Diaspora: How the Great Migrations of Black and White Southerners Transformed America* (Chapel Hill: University of North Carolina Press, 2005), 11–23; Daniel M. Johnson and Rex R. Campbell, *Black Migration in America: A Social Demographic History* (Durham, NC: Duke University Press, 1981), 44–70; Darlene Clark Hine, "Black Migration to the Urban Midwest: The Gender Dimension, 1915–1945," in *The Great Migration in Historical Perspective: New Dimensions of Race, Class, and Gender,* ed. Joe William Trotter, Jr. (Bloomington: Indiana University Press, 1991), 127–46; Masur, *Example for All the Land,* 261; U.S. Bureau of the Census, *Negro Population in the United States, 1790–1915* (1918; repr. New York: Arno Press and *New York Times,* 1968), 156; U.S. Bureau of the Census, *Negroes in the United States, 1915–1932* (1935; repr. New York: Arno Press and *New York Times,* 1968), 55, 85; James Borchert, *Alley Life in Washington: Family, Community, Religion, and Folklife in the City, 1850–1970* (Urbana: University of Illinois Press, 1980), 13–14; Elizabeth Clark-Lewis, *Living In, Living Out: African American Domestics in Washington, D.C., 1910–1940* (Washington, DC: Smithsonian Institution Press, 1994), 73–75.

33. Masur, *Example for All the Land,* 10; U.S. Bureau of the Census, *Negroes in the United States, 1915–1932,* 55, 517–21; Lause, *Free Labor,* 55; Constance M. Green, *American Cities in the Growth of the Nation* (New York: J. De Graff, 1957), 233; Clark-Lewis, *Living In, Living Out,* 9–11, 204n6.

34. Brian Kelly, *Race, Class, and Power in the Alabama Coalfields, 1908–1921* (Urbana: University of Illinois Press, 2001), 32; Lynne B. Feldman, *A Sense of Place: Birmingham's Black Middle Class Community, 1890–1930* (Tuscaloosa: University of Alabama Press, 1999), 7–9; Henry M. McKiven, Jr., *Iron and Steel: Class, Race, and Community in Birmingham, Alabama, 1875–1920* (Chapel Hill: University of North Carolina Press, 1995), 18, 42–47; Ronald Lewis, *Black Coal Miners in America: Race, Class, and Community Conflict, 1780–1980* (Lexington: University of Kentucky Press, 1987), 39–41, 167–93; Daniel Letwin, *The Challenge of Interracial Unionism: Alabama Coal Miners, 1878–1921* (Chapel Hill: University of North Carolina Press, 1998), 23; Eric Arnesen, *Brotherhoods of Color: Black Railroad Workers and the Struggle for Equality* (Cambridge: Harvard University Press, 2001), 29–30; Foner, *Organized Labor and the Black Worker*, 104–5; Sterling D. Spero and Abram L. Harris, *The Black Worker: The Negro and the Labor Movement* (1931; repr. New York: Atheneum, 1968), 250–51; Bruce Nelson, *Divided We Stand: American Workers and the Struggle for Black Equality* (Princeton: Princeton University Press, 2001), 24–25.

35. Georgina Hickey, *Hope and Danger in the New South City: Working Class Women and Urban Development in Atlanta, 1890–1940* (Athens: University of Georgia Press, 2003), 18–19; Mixon, *The Atlanta Riot*, 33–34; Tera W. Hunter, *To 'Joy My Freedom: Southern Black Women's Lives and Labors after the Civil War* (Cambridge: Harvard University Press, 1997), 114–20.

36. David M. Katzman, *Seven Days a Week: Women and Domestic Service in Industrializing America* (Urbana: University of Illinois Press, 1981), 271–73; U.S. Bureau of Census, *Negro Population in United States, 1790–1915,* 156; U.S. Bureau of Census, *Negroes in United States, 1915–1932,* 85; Hine, "Black Migration to the Urban Midwest" in Trotter, *Great Migration in Historical Perspective,* 127–46; Gregory, *Southern Diaspora,* 26; Florette Henri, *Black Migration: Movement North, 1900–1920* (Garden City, NJ: Anchor Press/Doubleday, 1975), 95–96; Jacqueline Jones, *Labor of Love, Labor of Sorrow: Black Women, Work, and the Family from Slavery to Freedom* (New York: Basic Books, 1985), 73–74; Gross, *Colored Amazons,* 43, 47.

37. Kelly, *Race, Class, and Power,* 32; Feldman, *Sense of Place,* 7–9; McKiven, *Iron and Steel,* 18, 42–47; Lewis, *Black Coal Miners,* 39–41, 167–93; Letwin, *Challenge of Interracial Unionism,* 23; Arnesen, *Brotherhoods of Color,* 29–30; Foner, *Organized Labor and the Black Worker,* 104–5; Spero and Harris, *The Black Worker,* 250–51; Nelson, *Divided We Stand,* 24–25.

38. Du Bois, *The Philadelphia Negro,* 129–31, quote, 131n14. Also see Arnesen, *Brotherhoods of Color,* 29–30; Foner, *Organized Labor and the Black Worker,* 104–5; Allan H. Spear, *Black Chicago: The Making of a Negro Ghetto, 1890–1920* (Chicago: University of Chicago Press, 1967), 40–41; Nelson, *Divided We Stand,* 24–25; Osofsky, *Harlem,* 42; Walter Licht, *Getting Work: Philadelphia, 1840–1950* (Cambridge: Harvard University Press, 1992), 46–47.

39. Arnesen, *Brotherhoods of Color,* 29–30; Nelson, *Divided We Stand,* 24–25; Zieger, *For Jobs and Freedom,* 63–64; Foner, *Organized Labor and the Black Worker,* 104–5; Osofsky, *Harlem,* 42; Spear, *Black Chicago,* 39–40, quote, 39.

40. Peter Gottlieb, *Making Their Own Way: Southern Blacks' Migration to Pittsburgh, 1916–30* (Urbana: University of Illinois Press, 1987), 90–91; Dennis Dickerson, *Out of the Crucible: Black Steelworkers in Western Pennsylvania, 1875–1980* (Albany: State University of New York Press, 1986), 20–21; John Hinshaw, *Steel and Steelworkers: Race and Class in Twentieth-Century Pittsburgh* (Albany: State University of New York Press), 18, 21, 28–29; Joe W. Trotter and Jared N. Day, *Race and Renaissance: African Americans in Pittsburgh since World War II* (Pittsburgh: University of Pittsburgh Press, 2010), 4–9; Joe W. Trotter, "Reflections on the Great Migration to Western Pennsylvania," *Pittsburgh History* 78, no. 4 (1995–96), 152–57.

41. Foner, *Organized Labor and the Black Worker,* quote, 24.

42. Spero and Harris, *The Black Worker,* 24–28; Zieger, *For Jobs and Freedom,* 25–26; William H. Harris, *The Harder We Run: Black Workers since the Civil War* (New York: Oxford University Press, 1982), 25–26; Foner, *Organized Labor and the Black Worker,* quote, 33; Meier, *Negro Thought in America,* quote, 9 .

43. Hunter, *To 'Joy My Freedom,* 88–97; Harris, *The Harder We Run,* 37; Zieger, *For Jobs and Freedom,* 146–47.

44. Zieger, *For Jobs and Freedom,* 51–69; Elizabeth Faue, *Rethinking the American Labor Movement* (New York: Routledge, 2017), 22; Harris, *The Harder We Run,* 27.

45. Foner, *Organized Labor and the Black Worker,* quotes, 7, 63.

46. Meier, *Negro Thought in America,* quote, 47–48; Emma Lou Thornbrough, *T. Thomas Fortune: Militant Journalist* (Chicago: University of Chicago Press, 1972), quote, 81–82; Spero and Harris, *The Black Worker,* quote, 43; Foner, *Organized Labor and the Black Worker,* 51–52.

47. Thornbrough, *T. Thomas Fortune,* 126–29; Marcy S. Sacks, "Re-Creating Black New York at Century's End," in *Slavery in New York,* ed. Ira Berlin and Leslie M. Harris (New York: New Press, 2005), 341–43; Hicks, *Talk with You Like a Woman,* 5–6, 92–93, 95–107; Stephanie J. Shaw, *What a Woman Ought to Be and to Do: Black Professional Women Workers during the Jim Crow Era* (Chicago: University of Chicago Press, 1996), 5–6.

48. Mark R. Schneider, *Boston Confronts Jim Crow, 1890–1930* (Boston: Northeastern University Press, 1997), 73–76; Meier, *Negro Thought in America,* 124–27; John N. Ingham and Lynne B. Feldman, *African-American Business Leaders: A Biographical Dictionary* (Westport, CT: Greenwood Press, 1994), 227.

49. Osofsky, *Harlem,* 33–34; Ingham and Feldman, *African-American Business Leaders,* 477, 680–93; Darlene Clark Hine and Kathleen Thompson, *A Shining Thread of Hope: The History of Black Women in America* (New York: Broadway Books, 1998), 203–5.

50. Bettye Collier-Thomas, *Jesus, Jobs, and Justice: African American Women and Religion* (New York: Alfred A. Knopf, 2010), 122–24; Sacks, "Re-Creating Black New York at Century's End," 327–28, 337–41, 344, 345, 348; Thornbrough, *T. Thomas Fortune,* 112–13.

51. Collier-Thomas, *Jesus, Jobs, and Justice,* 61, 77–78, quote, 123; Gaines, *Uplifting the Race,* 128–151, quote, 138; Evelyn Brooks Higginbotham, *Righteous Discon-*

tent: *The Women's Movement in the Black Baptist Church, 1880–1920* (Cambridge: Harvard University Press, 1993), 8, 151; Shaw, *What a Woman Ought to Be,* 1–10.

52. Hicks, *Talk with You Like a Woman,* 68–74, quote, 73–74.

53. Sacks, "Re-Creating Black New York at Century's End," 344, 348; Willard B. Gatewood, *Aristocrats of Color: The Black Elite, 1880–1920* (Bloomington: Indiana University Press, 1993), 277–79; Du Bois, *The Philadelphia Negro,* 10–12.

54. Gatewood, *Aristocrats of Color,* 96–103, 279–80; Du Bois, *The Philadelphia Negro,* 46–47; Robert Gregg, *Sparks from the Anvil of Oppression: Philadelphia's African Methodists and Southern Migrants, 1890–1940* (Philadelphia: Temple University Press, 1993), 46–47.

55. Sacks, "Re-Creating Black New York at Century's End," 344, 345, 348.

56. Shawn L. Alexander, *An Army of Lions: The Civil Rights Struggle before the NAACP* (Philadelphia: University of Pennsylvania, 2012), xiv, 21–22.

57. David Levering Lewis, *W. E. B. Du Bois: Biography of a Race, 1868–1919* (New York: Henry Holt, 1993), 408–34; Charles F. Kellogg, *NAACP: A History of the National Association for the Advancement of Colored People* (Baltimore: Johns Hopkins Press, 1967), 31–65; Touré Reed, *Not Alms But Opportunity: The Urban League and the Politics of Racial Uplift, 1910–1950* (Chapel Hill: University of North Carolina Press, 2008); Louis R. Harlan, *Booker T. Washington: The Wizard of Tuskegee, 1901–1915* (New York: Oxford University Press, 1983), 14–15, 359–78; Meier, *Negro Thought in America,* 182–83; Alexander, *Army of Lions,* 68–69.

CHAPTER FOUR

1. Ira Berlin, *The Making of African America: The Four Great Migrations* (New York: Viking, 2010), 153–56; James N. Gregory, *The Southern Diaspora: How the Great Migrations of Black and White Southerners Transformed America* (Chapel Hill: University of North Carolina Press, 2005), 14–15; Isabel Wilkerson, *The Warmth of Other Suns: The Epic Story of America's Great Migration* (New York: Random House, 2010), 8–15; Leah Platt Boustan, *Competition in the Promised Land: Black Migrants in Northern Cities and Labor Markets* (Princeton, NJ: Princeton University Press, 2017), 20–27.

2. Luther Adams, *Way Up North in Louisville: African American Migration in the Urban South, 1930–1970* (Chapel Hill: University of North Carolina Press, 2010), 24–25, 38–40; Bernadette Pruitt, *The Other Great Migration: The Movement of Rural African Americans to Houston, 1900–1941* (College Station: Texas A&M University Press, 2013), 3–4, 283–84; Earl Lewis, "Expectations, Economic Opportunities, and Life in the Industrial Age: Black Migration to Norfolk, Virginia, 1910–1945," in *The Great Migration in Historical Perspective: New Dimensions of Race, Class, and Gender,* ed. Joe William Trotter, Jr. (Bloomington: Indiana University Press, 1991), 22–25; Karl E. Taeuber and Alma F. Taeuber, *Negroes in Cities: Residential Segregation and Neighborhood Change* (Chicago: Aldine, 1965), 119.

3. Boustan, *Competition in the Promised Land,* 50–54; Clare Corbould, *Becoming African Americans: Black Public Life in Harlem, 1919–1939* (Cambridge: Harvard University Press, 2009), 6–7; Gilbert Osofsky, *Harlem: The Making of a Ghetto, Negro New York, 1890–1930,* 2nd ed. (1963; Chicago: Ivan R. Dee, 1996), 128–29; Joshua Sides, *L.A. City Limits: African American Los Angeles from the Great Depression to the Present* (Berkeley: University of California Press, 2004), 15; James R. Grossman, *Land of Hope: Chicago, Black Southerners, and the Great Migration* (Chicago: University of Chicago Press, 1989), 38–65; Earl Lewis, *In Their Own Interests: Race, Class, and Power in Twentieth-Century Norfolk, Virginia* (Berkeley: University of California Press, 1993), 29–32; Adams, *Way Up North in Louisville,* 24–27; Pruitt, *The Other Great Migration,* 41–43.

4. Peter Gottlieb, *Making Their Own Way: Southern Blacks' Migration to Pittsburgh, 1916–30* (Urbana: University of Illinois Press, 1987), 43–45, 55–59; Grossman, *Land of Hope,* 44–47, 72–73; Pruitt, *The Other Great Migration,* 42–44; Henry M. McKiven, Jr., *Iron and Steel: Class, Race, and Community in Birmingham, Alabama, 1875–1920* (Chapel Hill: University of North Carolina Press, 1995), 18, 42–47; Shirley Ann Moore, *To Place Our Deeds: The African American Community in Richmond, California, 1910–1963* (Berkeley: University of California Press, 2000), 46–47.

5. Philip S. Foner, *Organized Labor and the Black Worker, 1619–1973* (New York: Praeger, 1974), 130.

6. Marion Hayes, "A Century of Change: Negroes in the U.S. Economy, 1860–1960," *Monthly Labor Review,* December 1962, in *Negroes and Jobs: A Book of Readings,* ed. Louis A. Ferman, Joyce L. Kornbluh, and J. A. Miller (Ann Arbor: University of Michigan Press, 1968), 62; Bart Landry, *The New Black Middle Class* (Berkeley: University of California Press, 1987), 68; Steven A. Reich, *A Working People: A History of African American Workers since Emancipation* (Lanham, MD: Rowman and Littlefield, 2013), 69, 117.

7. Eric Arnesen, *Brotherhoods of Color: Black Railroad Workers and the Struggle for Equality* (Cambridge: Harvard University Press, 2001), 29–30; Foner, *Organized Labor and the Black Worker,* 104–5; Allan Spear, *Black Chicago: The Making of a Negro Ghetto, 1890–1920* (Chicago: University of Chicago Press, 1967), 40–41; Bruce Nelson, *Divided We Stand: American Workers and the Struggle for Black Equality* (Princeton, NJ: Princeton University Press, 2001), 24–25; Osofsky, *Harlem,* 42; W. E. B. Du Bois, *The Philadelphia Negro: A Social Study* (1899; repr., Philadelphia: University of Pennsylvania Press, 1996), 98, 100–103, 109, 129–31; Walter Licht, *Getting Work: Philadelphia, 1840–1950* (Cambridge: Harvard University Press, 1992), 46–47. In 1896, black domestics (and some general laborer jobs) averaged a high of just over $3.00–$4.00 per week, but blacks working at the Midvale company started out at a wage of $1.20 per day.

8. Dennis C. Dickerson, *Out of the Crucible: Black Steelworkers in Western Pennsylvania, 1875–1980* (Albany: State University of New York Press, 1986), 20–21, 33–53; Gottlieb, *Making Their Own Way,* 90–99; John Hinshaw, *Steel and Steelworkers: Race and Class Struggle in Twentieth-Century Pittsburgh* (Albany: State University of New York Press, 2002), 18, 21, 28–29, 35–38.

9. Joe William Trotter and Jared N. Day, *Race and Renaissance: African Americans in Pittsburgh since World War II* (Pittsburgh: University of Pittsburgh Press, 2010), 4–9; Joe W. Trotter, "Reflections on the Great Migration to Western Pennsylvania," *Pittsburgh History* 78, no. 4 (1995–96), 52–57.

10. Roger Horowitz, *"Negro and White, Unite and Fight!": A Social History of Industrial Unionism in Meatpacking, 1930–80* (Urbana: University of Illinois Press, 1999), 87–88; Walter A. Fogel, *The Negro in the Meat Industry* (Philadelphia: University of Pennsylvania Wharton School of Finance and Commerce, Report no.12, 1970), 46–47; Rick Halpern, *Down on the Killing Floor: Black and White Workers in Chicago's Packinghouses, 1904–54* (Urbana: University of Illinois Press, 1997), 47–48; Rick Halpern and Roger Horowitz, *Meatpackers: An Oral History of Black Packinghouse Workers and Their Struggle for Racial and Economic Equality* (New York: Monthly Review Press, 1999), 3–10; Grossman, *Land of Hope*, 187–99; Spear, *Black Chicago*, quote, 39–40, 151–53; Arnesen, *Brotherhoods of Color*, 29–30; Nelson, *Divided We Stand*, 24–25; Robert H. Zieger, *For Jobs and Freedom: Race and Labor in America since 1865* (Lexington: University Press of Kentucky, 2007), 63–64; Foner, *Organized Labor and the Black Worker*, 104–5; Spear, *Black Chicago*, 39–40, quote, 39; Christopher R. Reed, *The Rise of Chicago's Black Metropolis, 1920–1929* (Urbana: University of Illinois Press, 2011), 120–22.

11. Spear, *Black Chicago*, 133, 140; Grossman, *Land of Hope*, 44–47; John D. Finney, Jr., "A Study of Negro Labor During and After World War I" (PhD diss., Georgetown University, June 1967), 77–81; Trotter, *Great Migration in Historical Perspective*, 7–8; Wilkerson, *Warmth of Other Suns*, 161–63, 216; Florette Henri, *Black Migration: Movement North, 1900–1920* (Garden City, NJ: Anchor Press, 1975), 60–62, 67, 135–36.

12. Richard Walter Thomas, *Life for Us Is What We Make It: Building Black Community in Detroit, 1915–1945* (Bloomington: Indiana University Press, 1992), 28–30; August Meier and Elliot Rudwick, *Black Detroit and the Rise of the UAW* (New York: Oxford University Press, 1979), 9–16; David M. Lewis-Colman, *Race against Liberalism: Black Workers and the UAW in Detroit* (Urbana and Chicago: University of Illinois Press, 2008), 5–9.

13. Licht, *Getting Work*, 45–47; Theodore Kornwiebel, Jr., *Railroads in the African American Experience: A Photo Journey* (Baltimore: Johns Hopkins University Press, 2010), 52–53; Philip Scranton and Walter Licht, *Work Sights: Industrial Philadelphia, 1890–1950* (Philadelphia: Temple University Press, 1986), 203–4, 244–46; Lester Rubin, *The Negro in the Shipbuilding Industry* (Philadelphia: University of Pennsylvania Wharton School of Finance and Commerce, Report no. 17, 1970), 46.

14. Douglas Flamming, *Bound for Freedom: Black Los Angeles in Jim Crow America* (Berkeley: University of California, 2005), 245; Albert S. Broussard, *Black San Francisco: The Struggle for Racial Equality in the West, 1900–1954* (Lawrence: University Press of Kansas, 1993), 44–45; Quintard Taylor, *The Forging of a Black Community: Seattle's Central District from 1870 through the Civil Rights Era* (Seattle: University of Washington Press, 1994), 60–61; Scott Kurashige, *The Shifting Grounds of Race: Black and Japanese Americans in the Making of Multiethnic Los*

Angeles (Princeton, NJ: Princeton University Press, 2008), 67–69. Kurashige underscores how few African American and Asian American workers secured jobs in L.A.'s industrial workforce.

15. Moore, *To Place Our Deeds,* 46–47; Gretchen Lemke-Santangelo, *Abiding Courage: African American Women in the East Bay Community* (Chapel Hill: University of North Carolina Press, 1996), 50–51; Broussard, *Black San Francisco,* 134–35, 146, 209.

16. Lewis, *In Their Own Interests,* 30–32; Adams, *Way Up North in Louisville,* 1–2; McKiven, *Iron and Steel,* 18, 42–47.

17. Pruitt, *The Other Great Migration,* 42–44.

18. Pruitt, *The Other Great Migration,* 225–32. Ronald H. Bayor, *Race and the Shaping of Twentieth-Century Atlanta* (Chapel Hill: University of North Carolina Press, 1996), 96–98.

19. Brian Kelly, *Race, Class, and Power in the Alabama Coalfields, 1908–1921* (Urbana: University of Illinois Press, 2001), 137; Eric Arnesen, *Waterfront Workers of New Orleans: Race, Class, and Politics, 1863–1923* (New York: Oxford University Press, 1991), 220.

20. Arnesen, *Waterfront Workers of New Orleans,* 220; Kelly, *Race, Class, and Power in the Alabama Coalfields,* 138.

21. Kelly, *Race, Class, and Power in the Alabama Coalfields,* 137–39; Georgina Hickey, *Hope and Danger in the New South: Working Class Women and Urban Development in Atlanta, 1890–1940* (Athens: University of Georgia Press, 2003), quote, 174.

22. Lewis, *In Their Own Interests,* 29–30; Adams, *Way Up North in Louisville,* 13–14, 15.

23. Leslie Brown, *Upbuilding Black Durham: Gender, Class, and Black Community Development in the Jim Crow South* (Chapel Hill: University of North Carolina Press, 2008), quotes, 234.

24. Jacqueline Jones, *Labor of Love, Labor of Sorrow: Black Women, Work and the Family from Slavery to Freedom* (New York: Basic Books, 1985), 166–80; Sadie Tanner Mossell Alexander, "Negro Women in Our Economic Life," 201–3, quoted in *Words of Fire: An Anthology of African-American Feminist Thought,* ed. Beverly Guy-Sheftall (New York: New Press, 1995), 97–98, https://books.google.com/books/about /Words_of_Fire.html; Spear, *Black Chicago,* 151–58, quote, 157; Elaine G. Wrong, *The Negro in the Apparel Industry* (Philadelphia: University of Pennsylvania, Wharton School of Industrial Research, Report no. 31, 1974), 31–32; Thomas, *Life for Us,* 32–35; Tera Hunter, *To 'Joy My Freedom: Southern Black Women's Lives and Labors after the Civil War* (Cambridge: Harvard University Press, 1997), 224–25; David M. Katzman, *Seven Days a Week: Women and Domestic Service in Industrializing America* (Urbana: University of Illinois Press, 1981), 228–29; Gottlieb, *Making Their Own Way,* 108.

25. Thomas, *Life for Us,* 32–35; Victoria W. Wolcott, *Remaking Respectability: African American Women in Interwar Detroit* (Chapel Hill: University of North Carolina Press, 2001), 78–82; Gottlieb, *Making Their Own Way,* 107.

26. Jones, *Labor of Love,* 166–80; Alexander, "Negro Women in Our Economic Life," 201–3, quoted in Guy-Sheftall, *Words of Fire,* 97–98; Spear, *Black Chicago,* 151–58,

quote, 157; Reed, *Rise of Chicago's Black Metropolis*, 138; Wrong, *The Negro in the Apparel Industry*, 31–32; Thomas, *Life for Us*, 32–35; Hunter, *To 'Joy My Freedom*, 224–25; Katzman, *Seven Days a Week*, 228–29; Gottlieb, *Making Their Own Way*, 108; Cheryl D. Hicks, *Talk with You Like a Woman: African American Women, Justice, and Reform in New York, 1890–1935* (Chapel Hill: University of North Carolina Press, 2010), 40.

27. Brown, *Upbuilding Black Durham*, 235–37; Gregory, *Southern Diaspora*, 12–19; Berlin, *Making of African America*, 152–83; Peter M. Rutkoff and William Scott, *Fly Away: The Great African American Cultural Migrations* (Baltimore: Johns Hopkins University Press, 2010), 55–56, 144–47, 205–8; Wilkerson, *Warmth of Other Suns*, 8–15; Daniel M. Johnson and Rex R. Campbell, *Black Migration in America: A Social Demographic History* (Durham, NC: Duke University Press, 1981), 71–72.

28. Lewis, *In Their Own Interests*, 32–37; Pruitt, *The Other Great Migration*, 216, 223, 233.

29. Michael Honey, *Southern Labor and Black Civil Rights: Organizing Memphis Workers* (Urbana: University of Illinois Press, 1993), 35–38; Georgina Hickey, *Hope and Danger in the New South: Working Class Women and Urban Development in Atlanta, 1890–1940* (Athens: University of Georgia Press, 2003), 171; Bayor, *Race and the Shaping of Twentieth-Century Atlanta*, 97–101.

30. Adams, *Way Up North in Louisville*, 13–14, 15.

31. Thomas, *Life for Us*, 41–42; Wolcott, *Remaking Respectability*, 72–91; Meier and Rudwick, *Black Detroit and the Rise of the UAW*, 7–8.

32. Dickerson, *Out of the Crucible*, 49–53; Gottlieb, *Making Their Own Way*, 96–102, 119, 124–25; Thomas, *Life for Us*, 107; Halpern and Horowitz, *Meatpackers*, 6, 33–34, 52; Spear, *Black Chicago*, 158; Horowitz, *"Negro and White, Unite and Fight!,"* 23–24; Fogel, *The Negro in the Meat Industry*, 44–54.

33. Licht, *Getting Work*, 45–46.

34. McKiven, *Iron and Steel*, 121–23; Jacqueline Jones, *American Work: Four Centuries of Black and White Labor* (New York: W. W. Norton, 1998), 328–29; Robert J. Norrell, "Caste in Steel: Jim Crow Careers in Birmingham," *Journal of American History* 73 (December 1986): 669–94.

35. Pruitt, *The Other Great Migration*, 223–30; Jones, *Labor of Love*, 328–29.

36. Honey, *Southern Labor and Black Civil Rights*, 34; Lewis, *In Their Own Interests*, 34.

37. Flamming, *Bound for Freedom*, 71–73, 245–47, Johnson quote, 246; James Wolfinger, *Philadelphia Divided: Race and Politics in the City of Brotherly Love* (Chapel Hill: University of North Carolina Press, 2007), 114, 116–17; Sides, *L.A. City Limits*, 54–55.

38. Pruitt, *The Other Great Migration*, 222–23.

39. Foner, *Organized Labor and the Black Worker*, 141–43, 158–176; Arnesen, *Brotherhoods of Color*, 46, 67–83, 98, 142, 143–44; Spear, *Black Chicago*, 159–63; Halpern, *Down on the Killing Floor*, 50–59; Reed, *Rise of Chicago's Black Metropolis*, 120–24.

40. Arnesen, *Brotherhoods of Color*, 29–30; Nelson, *Divided We Stand*, 24–26; Zieger, *For Jobs and Freedom*, 63–64; Foner, *Organized Labor and the Black Worker*, 104–5; Osofsky, *Harlem*, 42; Spear, *Black Chicago*, 37, 39–41, quote, 39.

41. Halpern, *Down on the Killing Floor,* 41; Sylvia Hood Washington, *Packing Them In: An Archaeology of Environmental Racism in Chicago, 1865–1954* (Lanham, MD: Lexington Books, 2005), 77–79; Spear, *Black Chicago,* 37, 40–41; Nelson, *Divided We Stand,* 24–26; James R. Barrett, "Ethnic and Racial Fragmentation: Toward a Reinterpretation of a Local Labor Movement," in *The African American Urban Experience: Perspectives from the Colonial Period to the Present,* ed. Joe W. Trotter, Earl Lewis, and Tera Hunter (New York: Palgrave/Macmillan, 2004), 287–309.

42. Lewis, *In Their Own Interests,* 32–36; Pruitt, *The Other Great Migration,* 228; George C. Wright, *Life behind a Veil: Blacks in Louisville, Kentucky, 1865–1930* (Baton Rouge: Louisiana State University Press, 1985), 78–79; Taylor, *Forging of a Black Community,* 49; Gottlieb, *Making Their Own Way,* 91–92; Osofsky, *Harlem,* 136–37; Kornwiebel, *Railroads in the African American Experience,* quote, 115–16; Jack Santino, *Miles of Smiles, Years of Struggle: Stories of Black Pullman Porters* (Urbana: University of Illinois Press, 1989), 19–21; Arnesen, *Brotherhoods of Color,* 87–88.

43. Premilla Nadasen, *Household Workers Unite: The Untold Story of African American Women Who Built a Movement* (Boston: Beacon Press, 2015), 10–11, 16–17, 111–18.

44. Jones, *Labor of Love,* 167–68; Kimberley Phillips, *AlabamaNorth: African-American Migrants, Community, and Working-Class Activism, 1915–45* (Urbana: University of Illinois Press, 1999), 72; Hicks, *Talk with You Like a Woman,* 39.

45. Lewis, *In Their Own Interests,* 35–37; Pruitt, *The Other Great Migration,* 216; Honey, *Southern Labor and Black Civil Rights,* 35–38.

46. Brown, *Upbuilding Black Durham,* 228.

47. Thomas, *Life for Us,* 106–07.

48. Thomas, *Life for Us,* 106–07. On the notion of an "occupational ghetto," see Richard B. Pierce, *Polite Protest: The Political Economy of Race in Indianapolis, 1920–1970* (Bloomington: Indiana University Press, 2005), 93.

49. Cynthia M. Blair, *I've Got to Make My Livin': Black Women's Sex Work in Turn-of-the-Century Chicago* (Chicago: University of Chicago Press, 2010), 223–29, quote, 228; Kevin Mumford, *Interzones: Black/White Sex Districts in Chicago and New York in the Early Twentieth Century* (New York: Columbia University Press, 1997), 38–39; Khalil G. Muhammad, *The Condemnation of Blackness: Race, Crime, and the Making of Modern Urban America* (Cambridge: Harvard University Press, 2010), 121–22, 223–24.

50. Hicks, *Talk with You Like a Woman,* quote, 40–41; Cheryl L. Greenberg, *Or Does It Explode?: Black Harlem in the Great Depression* (New York: Oxford University Press, 1991), 77–80; Cheryl Greenberg, *To Ask for an Equal Chance: African Americans in the Great Depression* (Lanham, MD: Rowman and Littlefield, 2009), 27–28; Blair, *I've Got to Make My Livin',* 223–29; Ella Baker and Marvel Cooke, "Domestic Slavery: The Bronx Slave Market," in *Afro-American History: Primary Sources,* ed. Thomas R. Frazier (Chicago: Dorsey Press, 1970), 265–71. For similar patterns of policing, work, and prostitution in the urban South, see Talitha L. LeFlouria, *Chained in Silence: Black Women and Convict Labor in the New South* (Chapel Hill: University of North Carolina Press, 2015), 178–79.

51. Greenberg, *Or Does It Explode?*, 77–80; Greenberg, *To Ask for an Equal Chance*, 27–28; Baker and Cooke, "Domestic Slavery," in Frazier, *Afro-American History*, 265–71; Quintard Taylor, *In Search of the Racial Frontier: African Americans in the American West, 1528–1990* (New York: W.W. Norton, 1998), 229–30; Lewis, *In Their Own Interests*, 35, 112–13; Christopher R. Reed, *The Depression Comes to the South Side: Protest and Politics in the Black Metropolis, 1930–1933* (Bloomington: Indiana University Press, 2011), 9–34; Thomas, *Life for Us*, 45–46.

52. Boustan, *Competition in the Promised Land*, 87–88.

53. Richard Rothstein, *The Color of Law: A Forgotten History of How Our Government Segregated America* (New York: Liveright / W.W. Norton, 2017), ix.

54. Mitchell Duneier, *Ghetto: The Invention of a Place, the History of an Idea* (New York: Farrar, Straus, and Giroux, 2016), ix–xii, 217–37; Avigail Oren, "'Is a Negro District, in the Midst of Our Fairest Cities, to Become Connotative of the Ghetto . . . ?': Using Corpus Analysis to Trace the 'Ghetto' in the Black Press, 1900–1930," in *The Ghetto in Global History: 1500 to the Present*, ed. Wendy Z. Goldman and Joe William Trotter, Jr. (New York: Routledge, 2017).

55. Jeffrey D. Gonda, *Unjust Deeds: The Restrictive Covenant Cases and the Making of the Civil Rights Movement* (Chapel Hill: University of North Carolina Press, 2015), 4, 134; Kevin McGruder, *Race and Real Estate: Conflict and Cooperation in Harlem, 1890–1920* (New York: Columbia University Press, 2015), 94, 231–32n52; Carl Nightingale, *Segregation: A Global History of Divided Cities* (Chicago: University of Chicago Press, 2012), 306–7; Donald G. Nieman, *Promises to Keep: African Americans and the Constitutional Order, 1776 to the Present* (Oxford: Oxford University Press, 1991), 128–29; N.D.B. Connolly, *A World More Concrete: Real Estate and the Remaking of Jim Crow South Florida* (Chicago: University of Chicago Press, 2014), 39–40.

56. Gonda, *Unjust Deeds*, 4–5; McGruder, *Race and Real Estate*, 94–96; Nieman, *Promises to Keep*, 129; Connolly, *A World More Concrete*, 40–41.

57. Pierce, *Polite Protest*, 59, 61.

58. Kurashige, *Shifting Grounds of Race*, 163–64. A group of black business and professional men and women bought homes in the elite Adams Heights community, described as a "star-studded" area called "Sugar Hill" on Harvard and Hobart Streets. White residents soon rallied their forces, took the matter to court, and blocked African Americans (including well-known entertainers Hattie McDaniel, Louise Beavers, and Ethel Waters) from occupying their homes. Only in the aftermath of World War II were the homeowners able to occupy their property. In another Los Angeles case, after three years of litigation, a court ordered the family of Henry and Anna Laws to vacate their home in a South Los Angeles neighborhood in 1945.

59. Flamming, *Bound for Freedom*, 224–25.

60. Nightingale, *Segregation*, 1–3, 13; Osofsky, *Harlem*, 106–7; Spear, *Black Chicago*, 17–23; Reed, *Rise of Chicago's Black Metropolis*, 25–33, 46–47, 672–73; Douglas S. Massey and Nancy Denton, *American Apartheid: Segregation and the Making of the Underclass* (Cambridge: Harvard University Press, 1993), 20–22;

Stanley Lieberson, *A Piece of the Pie: Blacks and White Immigrants since 1880* (Berkeley: University of California Press, 1980), 265–67; Wright, *Life behind a Veil*, 237; Andor Skotnes, *A New Deal for All? Race and Class Struggles in Depression-Era Baltimore* (Durham, NC: Duke University Press, 2013), 275–76.

61. Bayor, *Race and the Shaping of Twentieth-Century Atlanta*, 55–58.

62. Wright, *Life behind a Veil*, 236; Adams, *Way Up North in Louisville*, 41, 46; Connolly, *A World More Concrete*, 38.

63. Pierce, *Polite Protest*, 59; Wright, *Life behind a Veil*, 236.

64. Kevin Boyle, *Arc of Justice: A Saga of Race, Civil Rights, and Murder in the Jazz Age* (New York: H. Holt, 2004), 17–43; Thomas, *Life for Us*, quote, 138–40, 230–31.

65. Thomas, *Life for Us*, 136.

66. Marcus A. Hunter, *Black Citymakers: How The Philadelphia Negro Changed Urban America* (New York: Oxford University Press, 2013), 75–76. See also V. P. Franklin, "The Philadelphia Race Riot of 1918," *Pennsylvania Magazine of History and Biography* 99 (July 1975), in *African Americans in Pennsylvania: Shifting Historical Perspectives*, ed. Joe William Trotter, Jr., and Eric L. Smith (Harrisburg and University Park: Pennsylvania State University Press, 1997), 316–19; Olivier Zunz, *The Changing Face of Inequality: Urbanization, Industrial Development, and Immigrants in Detroit, 1880–1920* (Chicago: University of Chicago Press, 1982), 374–75.

67. Jeffrey Hegelson, *Crucibles of Black Empowerment: Chicago's Neighborhood Politics from the New Deal to Harold Washington* (Chicago: University of Chicago Press, 2014), 31; Spear, *Black Chicago*, 22, 150, 210–12.

68. Reed, *Rise of Chicago's Black Metropolis*, 30, 31, 37, 147; Spear, *Black Chicago*, 221.

69. Flamming, *Bound for Freedom*, 351–52; Pierce, *Polite Protest*, 60–61; Connolly, *A World More Concrete*, 94–98. Also see Richard Rothstein, *The Color of Law*, 63–64.

70. Taeuber and Taeuber, *Negroes in Cities*, 47–55; Massey and Denton, *American Apartheid*, 23–42; Osofsky, *Harlem*, 135–41; Spear, *Black Chicago*, 23; Robert Gregg, *Sparks from the Anvil of Oppression: Philadelphia's African Methodists and Southern Migrants, 1890–1940* (Philadelphia: Temple University Press, 1993), 26–27, 30; Franklin, "Philadelphia Race Riot of 1918," in Trotter and Smith, *African Americans in Pennsylvania*, 316–29; Zunz, *Changing Face of Inequality*, 374–75; Thomas, *Life for Us*, 37–38, 89–93; Allen B. Ballard, *One More Day's Journey: The Making of Black Philadelphia* (Philadelphia: Institute for the Study of Human Issues, 1987), 234–36; Reed, *Rise of Chicago's Black Metropolis*, quote, 62.

71. Greenberg, *Or Does It Explode?*, 31–32.

72. Taeuber and Taeuber, *Negroes in Cities*, 47–55; Massey and Denton, *American Apartheid*, 23–42; Greenberg, *Or Does It Explode?*, 31–32; Osofsky, *Harlem*, 135–41; Gregg, *Sparks from the Anvil*, 26–27, 30; Ballard, *One More Day's Journey*, 234–36; Franklin, "Philadelphia Race Riot of 1918," in Trotter and Smith, *African Americans in Pennsylvania*, 316–29; Zunz, *Changing Face of Inequality*, 374–75;

Thomas, *Life for Us*, 37–38, 89–93; St. Clair Drake and Horace R. Cayton, *Black Metropolis: A Study of Negro Life in a Northern City*, vols. 1 and 2 (1945; rev. and enl., Chicago: University of Chicago Press, 1993), 61; Davarian L. Baldwin, *Chicago's New Negroes: Modernity, The Great Migration, and Black Urban Life* (Chapel Hill: University of North Carolina Press, 2007), 25; Touré Reed, *Not Alms but Opportunity: The Urban League and the Politics of Racial Uplift, 1910–1950* (Chapel Hill: University of North Carolina Press, 2008), 32–33.

73. Thomas, *Life for Us*, 100–01; Lemke-Santangelo, *Abiding Courage*, 80; Gottlieb, *Making Their Own Way*, 70.

74. Gottlieb, *Making Their Own Way*, 69–71; Gregg, *Sparks from the Anvil*, quote from Woodson, 29; Wolcott, *Remaking Respectability*, 111; Lemke-Santangelo, *Abiding Courage*, 81; Moore, *To Place Our Deeds*, 23; Laurie B. Green, *Battling the Plantation Mentality: Memphis and the Black Freedom Struggle* (Chapel Hill: University of North Carolina Press, 2007), 17–18.

75. Wolfinger, *Philadelphia Divided*, 53, 57–58; Hunter, *Black Citymakers*, 69–71.

76. Hunter, *Black Citymakers*, quote, 69; Wolfinger, *Philadelphia Divided*, 81, Faucet quote, 87, 89.

77. Gottlieb, *Making Their Own Way*, 75; Dickerson, *Out of the Crucible*, 55–56, 58; Taeuber and Taeuber, *Negroes in Cities*, 47–55; Massey and Denton, *American Apartheid*, 23–42; Osofsky, *Harlem*, 135–41; Gregg, *Sparks from the Anvil*, 26–27, 30; Franklin, "Philadelphia Race Riot of 1918," in Trotter and Smith, *African Americans in Pennsylvania*, 316–29; Zunz, *Changing Face of Inequality*, 374–75; Thomas, *Life for Us*, 37–38, 89–93; Ballard, *One More Day's Journey*, 234–36.

78. Greenberg, *Or Does It Explode?*, 28–29, 181–83; Lewis, *In Their Own Interests*, 171; Broussard, *Black San Francisco*, 35.

79. Lewis, *In Their Own Interests*, 80–81; Thomas, *Life for Us*, 104–5; Greenberg, *Or Does It Explode?*, 31–32, 186–87, 192; Hunter, *Black Citymakers*, 80–81; Dickerson, *Out of the Crucible*, 59.

80. Thomas, *Life for Us*, 111; Ballard, *One More Day's Journey*, 234–35; Osofsky, *Harlem*, 140–41; Joe W. Trotter, "Blacks in the Urban North: The 'Underclass Question' in Historical Perspective," in *The "Underclass Debate": Views from History*, ed. Michael Katz (Princeton, NJ: Princeton University Press, 1993), 61–62, 73–74; Osofsky, *Harlem*, 146–47; Muhammad, *Condemnation of Blackness*, 9–10, 226–29; Hicks, *Talk with You Like a Woman*, 130–31, 256–57; Sides, *L.A. City Limits*, 47.

81. Greenberg, *Or Does It Explode?*, 193; Green, *Battling the Plantation Mentality*, 14, 32–33, 89–90.

82. Thomas Sugrue, *Sweet Land of Liberty: The Forgotten Struggle for Civil Rights in the North* (New York: Random House, 2008), 154–56; Muhammad, *Condemnation of Blackness*, 235–36; Robert A. Caro, *The Power Broker: Robert Moses and the Fall of New York* (New York: Vintage Books, 1974), 512–13; Spear, *Black Chicago*, 205–8; Flamming, *Bound for Freedom*, 271–72; Sides, *L.A. City Limits*, 21; Victoria W. Wolcott, *Race, Riots, and Roller Coasters: The Struggle over Segregated Recreation in America* (Philadelphia: University of Pennsylvania Press), 25–31. For

helpful overviews of municipal policies governing public parks, playgrounds, and libraries, also see Henry J. McGuinn, "Part IV: Recreation," in *Negro Problems in Cities,* ed. T. J. Woofter, Jr. (1928; repr., New York: Harper and Row, 1969), 231–39; and Jearold W. Holland, *Black Recreation: A Historical Perspective* (Chicago: Burnham, 2002), 137–52.

83. Thomas, *Life for Us,* 127–28; Trotter and Day, *Race and Renaissance,* 14–15; Spear, *Black Chicago,* 206–7.

84. Chicago Commission on Race Relations, *The Negro in Chicago: A Study of Race Relations and a Race Riot* (Chicago: University of Chicago Press, 1922), 1–52; Drake and Cayton, *Black Metropolis,* 61; Reed, *Not Alms but Opportunity,* 32–33; Baldwin, *Chicago's New Negroes,* 25.

85. Kenneth Jackson, *The Ku Klux Klan in the City, 1915–1930* (New York: Oxford University Press, 1967), 94, 96, 108, 129–30; Kathleen M. Blee, *Women of the Klan: Racism and Gender in the 1920s* (Berkeley: University of California Press, 1991), quote, 177.

86. Hickey, *Hope and Danger in the New South,* 178–79; Blee, *Women of the Klan,* 172–78.

87. Charles L. Lumpkins, *American Pogrom: The East St. Louis Race Riot and Black Politics* (Athens: Ohio University Press, 2008), 74–108; Elliott M. Rudwick, *Race Riot at East St. Louis, July 2, 1917* (Carbondale: Southern Illinois University Press, 1964), 39–57; Alfred L. Brophy, *Reconstructing the Dreamland: The Tulsa Riot of 1921; Race, Reparations, and Reconciliation* (New York: Oxford University Press, 2002), 1–24; Scott Ellsworth, *Death in a Promised Land: The Tulsa Race Riot of 1921* (Baton Rouge: Louisiana State University Press, 1982), 45–70; William M. Tuttle, *Race Riot: Chicago in the Red Summer of 1919* (1966; repr., New York: Atheneum, 1970), 32–66; Herbert Shapiro, *White Violence and Black Response: From Reconstruction to Montgomery* (Amherst: University of Massachusetts Press, 1988), 150–52, 182–85.

CHAPTER FIVE

1. Clare Corbould, *Becoming African Americans: Black Public Life in Harlem, 1919–1939* (Cambridge: Harvard University Press, 2009), 11; Kevin Mumford, *Newark: A History of Race, Rights, and Riots in America* (New York: New York University Press, 2007), 6–7; Victoria W. Wolcott, *Remaking Respectability: African American Women in Interwar Detroit* (Chapel Hill: University of North Carolina Press, 2001), 149–57; Erik S. McDuffie, *Sojourning for Freedom: Black Women, American Communism, and the Making of a Black Left Feminism* (Durham, NC: Duke University Press, 2011), 2–34 .

2. Bruce Nelson, *Divided We Stand: American Workers and the Struggle for Black Equality* (Princeton, NJ: Princeton University Press, 2001), 204–37; Robert H. Zieger, *For Jobs and Freedom: Race and Labor in America since 1865* (Lexington: University Press of Kentucky, 2007), 112–23; Horace R. Cayton and George S.

Mitchell, *Black Workers and the New Unions* (1939; Westport, CT: Negro Universities Press, 1970), 257–79.

3. Rick Halpern, *Down on the Killing Floor: Black and White Workers in Chicago's Packinghouses, 1904–54* (Urbana: University of Illinois Press, 1997), 96–138; Rick Halpern and Roger Horowitz, *Meatpackers: An Oral History of Black Packinghouse Workers and their Struggle for Racial and Economic Equality* (New York: Twayne, 1996), quotes, 37, 38; Roger Horowitz, *"Negro and White, Unite and Fight!": A Social History of Industrial Unionism in Meatpacking, 1930–80* (Urbana: University of Illinois Press, 1999), 58–83; Walter A. Fogel, *The Negro in the Meat Industry* (Philadelphia: University of Pennsylvania Wharton School of Finance and Commerce, Report no. 12, 1970), 44–71.

4. August Meier and Elliot Rudwick, *Black Detroit and the Rise of the UAW* (New York: Oxford University Press, 1979), 40–41; Nelson, *Divided We Stand,* 192–93; Wolcott, *Remaking Respectability,* 207–40; Richard Walter Thomas, *Life for Us Is What We Make It: Building Black Community in Detroit, 1915–1945* (Bloomington: Indiana University Press, 1992), 139–41.

5. Philip S. Foner, *Organized Labor and the Black Worker, 1619–1973* (New York: Praeger, 1974), 204–37; Zieger, *For Jobs and Freedom,* 112–23; Nelson, *Divided We Stand,* 193–208.

6. Robert Francis quoted in Nelson, *Divided We Stand,* 96; Douglas Flamming, *Bound for Freedom: Black Los Angeles in Jim Crow America* (Berkeley: University of California, 2005), 360; Scott Kurashige, *The Shifting Grounds of Race: Black and Japanese Americans in the Making of Multiethnic Los Angeles* (Princeton, NJ: Princeton University Press, 2008), 67–69; Joshua Sides, *L.A. City Limits: African American Los Angeles from the Great Depression to the Present* (Berkeley: University of California Press, 2004), 71–74; Gerald Horne, *Red Seas: Ferdinand Smith and Radical Black Sailors in the United States and Jamaica* (New York: New York University Press, 2005), 32–35, 39–40, 48.

7. Albert S. Broussard, *Black San Francisco: The Struggle for Racial Equality in the West, 1900–1954* (Kansas: University Press of Kansas, 1993), 144–45; Shirley Ann Moore, *To Place Our Deeds: The African American Community in Richmond, California, 1910–1963* (Berkeley: University of California Press, 2000), 37–38, 60–61; Nelson, *Divided We Stand,* 96–97; Quintard Taylor, *The Forging of a Black Community: Seattle's Central District from 1870 through the Civil Rights Era* (Seattle: University of Washington Press, 1994), 68–69.

8. Broussard, *Black San Francisco,* 144–45; Moore, *To Place Our Deeds,* 37–38, 60–61; Nelson, *Divided We Stand,* 96–97; Taylor, *Forging of a Black Community,* 68–69.

9. Eric Arnesen, *Brotherhoods of Color: Black Railroad Workers and the Struggle for Equality* (Cambridge: Harvard University Press, 2001), 116, 139; Michael Honey, *Southern Labor and Black Civil Rights: Organizing Memphis Workers* (Urbana: University of Illinois Press, 1993), 1–6, 103–16; Laurie B. Green, *Battling the Plantation Mentality: Memphis and the Black Freedom Struggle* (Chapel Hill: University of North Carolina Press, 2007), 29–30.

10. Robin D. G. Kelley, *Hammer and Hoe: Alabama Communists during the Great Depression* (Chapel Hill: University of North Carolina Press, 1990), 143–44.

11. Robert H. Zieger, *For Jobs and Freedom: Race and Labor in America since 1865* (Lexington: University Press of Kentucky, 2007), 25–26; William H. Harris, *The Harder We Run: Black Workers since the Civil War* (New York: Oxford University Press, 1982), 25; August Meier, *Negro Thought in America, 1880–1915: Racial Ideologies in the Age of Booker T. Washington* (Ann Arbor: University of Michigan Press, 1973), 9. Sterling D. Spero and Abram L. Harris, *The Black Worker: The Negro and the Labor Movement* (1931; repr. New York: Athenaeum, 1968), quote, 43; Foner, *Organized Labor and the Black Worker*, 7, 51–52, 63; Andrew E. Kersten and Clarence Lang, "A Reintroduction to Asa Philip Randolph," in *Reframing Randolph: Labor, Black Freedom, and the Legacies of A. Philip Randolph*, ed. Andrew E. Kersten and Clarence Lang (New York: New York University Press, 2015), 1–20; Joe William Trotter, Jr., "Researching Randolph: Shifting Historiographic Perspectives," in Kersten and Lang, *Reframing Randolph*, 21–44.

12. Foner, *Organized Labor and the Black Worker*, 182–83; Jervis Anderson, *A. Philip Randolph: A Biographical Portrait* (1972; repr., Berkeley: University of California Press, 1986), 168–86; Jack Santino, *Miles of Smiles, Years of Struggle: Stories of Black Pullman Porters* (Urbana: University of Illinois Press, 1989), 13–14, 37–39; Beth Tompkins Bates, *Pullman Porters and the Rise of Protest Politics in Black America, 1925–1945* (Chapel Hill: University of North Carolina Press, 2001), 63–105; Cynthia Taylor, *A. Philip Randolph: The Religious Journey of an African American Labor Leader* (New York: New York University Press, 2006), 85–127; Paula F. Pfeffer, *A. Philip Randolph, Pioneer of the Civil Rights Movement* (Baton Rouge: Louisiana State University Press, 1990), 6–44; William H. Harris, *Keeping the Faith: A. Philip Randolph, Milton P. Webster, and the Brotherhood of Sleeping Car Porters, 1925–37* (Urbana: University of Illinois Press, 1977), 40–41; Deborah Gray White, *Too Heavy a Load: Black Women in Defense of Themselves, 1894–1994* (New York: W. W. Norton, 1999), 162–67.

13. Foner, *Organized Labor and the Black Worker*, 182–83; White, *Too Heavy a Load*, 162–67; Melinda Chateauvert, *Marching Together: Women of the Brotherhood of Sleeping Car Porters* (Urbana: University of Illinois Press, 1998), xii, 39, 54–55, 60–61, 83, 197.

14. Arnesen, *Brotherhoods of Color*, 84–115; Nelson, *Divided We Stand*, 193–200; Anderson, *A. Philip Randolph*, 224–25; Pfeffer, *A. Philip Randolph, Pioneer*, 29–44; Taylor, *A. Philip Randolph*, 123–27; Harris, *Keeping the Faith*, 206–16, 228.

15. Foner, *Organized Labor and the Black Worker*, 182–83; White, *Too Heavy a Load*, 162–67; Chateauvert, *Marching Together*, xii, 39, 54–55, 60–61, 83, 197. Ula Y. Taylor, *The Veiled Garvey: The Life and Times of Amy Jacques Garvey* (Chapel Hill: University of North Carolina Press, 2002), 2–3, 44–45, 63–64, 66–67.

16. Yevette Richards Jordan, *Maida Springer-Kemp: Pan-Africanist and International Labor Leader* (Pittsburgh: University of Pittsburgh Press, 2000), 34–35, 36–37, 43–44.

17. Premilla Nadasen, *Household Workers Unite: The Untold Story of African American Women Who Built a Movement* (Boston: Beacon Press, 2015), 10, 13–18; McDuffie, *Sojourning for Freedom*, 9, 11, 102.

18. Allan H. Spear, *Black Chicago: The Making of a Negro Ghetto, 1890–1920* (Chicago: University of Chicago Press, 1967), 156; Dennis Dickerson, *Out of the Crucible: Black Steelworkers in Western Pennsylvania, 1875–1980* (New York: State University of New York Press, 1986), 61; Peter Gottlieb, *Making Their Own Way: Southern Blacks' Migration to Pittsburgh, 1916–30* (Urbana: University of Illinois Press, 1987), 126–27, 135–36; Thomas, *Life for Us*, 35–36; Joe William Trotter, Jr., *River Jordan: African American Urban Life in the Ohio Valley* (Lexington: University Press of Kentucky, 1998), 103; Fidel Campet, "Black Housing in Pittsburgh: Community Struggles and the State, 1916–1973" (PhD diss., Carnegie Mellon University, 2011), 88–89; Gilbert Osofsky, *Harlem: The Making of a Ghetto, 1890–1930*, rev. ed. (1963; repr., New York: Harper Torchbooks, 1971), 139; Joe William Trotter, Jr., *The African American Experience* (Boston: Houghton Mifflin, 2001), 455–56.

19. Cayton and Mitchell, *Black Workers and the New Unions*, excerpt, in John H. Bracey, August Meier, and Elliott Rudwick, eds., *Black Workers and Organized Labor* (Belmont, CA: Wadsworth, 1971), 134–38; Taylor, *Forging of a Black Community*, 58–61; Nelson, *Divided We Stand*, 95, 167.

20. Jeffrey Helgeson, *Crucibles of Black Empowerment: Chicago's Neighborhood Politics from the New Deal to Harold Washington* (Chicago: University of Chicago Press, 2014), 42, 62–70, 78–79; Andor Skotnes, *A New Deal for All? Race and Class Struggles in Depression-Era Baltimore* (Durham, NC: Duke University Press, 2013), 181–82; James Wolfinger, *Philadelphia Divided: Race and Politics in the City of Brotherly Love* (Chapel Hill: University of North Carolina Press, 2007), 47–48; Nancy J. Weiss, *Farewell to the Party of Lincoln: Black Politics in the Age of FDR* (Princeton, NJ: Princeton University Press, 1983), 214; St. Clair Drake and Horace R. Cayton, *Black Metropolis: A Study of Negro Life in a Northern City*, vols. 1 and 2 (1945; rev. and enl., Chicago: University of Chicago Press, 1993), 354.

21. Jeffrey D. Gonda, *Unjust Deeds: The Restrictive Covenant Cases and the Making of the Civil Rights Movement* (Chapel Hill: University of North Carolina Press, 2015), 7–8; Carl Nightingale, *Segregation: A Global History of Divided Cities* (Chicago: University of Chicago Press, 2012), 1–3, 13; N. D. B. Connolly, *A World More Concrete: Real Estate and the Remaking of Jim Crow South Florida* (Chicago: University of Chicago Press, 2014), 94–98.

22. Helgeson, *Crucibles of Black Empowerment*, 34–35, 77, 78.

23. Wolfinger, *Philadelphia Divided*, 55–77, 63, 72; Marcus A. Hunter, *Black Citymakers: How* The Philadelphia Negro *Changed Urban America* (New York: Oxford University Press, 2013), 74–76, 94, 96, 98–99.

24. Skotnes, *A New Deal for All?*, 298–99.

25. Wolfinger, *Philadelphia Divided*, 93; Hunter, *Black Citymakers*, 77, quote, 9.

26. Hunter, *Black Citymakers*, 97; Helgeson, *Crucibles of Black Empowerment*, quote, 74.

27. Gretchen Lemke-Santangelo, *Abiding Courage: African American Women in the East Bay Community* (Chapel Hill: University of North Carolina Press, 1996), 87; Weiss, *Farewell to the Party of Lincoln,* 136–56, 209–66; Drake and Cayton, *Black Metropolis,* 354–55; Karen Ferguson, *Black Politics in New Deal Atlanta* (Chapel Hill: University of North Carolina Press, 2002), 174–75, 190–91, 207–8, 214; John B. Kirby, *Black Americans in the Roosevelt Era: Liberalism and Race* (Knoxville: University of Tennessee Press, 1980), 97–151.

28. Ferguson, *Black Politics in New Deal Atlanta,* quote, 218.

29. Spear, *Black Chicago,* 156; Dickerson, *Out of the Crucible,* 61; Gottlieb, *Making Their Own Way,* 126–27, 135–36; Thomas, *Life for Us,* 35–36; Trotter, *River Jordan,* 103; Campet, "Black Housing in Pittsburgh," 88–89; Osofsky, *Harlem,* 139; Trotter, *The African American Experience,* 455–56; Cheryl Greenberg, *To Ask for an Equal Chance: African Americans in the Great Depression* (Lanham, MD: Roman and Littlefield, 2009), 29–30.

30. Lemke-Santangelo, *Abiding Courage,* 80; Connolly, *A World More Concrete,* 35.

31. Georgina Hickey, *Hope and Danger in the New South City: Working Class Women and Urban Development in Atlanta, 1890–1940* (Athens: University of Georgia Press, 2003), 62–63; Lynne B. Feldman, *A Sense of Place: Birmingham's Black Middle Class Community, 1890–1930* (Tuscaloosa: University of Alabama Press, 1999), 68–69, 86–87; Clifford M. Kuhn, Harlon E. Joye, and E. B. West, *Living Atlanta: An Oral History of the City, 1914–1948* (Athens: Atlanta Historical Society and University of Georgia Press, 1990), 37–42, 301–2; Eileen Southern, *The Music of Black Americans: A History* (New York: W. W. Norton, 1971), 376, 382; Roland E. Wolseley, *The Black Press, U.S.A.,* 2nd ed. (Ames: Iowa State University Press, 1990), 75–78; Alexa B. Henderson, *Atlanta Life Insurance Company: Guardian of Black Economic Dignity* (Tuscaloosa: University of Alabama Press, 1990), 63–99.

32. Davarian L. Baldwin, *Chicago's New Negroes: Modernity, The Great Migration, and Black Urban Life* (Chapel Hill: University of North Carolina Press, 2007), 7, 21–52, particularly 39 and 46, on stroll; Corbould, *Becoming African Americans,* 11; Robin F. Bachin, "Mapping Out Space of Race Pride: The Social Geography of Leisure on the South Side of Chicago, 1900–1919," in *"We Shall Independent Be": African American Place Making and the Struggle to Claim Space in the United States,* ed. Angel D. Nieves and Leslie M. Alexander (Boulder: University of Colorado Press, 2008), 351–75; Wallace Thurman, *Negro Life in New York's Harlem: A Lively Picture of a Popular and Interesting Section* (Girard, KS: Haldeman-Julius Publications, 1928), 8–9.

33. Nick Salvatore, *Singing in a Strange Land: C. L. Franklin, the Black Church, and the Transformation of Black America* (Urbana: University of Illinois Press, 2006), 107–8; Joe W. Trotter and Jared N. Day, *Race and Renaissance: African Americans in Pittsburgh Since World War II* (Pittsburgh: University of Pittsburgh Press, 2010), 15–16; *Wylie Avenue Days: Pittsburgh's Hill District,* Doug Bolin, Christopher Moore, and Nancy Levin, film (Pittsburgh: QED Communications, 1991); Flamming, *Bound for Freedom,* 122.

34. Baldwin, *Chicago's New Negroes*, 44–52 (definition and discussion), 209–23, quote, 50; Harold F. Gosnell, *Negro Politicians: The Rise of Negro Politics in Chicago* (Chicago: University of Chicago Press, 1967), 115–35.

35. Rob Ruck, *Sandlot Seasons: Sport in Black Pittsburgh* (1987; repr., Urbana: University of Illinois Press, 1993), 140–52, quote, 150; Thomas, *Life for Us*, 116–17; Wolcott, *Remaking Respectability*, 121–25; Roger Lane, *William Dorsey's Philadelphia and Ours: On the Past and Future of the Black City in America* (New York: Oxford University Press, 1991), 129–30; Thurman, *Negro Life in New York's Harlem*, 44–47, quote, 47.

36. Wallace Best, *Passionately Human, No Less Divine: Religion and Culture in Black Chicago, 1915–1952* (Princeton, NJ: Princeton University Press, 2007), 1–11, 71–93, 118–46; Milton C. Sernett, *Bound for the Promised Land: African American Religion and the Great Migration* (Durham, NC: Duke University Press, 1997), 101–3; Spear, *Black Chicago*, 175–79; Christopher R. Reed, *The Rise of Chicago's Black Metropolis, 1920–1929* (Urbana: University of Illinois Press, 2011), 186–200.

37. Dickerson, *Out of the Crucible*, 65; Trotter, *River Jordan*, 111; Sernett, *Bound for the Promised Land*, 145–46, 149; Best, *Passionately Human, No Less Divine*, 13–15, 46–47, 74–77; Robert Gregg, *Sparks from the Anvil of Oppression: Philadelphia's African Methodists and Southern Migrants, 1890–1940* (Philadelphia: Temple University Press, 1993), 200–202; Bettye Collier-Thomas, *Jesus, Jobs, and Justice: African American Women and Religion* (New York: Alfred A. Knopf, 2010), 79–86; Evelyn Brooks Higginbotham, *Righteous Discontent: The Women's Movement in the Black Baptist Church, 1880–1920* (Cambridge: Harvard University Press, 1993), 171–80.

38. Sernett, *Bound for the Promised Land*, 145–46, 149; Gregg, *Sparks from the Anvil of Oppression*, 200–02.

39. Touré Reed, *Not Alms but Opportunity: The Urban League and the Politics of Racial Uplift, 1910–1950* (Chapel Hill: University of North Carolina Press, 2008), 30–31, 35–36, 43–78.

40. Reed, *Not Alms but Opportunity*, 30–31, 35–36, 43–78, 170–71; Felix L. Armfield, *Eugene Kinckle Jones: The National Urban League and Black Social Work* (Urbana: University of Illinois Press, 2012), 36–49; Thomas, *Life for Us*, 50–51, 58–59, 63–65; Nancy J. Weiss, *The National Urban League, 1910–1940* (New York: Oxford University Press, 1974), 112–54.

41. Christopher R. Reed, *The Chicago NAACP and the Rise of Black Professional Leadership, 1910–1966* (Bloomington: Indiana University Press, 1997), 47–48; Reed, *Rise of Chicago's Black Metropolis*, 164, 171–73, 175, 177–78; Charles F. Kellogg, *NAACP: A History of the National Association for the Advancement of Colored People* (Baltimore: Johns Hopkins University Press, 1967), 121, 125–26, 183–87, 205–8, 226–27, 242–45, photo, illustrations, 294; W. E. B. Du Bois, "Race Relations in the United States, 1917–1947," in *The Negro in Depression and War: Prelude to Revolution, 1930–1945*, ed. Bernard Sternsher (Chicago: Quadrangle Books, 1969), 30–31; Thomas, *Life for Us*, 138–40, 230–31; Donald G. Nieman, *Promises to Keep: African-Americans and the Constitutional Order, 1776 to the Present* (New York: Oxford University Press, 1991), 127–39.

42. Robert A. Hill, ed., *The Marcus Garvey and Universal Negro Improvement Association Paper,* vol. 1 (Berkeley: University of California Press, 1983–1986), xxxvi–viii; Claudrena N. Harold, *The Rise and Fall of the Garvey Movement in the Urban South, 1918–1942* (New York: Routledge, 2007), 17–27; Colin Grant, *Negro with a Hat: The Rise and Fall of Marcus Garvey* (New York: Oxford University Press, 2010), 164–65; Taylor, *The Veiled Garvey,* 27, 42–43, 89.

43. Reed, *Chicago NAACP,* 47–48; Reed, *Rise of Chicago's Black Metropolis,* 171–75; Kevin Boyle, *Arc of Justice: A Saga of Race, Civil Rights, and Murder in the Jazz Age* (New York: H. Holt, 2004), 17–43; Thomas, *Life for Us,* quote, 138–40, 230–31.

44. Broussard, *Black San Francisco,* 85–86; Flamming, *Bound for Freedom,* 144–48.

45. Kellogg, *NAACP,* 226–27, 294ff; Du Bois, "Race Relations in the United States," in Sternsher, *The Negro in Depression and War,* 29–52; Skotnes, *A New Deal for All?,* 37–38; Ronald H. Bayor, *Race and the Shaping of Twentieth-Century Atlanta* (Chapel Hill: University of North Carolina Press, 1996), 17–18.

46. Kersten and Lang, "Reintroduction to Asa Philip Randolph," in Kersten and Lang, *Reframing Randolph,* 10–11; Robert A. Hill, "Introduction: Racial and Radical: Cyril V. Briggs, *The Crusader* Magazine, and the African Blood Brotherhood," *Crusader* 1, September 1918–August 1919 (New York: Garland, 1987), v–lxxiii; Jeffrey B. Perry, *Hubert Harrison: The Voice of Harlem Radicalism, 1883–1918* (New York: Columbia University Press, 2009), 1–18, 296–99; Anderson, *A. Philip Randolph,* 85–119; Harris, *Keeping the Faith,* 26–65; Roi Ottley and William J. Weatherby, *The Negro in New York: An Informal History* (New York: New York Public Library, 1967), 253–78; Santino, *Miles of Smiles, Years of Struggle,* 13–14, 37–39; Bates, *Pullman Porters,* 63–105; Taylor, *A. Philip Randolph,* 37–125; Pfeffer, *A. Philip Randolph, Pioneer,* 6–44; Michael E. Deutsch, "The Improper Use of the Federal Grand Jury: An Instrument for the Internment of Political Activists," *Journal of Criminal Law and Criminology* 75, no. 4 (Winter 1984), 1159–96, https://scholarlycommons.law.northwestern.edu/jclc/vol75/iss4/6/.

47. Lara Putnam, *Radical Moves: Caribbean Migrants and the Politics of the Jazz Age* (Chapel Hill: University of North Carolina Press, 2013), 126–27; Minkah Makalani, *In the Cause of Freedom: Radical Black Internationalism from Harlem to London, 1917–1939* (Chapel Hill: University of North Carolina Press, 2011), 104–5, 116–31; Mark Naison, *Communists in Harlem During the Depression* (Urbana: University of Illinois Press, 1983), 42, 100, 173; Robin D. G. Kelley, "Afric's Sons with Banner Red," chap. 5 in *Race Rebels: Culture, Politics, and the Black Working Class* (New York: Free Press, 1996), 103, 110–11.

48. Hill, "Introduction: Racial and Radical: Cyril V. Briggs," v–lxxiii; Perry, *Hubert Harrison,* 1–18; Putnam, *Radical Moves,* 126–33; Anderson, *A. Philip Randolph,* 120–21; Grant, *Negro with a Hat,* 52–55; Tony Martin, *Race First: The Ideological Origins and Organizational Struggles of Marcus Garvey and the Universal Improvement Association* (Dover, MA: Majority Press, 1976), 236–43; Judith Stein, *The World of Marcus Garvey: Race and Class in Modern Society* (Baton Rouge: Loui-

siana State University Press, 1986), 43–48, 141–44; David J. Hellwig, "Black Meets Black: Afro-American Reactions to West Indian Immigrants in the 1920s," *South Atlantic Quarterly* 77, no. 2 (1978): 206–24.

49. Putnam, *Radical Moves*, 126–27; Makalani, *In the Cause of Freedom*, 104–5, 116–131; Naison, *Communists in Harlem*, 42, 100, 173; Kelley, "Afric's Sons with Banner Red," in Kelley, *Race Rebels*, 103, 110–11.

50. McDuffie, *Sojourning for Freedom*, 9–10, quote, 112.

51. Reed, *Chicago NAACP*, 67–89; Reed, *Rise of Chicago's Black Metropolis*, 182–85; Martin, *Race First*, 22–25, 41–45, 110–15, 273–77; Stein, *World of Marcus Garvey*, 7–23, 108–10, 223–27; Hellwig, "Black Meets Black," 206–24; Hill, *Marcus Garvey and UNIA Papers,* vols. 1–3, see volume introductions, 1:xxxv–xc, 2:xxxi–xxxiii, and 3:xxxiii–xxxvii; Hill, *Marcus Garvey and UNIA Papers,* vol. 1, xxxvi–viii.

52. Trotter, "Researching Randolph," in Kersten and Lang, *Reframing Randolph,* 21–44.

53. Martin, *Race First*, 275–76, 287; Anderson, *A. Philip Randolph*, 132–37; Hellwig, "Black Meets Black," 206–24, quote, 209; Hill, *Marcus Garvey and UNIA Papers,* vol. 1, xxxvi–viii; Trotter, "Researching Randolph," in Kersten and Lang, *Reframing Randolph,* 21–44.

54. White, *Too Heavy a Load*, 110–17; Stephanie J. Shaw, *What a Woman Ought to Be and to Do: Black Professional Women Workers during the Jim Crow Era* (Chicago: University of Chicago Press, 1996), 109–210; Paula Giddings, *When and Where I Enter: The Impact of Black Women on Race and Sex in America* (New York: W. Morrow, 1996), 159–70; Lisa G. Materson, *For the Freedom of Her Race: Black Women and Electoral Politics in Illinois, 1877–1932* (Chapel Hill: University of North Carolina Press, 2009); Elsa Barkley Brown, "Negotiating and Transforming the Public Sphere: African American Political Life in the Transition from Slavery to Freedom," *Public Culture* 7 (1994): 107–46; Elsa Barkley Brown, "To Catch the Vision of Freedom: Reconstructing Southern Black Women's Political History, 1865–1880," in *African American Women and the Vote, 1837–1865,* ed. Ann D. Gordon et al. (Amherst: University of Massachusetts Press, 1996).

55. For a recent assessment of black politics during the industrial era, see Lisa G. Materson and Joe William Trotter, Jr., "African American Urban Electoral Politics in the Age of Jim Crow," *Journal of Urban History*, vol. 44, no. 2 (March 2018): 123–33. For variations on the development of black politics in other cities, see Millington Bergeson-Lockwood, *Race over Party: Black Politics and Partisanship in Late Nineteenth-Century Boston* (Chapel Hill: University of North Carolina Press, 1918).

56. Reed, *Rise of Chicago's Black Metropolis*, 148–49; Martin Kilson, "Politics Change in the Negro Ghetto, 1900–1940s," in *Key Issues in the Afro-American Experience,* ed. Nathan Huggins et al., vol. 2 (New York: Harcourt Brace Jovanovich, 1971), 167–92; Gosnell, *Negro Politicians*, 67–114, 136–52; Hanes Walton, Jr., *Black Politics: A Theoretical and Structural Analysis* (Philadelphia: J. B. Lippincott, 1972), 51–69, 94–98, 104–117; Spear, *Black Chicago*, 186–92; Weiss, *Farewell to the Party of Lincoln*, 3–33; Lucius J. Barker and Mack H. Jones, *African Americans and*

the *American Political System* (Englewood Cliffs, NJ: Prentice Hall, 1994), 18; Thomas, *Life for Us,* 67–68, 253–54, 258; Trotter and Day, *Race and Renaissance,* 22–23; Wolfinger, *Philadelphia Divided,* 28–31; V.P. Franklin, *The Education of Black Philadelphia: The Social and Educational History of a Minority Community, 1900–1950* (Philadelphia: University of Pennsylvania Press, 1979), 121–22; Taylor, *Forging of a Black Community,* 103. For variations on the rise of black machine politics in other cities, see Osofsky, *Harlem,* 160–61, 165; Bergeson-Lockwood, *Race over Party;* Richard B. Pierce, *Polite Protest: The Political Economy of Race in Indianapolis, 1920–1970* (Bloomington: Indiana University Press, 2005).

57. Wolfinger, *Philadelphia Divided,* 72; Erik S. Gellman, *Death Blow to Jim Crow: The National Negro Congress and the Rise of Militant Civil Rights* (Chapel Hill: University of North Carolina Press, 2012), 209–17; Paul Moreno, *From Direct Action to Affirmative Action: Fair Employment Law and Policy in America, 1933–1972* (Baton Rouge: Louisiana State University Press, 1997), 4–5, 30–54; Cheryl L. Greenberg, *Or Does It Explode?: Black Harlem in the Great Depression* (New York: Oxford University Press, 1991), 114–39; Greenberg, *To Ask for an Equal Chance,* 27–29; Naison, *Communists in Harlem,* 50–51, 100–02; Drake and Cayton, *Black Metropolis,* 84–85; White, *Too Heavy a Load,* 165–73; Jacqueline Jones, *Labor of Love, Labor of Sorrow: Black Women, Work, and the Family, from Slavery to the Present* (New York: Basic Books, 1985), 215; Will P. Jones, *the March on Washington: Jobs, Freedom, and the Forgotten History of Civil Rights* (New York: W.W. Norton, 2013), 1–40, 41–78; Jennifer Delton, *Racial Integration in Corporate America, 1940–1990* (Cambridge: Cambridge University Press, 2009), 17–41; Kurashige, *Shifting Grounds of Race,* 158–85.

58. Herbert Garfinkel, *When Negroes March: The March on Washington Movement in the Organizational Politics for FEPC* (Glencoe, IL: Free Press, 1959), 37–61; Martha Biondi, *To Stand and Fight: The Struggle for Civil Rights in Postwar New York City* (Cambridge: Harvard University Press, 2003), 4, 7–16; Bates, *Pullman Porters,* 148–87; Pfeffer, *A. Philip Randolph, Pioneer,* 45–88; Charles D. Chamberlain, *Victory at Home: Manpower and Race in the American South during World War II* (Athens: University of Georgia Press, 2003), 46–59; Anderson, *A. Philip Randolph,* 241–74; Reed, *Not Alms But Opportunity,* 140–59; Harvard Sitkoff, "African American Militancy in the World War II South: Another Perspective," in *Remaking Dixie: The Impact of World War II on the American South,* ed. Neil R. McMillen (Jackson: University of Mississippi, 1997), 70–92; Megan T. Shockley, *"We, Too, Are Americans": African American Women in Detroit and Richmond, 1940–54* (Urbana: University of Illinois Press, 2004), 12–13, 22–23, 25–26, 29–62, 63–102; Drake and Cayton, *Black Metropolis,* 89–97; Nico Slate, *Colored Cosmopolitanism: The Shared Struggle for Freedom in the United States and India* (Cambridge: Harvard University Press, 2012), 2–3, quote, 144, 212–13.

59. For the "call" to march, see edited volume of documents, Thomas R. Frazier, ed., *Afro-American History: Primary Sources* (1970; repr. Chicago: Dorsey Press, 1988), 291–94; Anderson, *A. Philip Randolph,* 249–51; Herbert Hill, *Black Labor and the American Legal System* (Madison: University of Wisconsin Press, 1985), 173–84.

60. Jones, *March on Washington,* ix, 163–200.

61. Clarence Lang, *Grassroots at the Gateway: Class Politics and Black Freedom Struggle in St. Louis, 1936–75* (Ann Arbor: University of Michigan Press, 2009), 44, 46, 47, 63.

62. Chamberlain, *Victory at Home,* 123.

63. Shockley, *"We, Too, Are Americans,"* 65; Chamberlain, *Victory at Home,* 123–24.

64. Dominic J. Capeci, Jr., and Margaret Wilkerson, *Layered Violence: The Detroit Rioters of 1943* (Jackson: University of Mississippi Press, 1991), 144–73; Meier and Rudwick, *Black Detroit and the Rise of the UAW,* 176–206; Wolcott, *Remaking Respectability,* 243–44; Thomas, *Life for Us,* 143–48; Robin D. G. Kelley, "The Riddle of the Zoot: Malcolm Little and Black Cultural Politics During World War II," chap. 7 in Kelley, *Race Rebels,* 61–82.

65. Nieman, *Promises to Keep,* 140–41; Garfinkel, *When Negroes March,* 150–51; Sitkoff, "African American Militancy," in McMillen, *Remaking Dixie,* 76–77; Lang, *Grassroots at the Gateway,* 60–70; August Meier and Elliott Rudwick, *CORE: A Study in the Civil Rights Movement, 1942–1968* (Urbana: University of Illinois Press, 1975), 3–39.

CHAPTER SIX

1. William Jones, *The March on Washington: Jobs, Freedom, and the Forgotten History of Civil Rights* (New York: W. W. Norton, 2013), ix, 163–200; Martha Biondi, *To Stand and Fight: The Struggle for Civil Rights in Postwar New York City* (Cambridge: Harvard University Press, 2003), 17–21; Matthew Countryman, *Up South: Civil Rights and Black Power in Philadelphia* (Philadelphia: University of Pennsylvania Press, 2006), 50–51, 62–64; Thomas J. Sugrue, *The Origins of the Urban Crisis: Race and Inequality in Postwar Detroit* (Princeton, NJ: Princeton University Press, 1996), 100, 103; Dennis C. Dickerson, *Out of the Crucible: Black Steelworkers, 1875–1980* (Albany: State University of New York Press, 1986), 177, 194–95, 217; Joe W. Trotter and Jared N. Day, *Race and Renaissance: African Americans in Pittsburgh since World War II* (Pittsburgh: University of Pittsburgh Press, 2010), 43; Andrew E. Kersten and Clarence Lang, eds., *Reframing Randolph: Labor, Black Freedom, and the Legacies of A. Philip Randolph* (New York: New York University Press, 2015), 26–27.

2. Sugrue, *Origins of the Urban Crisis,* 132–34, 144–45.

3. Roger Horowitz, *"Negro and White, Unite and Fight!": A Social History of Industrial Unionism in Meatpacking, 1930–90* (Urbana: University of Illinois Press, 1997), 253–54; Biondi, *To Stand and Fight,* 251–56.

4. Daniel R. Fusfeld and Timothy Bates, *The Political Economy of the Urban Ghetto* (Carbondale: Southern Illinois University Press, 1984), 115–19; William H. Harris, *The Harder We Run: Black Workers since the Civil War* (New York: Oxford University Press, 1982), 132, 155; Arthur M. Ross and Herbert Hill, eds., *Employment,*

Race, and Poverty: A Critical Study of the Disadvantaged Status of Negro Workers from 1865–1965 (New York: Harcourt, Brace, and World, 1967), 30–35; Biondi, To Stand and Fight, 269.

5. Jacqueline Jones, Labor of Love, Labor of Sorrow: Black Women, Work, and the Family from Slavery to the Present (New York: Basic Books, 1985), 256–60, 262; Biondi, To Stand and Fight, 24–25.

6. Grace Palladino, Skilled Hands, Strong Spirits: A Century of Building Trades History (Ithaca, NY: Cornell University Press, 2005), 140–41, 156–57; Bruce E. Seely, Building the American Highway System: Engineers as Policy Makers (Philadelphia: Temple University Press, 1987), 196–223; Tom Lewis, Divided Highways: Building the Interstate Highways, Transforming American Life (New York: Viking, 1997), 118–23; F. Ray Marshall and Vernon M. Briggs, Jr., The Negro and Apprenticeship (Baltimore: Johns Hopkins University Press, 1967), 113–20; David Goldberg and Trevor Griffey, eds., Black Power at Work: Community Control, Affirmative Action, and the Construction Industry (Ithaca, NY: Cornell University Press, 2010); Countryman, Up South, 64; Philip Foner, Organized Labor and the Black Worker, 1619–1973 (New York: Praeger, 1974), 338–39.

7. Marshall and Briggs, The Negro and Apprenticeship, 113–20; Irwin Dubinsky, Reform in Trade Union Discrimination in the Construction Industry: Operation Dig and Its Legacy (New York: Praeger Books, 1973), 3–50; E. Barbour, "City, Union 'Pass Buck' on Negro Electrician," Pittsburgh Courier, 25 November 1961; Foner, Organized Labor and the Black Worker, 338–39.

8. Charles R. Perry, The Negro in the Department Store Industry, Report no. 22 (Philadelphia: Wharton School of Finance and Commerce, University of Pennsylvania, 1971), 5, 31–32, 42–43; Sugrue, Origins of the Urban Crisis, 110–14; Arthur J. Edmunds and Esther L. Bush, Daybreakers: The Story of the Urban League of Pittsburgh: The First Eighty Years, rev. ed. (1983; Pittsburgh: Urban League of Pittsburgh, 1999), 120–21; Holland F. Kelley, "Spur Dept. Store Fight," Pittsburgh Courier, 9 November 1946; "Store Heads Still Dodge Race Issue," Pittsburgh Courier, 16 November 1946.

9. Jeffrey D. Gonda, Unjust Deeds: The Restrictive Covenant Cases and the Making of the Civil Rights Movement (Chapel Hill: University of North Carolina Press, 2015), 1–15; Carl Nightingale, Segregation: A Global History of Divided Cities (Chicago: University of Chicago Press, 2012), 356–57; Donald G. Nieman, Promises to Keep: African-Americans and the Constitutional Order, 1776 to the Present (New York: Oxford University Press, 1991), 144; Evan McKenzie, Privatopia: Homeowner Associations and the Rise of Residential Private Government (New Haven, CT: Yale, 1994), 75–76, 82.

10. Kenneth Jackson, Crabgrass Frontier: The Suburbanization of the United States (New York: Oxford University Press, 1985), 227, 234–42; Robert A. Caro, The Power Broker: Robert Moses and the Fall of New York (New York: Vintage Books, 1975), 12–13; Biondi, To Stand and Fight, 230–32; Countryman, Up South, 53–57; Colin Gordon, Mapping Decline: St. Louis and the Fate of the American City (Philadelphia: University of Pennsylvania Press, 2008), 96–98.

11. Jackson, *Crabgrass Frontier*, 190–218; Quintard Taylor, *The Forging of a Black Community: Seattle's Central District, from 1870 through the Civil Rights Era* (Seattle: University of Washington Press, 1994), 180–81.

12. John F. Bauman, *Public Housing, Race, and Renewal: Urban Planning in Philadelphia, 1920–1974* (Philadelphia: Temple University Press, 1987), 161–62; Countryman, *Up South*, 52–53, 55–56; Harold X. Connolly, *A Ghetto Grows in Brooklyn* (New York: New York University Press, 1977), 134–36; Sugrue, *Origins of the Urban Crisis*, 221, 232–48, 252; Arnold Hirsch, *Making the Second Ghetto: Race and Housing in Chicago, 1940–1960* (Cambridge: Cambridge University Press, 1983), 52–53, 68–99; Robert Weisbrot, *Freedom Bound: A History of America's Civil Rights Movement* (New York: Norton, 1990), 154–55, 178–79; Henry Hampton and Steve Fayer, with Sarah Flynn, *Voices of Freedom: An Oral History of the Civil Rights Movement from the 1950s through the 1980s* (New York: Bantam Books, 1990), 297–319.

13. Todd Michney, *Neighborhoods: Black Upward Mobility in Cleveland, 1900–1980* (Chapel Hill: University of North Carolina, 2016); Abigail Perkiss, *Making Good Neighbors: Civil Rights, Liberalism, and Integration in Postwar Philadelphia* (Ithaca, NY: Cornell University Press, 2014), 2.

14. Mindy T. Fullilove, *Root Shock: How Tearing Up City Neighborhoods Hurts America, and What We Can Do about It* (New York: Ballantine Books, One World, 2005), 4–5; Josh Sides, *L.A. City Limits* (Berkeley: University of California Press, 2003), 118–20; Trotter and Day, *Race and Renaissance*, 69–73; Sugrue, *Origins of the Urban Crisis*, 47–50; Robert Self, *American Babylon: Race and the Struggle for Postwar Oakland* (Princeton, NJ: Princeton University Press, 2003), quote, 137.

15. Self, *American Babylon*, 137–49.

16. Trotter and Day, *Race and Renaissance*, quote, 78–80.

17. Lawrence Vale, *Reclaiming Public Housing: A Half Century of Struggle in Three Public Housing Projects* (Cambridge: Harvard University Press, 2002), 14–16; J.S. Fuerst, *When Public Housing Was Paradise: Building Community in Chicago* (Westport, CT: Praeger, 2003), 105, 194; Sugrue, *Origins of the Urban Crisis*, 50, 86; Hirsch, *Making the Second Ghetto*, 4–7, 120–28; Wendell E. Pritchett, *Brownsville, Brooklyn: Blacks, Jews, and the Changing Face of the Ghetto* (Chicago: University of Chicago, 2002), 148–49; Sides, *L.A. City Limits*, 116–17, 120–24, quote, 120; Taylor, *Forging of a Black Community*, 169–70; Bauman, *Public Housing, Race, and Renewal*, 125–35; Self, *American Babylon*, 145–46; Gordon, *Mapping Decline*, 98–100; Trotter and Day, *Race and Renaissance*, 74–78.

18. Hirsch, *Making the Second Ghetto*, 4–7; Amanda I. Seligman, *Block by Block: Neighborhoods and Public Policy on Chicago's West Side* (Chicago: University of Chicago Press, 2004), 6–7, 161–62; Roy Lubove, *Twentieth-Century Pittsburgh*, vol. 1 (Pittsburgh: University of Pittsburgh Press, 1996), 130–32; Biondi, *To Stand and Fight*, 237–41; Pritchett, *Brownsville, Brooklyn*, 148–49; Sides, *L.A. City Limits*, 120–30.

19. Jeanne F. Theoharis and Komozi Woodard, eds., *Freedom North: Black Freedom Struggles outside the South, 1940–1980* (New York: Palgrave/Macmillan, 2003), 1–15; Trotter and Day, *Race and Renaissance*, 58–59; Biondi, *To Stand and Fight*, 36–37.

20. Clarence Lang, *Grassroots at the Gateway: Class Politics and Black Freedom Struggle in St. Louis, 1936–75* (Ann Arbor: University of Michigan Press, 2009), 80–82; George Lipsitz, *A Life of Struggle: Ivory Perry and the Culture of Opposition* (Philadelphia: Temple University Press, 1988), 1–14.

21. Countryman, *Up South,* 104–5.

22. David Garrow, *Bearing the Cross: Martin Luther King, Jr., and the Southern Christian Leadership Conference* (New York: Vintage Books, 1986), 223–24; Clayborne Carson, ed., *The Autobiography of Martin Luther King, Jr.* (New York: Warner Books, 1998), 308–9; Marshall Frady, *Jesse: The Life and Pilgrimage of Jesse Jackson* (New York: Simon and Schuster, 2006), 199–200; Hampton and Fayer, *Voices of Freedom,* 301, 314–15, 576.

23. Biondi, *To Stand and Fight,* 263–68; Robert H. Zieger, *For Jobs and Freedom: Race and Labor in America since 1865* (Lexington: University Press of Kentucky, 2007), 167–71; Harris, *The Harder We Run,* 139–41; Foner, *Organized Labor and the Black Worker,* 293–311, 333–35; William R. Hood, "Labor Will Lead Our People to First Class Citizenship," in *The Black Worker from the Founding of the CIO to the AFL-CIO Merger, 1936–1955,* vol. 7, ed. Philip Foner and Ronald Lewis (Philadelphia: Temple University Press, 1983), 560–61.

24. Erik S. McDuffie, *Sojourning for Freedom: Black Women, American Communism, and the Making of a Black Left Feminism* (Durham, NC: Duke University Press, 2011), 173–82, quote, 175, 183–85, 205.

25. "Labor Unit Set Up for Negro Rights: 75 Anti-Communist Unions Form Committee," in Foner and Lewis, *The Black Worker,* 580–81; Yevette Richards Jordan, *Maida Springer-Kemp: Pan-Africanist and International Labor Leader* (Pittsburgh: University of Pittsburgh Press, 2000), 5, 77–78, 94–95, 176–77.

26. Marcia Walker-McWilliams, *Reverend Addie Wyatt: Faith and the Fight for Labor, Gender, and Racial Equality* (Urbana: University of Illinois Press, 2016), 1–5, 48–49, 52–53, 188.

27. Jones, *March on Washington,* ix, 163–200; August Meier and Elliott Rudwick, *CORE: A Study in the Civil Rights Movement, 1942–1968* (Urbana: University of Illinois Press, 1975), 238–40, 290.

28. Sides, *L.A. City Limits,* 136; Meier and Rudwick, *CORE,* 228, 237, 248–50.

29. Lang, *Grassroots at the Gateway,* 160–75.

30. Rhonda Y. Williams, *Concrete Demands: The Search for Black Power in the 20th Century* (New York: Routledge, 2015), 5,

31. Peniel E. Joseph, *Waiting 'til the Midnight Hour: A Narrative History of Black Power in America* (New York: Henry Holt, 2006); Joshua Bloom and Waldo Martin, *Black against Empire: The History and Politics of the Black Panther Party* (Berkeley: University of California, 2013); Manning Marable, *Malcolm X: A Life of Reinvention* (New York: Viking, 2011); Theoharis and Woodard, *Freedom North.*

32. Robyn C. Spencer, *The Revolution Has Come: Black Power, Gender, and the Black Panther Party in Oakland* (Durham, NC: Duke University Press, 2016), 1–5, 14–25; Donna Murch, *Living for the City: Migration, Education, and the Rise of the*

Black Panther Party in Oakland, California (Chapel Hill: University of North Carolina Press, 2010), 6–7; Self, *American Babylon*, 217–19.

33. Kevin Mumford, "Harvesting the Crisis: The Newark Uprising, the Kerner Commission, and Writings on Riots," in *African American Urban History since World War II,* ed. Kenneth L. Kusmer and Joe W. Trotter (Chicago: University of Chicago Press, 2010), 203–19; Kevin Mumford, *Newark: A History of Race, Rights, and Riots in America* (New York: New York University Press, 2007), 125–40; Scot Brown, *Fighting for US: Maulana Karenga, the US Organization, and Black Cultural Nationalism* (New York: New York University Press, 2005), 29–33.

34. Kimberley L. Phillips, *War! What Is It Good For? Black Freedom Struggles and the U.S. Military from World War II to Iraq* (Chapel Hill: University of North Carolina Press, 2012), 1–15, 188–227, 248–52, 273–85; Clayborne Carson, *In Struggle: SNCC and the Black Awakening of the 1960s* (1981; repr., Cambridge: Harvard University Press, 1995), 183–90; Carson, *Autobiography of Martin Luther King,* 333–45.

35. M. Honey, *Going Down Jericho Road* (New York: W. W. Norton, 2005), 93–95; M. Marable and L. Mullings, ed., *Let Nobody Turn Us Around* (Lanham: Roman and Littlefield, 2000), 463.

36. Spencer, *The Revolution Has Come,* quote, 1, 25–34; Murch, *Living for the City,* 4–5, 15–68; Self, *American Babylon,* 217–55.

37. Charles E. Jones, *The Black Panther Party [Reconsidered]* (Baltimore: Black Classic Press, 1998), 37; Joseph, *Waiting 'til the Midnight Hour,* 66–67, 92–94; Bloom and Martin, *Black against Empire,* 197; Spencer, *The Revolution Has Come,* 52–55.

38. Murch, *Living for the City,* 4; Self, *American Babylon,* 217; Heather A. Thompson, *Whose Detroit?: Politics, Labor, and Race in a Modern American City* (Ithaca, NY: Cornell University Press, 2001), 109–10; Jeffrey O. G. Ogbar, "Rainbow Radicalism: The Rise of the Radical Ethnic Nationalism," in *The Black Power Movement: Rethinking the Civil Rights–Black Power Era,* ed. Peniel E. Joseph (New York: Routledge, 2006), 193–228; Nico Slate, ed., *Black Power beyond Borders: The Global Dimensions of Black Power* (New York: Palgrave Macmillan, 2012), 1–33.

39. Nico Slate, "The Dalit Panthers: Race, Caste, and Black Power in India," in Slate, *Black Power beyond Borders,* 127–28; Robbie Shillian, "The Polynesian Panthers and the Black Power Gang: Surviving Racism and Colonialism in Aotearoa New Zealand," in Slate, *Black Power beyond Borders,* 107–11; Oz Frankel, "The Black Panthers of Israel and the Politics of the Radical Analogy," in Slate, *Black Power beyond Borders,* 81–83.

40. Thompson, *Whose Detroit?,* 109–10; Ogbar, "Rainbow Radicalism," in Joseph, *Black Power Movement,* 193–228; Slate, *Black Power beyond Borders,* 1–33.

41. Thompson, *Whose Detroit?,* 82–83, 109–11, 119; William L. Van Deburg, *New Day in Babylon: The Black Power Movement and American Culture, 1965–1975* (Chicago: University of Chicago Press, 1992), 92–97; Jones, *Black Panther Party [Reconsidered],* 342–43.

42. Jones, *Black Panther Party [Reconsidered],* 136–37, 366–67; Clayborne Carson, ed., *Malcolm X: FBI File* (New York: Carroll and Graf, 1991), 26, 30, 44–49; Thomas J. Sugrue, *Sweet Land of Liberty: The Forgotten Struggle for Civil Rights in*

the North (New York: Random House, 2008), 353–54; Van Deburg, *New Day in Babylon,* 302–3; Hampton and Fayer, *Voices of Freedom,* quote, 530.

43. Murch, *Living for the City,* 178, 185–89, quote, 188; Yohuru Williams, *Black Politics/White Power: Civil Rights, Black Power, and the Black Panthers in New Haven* (Malden, MA: Blackwell, 2008), 160–68; Brown, *Fighting for US,* 99–106.

44. Jones, *March on Washington,* 174–75; Sara Evans, *Personal Politics: The Roots of Women's Liberation in the Civil Rights Movement and the New Left* (New York: Alfred A. Knopf, 1979), pp. 85–86; Carson, *In Struggle,* 148–49.

45. Murch, *Living for the City,* 133; Tracye Matthews, "'No One Ever Asks, What a Man's Place in the Revolution Is': Gender and the Politics of the Black Panther Party, 1966–1971," in Jones, *Black Panther Party [Reconsidered],* 267–304, quote, 270; Countryman, *Up South,* 260–61; Paula Giddings, *When and Where I Enter: The Impact of Black Women on Race and Sex in America* (New York: W. Morrow, 1996), 314–15, 337–40; Darlene Clark Hine and Kathleen Thompson, *A Shining Thread of Hope: The History of Black Women in America* (New York: Broadway Books, 1998); Rhonda Williams, "Black Women, Urban Politics, and Engendering Black Power," in Joseph, *Black Power Movement,* 79–103; Kimberly Springer, "Black Feminists Respond to Black Power Masculinism," in Joseph, *Black Power Movement,* 105–18; and Stephen Ward, "The Third World Women's Alliance: Black Feminist Radicalism and Black Power Politics," in Joseph, *Black Power Movement,* 145–65.

46. Barbara Ransby, *Ella Baker and the Black Freedom Movement: A Radical Democratic Vision* (Chapel Hill: University of North Carolina Press, 2005), 174–76, 231–38, 286–98; Carson, *In Struggle,* 51–55.

47. Bart Landry, *The New Black Middle Class* (Berkeley: University of California Press, 1987), quote, 86.

48. John Higham, "Introduction: A Historical Perspective," in *Civil Rights and Social Wrongs: Black-White Relations since World War II,* ed. John Higham (University Park: Pennsylvania State University Press, 1997), 1–30; Lawrence H. Fuchs, "The Changing Meaning of Civil Rights, 1954–1994," in Higham, *Civil Rights and Social Wrongs,* 59–85; Paul D. Moreno, *From Direct Action to Affirmative Action: Fair Employment Law and Policy in America, 1933–1972* (Baton Rouge: Louisiana State University Press, 1997), 162–215; Nieman, *Promises to Keep,* 148–215; Venus Green, *Race on the Line: Gender, Labor, and Technology in the Bell System, 1880–1980* (Durham, NC: Duke University Press, 2001), 227–57.

49. Jennifer Delton, *Racial Integration in Corporate America, 1940–1990* (Cambridge: Cambridge University Press, 2009), 194–224; Carol A. Horton, *Race and the Making of American Liberalism* (New York: Oxford University Press, 2005), 139–99; Moreno, *From Direct Action to Affirmative Action,* 231–82; Stephen Steinberg, *Turning Back: The Retreat from Racial Justice in American Thought and Policy* (Boston: Beacon Press, 1995), 97, 101–3; Green, *Race on the Line,* 227–57; Reynolds Farley and Walter R. Allen, *The Color Line and the Quality of Life in America* (New York: Oxford University Press, 1987), 203; Gerald David Jaynes and Robin M. Williams, Jr., eds., *A Common Destiny: Blacks and American Society* (Washington, DC: National Academy Press, 1989), 35; Zieger, *For Jobs and Freedom,* 178–79, 217.

50. Landry, *New Black Middle Class*, 67–93; Manning Marable, *Race and Reform, and Rebellion: The Second Reconstruction and Beyond in Black America* (Jackson: University Press of Mississippi, 2007), 93; Mumford, "Harvesting the Crisis," in Kusmer and Trotter, *African American Urban History*, 203–19, quote, 202; Mumford, *Newark*, 156–57; Eric Brown, "The Black Professional Middle Class and the Black Community: Racialized Class Formation in Oakland and the East Bay," in Kusmer and Trotter, *African American Urban History*, 263–91.

CHAPTER SEVEN

1. William J. Wilson, *When Work Disappears: The World of the New Urban Poor* (Chicago: University of Illinois Press, 1996), 29–31, 42, 138–39; Sudhir Alladi Venkatesh, *American Project: The Rise and Fall of a Modern Ghetto* (Cambridge: Harvard University Press, 2000), 118; Heather A. Thompson, *Whose Detroit?: Politics, Labor, and Race in a Modern American City* (Ithaca, NY: Cornell University Press, 2001), 207–8, 218; Reynolds Farley, Sheldon Danziger, and Harry J. Holzer, *Detroit Divided: A Volume in the Multi-City Study of Urban Inequality* (New York: Russell Sage Foundation, 2000), 63, 65; Wendell E. Pritchett, *Brownsville, Brooklyn: Blacks, Jews, and the Changing Face of the Ghetto* (Chicago: University of Chicago, 2002), 251; David Fasenfest, "Race, Class, and Community Redevelopment: A Comparison of Detroit's Poletown and Chicago's Goose Island," in *Race, Class, and Urban Social Change*, ed. Jerry Lembcke (Greenwich, CT: JAI Press, 1989), 114; Mike Davis, *City of Quartz: Excavating the Future in Los Angeles* (London: Verso Press, 2006), 304–5; Robert H. Zieger, *For Jobs and Freedom: Race and Labor in America since 1865* (Lexington: University Press of Kentucky, 2007), 223–33; John P. Hoerr, *And the Wolf Finally Came: The Decline of the American Steel Industry* (Pittsburgh: University of Pittsburgh Press, 1988), 1, 3.

2. Zieger, *For Jobs and Freedom*, 217–19 (on nationwide manufacturing employment decline); Wilson, *When Work Disappears*, 29–31 (on job losses in Chicago and other cities), 42, 138–39; Thompson, *Whose Detroit?*, 207–8, 218; Farley, Danziger, and Holzer, *Detroit Divided*, 63, 65; Pritchett, *Brownsville, Brooklyn*, 251; Fasenfest, "Race, Class, and Community Redevelopment," in Lembcke, *Race, Class, and Urban Social Change*, 114; Davis, *City of Quartz*, 304–5; Daniel R. Fusfeld and Timothy Bates, *The Political Economy of the Urban Ghetto* (Carbondale: Southern Illinois University Press, 1984), 115–19; Arthur M. Ross and Herbert Hill, eds., *Employment, Race, and Poverty: A Critical Study of the Disadvantaged Status of Negro Workers from 1865 to 1965* (New York: Harcourt, Brace & World, 1967), 24–27, 30–32, 36–37, 39, 44–45.

3. Farley, Danziger, and Holzer, *Detroit Divided*, 67, 69, 82; Lawrence D. Bobo, Melvin L. Oliver, James H. Johnson, Jr., and Abel Valenzuela, Jr., *The Prismatic Metropolis: Inequality in Los Angeles* (New York: Russell Sage Foundation, 2000), 19–20, 222; Barry Bluestone and Mary H. Stevenson, *The Boston Renaissance: Race, Space, and Economic Change in an American Metropolis* (New York: Russell Sage Foundation, 2000), 1, 3–5, 108, 117, 199, 221–22, 226.

4. William J. Wilson, *The Truly Disadvantaged: The Inner City, the Underclass, and Public Policy* (Chicago: University of Chicago Press, 1987), 172–73; Wilson, *When Work Disappears*, 15–16; Paul A. Jargowsky and Mary Jo Bane, "Ghetto Poverty in the United States, 1970–1980," in *The Urban Underclass*, ed. Christopher Jencks and Paul E. Peterson (Washington, DC: Brookings Institution, 1991), 254–55; Paul Osterman, "Gains from Growth?: The Impact of Full Employment on Poverty in Boston," in Jencks and Peterson, *Urban Underclass*, 125–27; Reynolds Farley, "Metropolises of the Multi-City Study of Urban Inequality: Social, Economic, Demographic, and Racial Issues in Atlanta, Boston, Detroit, and Los Angeles," in *Urban Inequality: Evidence from Four Cities*, ed. Alice O'Connor, Chris Tilly, and Lawrence D. Bobo (New York: Russell Sage Foundation, 2001), 49–53; Farley, Danziger, and Holzer, *Detroit Divided*, 49–51.

5. John M. R. Bull, "Patterns of Racial Division: Pittsburgh's Housing Projects among Nation's Most Segregated," *Pittsburgh Post-Gazette*, 14 April 1996; Lawrence Vale, *Reclaiming Public Housing: A Half Century of Struggle in Three Public Housing Projects* (Cambridge: Harvard University Press, 2002), 22–36, 219–20; Wilson, *The Truly Disadvantaged*, 25–26.

6. Vale, *Reclaiming Public Housing*, 30–31; Venkatesh, *American Project*, 118–19, 130; Mary Pattillo-McCoy, *Black Picket Fences: Privilege and Peril among the Black Middle Class* (Chicago: University of Chicago Press, 1999), 91–92.

7. Tricia Rose, *Black Noise: Rap Music, and Black Culture in Contemporary America* (Hanover, NH: University Presses of New England, 1994), 177–79; Nelson George, *Hip-Hop America* (New York: Plume, 1998), 188–92; Jeff Chang, *Can't Stop, Won't Stop: A History of the Hip-Hop Generation* (New York: St. Martins Press, 2005), 451–53; Joe William Trotter, Jr., *The African American Experience* (Boston: Houghton Mifflin, 2001), quote, 636.

8. Michelle Alexander, *The New Jim Crow: Mass Incarceration in the Age of Colorblindness* (New York: New Press, 2012), 5–9, 52–53, 86–91, Illinois prison, education statistics, 185; Michael Katz, *Why Don't American Cities Burn?* (Philadelphia: University of Pennsylvania Press, 2012), 54–57; Roy L. Austin and Mark D. Allen, "Racial Disparity in Arrest Rates as an Explanation of Racial Disparity in Commitment to Pennsylvania's Prisons," *Journal of Research on Crime and Delinquency* 37, no. 2 (May 2000), 200–220; Wilson, *The Truly Disadvantaged*, 25–27, quote, 26; Coramae R. Mann, *Unequal Justice: A Question of Color* (Bloomington: Indiana University Press, 1993), vii–viii, 220–21; Othello Harris and R. Robin Miller, eds., *Impacts of Incarceration on the African American Family* (New Brunswick, NJ: Transaction, 2003), 4–5.

9. Alexander, *New Jim Crow*, 1–19; Kelly Lytle Hernandez, Khalil Gibran Muhammad, and Heather Ann Thompson, "Introduction: Constructing the Carceral State," *Journal of American History*, 102, no. 1 (June 2015): 18–24; Kali N. Gross and Cheryl D. Hicks, "Gendering the Carceral State: African American Women, History, and the Criminal Justice System," *Journal of African American History* 100, no. 3 (Summer 2015): 357–65; Patricia O'Connor, "The Prison Cage as Home for African American Men," in Harris and Miller, *Impacts*

of Incarceration, 81; Geoffrey DeVerteuil, Heidi Sommer, Jennifer Wolch, and Lois Takahashi, "The Local Welfare State in Transition: Welfare Reform in Los Angeles," in *New York and Los Angeles: Politics, Society, and Culture, A Comparative View,* ed. David Halle (Chicago: University of Chicago Press, 2003), 269–70, 276, 282–83.

10. Carol A. Horton, *Race and the Making of American Liberalism* (New York: Oxford University Press, 2005), 9–12, 39–40, 157–58, 165, 196–97; Paul D. Moreno, *From Direct Action to Affirmative Action: Fair Employment Law and Policy in America, 1933–1972* (Baton Rouge: Louisiana State University Press, 1997), 188–90; Stephen Steinberg, *Turning Back: The Retreat from Racial Justice in American Thought and Policy* (Boston: Beacon Press, 1995), 97–100; DeVerteuil, Sommer, Wolch, and Takahashi, "The Local Welfare State in Transition," in Halle, *New York and Los Angeles,* 269–70; Jennifer Delton, *Racial Integration in Corporate America, 1940–1990* (Cambridge: Cambridge University Press, 2009), 278–79; David O. Sears, "Black-White Conflict: A Model for the Future of Ethnic Politics in Los Angeles," in Halle, *New York and Los Angeles,* 373–74; Thomas Sugrue, *Sweet Land of Liberty: The Forgotten Struggle for Civil Rights in the North* (New York: Random House, 2009), quote, 523–25.

11. Carol Stack, *Call to Home: African Americans Reclaim the Rural South* (New York: Basic Books, 1996), xi–xii, 25–26, 118; James N. Gregory, *The Southern Diaspora: How the Great Migrations of Black and White Southerners Transformed America* (Chapel Hill: University of North Carolina Press, 2005), 322–23; Ira Berlin, *The Making of African America: The Four Great Migrations* (New York: Viking Books, 2010), 201; Isabel Wilkerson, *The Warmth of Other Suns: The Epic Story of America's Great Migration* (New York: Random House, 2010), 486–87. For a stellar forthcoming study of the reverse migration, see Sabrina Pendergrass, *The Black Reverse Migration Unfolds: Black Americans Move to the Urban South* (New York: Oxford University Press, forthcoming).

12. Berlin, *Making of African America,* 201–2; James S. Hirsch and Suzanne Alexander, "Reverse Exodus: Middle Class Blacks Quit Northern Cities and Settle in the South," *Wall Street Journal,* 22 May 1990. Cf. Michelle Nickerson and Darren Dochuk, eds., *Sunbelt Rising: The Politics of Space, Place, and Region* (Philadelphia: University of Pennsylvania Press, 2011), 1–28.

13. Paul Spickard, *Almost All Aliens: Immigration, Race, and Colonialism in American History and Identity* (New York: Routledge, 2007), 339, 341–42, 385–86; Albert Camarillo, "Blacks, Latinos, and the New Racial Frontier in American Cities of Color: California's Emerging Minority-Majority Cities," in *African American Urban History since World War II,* ed. Kenneth L. Kusmer and Joe W. Trotter (Chicago: University of Chicago Press, 2010), 41–42; Nancy Foner, "West Indian Migration to New York: An Overview," in *Islands in the City: West Indian Migration to New York,* ed. Nancy Foner (Berkeley: University of California Press, 2001), 3–7; Berlin, *Making of African America,* 4–7; Jorge Duany, *Blurred Borders: Transnational Migration between the Hispanic Caribbean and the United States* (Chapel Hill: University of North Carolina Press, 2011), 63–68.

14. Berlin, *Making of African America*, 4–7, 216–25; James Campbell, *Middle Passages: African American Journeys to Africa, 1787–2005* (New York: Penguin Press, 2006), 371–73.

15. Premilla Nadasen, *Household Workers Unite: The Untold Story of African American Women Who Built a Movement* (Boston: Beacon Press, 2015), 34–35, 42–44, 98–99, 104–5, 119, 175.

16. Robert Gioielli, *Environmental Activism and the Urban Crisis: Baltimore, St. Louis, and Chicago* (Philadelphia: Temple University Press, 2014), 50–65, 81–87, 99–103.

17. Joe W. Trotter and Jared N. Day, *Race and Renaissance: African Americans in Pittsburgh since World War II* (Pittsburgh: University of Pittsburgh Press, 2010), 174–75.

18. Rhonda Williams, *The Politics of Public Housing: Black Women's Struggles against Urban Inequality* (New York: Oxford University Press, 2004), 222–28; Lisa Levenstein, *A Movement without Marches: African American Women and the Politics of Poverty in Postwar Philadelphia* (Chapel Hill: University of North Carolina Press, 2009), 181–91; Nadasen, *Household Workers Unite*, 152–53, 166–80.

19. Brian Purnell, "Unmaking the Ghetto: Community Development and Persistent Social Inequality in Brooklyn, Los Angeles, and Philadelphia," in *The Ghetto in Global History: 1500 to the Present*, ed. Wendy Z. Goldman and Joe W. Trotter (New York: Routledge, 2018).

20. Richard Walter Thomas, "The Black Community Building Process in Post-Urban Disorder Detroit, 1967–1997," in *African American Urban Experience: Perspectives from the Colonial Era to the Present*, ed. Joe W. Trotter, Earl Lewis, and Tera Hunter (New York: Palgrave/Macmillan, 2004), 209–40; Robin D. G. Kelley, *Yo' Mama's Disfunktional!: Fighting the Culture Wars in Urban America* (New York: Beacon, 1997), 146–47; Sugrue, *Sweet Land of Liberty*, 525.

21. Marcus A. Hunter, *Black Citymakers: How* The Philadelphia Negro *Changed Urban America* (New York: Oxford University Press, 2013); Jeffrey Helgeson, *Crucibles of Black Empowerment: Chicago's Neighborhood Politics from the New Deal to Harold Washington* (Chicago: University of Chicago Press, 2014); Zieger, *For Jobs and Freedom*, 233; Nancy Maclean, *Freedom Is Not Enough: The Opening of the American Workplace* (New York and Cambridge: Russell Sage and Harvard University Press, 2006), 289–90; Jacqueline Jones, *American Work: Four Centuries of Black and White Labor* (New York: W. W. Norton, 1998), 370; David R. Colburn and Jeffrey S. Adler, *African American Mayors: Race, Politics, and the American City* (Urbana: University of Illinois Press, 2005); Sears, "Black-White Conflict," in Halle, *New York and Los Angeles*, 370–71, 375–76.

22. Peniel E. Joseph, *Waiting 'til the Midnight Hour: A Narrative History of Black Power in America* (New York: Henry Holt, 2006), 276–83; Lucius J. Barker and Mack H. Jones, *African Americans and the American Political System* (Englewood Cliffs, NJ: Prentice Hall, 1994), 81–84; Henry Hampton and Steve Fayer, with Sarah Flynn, *Voices of Freedom: An Oral History of the Civil Rights Movement from the 1950s through the 1980s* (New York: Bantam Books, 1990), 565–86.

23. Komozi Woodard, "It's Nation Time in Newark: Amiri Baraka and the Black Power Experiments in Newark, New Jersey," in *Freedom North: Black Freedom Struggles Outside the South, 1940–1980*, ed. Jeanne F. Theoharis and Komozi Woodard (New York: Palgrave Macmillan, 2003), 287–311; Komozi Woodard, "Amiri Baraka, the Congress of African People, and Black Power Politics from the 1961 United Nations Protest to the 1972 Gary Convention," in *The Black Power Movement: Rethinking the Civil Rights–Black Power Era*, ed. Peniel Joseph (New York: Routledge, 2006), 55–78; Kevin Mumford, *Newark: A History of Race, Rights, and Riots in America* (New York: New York University Press, 2007), 197–212; Scot Brown, *Fighting for US: Maulana Karenga, the US Organization, and Black Cultural Nationalism* (New York: New York University Press, 2003), 99–103; Joseph, *Waiting 'til the Midnight Hour*, 276–83; Barker and Jones, *African Americans*, 81–84; Hampton and Fayer, *Voices of Freedom*, 565–86; Donna Murch, *Living for the City: Migration, Education, and the Rise of the Black Panther Party in Oakland, California* (Chapel Hill: University of North Carolina Press, 2010), 195–96; Manning Marable, *Race and Reform, and Rebellion: The Second Reconstruction and Beyond in Black America, 1945–2006* (Jackson: University Press of Mississippi, 2007), 122–23.

24. Zieger, *For Jobs and Freedom*, 223–33.

25. Heather R. Parker, "Tom Bradley and the Politics of Race," in Colburn and Adler, *African American Mayors*, 153–77; Camarillo, "Blacks, Latinos, and the New Racial Frontier," in Kusmer and Trotter, *African American Urban History*, 41–42; Raphael J. Sonenshein, *Politics in Black and White: Race and Power in Los Angeles* (Princeton, NJ: Princeton University Press, 1993), 85–100, 101–13; Sears, "Black-White Conflict," in Halle, *New York and Los Angeles*, 370–71, 375–76; Joshua Sides, *L.A. City Limits: African American Los Angeles from the Great Depression to the Present* (Berkeley: University of California Press, 2004), 193–94.

26. Heather Ann Thompson, "Rethinking the Collapse of Postwar Liberalism: The Rise of Mayor Coleman Young and the Politics of Race in Detroit," in Colburn and Adler, *African American Mayors*, 223–48; Thompson, *Whose Detroit?*, 80–81, 192, 195–96, 197, 199; Sidney Fine, *Violence in the Model City: The Cavanagh Administration, Race Relations, and the Detroit Riot of 1967* (Ann Arbor: University of Michigan Press, 1989), 31–32, 456, 457; Sugrue, *Sweet Land of Liberty*, 504.

27. Helgeson, *Crucibles of Black Empowerment*, 240–42; Walda Katz Fishman, Jerome Scott, Ralph C. Gomes, and Robert Newby, "The Politics of Race and Class in City Hall: 'Race Politics' and the Class Question," in Lembcke, *Race, Class, and Urban Social Change*, 135–77; Thomas L. Blair, *Retreat to the Ghetto: End of a Dream?* (New York: Hill and Wang, 1978), 202–7; Paul Kleppner, *Chicago Divided: The Making of a Black Mayor* (DeKalb: Northern Illinois University Press, 1985), 134–37, 149, 183–85; Sugrue, *Sweet Land of Liberty*, 503; Arnold R. Hirsch, "Harold and Dutch Revisited: A Comparative Look at the First Black Mayors of Chicago and New Orleans," in Colburn and Adler, *African American Mayors*, 107–29.

28. Helgeson, *Crucibles of Black Empowerment*, 240–42; Kleppner, *Chicago Divided*, 187, 217, 241.

29. Sugrue, *Sweet Land of Liberty*, 504–5; Roger Biles, "Mayor David Dinkins and the Politics of Race in New York City," in Colburn and Adler, *African American Mayors,* 130–52; Karen M. Kaufmann, "Mayoral Politics of New York and Los Angeles," in Halle, *New York and Los Angeles,* 324–29; Wilkerson, *Warmth of Other Suns,* 529.

30. David L. Sjoquist, ed., *The Atlanta Paradox* (New York: Russell Sage Foundation, 2000), 1–2; Farley, "Metropolises of the Multi-City Study," in O'Connor, Tilly, and Bobo, *Urban Inequality,* 49; Glenn Feldman, ed., *Painting Dixie Red: When, Where, Why, and How the South Became Republican* (Gainesville: University Press of Florida, 2011), 1–18, 91–94; Ronald H. Bayor, "African American Mayors in Atlanta," in Colburn and Adler, *African American Mayors,* 178–99; Kevin Kruse, *White Flight: Atlanta and the Making of Modern Conservatism* (Princeton, NJ: Princeton University Press, 2005), 240–41; Clarence N. Stone, *Regime Politics: Governing Atlanta, 1946–1988* (Lawrence: University Press of Kansas, 1989), 80–81, 87–88; Howard Gillette, Jr., "Protest and Power in Washington, D.C.: The Troubled Legacy of Marion Barry," in Colburn and Adler, *African American Mayors,* 200–222; Jonathan J. Z. Agronsky, *Marion Barry: The Politics of Race* (Latham, NY: British American Publishing, 1991), 13–53, 181–235.

31. Lawrence Otis Graham, *Our Kind of People: Inside America's Black Upper Class* (New York: HarperCollins, 1999), quote, 267; Helgeson, *Crucibles of Black Empowerment,* 255–56, 258, 260–61; Fishman, Scott, Gomes, and Newby, "Politics of Race and Class," in Lembcke, *Race, Class, and Urban Social Change,* 150–51; Kleppner, *Chicago Divided,* 145, 154; Thompson, *Whose Detroit?,* 171, 221.

32. Fishman, Scott, Gomes, and Newby, "Politics of Race and Class," in Lembcke, *Race, Class, and Urban Social Change,* 150–51; Kleppner, *Chicago Divided,* 145, 154.

33. Thompson, *Whose Detroit?,* 171, 221.

34. Matthew Countryman, *Up South: Civil Rights and Black Power in Philadelphia* (Philadelphia: University of Pennsylvania Press, 2006), 323–25; Hunter, *Black Citymakers,* 180–89.

35. Fishman, Scott, Gomes, and Newby, "Politics of Race and Class," in Lembcke, *Race, Class, and Urban Social Change,* 150–51; Manning Marable, "Harold Washington's Chicago: Race, Class Conflict and Political Change," in Lembcke, *Race, Class, and Urban Social Change,* 82, 84–85; Helgeson, *Crucibles of Black Empowerment,* 262–63, 274–75; Graham, *Our Kind of People,* 209; Katz, *Why Don't American Cities Burn?,* 58–60; Sugrue, *Sweet Land of Liberty,* 504–05.

36. Bayor, "African American Mayors in Atlanta," in Colburn and Adler, *African American Mayors,* 178–99; Kruse, *White Flight,* 240–41; Stone, *Regime Politics,* 80–81, 87–88.

37. Arnold Hirsch, "Harold and Dutch Revisited," in Colburn and Adler, *African American Mayors,* 107–29; Arnold Hirsch, "Simply a Matter of Black and White: The Transformation of Race and Politics in New Orleans in Twentieth-Century New Orleans," in Arnold Hirsch and Joseph Logsdon, eds., *Creole New Orleans: Race and Americanization* (Baton Rouge: Louisiana State University Press, 1992), 304–19; Arnold Hirsch, "(Almost) A Closer Walk with Thee: Historical

Reflections on New Orleans and Hurricane Katrina," *Journal of Urban History*, 35, no. 5 (July 2009): 623–24; Gillette, "Protest and Power in Washington, D.C.," in Colburn and Adler, *African American Mayors*, 200–22; Agronsky, *Marion Barry*, 13–53, 181–235.

38. Thompson, *Whose Detroit?*, 81.

39. Sjoquist, *Atlanta Paradox*, 1–2; Farley, "Metropolises of the Multi-City Study," in O'Connor, Tilly, and Bobo, *Urban Inequality*, 49; Trotter, *The African American Experience*, 610–11; Feldman, *Painting Dixie Red*, 1–18, 91–94.

40. Hirsch, "Harold and Dutch Revisited," in Colburn and Adler, *African American Mayors*, 107–29; Hirsch, "Simply a Matter of Black and White," in Hirsch and Logsdon, *Creole New Orleans*, 304–19; Hirsch, "(Almost) A Closer Walk with Thee," 623–24; Gillette, "Protest and Power in Washington, D.C.," in Colburn and Adler, *African American Mayors*, 200–22; Agronsky, *Marion Barry*, 13–53, 181–235.

41. Kwame Holmes, "Chocolate to Rainbow City: Liberalism and Displacement in the Nation's Capital" (unpublished manuscript, 2013). Also see Kevin Mumford, *Not Straight, Not White: Black Gay Men from the March on Washington to the AIDS Crisis* (Chapel Hill: University of North Carolina Press, 2016).

42. Peniel Joseph, *Dark Days, Bright Nights: From Black Power to Barack Obama* (New York: Basic/Civitas Books, 2010), 188–89.

EPILOGUE

1. On perquisites of citizenship, see James Grossman, *Land of Hope: Chicago, Black Southerners, and the Great Migration* (Chicago: University of Chicago Press, 1989), 8; Doug Henwood, quoted in Michael Zweig, *The Working Class Majority: America's Best Kept Secret* (Ithaca, NY: Cornell University, ILR Press, 2001), 33.

2. Clarence Lang, *Black America in the Shadow of the Sixties: Notes on the Civil Rights Movement, Neoliberalism, and Politics* (Ann Arbor: University of Michigan, 2015), xi, xvi.

3. Michelle Alexander, *The New Jim Crow: Mass Incarceration in the Age of Colorblindness* (New York: New Press, 2010), 2, 13.

4. Heather Ann Thompson, *Blood in the Water: The Attica Prison Uprising of 1971 and Its Legacy* (New York: Pantheon Books, 2017), 558–71.

5. Premilla Nadasen, *Household Workers Unite: The Untold Story of African American Women Who Built a Movement* (Boston: Beacon Press, 2015), 34–35, 42–44, 98–99, 104–05, 119, 175.

6. Philip F. Rubio, *There's Always Work at the Post Office: African American Postal Workers and the Fight for Jobs, Justice, and Equality* (Chapel Hill: University of North Carolina Press, 2010); Francis Ryan, *AFSCME's Philadelphia Story: Municipal Workers and Urban Power in the Twentieth Century* (Philadelphia: Temple University Press, 2011); Leon Fink and Brian Greenberg, *Upheaval in the Quiet Zone: 1199SEIU and the Politics of Health Care Unionism*, 2nd ed. (Urbana: University of

Illinois Press, 2009); Robert H. Zieger, *For Jobs and Freedom: Race and Labor in America since 1865* (Lexington: University Press of Kentucky, 2007), quote, 229.

7. Elizabeth Faue, *Rethinking the American Labor Movement* (New York: Routledge, 2017), 207.

8. Michael Zweig, "White Working-Class Voters and the Future of Progressive Politics," *New Labor Forum* 26, no. 2 (11 May 2017), http://newlaborforum.cuny.edu/2017/05/11/white-working-class-voters-and-the-future-of-progressive-politics/; Robin D. G. Kelley, "After Trump," Forum Response, *Boston Review*, 15 November 2016, http://bostonreview.net/forum/after-trump/robin-d-g-kelley-trump-says-go-back-we-say-fight-back.

9. Zweig, "White Working-Class Voters."

10. For a recent set of essays addressing the ongoing historical connection between electoral politics and grassroots black activism, see Lisa Materson and Joe W. Trotter, eds., "African American Urban Electoral Politics in the Age of Jim Crow," special section, *Journal of Urban History* (March 2018).

11. Marcia Walker-McWilliams, *Reverend Addie Wyatt: Faith and the Fight for Labor, Gender, and Racial Equality* (Urbana: University of Illinois Press, 2016), 1–5, 48–49, 52–53, 188; Peniel Joseph, *Dark Days, Bright Nights: From Black Power to Barack Obama* (New York: Basic/Civitas Books, 2010), 188–89.

12. Elizabeth Day, "#BlackLivesMatter: The Birth of a New Civil Rights Movement," *Guardian*, 19 July 2015, www.theguardian.com/world/2015/jul/19/blacklivesmatter-birth-civil-rights-movement; Lang, *Black America in the Shadow of the Sixties*, xv, 13, 34, 126–27, 130. For a pioneering study of the increasing movement of racialized poverty to the suburbs, see sociologist Alexandra Murphy, *When the Sidewalks End: Poverty and Race in an American Suburb* (New York: Oxford University Press, forthcoming).

13. Garza quoted in Bryan Tarnowski and Janell Ross, "Black Lives Matter Shifts from Protests to Policy under Trump," *Washington Post*, 4 May 2017, www.washingtonpost.com/national/in-trumps-america-black-lives-matter-shifts-from-protests-to-policy/2017/05/04/a2acf37a-28fe-11e7-b605–33413c691853_story.html. Also see Brandon E. Patterson, "How the Black Lives Matter Movement is Mobilizing Against Trump," *Mother Jones*, 7 February 2017, www.motherjones.com/politics/2017/02/black-lives-matter-versus-trump/.

14. N. D. B. Connolly, *A World More Concrete: Real Estate and the Remaking of Jim Crow South Florida* (Chicago: University of Chicago Press, 2014), 202.

APPENDIX

1. Pero Dagbovie, *African American History Reconsidered: New Perspectives on Black History and Its Profession* (Urbana: University of Illinois Press, 2010); Francille R. Wilson, *The Segregated Scholars: Black Social Scientists and the Creation of Black Labor Studies, 1890–1950* (Charlottesville: University of Virginia Press, 2006); Arvarh E. Strickland and Robert E. Weems, Jr., eds., *The African American Experience: An Histo-*

riographical and Bibliographical Guide (Westport, CT: Greenwood Press, 2001); Darlene Clark Hine, ed., State of Afro-American History: Past, Present, and Future (Baton Rouge: Louisiana State University Press, 1986); August Meier and Elliott Rudwick, Black History and the Historical Profession (Urbana: University of Illinois Press, 1986).

2. Ulrich Bonnell Phillips, American Negro Slavery: A Survey of the Supply, Employment and Control of Negro Labor as Determined by the Plantation Regime (1918; repr., New York: Appleton-Century, 1940), 292–93. This section is drawn from Joe W. Trotter, "African-American Workers: New Directions in U.S. Labor Historiography," Labor History 35, no. 4 (Fall 1994): 495–523, quotes, 497.

3. W. E. B. Du Bois, The Philadelphia Negro: A Social Study (1899; repr. Philadelphia: University of Pennsylvania, 1996), 5–9; Charles S. Johnson, for the Chicago Commission on Race Relations, The Negro in Chicago: A Study of Race Relations and a Race Riot (Chicago: University of Chicago Press, 1922); Louise V. Kennedy, The Negro Peasant Turns Cityward: Effects of Recent Migrations to Northern Cities (1930; repr., College Park, MD: McGrath, 1969); Franklin Frazier, The Negro Family in Chicago (Chicago: University of Chicago Press, 1932); E. F. Frazier, The Negro Family in the United States, rev. ed. (1939; New York: Macmillan, 1957); St. Clair Drake and Horace R. Cayton, Black Metropolis: A Study of Negro Life in a Northern City, vols. 1 and 2, rev. and enl. (1945; Chicago: University of Chicago Press, 1993); Robert Weaver, The Negro Ghetto (New York: Harcourt, Brace, 1948).

For specifically labor studies of this era, see W. E. B. Du Bois, ed., The Negro Artisan, Atlanta University Publications no. 7 (Atlanta: Atlanta University Press, 1902), https://catalog.hathitrust.org/Record/100775479; W. E. B. Du Bois and Augustus Dill, eds., The Negro Artisan, Atlanta University Publications no. 17 (Atlanta: Atlanta University, 1912), in Trotter, "African-American Workers," quote, 499; Charles H. Wesley, Negro Labor in the United States, 1850–1925: A Study in American Economic History (1927; repr. New York: Russell and Russell, 1967); Lorenzo J. Greene and Carter G. Woodson, The Negro Wage Earner (1930; repr. New York: Russell and Russell, 1969); Sterling D. Spero and Abram L. Harris, The Black Worker: The Negro and the Labor Movement (1930; repr. New York: Atheneum, 1968); Ira De Augustine Reid, Negro Membership in American Labor Unions (New York: National Urban League, Department of Research and Investigation, 1930); Horace R. Cayton and George S. Mitchell, Black Workers and the New Unions (Chapel Hill: University of North Carolina Press, 1939).

Although emphasis on the centrality of race relations would dissipate in the years after World War II, some works carried the primary focus on black-white interactions forward into the late twentieth century and beyond. See Constance M. Green, Secret City: A History of Race Relations in the Nation's Capital (Princeton, NJ: Princeton University Press, 1967); Chris M. Asch and George D. Musgrove, Chocolate City: A History of Race and Democracy in the Nation's Capital (Chapel Hill: University of North Carolina Press, 2017). Unlike Greens, Asch and Musgrove's book defines race and race relations to include "all races," not just blacks and whites.

4. Gilbert Osofsky, Harlem: The Making of a Ghetto, 1890–1930, rev. ed. (1963; repr., New York: Harper Torchbooks, 1971); Allan H. Spear, Black Chicago: The

Making of a Negro Ghetto, 1890–1920 (Chicago: University of Chicago Press, 1967); Kenneth L. Kusmer, *A Ghetto Takes Shape: Black Cleveland, 1870–1930* (Urbana: University of Illinois Press, 1976); David M. Katzman, *Before the Ghetto: Black Detroit in the Nineteenth Century* (Urbana: University of Illinois Press, 1973).

5. For subsequent critiques of this scholarship, see Kevin Gaines, "African-American History," in *American History Now,* ed. Eric Foner and Lisa McGirr (Philadelphia: Temple University Press, 2011), 400–420; Earl Lewis, "'To Turn as on a Pivot': Writing African Americans into a History of Overlapping Diasporas," *American Historical Review* 100 (June 1995), 765–87; Strickland and Weems, *African American Experience*; Kenneth W. Goings and Raymond A. Mohl, eds., *The New African American Urban History* (Thousand Oaks, CA: Sage Publications, 1996); Kenneth L. Kusmer and Joe W. Trotter, eds., *African American Urban History since World War II* (Chicago: University of Chicago Press, 2009); Meier and Rudwick, *Black History and the Historical Profession;* Hine, *State of Afro-American History;* Joe William Trotter, Jr., Earl Lewis, and Tera Hunter, eds., *African American Urban Experience: Perspectives from the Colonial Period to the Present* (New York: Palgrave, 2004).

6. John Blassingame, *Black New Orleans, 1865–1880* (Chicago: University of Chicago Press, 1973); Howard N. Rabinowitz, *Race Relations in the Urban South, 1865–1890* (New York: Oxford University Press, 1978); Robert E. Perdue, *The Negro in Savannah* (New York: Exposition Press, 1973); George C. Wright, *Life Behind a Veil: Blacks in Louisville, Kentucky, 1865–1930* (Baton Rouge: Louisiana State University Press, 1985); Zane L. Miller, "Urban Blacks in the South, 1865–1920: The Richmond, Savannah, New Orleans, Louisville, and Birmingham Experience," in *The New Urban History: Quantitative Explorations by American Historians,* ed. Leo F. Schnore (Princeton, NJ: Princeton University Press, 1975), 184–227.

7. Wright, *Life Behind a Veil,* 5, 6–7, 9–10.

8. Douglas Daniels, *Pioneer Urbanites: A Social and Cultural History of Black San Francisco* (Philadelphia: Temple University Press, 1980); Quintard Taylor, *The Forging of a Black Community: Seattle's Central District from 1870 through the Civil Rights Era* (Seattle: University of Washington Press, 1994); Albert S. Broussard, *Black San Francisco: The Struggle for Racial Equality in the West, 1900–1954* (Lawrence: University of Kansas, 1993); Douglas Flamming, *Bound for Freedom: Black Los Angeles in Jim Crow America* (Berkeley: University of California Press, 2005); Matthew C. Whitaker, *Race Work: The Rise of Civil Rights in the Urban West* (Lincoln: University of Nebraska Press, 2005); Scott Kurashige, *The Shifting Grounds of Race: Black and Japanese Americans in the Making of Multiethnic Los Angeles* (Princeton, NJ: Princeton University Press, 2008); Shirley Ann Wilson Moore, *To Place Our Deeds: The African American Community in Richmond, California, 1910–1963* (Berkeley: University of California Press, 2000). Also see Quintard Taylor, *In Search of the Racial Frontier: African Americans in the American West, 1528–1990* (New York: W. W. Norton, 1998).

9. Flamming, *Bound for Freedom,* 4; Moore, *To Place Our Deeds,* 2; Kurashige, *The Shifting Grounds of Race,* 186–95.

10. James Grossman, *Land of Hope: Chicago, Black Southerners, and the Great Migration* (Chicago: University of Chicago Press, 1989); Peter Gottlieb, *Making Their Own Way: Southern Blacks' Migration to Pittsburgh, 1916–30* (Urbana: University of Illinois Press, 1987); Richard Walter Thomas, *Life for Us Is What We Make It: Building Black Community in Detroit, 1915–1945* (Bloomington: Indiana University Press, 1992); Joe William Trotter, Jr., *Black Milwaukee: The Making of an Industrial Proletariat, 1915–45*, 2nd ed. (1985; Urbana: University of Illinois Press, 2007). See also Dennis Dickerson, *Out of the Crucible: Black Steelworkers in Western Pennsylvania, 1875–1980* (Albany: State University of New York Press, 1986); Henry Louis Taylor, Jr., ed., *Race and the City: Work, Community, and Protest in Cincinnati, 1820–1970* (Urbana: University of Illinois Press, 1993); Lillian Serece Williams, *Strangers in the Land of Paradise: The Creation of an African American Community, Buffalo, New York, 1900–1940* (Bloomington: Indiana University Press, 1999).

11. Peter Rachleff, *Black Labor in Richmond, 1865–1890* (1984; repr. Urbana: University of Illinois Press, 1989), quote, 15; Robin D. G. Kelley, *Hammer and Hoe: Alabama Communists during the Great Depression* (Chapel Hill: University of North Carolina Press, 1990), xiii, 1; Robin D. G. Kelley, *Race Rebels: Culture, Politics, and the Black Working Class* (New York: Free Press, 1994); Michael Honey, *Southern Labor and Black Civil Rights: Organizing Memphis Workers, 1929–1955* (Urbana: University of Illinois Press, 1993); Robert Korstad, *Civil Rights Unionism: Tobacco Workers and the Struggle for Democracy in the Mid-Twentieth-Century South* (Chapel Hill: University of North Carolina Press, 2003); Eric Arnesen, *Waterfront Workers of New Orleans: Race, Class, and Politics, 1863–1923* (New York: Oxford University Press, 1991); Earl Lewis, *In Their Own Interests: Race, Class, and Power in Twentieth-Century Norfolk, Virginia* (Berkeley: University of California Press, 1991). See also Lynne B. Feldman, *A Sense of Place: Birmingham's Black Middle-Class Community, 1890–1930* (Tuscaloosa: University of Alabama Press, 1999); Brian Kelly, *Race and Power in the Alabama Coalfields, 1908–21* (Urbana: University of Illinois Press, 2001); Henry M. McKiven, Jr., *Iron and Steel: Class, Race and Community in Birmingham, Alabama, 1875–1920* (Chapel Hill: University of North Carolina Press, 1995); Justin A. Nystrom, *New Orleans after the Civil War: Race, Politics, and a New Birth of Freedom* (Baltimore: Johns Hopkins University Press, 2010); Bernadette Pruitt, *The Other Great Migration: The Movement of Rural African Americans to Houston, 1900–1941* (College Station: Texas A&M University Press, 2013); Luther Adams, *Way Up North in Louisville: African American Migration in the Urban South, 1930–1970* (Chapel Hill: University of North Carolina Press, 2010).

12. Kelley, *Hammer and Hoe*, xiii, 1; Arnesen, *Waterfront Workers of New Orleans*; Honey, *Southern Labor and Black Civil Rights*, 8–9; Korstad, *Civil Rights Unionism*, 1.

13. Lewis, *In Their Own Interests*, 5.

14. Jacqueline Jones, *Labor of Love, Labor of Sorrow: Black Women, Work, and the Family, from Slavery to the Present* (New York: Basic Books, 1985), 5.

15. For 1990s scholarship, Tera Hunter, *To 'Joy My Freedom: Southern Black Women's Lives and Labors after the Civil War* (Cambridge: Harvard University

Press, 1997); Elizabeth Clark-Lewis, *Living In, Living Out: African American Domestics in Washington, D.C., 1910–1940* (Washington, DC: Smithsonian Institution Press, 1994); see also Kimberley Phillips, *AlabamaNorth: African-American Migrants, Community, and Working-Class Activism in Cleveland, 1915–45* (Urbana: University of Illinois Press, 1999). For twenty-first-century scholarship, Victoria Wolcott, *Remaking Respectability: African American Women in Interwar Detroit* (Chapel Hill: University of North Carolina Press, 2001); Georgina Hickey, *Hope and Danger in the New South: Working Class Women and Urban Development in Atlanta, 1890–1940* (Athens: University of Georgia Press, 2003); Leslie Brown, *Upbuilding Black Durham: Gender, Class, and Black Community Development in the Jim Crow South* (Chapel Hill: University of North Carolina Press, 2008). See also Darlene Clark Hine, "Black Migration to the Urban Midwest: The Gender Dimension, 1915–1945," in *The Great Migration in Historical Perspective: New Dimensions of Race, Class, and Gender*, ed. Joe William Trotter, Jr. (Bloomington: Indiana University Press, 1991), 127–54.

16. Wolcott, *Remaking Respectability*, 2–4.

17. Hickey, *Hope and Danger in the New South*, 3–5.

18. Brown, *Upbuilding Black Durham*, 15–16, 20.

19. Khalil G. Muhammad, *The Condemnation of Blackness: Race, Crime, and the Making of Modern Urban America* (Cambridge: Harvard University Press, 2010), 1–14.

20. Kevin Mumford, *Interzones: Black/White Sex Districts in Chicago and New York in the Early Twentieth Century* (New York: Columbia University Press, 1997), 38–39.

21. Kali N. Gross, *Colored Amazons: Crime, Violence, and Black Women in the City of Brotherly Love, 1880–1910* (Durham, NC: Duke University Press, 2006); Cheryl D. Hicks, *Talk with You Like a Woman: African American Women, Justice, and Reform in New York, 1890–1935* (Chapel Hill: University of North Carolina Press, 2010); Cynthia M. Blair, *I've Got to Make My Livin': Black Women's Sex Work in Turn-of-the-Century Chicago* (Chicago: University of Chicago Press, 2010); Talitha L. LeFlouria, *Chained in Silence: Black Women and Convict Labor in the New South* (Chapel Hill: University of North Carolina Press, 2015); Sarah Haley, *No Mercy Here: Gender, Punishment, and the Making of Jim Crow Modernity* (Chapel Hill: University of North Carolina Press, 2016).

22. Blair, *I've Got to Make My Livin'*, 2–3.

23. Hicks, *Talk with You Like a Woman*, 3, 12–13; Kali N. Gross, *Colored Amazons: Crime, Violence, and Black Women in the City of Brotherly Love, 1880–1910* (Durham, NC: Duke University Press, 2006), 11–12.

24. LeFlouria, *Chained in Silence*, 8, 172–73.

25. Haley, *No Mercy Here*, quote, 6; Kali N. Gross and Cheryl D. Hicks, "Gendering the Carceral State: African American Women, History, and the Criminal Justice System," *Journal of African American History* 100, no. 3 (Summer 2015): 357–65.

26. Davarian L. Baldwin, *Chicago's New Negroes: Modernity, the Great Migration, and Black Urban Life* (Chapel Hill: University of North Carolina Press, 2007);

Adam Green, *Selling the Race: Culture, Community, and Black Chicago, 1940–1955;* Wallace Best, *Passionately Human, No Less Divine: Religion and Culture in Black Chicago, 1915–1952* (Princeton, NJ: Princeton University Press, 2007), 1–3, 76–77, 93; Clare Corbould, *Becoming African Americans: Black Public Life in Harlem, 1919–1939* (Cambridge: Harvard University Press, 2009); Christopher R. Reed, *The Rise of Chicago's Black Metropolis, 1920–1929* (Urbana: University of Illinois Press, 2011).

   27. Baldwin, *Chicago's New Negroes,* 1–17. Also see Reed, *Rise of Chicago's Black Metropolis,* 1–8.

   28. Corbould, *Becoming African Americans,* 11–12, 16–17.

   29. Kevin Mumford, *Newark: A History of Race, Rights, and Riots in America* (New York: New York University Press, 2007), 6–7.

   30. Best, *Passionately Human, No Less Divine,* quote, 93.

   31. Green, *Selling the Race,* 1–17, 61–81.

   32. Arnesen, *Waterfront Workers of New Orleans;* Eric Arnesen, *Brotherhoods of Color: Black Railroad Workers and the Struggle for Equality* (Cambridge: Harvard University Press, 2001); Rick Halpern, *Down on the Killing Floor: Black and White Workers in Chicago's Packinghouses, 1904–1954* (Urbana: University of Chicago Press, 1997); John Hinshaw, *Steel and Steelworkers: Race and Class Struggle in Twentieth-Century Pittsburgh* (Albany: State University of New York Press, 2002); David Lewis-Colman, *Race against Liberalism: Black Workers and the UAW in Detroit* (Urbana: University of Illinois Press, 2008); Dickerson, *Out of the Crucible;* August Meier and Elliott Rudwick, *Black Detroit and the Rise of the UAW* (New York: Oxford University Press, 1979). For studies on black women household workers, see Clark-Lewis, *Living In, Living Out;* Hunter, *To 'Joy My Freedom;* Premilla Nadasen, *Household Workers Unite: The Untold Story of African American Women Who Built a Movement* (Boston: Beacon Press, 2015).

   33. Andrew E. Kersten and Clarence Lang, eds., *Reframing Randolph: Labor, Black Freedom, and the Legacies of A. Philip Randolph* (New York: New York University Press, 2015), 1–20.

   34. William Hamilton Harris, *Keeping the Faith: A. Philip Randolph, Milton P. Webster, and the Brotherhood of Sleeping Car Porters, 1925–37* (Urbana: University of Illinois Press, 1977); Paula F. Pfeffer, *A. Philip Randolph, Pioneer of the Civil Rights Movement* (Baton Rouge: Louisiana State University Press, 1990); Melinda Chateauvert, *Marching Together: Women of the Brotherhood of Sleeping Car Porters* (Urbana: University of Illinois Press, 1998); Beth Tompkins Bates, *Pullman Porters and the Rise of Protest Politics in Black America 1925–1945* (Chapel Hill: University of North Carolina Press, 2001), 63–105; Cornelius L. Bynum, *A. Philip Randolph and the Struggle for Civil Rights* (Urbana: University of Illinois Press, 2010); Cynthia Taylor, *A. Philip Randolph: The Religious Journey of an African American Labor Leader* (New York: New York University Press, 2006).

   35. Leon Litwack, *North of Slavery: The Negro in the Free States, 1790–1860* (Chicago: University of Chicago Press, 1961), viii, ix.

   36. Ira Berlin, *Slaves without Masters: The Free Negro in the Antebellum South* (New York: Oxford University Press, 1974), 221–22.

37. Richard C. Wade, *Slavery in the Cities: The South, 1820–1860* (New York: Oxford University Press, 1964), ix, 3, 17, 245.

38. Claudia Goldin, *Urban Slavery in the American South, 1820–1860: A Quantitative Study* (Chicago: University of Chicago Press, 1976), quote, xiii–xiv, 1, 87; Robert S. Starobin, *Industrial Slavery in the Old South* (New York: Oxford University Press, 1970), vii–ix; Ronald L. Lewis, *Coal, Iron, and Slaves: Industrial Slavery in Maryland and Virginia, 1715–1865* (Westport, CT: Greenwood Press, 1979), 1–10.

39. Mariana L. R. Dantas, *Black Townsmen: Urban Slavery and Freedom in the Eighteenth-Century Americas* (New York: Palgrave, 2008), quote, 5; Nathalie Dessens, *From Saint-Domingue to New Orleans: Migration and Influences* (Gainesville: University Press of Florida, 2007). Also see Catherine W. Bishir, *Crafting Lives: African American Artisans in New Bern, North Carolina, 1770–1900* (Chapel Hill: University of North Carolina Press, 2013), 6–18; L. Diane Barnes, *Artisan Workers in the Upper South: Petersburg, Virginia, 1820–1865* (Baton Rouge: Louisiana State University Press, 2008); Douglas W. Bristol, Jr., *Knights of the Razor: Black Barbers in Slavery and Freedom* (Baltimore: Johns Hopkins University Press, 2009).

40. Marisa J. Fuentes, *Dispossessed Lives: Enslaved Women, Violence, and the Archive* (Philadelphia: University of Pennsylvania Press, 2016), 8–9.

41. James O. Horton and Lois E. Horton, *Black Bostonians: Family Life and Community Struggle in the Antebellum North* (New York: Holmes and Meier, 1979); Robert J. Cottrol, *The Afro-Yankees: Providence's Black Community in the Antebellum Era* (Westport, CT: Greenwood Press, 1982); Gary B. Nash, *Forging Freedom: The Formation of Philadelphia's Black Community 1720–1840* (Cambridge: Harvard University Press, 1988); Julie Winch, *Philadelphia's Black Elite: Activism, Accommodation, and the Struggle for Autonomy, 1787–1848* (Philadelphia: Temple University Press, 1988). See also Adelaide M. Cromwell, *The Other Brahmins: Boston's Black Upper Class, 1750–1950* (Fayetteville: University of Arkansas Press, 1994); Deborah B. Van Broekhoven, *The Devotion of These Women: Rhode Island in the Antislavery Network* (Amherst: University of Massachusetts Press, 2002).

42. Shane White, *Somewhat More Independent: The End of Slavery in New York City, 1770–1810* (Athens: University of Georgia Press, 1991); Harry Reed, *Platform for Change: The Foundation of the Northern Free Black Community, 1775–1865* (East Lansing: Michigan State University Press, 1994); Leslie M. Harris, *In the Shadow of Slavery: African Americans in New York City, 1626–1863* (Chicago: University of Chicago Press, 2003); Leslie Alexander, *African or American? Black Identity in New York City, 1784–1861* (Chicago: University of Illinois Press, 2008); Jane E. Dabel, *A Respectable Woman: The Public Roles of African American Women in Nineteenth-Century New York* (New York: New York University Press, 2008). See also Thelma W. Foote, *Black and White Manhattan: The History of Racial Formation in Colonial New York City* (New York: Oxford University Press, 2004); George E. Walker, *The Afro-American in New York City, 1827–1860* (New York: Garland Publishing, 1993); Craig S. Wilder, *In the Company of Black Men: The Influence on African American Culture in New York City* (New York: New York University Press, 2001); David Gellman, *Emancipating New York: The Politics of Slavery and Freedom, 1777–1827*

(Baton Rouge: Louisiana University Press, 2006); Erica Dunbar, *A Fragile Freedom: African American Freedom and Emancipation in the Antebellum City* (New Haven, CT: Yale University Press, 2008); Catherine Adams and Elizabeth H. Pleck, *Love of Freedom: Black Women in Colonial and Revolutionary New England* (New York: Oxford University Press, 2010); Nikki M. Taylor, *Frontiers of Freedom: Cincinnati's Black Community, 1802–1868* (Athens: Ohio University Press, 2005).

43. Harris, *In the Shadow of Slavery*, 4; Dabel, *A Respectable Woman*, 6.

44. Alexander, *African or American?*, xv. Efforts to understand the complicated impact of African and New World influences on urban blacks include a significant body of scholarship on slave rebellions and plots to rebel in early colonial New York. See Jill Lepore, *New York Burning: Liberty, Slavery, and Conspiracy in Eighteenth-Century Manhattan* (New York: Vintage Books, 2005), 170–71; Thomas J. Davis, *A Rumor of Revolt: "The Great Negro Plot" in Colonial New York* (Amherst: University of Massachusetts Press, 1990), ix–xiii, 1–97; Mat Johnson, *The Great Negro Plot: A Tale of Conspiracy and Murder in Eighteenth-Century New York* (New York: Bloomsbury USA, 2007).

Thematic and topical studies of such subjects as religion, fraternal orders, and black manhood also buttress scholarship on the preindustrial black working class. See Eddie Claude, *Exodus! Religion, Race, and Nation in Early Nineteenth-Century Black America* (Chicago: University of Chicago Press, 2000); Clarence E. Walker, *A Rock in a Weary Land: The African Methodist Episcopal Church during the Civil War and Reconstruction* (Baton Rouge: Louisiana State University Press, 1982); Theda Skocpol, Ariane Liazos, and Marshall Ganz, *What a Mighty Power We Can Be: African American Fraternal Groups and the Struggle for Racial Equality* (Princeton, NJ: Princeton University Press, 2006), 2–3, 34; Martin Sommers, *Manliness and Its Discontents: The Black Middle Class and the Transformation of Masculinity, 1900–1930* (Chapel Hill: University of North Carolina Press, 2004).

45. Daniel E. Walker, *No More: Slavery and Cultural Resistance in Havana and New Orleans* (Minneapolis: University of Minnesota Press, 2004); Shannon L. Dawdy, *Building the Devil's Empire: French Colonial New Orleans* (Chicago: University of Chicago Press, 2008), particularly 83, 156–58, 175–76; Kimberly S. Hanger, *Bounded Lives, Bounded Places: Free Black Society in Colonial New Orleans, 1769–1803* (Durham: Duke University Press, 1997); Daniel H. Usner, "Colonial Projects and Frontier Practices: The First Century of New Orleans History," in *Frontier Cities: Encounters at the Crossroads of Empire,* ed. Jay Gitlin, Barbara Berglund, and Adam Arenson (Philadelphia: University of Pennsylvania Press, 2013), 36–40; Daniel H. Usner, Jr., "From African Captivity to American Slavery: The Introduction of Black Laborers to Colonial Louisiana," *Louisiana History,* 20 (1979), 25–29; Daniel H. Usner, Jr., *Indians, Settlers, and Slaves in a Frontier Exchange Economy: The Lower Mississippi Valley Before 1783* (Chapel Hill: University of North Carolina Press, 1992), 25, 33, 41; Ari Kelman, *A River and Its City: The Nature of Landscape in New Orleans* (Berkeley: University of California Press, 2003); Gwendolyn Midlo Hall, *Africans in Colonial Louisiana: The Development of Afro-Creole Culture in the Eighteenth Century* (Baton Rouge: Louisiana State University Press, 1992), 29, 57–60;

Midori Takagi, *"Rearing Wolves to Our Own Destruction": Slavery in Richmond, Virginia, 1782–1865* (Charlottesville: University Press of Virginia, 1999), 14–15; Gregg D. Kimball, *American City, Southern Place: A Cultural History of Antebellum Richmond* (Athens: University of Georgia Press, 2012); Christopher Phillips, *Freedom's Port: The African American Community of Baltimore, 1790–1860* (Urbana: University of Illinois Press, 1997); T. Stephen Whitman, *The Price of Freedom: Slavery and Manumission in Baltimore and Early National Maryland* (Lexington: University Press of Kentucky, 1997); Barbara Jean Fields, *Slavery and Freedom on the Middle Ground: Maryland during the Nineteenth Century* (New Haven, CT: Yale University Press, 1985); Charles G. Steffen, *The Mechanics of Baltimore: Workers and Politics in the Age of Revolution, 1763–1812* (Urbana: University of Illinois Press, 1984); Bernard E. Powers, Jr., *Black Charlestonians: A Social History, 1822–1885* (Fayetteville: University of Arkansas Press, 1994); Robert Olwell, *Masters, Slaves, and Subjects: The Culture of Power in the South Carolina Low Country, 1740–1790* (Ithaca, NY: Cornell University Press, 1998), quote, 1–2, 11, 27–29; Emma Hart, *Building Charleston: Town and Society in the Eighteenth-Century British Atlantic World* (Charlottesville: University of Virginia, 2010), 25, 32–33; Ras M. Brown, *African-Atlantic Cultures and the South Carolina Lowcountry* (New York: Cambridge University Press, 2012); Michael Gomez, *Exchanging Our Country Marks: The Transformation of African Identities in the Colonial and Antebellum South* (Chapel Hill: University of North Carolina Press, 1998); Margaret Washington Creel, *"A Peculiar People": Slave Religion and Community-Culture among the Gullahs* (New York: New York University Press, 1988); Amrita Chakrabarti Myers, *Forging Freedom: Black Women and the Pursuit of Liberty in Antebellum Charleston* (Chapel Hill: University of North Carolina Press, 2011), xi, 1–3, 5–6; Cynthia M. Kennedy, *Braided Relations, Entwined Lives: The Women of Charleston's Urban Slave Society* (Bloomington: Indiana University Press, 2005); Wilma King, *The Essence of Liberty: Free Black Women during the Slave Era* (Columbia: University of Missouri Press, 2006); Whittington B. Johnson, *Black Savannah, 1788–1864* (Fayetteville: University of Arkansas Press, 1996); Leslie M. Harris and Daina R. Berry, eds., *Slavery and Freedom in Savannah* (Athens: University of Georgia Press, 2014); Jacqueline Jones, *Saving Savannah: The City in the Civil War* (New York: Alfred A. Knopf, 2009); Kate Masur, *An Example for All the Land: Emancipation and the Struggle over Equality in Washington, D.C.* (Chapel Hill: University of North Carolina Press, 2010); Stanley Harrold, *Subversives: Antislavery Community in Washington, D.C., 1828–1865* (Baton Rouge: Louisiana State University Press, 2003).

For rural and small-town dimensions of proletarianization, see Max Grivno, *Gleanings of Freedom: Free and Slave Labor along the Mason-Dixon Line, 1790–1860* (Urbana and Chicago: University of Illinois Press, 2011); Jennifer H. Dorsey, *Hirelings: African American Workers and Free Labor in Early Maryland* (Ithaca, NY: Cornell University Press, 2011); Bishir, *Crafting Lives;* Barnes, *Artisan Workers in the Upper South;* Suzanne Lebsock, *The Free Women of Petersburg: Status and Culture in a Southern Town, 1784–1860* (New York: W. W. Norton, 1984).

46. Powers, *Black Charlestonians,* 36–37, 48–49.

47. Johnson, *Black Savannah*, 2, 6.

48. Harris and Berry, ed., *Slavery and Freedom in Savannah*, particularly the entry by Janice L. Sumler-Edmund, 130–31.

49. Phillips, *Freedom's Port*, 2–3.

50. Myers, *Forging Freedom*, xi, 1–3, 5–6; King, *Essence of Liberty*; Hanger, *Bounded Lives, Bounded Places*, 2–3, 6, 16; Harris, *In the Shadow of Slavery*, 179; Kennedy, *Braided Relations, Entwined Lives*; Lebsock, *Free Women of Petersburg*; Dunbar, *A Fragile Freedom*; Adams and Pleck, *Love of Freedom*.

51. Ousmane Powers-Greene, *Against the Wind and Tide: The African American Struggle against the Colonization Movement* (New York: New York University Press, 2014); P. J. Staudenraus, *The African Colonization Movement, 1816–1865* (New York: Octagon Books, 1980), 32–35; Floyd J. Miller, *The Search for a Black Nationality: Black Emigration and Colonization, 1787–1863* (Urbana: University of Illinois Press, 1975), 47–53; Claude A. Clegg III, *The Price of Liberty: African Americans and the Making of Liberia* (Chapel Hill: University of North Carolina Press, 2004), 30–31.

52. Keith Griffler, *Frontline of Freedom: African Americans and the Forging of the Underground Railroad in the Ohio Valley* (Lexington: University Press of Kentucky, 2004); R. J. M. Blackett, *Making Freedom: The Underground Railroad and the Politics of Slavery* (Chapel Hill: University of North Carolina Press, 2013); Graham Russell G. Hodges, *David Ruggles: A Radical Black Abolitionist and the Underground Railroad in New York City* (Chapel Hill: University of North Carolina Press, 2010); Fergus M. Bordewich, *Bound for Canaan: The Underground Railroad and the War for the Soul of America* (New York: HarperCollins, 2005); Richard Newman and James Mueller, eds., *Antislavery and Abolition in Philadelphia: Emancipation and the Long Struggle for Racial Justice in the City of Brotherly Love* (Baton Rouge: Louisiana State University Press, 2011); Thomas C. Buchanan, *Black Life on the Mississippi: Slaves, Free Blacks, and the Western Steamboat World* (Chapel Hill: University of North Carolina Press, 2004).

53. William J. Wilson, *The Declining Significance of Race: Blacks and Changing American Institutions* (Chicago: University of Chicago Press, 1978).

54. William J. Wilson, *The Truly Disadvantaged: The Inner City, the Underclass, and Public Policy* (Chicago: University of Chicago Press, 1987).

55. Douglas S. Massey and Nancy Denton, *American Apartheid: Segregation and the Making of the Underclass* (Cambridge: Harvard University Press, 1993).

56. Thomas J. Sugrue, *The Origins of the Urban Crisis: Race and Inequality in Postwar Detroit* (Princeton, NJ: Princeton University Press, 1996). Sugrue's study built partly upon Arnold Hirsch's conceptualization of the "second ghetto." See Arnold Hirsch, *Making the Second Ghetto: Race and Housing in Chicago 1940–1960* (Chicago: University of Chicago Press, 1983). See also Thomas J. Sugrue, *Sweet Land of Liberty: The Forgotten Struggle for Civil Rights in the North* (New York: Random House, 2008).

57. Donna Murch, *Living for the City: Migration, Education, and the Rise of the Black Panther Party in Oakland, California* (Chapel Hill: University of North Carolina Press, 2010); Clarence Lang, *Grassroots at the Gateway: Class Politics and*

Black Freedom Struggle in St. Louis, 1936–75 (Ann Arbor: University of Michigan Press, 2009); Adams, *Way Up North in Louisville*, 1–12; Rhonda Williams, *The Politics of Public Housing: Black Women's Struggles against Urban Inequality* (New York: Oxford University Press, 2004); Mumford, *Newark;* Robert Self, *American Babylon: Race and the Struggle for Postwar Oakland* (Princeton, NJ: Princeton University Press, 2003); Wendell E. Pritchett, *Brownsville, Brooklyn: Blacks, Jews, and the Changing Face of the Ghetto* (Chicago: University of Chicago Press, 2002); Marcus Hunter, *Black Citymakers: How* The Philadelphia Negro *Changed Urban America* (New York: Oxford University Press, 2013); Martha Biondi, *To Stand and Fight : The Struggle for Civil Rights in Postwar New York City* (Cambridge: Harvard University Press, 2003); Matthew Countryman, *Up South: Civil Rights and Black Power in Philadelphia* (Philadelphia: University of Pennsylvania Press, 2006); Heather Thompson, *Whose Detroit?: Politics, Labor, and Race in a Modern American City* (Ithaca, NY: Cornell University Press, 2001); Lisa Levenstein, *A Movement without Marches: African American Women and the Politics of Poverty in Postwar Philadelphia* (Chapel Hill: University of North Carolina Press, 2009).

58. Murch, *Living for the City*, 1–11; Adams, *Way Up North in Louisville*, 1–12.

59. Williams, *Politics of Public Housing*, 1–17; Levenstein, *A Movement without Marches*, 1–29, 47–48.

60. Mumford, *Interzones*, 3–35; Mumford, *Newark*, 1–9, 152–53.

61. Kwame Holmes, "Chocolate to Rainbow City: Liberalism and Displacement in the Nation's Capital" (unpublished manuscript, 2014).

62. Jacquelyn Dowd Hall, "The Long Civil Rights Movement and the Political Uses of the Past," *Journal of American History* 91, no. 4 (March 2005); Sundiata Keita Cha-Jua and Clarence Lang, "The 'Long Movement' as Vampire: Temporal and Spatial Fallacies in Recent Black Freedom Studies," *Journal of African American History* 92, no. 2 (Spring 2007): 265–88.

63. Clarence Lang, *Grassroots at the Gateway: Class Politics and Black Freedom Struggle in St. Louis, 1936–75* (Ann Arbor: University of Michigan Press, 2009); Heather Thompson, *Whose Detroit?: Politics, Labor, and Race in a Modern American City* (Ithaca, NY: Cornell University Press, 2001).

64. Todd Michney, *Surrogate Suburbs: Black Upward Mobility and Neighborhood Change in Cleveland, 1900–1980* (Chapel Hill: University of North Carolina Press, 2017); Abigail Perkiss, *Making Good Neighbors: Civil Rights, Liberalism, and Integration in Postwar Philadelphia* (Ithaca, NY: Cornell University Press, 2014); Robert Gioielli, *Environmental Activism and the Urban Crisis: Baltimore, St. Louis, and Chicago* (Philadelphia: Temple University Press, 2014); Amanda I. Seligman, *Block by Block: Neighborhoods and Public Policy on Chicago's West Side* (Chicago: University of Chicago Press, 2004); Brian Purnell, "Unmaking the Ghetto," in *The Ghetto in Global History: 1500 to the Present*, ed. Wendy Z. Goldman and J. W. Trotter (New York: Routledge, 2018).

65. Michney, *Surrogate Suburbs.*

66. Gioielli, *Environmental Activism and the Urban Crisis*, 2–5, 8–9.

67. Purnell, "Unmaking the Ghetto," in Goldman and Trotter, *The Ghetto in Global History.*

68. Michelle Alexander, *The New Jim Crow: Mass Incarceration in the Age of Colorblindness* (New York: New Press, 2010), 2, 13.

69. N. D. B. Connolly, *A World More Concrete: Real Estate and the Remaking of Jim Crow South Florida* (Chicago: University of Chicago Press, 2014), 11–12, 16.

70. Kelly Lytle Hernandez, Khalil Gibran Muhammad, and Heather Ann Thompson, "Introduction: Constructing the Carceral State," *Journal of American History,* 102, no. 1 (June 2015): 18–24; Gross and Hicks, "Gendering the Carceral State."

71. Lewis, "'To Turn as on a Pivot,'" 765–87.

72. Jeffrey Bolster, *Black Jacks: African American Seamen in the Age of Sail* (Cambridge: Harvard University Press, 1997), 6; Peter Linebaugh and Marcus Rediker, *The Many-Headed Hydra: Sailors, Slaves, Commoners, and the Hidden History of the Revolutionary Atlantic* (Boston: Beacon Press, 2000), 174–210, 226–47; Paul Gilroy, *The Black Atlantic: Modernity and Double Consciousness* (Cambridge: Harvard University Press, 1993), 4; Jorge Cañizares-Esguerra, Matt D. Childs, and James Sidbury, eds., *The Black Urban Atlantic in the Age of the Slave Trade* (Philadelphia: University of Pennsylvania Press, 2013), "Introduction," 5; Kevin Dawson, "The Cultural Geography of Enslaved Ship Pilots," in Cañizares-Esguerra, Childs, and Sidbury, *Black Urban Atlantic,* 178.

73. Dantas, *Black Townsmen,* 5; Gomez, *Exchanging Our Country Marks,* 128–29, 255–56; Washington Creel, *"A Peculiar People,"* 4–5.

74. Walker, *No More,* vii–xiv; Rebecca Scott, *Degrees of Freedom: Louisiana and Cuba after Slavery* (Cambridge: Harvard University Press, 2005), 1–10.

75. Carl Nightingale, *Segregation: A Global History of Divided Cities* (Chicago: University of Chicago Press, 2012), quote, 3; Minkah Makalani, *In the Cause of Freedom: Radical Black Internationalism from Harlem to London, 1917–1939* (Chapel Hill: University of North Carolina Press, 2011), 6–7, 11; Nico Slate, *Colored Cosmopolitanism: The Shared Struggle for Freedom in the United States and India* (Cambridge: Harvard University Press, 2011); Nico Slate, *The Prism of Race: W. E. B. Du Bois, Langston Hughes, Paul Robeson, and the Colored World of Cedric Dover* (New York: Palgrave/Macmillan, 2014); Gerald Horne, *Red Seas: Ferdinand Smith and Radical Black Sailors in the United States and Jamaica* (New York: New York University Press, 2005); also see the special *Journal of African American History* (Fall 2011) on Horne's scholarship; Kevin Gaines, *American Africans in Ghana: Black Expatriates and the Civil Rights Era* (Chapel Hill: University of North Carolina Press, 2006); Yevette Richards Jordan, *Maida Springer-Kemp: Pan-Africanist and International Labor Leader* (Pittsburgh: University of Pittsburgh Press, 2000); Erik S. McDuffie, *Sojourning for Freedom: Black Women, American Communism, and the Making of a Black Left Feminism* (Durham: Duke University Press, 2011); Keisha N. Blain, *Set the World on Fire: Black Nationalist Women and the Global Struggle for Freedom* (Philadelphia: University of Pennsylvania Press, 2018). See also Lara Putnam, *Radical Moves: Caribbean Migrants and the Politics of the Jazz Age* (Chapel Hill: University of North Carolina Press, 2013); and Ula Y. Taylor, *The Veiled*

Garvey: The Life and Times of Amy Jacques-Garvey (Chapel Hill: University of North Carolina Press, 2002).

76. Tobias Brinkmann, "Shifting 'Ghettos': Established Jews, Jewish Immigrants, and African Americans in Chicago, 1880–1960," in *The Ghetto in Global History: 1500 to the Present*, ed. Wendy Z. Goldman and J. W. Trotter (New York: Routledge, 2018), 189–205; Jeffrey D. Gonda, "The American Ghetto as an International Human Rights Crisis: The Fight Against Racial Restrictive Covenants, 1945–1948," in Goldman and Trotter, *Ghetto in Global History*, 239–55. This volume is the product of a year-long A. W. Mellon–funded Sawyer Seminar on the ghetto in transnational perspective.

77. Makalani, *In the Cause of Freedom*, 6–7, 11.

78. Slate, *Colored Cosmopolitanism*, 212–13.

79. Gaines, *American Africans in Ghana*, 8–13; Nico Slate, ed., *Black Power beyond Borders: The Global Dimensions of Black Power* (New York: Palgrave Macmillan, 2012).

80. Richards Jordan, *Maida Springer-Kemp*, 1–12.

81. McDuffie, *Sojourning for Freedom*, 3–23.

82. Blain, *Set the World on Fire*, 1–5.

INDEX

20th century
  interwar period, 110, 134–139
  last half of. See industrial working class,
    demise of
  World War I, 56–57, 85
  World War II, 85
21st century
  economy in. See global capitalist
    economy
  global research in, 205–210
  perspective shift during, 198–205
400 Ministers, 148

A. Krolik Garment Company, 84
A&P grocery chain, 134
ABB (African Blood Brotherhood), 131
Abernathy, Ralph, 148
ACS (American Colonization Society). See
  American Colonization Society (ACS)
Adams, Catherine, 12
Adams, Harvey, 168
Adams, Luther, 201
AFDC (Aid to Families with Dependent
  Children), 170
affirmative action, 158, 166
AFL (American Federation of Labor), 111,
  114–115
AFL-CIO (American Federation of Labor-
  Congress of Industrial Organizations)
  AFL in, 111, 114–115
  CIO in. See Congress of Industrial
    Organizations (CIO)
  creation of, 142

electoral politics and, 172
political endorsements by, 172
Springer and, 150
African American organizations. See also
  specific organizations
  for Black Metropolis, 124–126
  for blacks only, 113–116
  for housing equality, 119–124
  interracial, 110–113
  during interwar period, generally, 110,
    134–139
  March on Washington Movement and,
    134–140, 150, 208
  National Urban League. See National
    Urban League (NUL)
  for sacred order, 126–127
  for social change, generally, 128–134
  for wage equality, 117–119
  women in, 116–117
*African Americans in Ghana: Black Expa-
  triates and the Civil Rights Era,*
  208–209
African Blood Brotherhood (ABB), 131
African Civilization Society, 44
African Company of Boston, 43
African heritage, 32
African Meeting House, 29
African Methodist Bethel Society, 30–31
African Methodist Episcopal (AME)
  Church
  closing of, 42
  coloured aristocracy in, 72
  community-building and, 30, 39

African Methodist Episcopal (AME)
  Church *(continued)*
  on free vs. enslaved blacks, 45
  housing and, 127
African Methodist Episcopal Zion
  (AMEZ) Church, 30–33
African Repository, 23
agricultural labor, 53–59
Aid to Families with Dependent Children
  (AFDC), 170
Alexander, Leslie, 32
Alexander, Michelle, 180, 204–205, 210
Alexander, Mitchell, 165
Alexander, Shawn, 72
Allen, Bishop Richard, 29–30, 39, 45
AME (African Methodist Episcopal)
  Church. See African Methodist Episco-
  pal (AME) Church
American, 147
American Anti-Slavery Society, 40
American Casting Company, 114
American Colonization Society (ACS)
  black working class and, 22–24
  Douglass opposing, 39–40
  Lincoln promoting, 51–52
American Federation of Labor (AFL). See
  also AFL-CIO (American Federation of
  Labor-Congress of Industrial Organiza-
  tions), 111, 114–115
American Federation of Labor-Congress of
  Industrial Organizations (AFL-CIO)
  AFL in. See also AFL-CIO (American
    Federation of Labor-Congress of
    Industrial Organizations), 111, 114–115
  CIO in. See Congress of Industrial
    Organizations (CIO)
  creation of, 142
  electoral politics and, 172
  political endorsements by, 172
  Springer and, 150
American Federationist, 142
American Institute of Architecture, 128
American League of Colored Laborers, 33
American Negro Labor Congress (ANLC),
  131
American Railway Union, 90
American Revolution
  black working class and, 11

completing the work of, 48
free black proletariat and, 11–16
AMEZ (African Methodist Episcopal
  Zion) Church, 30–33
Amsterdam News, 135, 167
Anderson, Joseph, 15
ANLC (American Negro Labor Congress),
  131
antebellum period, 27, 46, 195
anticolonization efforts, 38–39
antislavery efforts, 39–42
antiwar freedom movement, 153–154
apartheid, 199
"Appeal," 40
Argus, 136, 147
armed defense of black homes, 100–101
Arnesen, Eric, 114, 194
Associated Negro Press, 80
Association of Washer Women, 67
AT&T consent decree, 158–159
Atlanta
  black mayors of, 174–175
  boycotts in, 148
  Ku Klux Klan in, 107
  NAACP in, 130
  paradox, 176
  in postbellum era, 63–64, 67
  Race Riot of 1906 in, 61–62
  residential segregation in, 98–99, 122–124
  women workers in, 84–85, 190
Atlanta Constitution, 67
Atlanta Journal, 62
Attica prison revolt, 180
Attucks, Crispus, 25
Auburn Avenue, 124
Augustine, Peter, 33–34
Augustus Transcript, 54
Austin, Gail, 146
Avery, Revered Charles, 24

Baker, Ella, 117, 158
Baker, General, 156
Baldwin, Davarian, 193–194
Baltimore Association of Black Caulkers,
  33
Baltimore Citizens Housing Committee
  (BCHA), 121
bank boycotts, 150–152

Banks, Nathaniel, 51
Baptist churches. See also *specific churches*, 126–127
barber trade, 19–21, 34
Barfield, Clementine, 171
Barry, Marion S., 177
Battle, Will, 88
Bauman, John, 143
Bayor, Ronald, 98–99
BBDs (black business districts), 124–125
BCHA (Baltimore Citizens Housing Committee), 121
Bennett, George W., 83
Bennett, Thomas, 5
Berlin, Ira, 16, 166, 195
Best, Wallace, 126, 193–194
Bethel African Methodist Church, 30
Bibb, Henry, 41
Binga, Jesse, 101
The Birth of a Nation, 130
Black Atlantic, 205
Black Belt sex industry, 94
black business districts (BBDs), 124–125
Black Jacks: African American Seamen in the Age of Sail, 205
black labor studies
    carceral studies in, 191–194
    community studies in, 191–194
    conclusions about, 210
    cultural studies in, 191–194
    gender dynamics in. See also women, 189–190
    global research and, 205–210
    historiography in, 185–187
    in industrial era, 187–194
    in late 20th century, 198–205
    overview of, 185
    in preindustrial era, 194–198
    transformation of, 187–194
    white supremacist scholars in, 185–186
Black Lives Matter (BLM), 181–182, 210
Black Metropolis, 110, 124–126
black nationalism, 153
Black Panther Party (BPP), 154–157, 200, 209
Black Political Forum (BPF), 175
Black Power beyond Borders, 209
Black Power movement. See also Modern Black Freedom Movement, 152–157

black public sphere, 110
Black, Timuel D., Jr., 103
The Black Urban Atlantic in the Age of the Slave Trade, 205–206
The Black Worker, 135
black working class, genesis of
    American Revolution and, 11–16
    colonization and, 3–11, 22–25
    conclusions about, 26
    Fugitive Slave Act and, 22–25
    immigration and, 16–22
    introduction to, 3
Blackett, R.J.M., 39
blacks only labor organizations, 113–116
Blackwell, Raymond, 104
Blain, Keisha N., 209
Blair, Cynthia, 94, 191
Blee, Kathleen, 107
BLM (Black Lives Matter), 181–182, 210
Blood in the Water, 180
Bluestone, Barry, 163
Blumenstein's Department Store, 134
Bogle, Robert, 33
Bolster, Jeffrey, 205
Book of Ruth, 105
Boston
    abolitionists in, 40–41
    blacks in military in, 48
    colonization in, 24–25
    deindustrialization in, 163
    genesis of black working class in, 3–4, 7
    residential segregation in, 28–29, 103
Boston Chronicle, 4
Boston Gazette, 4
Boustan, Leah, 94–96
boycotts
    of banks, 150–152
    ChicagoFest, 174
    Don't Buy Where You Can't Work and, 134
    postwar employment discrimination and, 148
BPF (Black Political Forum), 175
BPP (Black Panther Party), 154–157, 200, 209
Bradley, Tom, 172
Branagan, Thomas, 23–24
Bridges, Harry, 112–113

Cleaver, Eldridge, 157
Clinton, President Bill, 166
CMEBA (Colored Marine Employees
Benevolent Association), 113–114
CNLU (Colored National Labor Union),
67, 114
coal mines, 57
Coalition of Black Trade Unionists
(CBTU), 172
Colden, Cadwallader, 7
colonization, 3–11, 22–25
Colored American magazine, 21
Colored Board of Trade, 123–124
Colored Cosmopolitanism, 208
Colored Marine Employees Benevolent
Association (CMEBA), 113–114
Colored National Labor Union (CNLU),
67, 114
Colored Poet of America, 19
Committee of Fourteen, 106
Committee on Rent Profiteering, 105
Communist Party (CP)
American Negro Labor Congress and,
131
emergence of, 110–111, 113
postwar agenda of, 149
women in, 117
community-building
in antebellum period, generally, 27, 46
anticolonization efforts and, 38–39
antislavery efforts and, 39–42
emigration efforts and, 42–44
entrepreneurship and, 33–37
independent black institutions for, 29–33
internal social conflicts in, 44–46
mob violence and, 28
property ownership in, 38
residential segregation and, 28–29
Community Development Corporations, 171
community fragmentation, 72
community studies, 191–194
Comprehensive Crime Control Act of 1985,
165
*The Condition, Elevation, Emigration, and
Destiny of the Colored People of the
United States Politically Considered*, 44
Congress of Industrial Organizations
(CIO). See also AFL-CIO (American

Federation of Labor-Congress of Industrial Organizations)
in postwar era, 147, 149–150
in pre-WWI era, 69
Congress of Racial Equality (CORE), 147,
150–152
Connolly, Nathan, 182–183, 204
conscription, 51–52
construction industry, 142
containerization, 141
convict labor, 56–59
Cooke, Marvel, 117
Cooper, Anna Julia, 70
Corbould, Claire, 193
Corcraft (Division of Correctional Industries), 180
CORE (Congress of Racial Equality), 147,
150–152
Cottenham, Green, 57
cotton plantations, 16
Countryman, Matthew, 200
courts
California Supreme, 97–98
Chicago Morals, 106
on housing segregation, 97–98
U.S. Supreme. See U.S. Supreme Court
CP (Communist Party). See Communist
Party (CP)
CPINTELPRO, 157
Creel, Washington, 206
creolization, 196
crime, war on, 165
criminalization of blacks
in global capitalist economy, 180
in industrial working class, 106
during interwar period, 106
job ceilings and, 94
scholarship on, 191–192
Crisis magazine, 72, 130
Crusader, 131
Cuffee, Paul, 34, 43
cultural studies, 191–194
Curtin, Mary Ellen, 57

Dabel, Jane, 196–197
Dalit Panthers, 155
Dantas, Mariana, 196
Daughters of New York, 71

urban industrial working class and,
59–66
Emancipation Proclamation, 48–49
emigration, 42–44
entrepreneurship, 33–37
Equal Employment Opportunity Commission (EEOC), 159, 166
Equiano, Olaudah, 8–10
Executive Order 8802, 135

Fair Employment Practices Committee
(FEPC), 135–138, 140
FAS (Free African Society), 29–30
Faucet, Arthur, 104–105
Faue, Liz, 181
Fauset, Crystal Bird, 119
FBI (Federal Bureau of Investigation), 157
FDR (Roosevelt, President Franklin Delano), 119, 135
Federal Barge Line, 114
Federal Bureau of Investigation (FBI), 157
Federal Housing Administration (FHA), 102
federal urban renewal programs, 144
felons. See also criminalization of blacks, 180
females. See women
fence building, 99
FEPC (Fair Employment Practices Committee), 135–138, 140
Ferguson, Karen, 122–123
Ferrell, Frank, 68
FHA (Federal Housing Administration), 102
Fies, Milton, 82
Fifteen Amendment, 53
Fifth Massachusetts Regiment, 49
Fight for $15, 181
film industry, 130
Firestone Company, 88
First African Baptist Church, 29, 31–32
Ford Motor Company
death traps at, 93–94
in postwar era, 141
racial job ceilings at, 86
recruiting workers for, 80–81
UAW and, 112
Forten, James, 34, 39, 43
Fortune, Thomas T., 68–69, 71

Foster, A.L., 119, 120
Foster, George G., 28
Fourteenth Amendment, 53, 97
Francis, Robert, 112
Franklin, Aretha, 125
Franklin, Revered C.L., 125
Frazier, Garrison, 51
Free African Society (FAS), 29–30
Free and Equal, 130
free wage labor, 16–22, 47–53
Freedmen's Bureau, 56, 60
Fuentes, Marissa J., 196
Fugitive Slave Law of 1850, 22–26
Fulton Bag and Cotton Company, 64

Gaines, Kevin, 208
Gandhi, Mahatma, 135, 208
garment industry, 35, 83–84
Garnet, Reverend Henry Highland, 43–44
Garrison, William Lloyd, 40
Garvey, Marcus, 129, 132
Garvey Movement, 129, 132, 209–210
Garza, Alicia, 182
Gatewood, Willard, 71
gender dynamics. See women
General Conference of the AME Church, 127
General Motors, 112
genocide, 166
George, Henry, 68
Ghana, 208–209
ghetto-formation scholarship, 187
Ghetto: The Invention of a Place, the History of an Idea, 96
Giesberg, Judith, 53
Gilroy, Paul, 205
Gioielli, Robert R., 203–204
global capitalist economy, 179–184
global research, 205–210
Goldin, Claudia, 196
Goode, Wilson, 175, 200
Graham, George, 100–101
Great Depression, 94, 110–111
Great Migration. See also industrial working class, rise of
overview of, 72–73, 77–78, 108–109
in postbellum era, 62–63
racial job ceilings in, 87–96

March on Washington Movement
(MOWM), 134–140, 150, 208
Marine Cooks and Stewards Association of
the Pacific (MCSAP), 113–114
Maritime Strike of 1934, 112
Martin, Trayvon, 182
Martin, Waldo, 47–48
Massey, Douglas, 199
Masur, Kate, 50, 63
Matthews, Tracye, 158
Matthews, Victoria Earle, 69, 71
mayoral elections, 172–177
McCarthy era, 149
McCarty, Margaret (Peggy), 170
McCloudy, Josephine, 141
McDuffie, Erik S., 131
McNeal, Theodore D., 136
MCSAP (Marine Cooks and Stewards
Association of the Pacific), 113–114
meatpacking industry, 87–88, 141
media, 107
MELA (Mothers of East Los Angeles), 171
menial service, 18–19
Messenger, 130–131
Mexicans, 89
Meyers, Amrita, 45
Meyers, Isaac, 67
Michney, Todd, 144, 203
Midvale Steel Works, 65, 80
military service, 48–49, 51–52
Miller, Dora Scott, 93
Miller, William, 43
Mitchell, Gladys, 100
mob violence. See also violent resistance,
28
Modern Black Freedom Movement
black labor studies and, 187
Black Power phase of, 152–157
during interwar period, 110, 139
during postwar period, generally,
157–159
Morial, Ernest ("Dutch"), 175
Morris, Anna, 164
Mother Bethel, 30, 39
Mother Rescuers, 170
Mothers of East Los Angeles (MELA), 171
Mothers ROC (Reclaiming Our Children),
171

Movement Against Destruction (MAD),
168
MOWM (March on Washington Move-
ment), 134–140, 150, 208
Muhammad, Elijah, 152
Muhammad, Khalil, 106, 191
Multi-City Study of Urban Inequity, 176
Mumford, Kevin, 191, 193, 201
Murch, Donna, 153, 200
Myers, Amrita, 36, 198
Myers, Isaac, 114

NAACP (National Association for the
Advancement of Colored People)
on department store discrimination, 147
formation of, 72
on housing segregation, 100
National Black Political Convention
and, 172
on Oakland redevelopment program, 145
Pittsburgh branch of, 170
on police brutality, 106
on racial discrimination, generally,
129–130
Springer and, 117
Nashville Banner, 60
Nation of Islam, 152, 154
National Association for the Advancement
of Colored People (NAACP). See
NAACP (National Association for the
Advancement of Colored People)
National Black Political Assembly, 172
National Committee Against Discrimina-
tion in Housing, 143
National Committee to Free Angela Davis,
158
National Domestic Workers Alliance,
181–182
National League for the Protection of
Colored Women (NLPCW), 69
National Maritime Union (NMU), 110–
114, 208
National Negro Baseball League, 126
National Negro Business League (NNBL),
69–70
National Negro Congress (NNC), 120, 134
National Negro Labor Council (NNLC),
148–149

Omnibus Budgetary Reconciliation Act, 166
"Open Letter to City Council," 123–124
Operation Breadbasket, 148
Origins of the Urban Crisis: Race and Inequality in Postwar Detroit, 199
Osofsky, Gilbert, 187
"Outline for a Black Agenda," 172
Owen, Chandler, 130–131
oyster suppliers, 36

Packinghouse Workers Organizing Committee (PWOC), 111
Parchman Farm, 59
Parker, John, 41
Parks, Sam, 88
past discrimination, damages for, 158–159
Patterson, Louise Thompson, 132
Paul the Apostle, 44
Penningroth, Dylan, 8
Pennsylvania Gazette, 4
Pentecostal churches, 126–127
People's Coalition Against Lead Poisoning, 168
Perkiss, Abigail, 144
Perry, Ivory, 168
Personal Responsibility and Work Opportunity Act (PRWORA), 166
Peterson, Carlos, 145
Pettis, F.H., 25
Philadelphia
   black migration to, 64
   civil rights movement in, 170–171
   colonial generation in, 3–4, 8, 10–11
   colonization and, 23–25
   decline of manufacturing sector in, 162
   demise of industrial working class in, 139, 142
   Don't Buy Where You Can't Work in, 148
   early labor organizations in, 33–35
   immigration and, 16–19
   interwar period in, 79–80, 88, 92
   National Negro Congress in, 120–121
   residential segregation in, 38, 71, 103–105
   violent resistance in, 28–31, 61
Philadelphia Housing Authority, 120
Philadelphia Plan, 158

Philadelphia Record, 104
Philadelphia Tribune, 61, 104
Philbrick, Edward, 55–56
Phillips, Christopher, 197
Phillips, Kimberley, 153
PIAC (Pittsburgh Interracial Action Council), 147
Pierce, Richard, 99
pilots, 8–10, 18
Pitts, Alex D., 82
Pittsburgh Courier, 135, 142
Pittsburgh Interracial Action Council (PIAC), 147
Pittsburgh Urban League, 123
A Plea for Emigration or Notes of Canada West, 43
Pleck, Elizabeth H., 12
police brutality, 106, 182
politics. See electoral politics
Polynesian Panther Party, 155
Poor People's Campaign, 154
porters, 90–91
postbellum era
   Great Migration in, 62–63
   Jim Crow order in, 62
   legislation in, 55–56, 60
   Pullman Company in, 65
   race riots in, 61–62
   women in, 57–59
Powell, Lawrence, 4
Powers, Bernard, 197
PPMA (Pullman Porters and Maids Protective Association), 115
preindustrial era, scholarship on, 194–198
Prince Hall Masonic order, 29
prison systems. See also criminalization of blacks, 56–59
proletarian perspectives, 188–189
property ownership. See also residential segregation, 38
Proposition 209, 166
Prosser, Gabriel, 42
prostitution, 36
Protective Circle of Chicago, 101
Providence Gazette, 6
Pruitt, Bernadette, 81
PRWORA (Personal Responsibility and Work Opportunity Act), 166